Obsessive–Compulsive Disorder: Subtypes and Spectrum Conditions

OBSESSIVE–COMPULSIVE DISORDER: SUBTYPES AND SPECTRUM CONDITIONS

Jonathan S. Abramowitz
Associate Professor, Department of Psychology,
University of North Carolina at Chapel Hill

Dean McKay
Associate Professor, Department of Psychology,
Fordham University

and

Steven Taylor
Professor, Department of Psychiatry,
University of British Columbia

ELSEVIER

AMSTERDAM • BOSTON • HEIDELBERG • LONDON • NEW YORK • OXFORD
PARIS • SAN DIEGO • SAN FRANCISCO • SINGAPORE • SYDNEY • TOKYO

KH

Elsevier
360 Park Avenue South, New York, NY 10010-1710, USA
84 Theobald's Road, London WC1X 8RR, UK
30 Corporate Drive, Suite 400, Burlington, MA 01803, USA
525 B Street, Suite 1900, San Diego, California 92101-4495, USA

First edition 2008

Notice
No responsibility is assumed by the publisher for any injury and/or damage to persons
or property as a matter of products liability, negligence or otherwise, or from any use
or operation of any methods, products, instructions or ideas contained in the material
herein. Because of rapid advances in the medical sciences, in particular, independent
verification of diagnoses and drug dosages should be made

British Library Cataloguing in Publication Data
A catalogue record for this book is available from the British Library

Library of Congress Cataloging in Publication Data
A catalog record for this book is available from the Library of Congress

ISBN 978-0-08-044701-8

For information on all Elsevier publications
visit our web site at http://books.elsevier.com

Transferred to Digital Printing in 2010

11/17/16

CONTENTS

PART I

SUBTYPES OF OBSESSIVE–COMPULSIVE DISORDER

PART II

POSSIBLE OBSESSIVE–COMPULSIVE SPECTRUM
DISORDERS

CONTRIBUTORS

Numbers in parentheses indicate the pages on which the authors' contributions begin.

Jonathan S. Abramowitz, PhD, ABPP (127, 271, 287) Associate Professor, Department of Psychology, University of North Carolina at Chapel Hill, Chapel Hill, North Carolina, USA

Andrea R. Ashbaugh, BA (19) Department of Psychology, Concordia University, Montreal, Quebec, Canada

Theo K. Bouman, PhD (196) Department of Clinical and Developmental Psychology, University of Groningen, Groningen, The Netherlands

David A. Clark, PhD (53) Professor, Department of Psychology, University of New Brunswick, Fredricton, New Brunswick, Canada

Meredith E. Coles, PhD (36) Assistant Professor, Department of Psychology, Binghamton University (SUNY), Binghamton, New York, USA

Kristen M. Culbert, BA (230) Department of Psychology, Michigan State University, East Lansing, Michigan, USA

Thilo Deckersbach, PhD (94) Assistant Professor, Department of Psychiatry, Massachusetts General Hospital and Harvard Medical School, Boston, Massachusetts, USA

Gretchen J. Diefenbach, PhD (139) Postdoctoral Fellow, The Institute of Living, Hartford, Connecticut, USA

Michel J. Dugas, PhD (19) Associate Professor, Department of Psychology, Concordia University, Montreal, Quebec, Canada

Heather Durdle, MA (160) Department of Psychology, University of Windsor, Windsor, Ontario, Canada

Jane L. Eisen, MD (246) Associate Professor, Department of Psychiatry and Human Behavior, Butler Hospital and Brown Medical School, Providence, Rhode Island, USA

Martin E. Franklin, PhD (139) Associate Professor, Department of Psychiatry, University of Pennsylvania, Philadelphia, Pennsylvania, USA

Randy O. Frost, PhD (76) Professor, Department of Psychology, Smith College, Northampton, Massachusetts, USA

Laurie A. Gelfand, BA (19) Department of Psychology, Concordia University, Montreal, Quebec, Canada

Jennifer T. Gosselin, BA (177) Department of Psychology, Fordham University, Bronx, New York, USA

Sapna Gupta, BA (177) Department of Psychology, Fordham University, Bronx, New York, USA

Brendan D. Guyitt, BA (53) Department of Psychology, University of New Brunswick, Fredricton, New Brunswick, Canada

Kelly L. Klump, PhD (230) Assistant Professor, Department of Psychology, Michigan State University, East Lansing, Michigan, USA

Julie Leclerc, PhD (212) Fernand–Seguin Research Centre, University of Montreal, Montreal, Quebec, Canada

Han-Joo Lee, BA (107) Department of Psychology, University of Texas at Austin, Austin, Texas, USA

Maria C. Mancebo, PhD (246) Instructor, Department of Psychiatry and Human Behavior, Butler Hospital and Brown Medical School, Providence, Rhode Island, USA

Dean McKay, PhD, ABPP (127, 177, 287) Associate Professor, Department of Psychology, Fordham University, Bronx, New York, USA

Suzanne A. Meunier, PhD (3) Postdoctoral fellow, Anxiety Disorders Center, The Institute of Living, Hartford, Connecticut, USA

Kieron O'Connor, PhD (212) Fernand–Seguin Research Centre, University of Montreal, Montreal, Quebec, Canada

Bunmi O. Olatunji, PhD (94) Assistant Professor, Department of Psychology, Vanderbilt University, Nashville, Tennessee, USA

Ashley S. Pietrefesa, BA (36) Department of Psychology, Binghamton University (SUNY), Binghamton, New York, USA

Anthony Pinto, PhD (246) Assistant Professor, Department of Psychiatry and Human Behavior, Butler Hospital and Brown Medical School, Providence, Rhode Island, USA

Adam S. Radomsky, PhD (19) Associate Professor, Department of Psychology, Concordia University, Montreal, Quebec, Canada

Steven A. Rasmussen, PhD (246) Associate Professor, Department of Psychiatry and Human Behavior, Butler Hospital and Brown Medical School, Providence, Rhode Island, USA

Gail Steketee, PhD (76) Professor, School of Social Work, Boston University, Boston, Massachusetts, USA

Sherry H. Stewart, PhD (160) Professor, Departments of Psychiatry and Psychology, Dalhousie University, Halifax, Nova Scotia, Canada

Steven Taylor, PhD, ABPP (127, 287) Professor, Department of Psychiatry, University of British Columbia, Vancouver, British Columbia, Canada

Michael J. Telch, PhD (107) Professor, Department of Psychology, University of Texas at Austin, Austin, Texas, USA

David F. Tolin, PhD (3, 139) Director, Anxiety Disorders Center, The Institute of Living, Hartford, Connecticut, USA

Sabine Wilhelm, PhD (94) Associate Professor, Department of Psychiatry, Massachusetts General Hospital and Harvard Medical School, Boston, Massachusetts, USA

PREFACE: WHY SUBTYPES? WHY SPECTRUM DISORDERS?

OCD ACCORDING TO THE *DSM-IV*

According to the *Diagnostic and Statistical Manual of Mental Disorders* (*DSM-IV-TR*; American Psychiatric Association, 2000), obsessive–compulsive disorder (OCD) is an anxiety disorder defined by the presence of *obsessions* or *compulsions* that produce significant distress and cause noticeable interference with functioning in domains such as work and school, social and leisure activities, and family settings. Table 1 shows a summary of the *DSM-IV-TR* criteria for OCD. *Obsessions* are defined as intrusive thoughts, ideas, images, impulses, or doubts that the person experiences in some way as senseless and that evoke affective distress (typically in the form of anxiety). Classic examples include preoccupation with germs and contamination, doubts about having caused harm, and unwanted sexual, blasphemous, and violent impulses. *Compulsions* are urges to perform behavioral rituals (e.g., washing, checking) or mental rituals (e.g., praying) that are senseless, excessive, and often conforming to strict idiosyncratic rules imposed by the individual (e.g., washing according to a specified routine, checking 15 times).

LIMITATIONS OF THE *DSM* DEFINITION

Research on the phenomenology of OCD, however, suggests that the *DSM-IV-TR* definition of OCD has several limitations. First, the definition implies that obsessions and compulsions are independent phenomena – that one *or* the other is necessary and sufficient for a diagnosis of OCD. Prior to deciding upon the diagnostic criteria for OCD during the drafting of the *DSM-IV* (the diagnostic criteria in *DSM-IV-TR* [2000] are unchanged from *DSM-IV* [1994]), some experts argued that OCD ought to be defined by the presence of obsessions *and* compulsions. In fact, data from a large multi-site field trial that was conducted during the early 1990s (in conjunction with the preparation of the *DSM-IV*; Foa et al., 1995) revealed that 96% of 411 OCD patients exhibited both obsessions and compulsions. Only 2.1% evidenced obsessions in the absence of compulsive rituals; and only 1.7% evidenced

TABLE 1   *DSM-IV-TR* diagnostic criteria for OCD

A. Either obsessions or compulsions.

Obsessions are defined by (1), (2), (3), and (4):
   (1) repetitive and persistent thoughts, images or impulses that are experienced, at some point, as
       intrusive and inappropriate and that cause marked anxiety or distress
   (2) the thoughts, images or impulses are not worries about real-life problems
   (3) the person tries to ignore or suppress the thoughts, images or impulses, or neutralize them
       with some other thought or action
   (4) the thoughts, images or impulses are recognized as a product of one's own mind and not
       imposed from without

Compulsions are defined as (1) and (2):
   (1) repetitive behaviors or mental acts that one feels driven to perform in response to an
       obsession or according to certain rules
   (2) the behaviors or mental acts are aimed at preventing or reducing distress or preventing feared
       consequences; however the behaviors or mental acts are clearly excessive or are not
       connected in a realistic way with what they are designed to neutralize or prevent.

B. At some point during the disorder the person has recognized that the obsessions or compulsions
   are excessive or unreasonable.

C. The obsessions or compulsions cause marked distress, are time-consuming (take more than 1
   hour a day), or significantly interfere with usual daily functioning.

D. The content of the obsessions or compulsions is not better accounted for by another Axis I
   disorder, if present. (e.g., concern with appearance in the presence of Body Dysmorphic
   Disorder, or preoccupation with having a serious illness in the presence of hypochondriasis).

E. Symptoms are not due to the direct physiological effects of a substance or a general medical
   condition.

Specify if:
With poor insight: if for most of the time the person does not recognize that their obsessions and
compulsions are excessive or unreasonable.

Reprinted with permission from the *Diagnostic and Statistical Manual of Mental Disorders,
Text Revision*, Copyright 2000. American Psychiatric Association.

compulsions without obsessions. Thus, the current diagnostic criteria appear to be
at odds with the fact that virtually everyone with OCD experiences both obsessions
and compulsions.

As we will see in the chapters of this volume, this discrepancy has had no small
effect on the tendency to draw parallels between OCD and other disorders involving obsession-like and compulsive-like behaviors. A number of disorders labeled
as 'obsessive–compulsive spectrum (OCS) disorders', e.g., conditions presumed
related to OCD primarily on the basis of symptom overlap, involve obsessions
without compulsions and compulsions without obsessions. As many of the
authors in Part II of this volume point out, the lack of both obsessions *and* compulsions in these OCS disorders is a main reason for concluding that such disorders are probably *not* related to OCD.

Along with their co-existence in virtually all OCD patients, obsessions and
compulsions demonstrate a sort of internal validity, even if irrational. For example, patients with compulsive washing rituals are typically the same individuals

with obsessions about germs. Similarly, those with checking rituals are the same patients with obsessional doubts that they might be responsible for some sort of harm. Thus, a second limitation of the *DSM* definition is that it portrays compulsive rituals as devoid of intent and does not include the clinically meaningful relationship discussed above. This relationship, however, has been demonstrated in both experimental laboratory research (e.g., Rachman & Hodgson, 1980) and in the *DSM-IV* field trial mentioned previously: 84% of patients indicated that they performed compulsive rituals to reduce obsessional distress, often articulated in terms of the probability of some specific feared consequence. Thus, contrary to what the *DSM* definition implies, these data suggest that compulsive rituals are not simply senseless, excessive, or rule-bound actions or movements. Rather, rituals have a purpose for the person with OCD.

Further support for the ideas that obsessions and compulsions co-occur and are closely related in a functional manner comes via a number of studies that have identified symptom dimensions and 'subtypes' of OCD. These investigations consistently find that specific obsessions and compulsions load together on the same symptom-based factors and clusters (such as contamination obsessions with washing rituals; e.g., Leckman et al., 1997) as well as on measures of symptom severity (e.g., Deacon & Abramowitz, 2005). These symptom-based subtypes of OCD comprise the focus of the chapters in Part I of this book. These chapters will convince the reader that as much as the distinction between obsessions and compulsions is intuitively appealing, OCD phenomenology does not distill neatly into these two categories.

The *DSM*'s emphasis on the *repetitiveness* and *persistent* nature of obsessions and compulsions represents a third limitation of these diagnostic criteria. Whereas these descriptions characterize *some* symptoms of OCD, the *defining* feature (as we have mentioned previously) is the relationship *between* obsessions (which evoke distress) and efforts to reduce this distress (e.g., compulsions). Few other disorders in the *DSM* have symptoms characterized by such a relationship. Moreover, as is revealed in the chapters of Part I, quintessential compulsive rituals such as washing and checking represent only one class of tactics that patients with OCD use in response to their distressing obsessional thoughts.

PURPOSE OF THIS BOOK

A scientific understanding of OCD and other psychological disorders entails an attempt, in Plato's words, to 'carve nature at its joints' (Hackforth, 1952). As research on the nature and treatment of OCD has accrued it has become increasingly apparent that this disorder is heterogeneous, and possibly composed of many different subtypes. Indeed, the specific themes of obsessions and compulsions represent an endless array of topics constrained only by the sufferer's idiosyncratic personal concerns and experiences. Obsessions might relate to contamination, harm, morality, exactness, sexual behavior, or religion. Compulsive behaviors typically take the form of washing, checking, arranging, or mentally neutralizing; as

well as avoidance of situations that provoke the obsessions. Although these subtypes may share overlapping etiologic mechanisms and may respond to similar
treatments, there also appear to be some important differences. We feel that a clearer
understanding of the essential similarities and differences among these subtypes
will lead to advances in understanding and treating OCD.

Some authors have also noted that OCD appears to share characteristics with
other disorders. The OCS concept described earlier represents one manifestation
of this notion. As the reader will see later in this volume, the OCS is considered to
encompass between 10 and 20 conditions such as trichotillomania, body dysmorphic disorder, and Tourette syndrome. Such problems not only seem to have
symptoms similar to obsessions and compulsions, but many also seem to respond
to treatments similar to those used for OCD. Although the concept of an OCS
remains highly controversial, especially as work begins on the next iteration of the
DSM, it is our feeling that advances in understanding and treating these putative
(and understudied) OCS disorders can arise from a more critical examination of
how they are similar to, and different from OCD. Each chapter in Part II of this
book undertakes such an analysis.

It is with these points in mind that we developed the concept for the present
volume. The chapters within provide empirically based reviews of clinical observations, theoretical, and treatment data on proposed OCD subtypes and spectrum
disorders. Researchers and clinicians continue to disagree about the value of the
concepts of OCD subtypes and spectra. The chapters in this volume, however,
attempt to explore these controversies in order to arrive at a deeper understanding
of the causes and treatments for the many different clinical presentations covered
in the book.

This book also has implications for the classification of psychological disorders in general. As the field of mental health begins to consider the next iteration
of the diagnostic manual (*DSM-V* is planned for release in 2012), an entire
research agenda is being implemented to elucidate issues such as how best to
understand and classify OCD. The questions of subtypes and spectrum disorders
are at the forefront of this issue and will guide how OCD is conceptualized in the
DSM-V. To 'weigh in' on this aspect of the field, the chapters in this book have
been contributed by scientist-practitioners who have the benefit of empirical data
and clinical observation.

The book is divided into two parts. Part I, which addresses the heterogeneity of
OCD, contains chapters addressing a variety of proposed OCD 'subtypes'. These
chapters critically review the literature and address the following aspects of each
presentation: (a) symptomatology, (b) empirically supported etiologic and conceptual models, (c) support for the particular symptom presentation as a valid
OCD subtype, (d) a review of the subtype-specific treatment literature. A concluding chapter by the editors synthesizes and discusses conceptual issues raised in the
preceding chapters.

The chapters included in Part II address a number of proposed OCS disorders
and cover the following aspects of each condition: (a) clinical presentation and

important features, (b) etiologic and conceptual models, (c) a review of the empirical evidence pertaining to the disorder's standing as a possible OCS condition (e.g., its similarity and relationship to OCD), and (d) treatment issues. As in Part I, Part II concludes with our own discussion and critical review of the literature on the OCS hypothesis, drawing on conclusions from the chapters within Part II.

The Editors

REFERENCES

American Psychiatric Association (2000). *Diagnostic and statistical manual of mental disorders* (4th ed., text rev.) (*DSM-IV-TR*). Washington, DC: APA.

Deacon, B. J., & Abramowitz, J. S. (2005). The Yale–Brown obsessive compulsive scale: Factor analysis, construct validity, and suggestions for refinement. *Journal of Anxiety Disorders, 19*, 573–585.

Foa, E. B., Kozak, M. J., Goodman, W. K., Hollander, E., Jenike, M.A., & Rasmussen, S. (1995). DSM-IV field trial: Obsessive compulsive disorder. *American Journal of Psychiatry, 152*, 90–96.

Hackforth, R. (1952). *Plato's Phaedrus*. Cambridge: Cambridge University Press.

Leckman, J. F., Grice, D. E., Boardman, J., Zhang, H., Vitale, A., Bondi, C., et al. (1997). Symptoms of obsessive–compulsive disorder. *American Journal of Psychiatry, 154*, 911–917.

Rachman, S., & Hodgson, R. (1980). *Obsessions and compulsions*. New York: Prentice Hall.

SUBTYPES OF OBSESSIVE– COMPULSIVE DISORDER

1

CONTAMINATION AND DECONTAMINATION

DAVID F. TOLIN[1, 2] AND SUZANNE A. MEUNIER[1]

[1]The Institute of Living/Hartford Hospital;
[2]University of Connecticut School of Medicine

PHENOMENOLOGY[1]

Gretchen is a 22-year-old woman who came to the Anxiety Disorders Center for treatment of her intense fears of contamination from HIV. She was afraid to come into contact with anyone whom she perceived as being homosexual or sexually promiscuous because she feared that these people had a high likelihood of being HIV positive and spreading the virus to her. She also avoided certain stores and restaurants that she worried were frequented by homosexual or promiscuous customers because she was afraid to touch items that they had touched. During her first therapy session, she found it difficult to sit in a chair or touch the doorknob in the therapist's office because 'I don't know who's touched it.' She further described a concern that someone else's semen or other bodily fluids might be on the chair or doorknob, that these fluids would contain live HIV virus, and that the virus would jump onto her or seep through her clothing and into bodily orifices or microscopic cuts on her skin. When she felt contaminated, she was reluctant to touch her car or house for fear of contaminating those previously 'clean' places.

Correspondence to: David F. Tolin, Anxiety Disorders Center, The Institute of Living, 200 Retreat Avenue, Hartford, CT 06106.

[1]Names and other identifying information have been altered.

Nicholas is a 43-year-old man who also presented with contamination-related OCD. Unlike Gretchen, however, Nicholas did not fear contracting a disease. Rather, he reported fears of being contaminated by his alma mater, the University of Washington. He reported that, shortly after graduating and leaving the campus, he began to think that the University and everything associated with it was contaminated in some way. He was unable to go to the campus or even the state of Washington. If he saw someone wearing a t-shirt from that University, or saw a bumper sticker on a car, he would immediately have to go home to shower and change his clothes. When his therapist suggested experimenting by looking at pictures of the University of Washington on the Internet, Nicholas became visibly anxious and stated that this would make him feel contaminated. When asked what he feared would happen if he became contaminated by his former University, he replied, 'Nothing bad would happen. I wouldn't get sick or anything. I'd just feel really contaminated and would have to wash or else I would go crazy.'

As is evident from the above examples, contamination-related obsessive–compulsive disorder (OCD) can take many forms. Across all variants of this particular symptom dimension, patients report an intense and often overwhelming fear that they will become contaminated in some way or that they will accidentally spread contamination to another person or place. In addition, across all variants of contamination-related OCD, patients' fears of contamination are clearly in excess of any actual risk. There are, however, a number of variations within the contamination symptom dimension. For example, some patients (such as Gretchen) fear contamination from germs or other physical contaminants, whereas others (such as Nicholas) fear contamination by unlikely sources that most people would not consider to be contaminants. In addition, although many patients (such as Gretchen) express an exaggerated belief that they will become ill if contaminated, others (such as Nicholas) deny any illness-related fears but instead express a more vague concern about feeling 'dirty' and a fear that their emotional reaction to contamination will be extreme or long-lasting. Contamination-related obsessions are typically (although not always) associated with washing and cleaning compulsions.

FEATURES OF CONTAMINATION-RELATED OCD

The essential feature of contamination-related OCD is a fear of spreading contagion. What is meant by 'contagion', however, may vary widely across individuals. In many cases, such as the example of Gretchen above, there is a clear fear of contact with physical contaminants such as viruses, bacteria, poisons, etc. In such instances, the fear is typically related to the known effects of the contaminant – e.g., that one will develop AIDS from contact with the HIV virus, that one will be poisoned by ingesting toxins, etc. In Gretchen's case, for the most part she feared that contaminants would enter her body through physical contact such as sitting on a chair, touching a doorknob, etc. Like many other individuals with contamination-related OCD, Gretchen's beliefs about the 'behavior' of germs was clearly irrational, such as her belief that the germs could survive for hours or even days on a chair, or her concern that the germs would 'jump' on her if she got too close. In other cases, however, the person's concept of contagion is less clear. Nicholas, described above, did not believe that there was some kind of substance on the University of Washington that would somehow get on him; rather, he held the (physically implausible) belief that the mere sight of, proximity to, or even thoughts about, University-related stimuli would somehow lead him to become 'dirty'. He denied a concern that he would become ill from this contagion; rather, he seemed to fear the feeling of being contaminated in its own right.

Nicholas's concerns are consistent with the concept, advanced by Rachman (1994), of *mental pollution*: a sense of 'internal dirtiness' that can be elicited by thoughts, words, or memories as well as by physical contact. Although mental pollution may at times be associated with concerns about threat (e.g., disease), it may also be associated with other emotional features such as disgust, shame, responsibility, and moral outrage. In studies of sexual assault survivors as well as college students asked to imagine an unwanted sexual contact, participants reported that their feelings of mental pollution led to handwashing behaviors (Fairbrother, Newth, & Rachman, 2005; Fairbrother & Rachman, 2004).

Contamination fears have been closely associated with the phenomenon of *sympathetic magic*, or implausible beliefs about the nature of contagion. These beliefs can manifest in two ways. The first, *contagion*, can be worded as 'once in contact, always in contact'. That is, the transfer of contaminating properties can remain even after the actual physical contact has ended. In addition, an object that has acquired properties through contagion can then spread the same properties to other objects. One study demonstrated the 'chain of contagion' by touching a new pencil to an object perceived to be highly contaminated, such as the toilet (Tolin, Worhunsky, & Maltby, 2004). That pencil was then touched to a new pencil, which in turn was touched to another pencil, and so on for a chain of 12 pencils. At each step, OCD patients and controls were asked to rate how contaminated each pencil was. Non-anxious participants perceived a 'chain of contagion' through two pencils (meaning that they perceived pencils 1 and 2 as contaminated, but not pencils 3 or higher), and anxious control participants (individuals with anxiety disorders other than OCD) perceived a 'chain of contagion' through six pencils. Individuals with OCD, however, perceived a chain of contagion through the entire set of 12 pencils.

The second form of sympathetic magic beliefs is *similarity*, which can be worded as 'appearance is reality'. When things appear superficially similar, they are thought to be equally contaminated and therefore might be avoided as if they were contaminated. For example, participants rated substances that resembled contaminants (e.g. chocolate fudge in the shape of dog feces) as less desirable when compared to the same substance in a different form (e.g., chocolate fudge in the shape of a disc) (Rozin, Millman, & Nemeroff, 1986). In a study of analogue volunteers, participants with high contamination fear, but not those with high trait anxiety, were reluctant to drink water from a cup labeled 'saliva', even though they were assured that the water was clean and safe to drink (Tsao & McKay, 2004). Similarity beliefs may explain why some OCD patients find that the cues leading them to feel contaminated generalize over time such that even benign stimuli such as words or pictures can be perceived as contaminants (as was the case with Nicholas, described above).

ETIOLOGICAL AND CONCEPTUAL MODELS AND ISSUES

BEHAVIORAL MODELS

Behavioral models of OCD (e.g., Kozak & Foa, 1997) emphasize the role of avoidance behavior in maintaining conditioned fear reactions. In the case of contamination-related OCD, compulsive washing and cleaning behaviors are conceptualized as a form of active avoidance which, in addition to more passive avoidance strategies (e.g., refusing to touch 'contaminated' objects), is thought to maintain contamination fears by diminishing the person's capacity to habituate to 'contaminated' objects and to realistically distinguish safe from unsafe situations. In many cases, avoidance behavior is quite obvious, such as the patient who washes her hands repeatedly, refuses to touch objects in her home, etc. In other cases, however, the avoidance is subtler, such as the person who pulls his sleeve down over his hand before opening the door. Because compulsive behavior (e.g., washing) results in anxiety reduction, the behavior is negatively reinforced, thus increasing the likelihood that the behavior will recur (Hodgson & Rachman, 1972).

COGNITIVE MODELS

Cognitive models of OCD have traditionally been 'top-down', e.g., they emphasize the role of dysfunctional cognitions in the etiology and maintenance of disorders (Beck, Emery, & Greenberg, 1985). According to such models, obsessive fears and behaviors are maintained by dysfunctional assumptions and maladaptive beliefs. The Obsessive Compulsive Cognitions Working Group (OCCWG, 1997) identified six domains of obsessional beliefs that appeared to distinguish OCD patients from nonclinical controls and, to a lesser extent, anxious controls: overestimation of threat, intolerance of uncertainty, importance of thoughts, need to control thoughts, responsibility, and perfectionism. In both clinical and nonclinical samples, contamination fears and washing/cleaning behaviors were specifically predicted by overestimation of threat (OCCWG, 2005; Tolin, Brady, & Hannan, 2005; Tolin, Woods, & Abramowitz, 2003). Thus, 'top-down' cognitive models suggest that contamination-related OCD is characterized by exaggerated beliefs about the risk of harm to oneself or others. Such beliefs are thought to be strengthened when neutralizing strategies lead to decreased anxiety, a factor that overlaps with the behavioral model (Rachman, 1998; Salkovskis, 1985).

By comparison, 'bottom-up' cognitive models of OCD reflect an emphasis not on declarative, verbal beliefs, but rather on the processes of mental activity (Williams, Watts, MacLeod, & Mathews, 1997). Information-processing studies have shown that individuals with contamination-related OCD patients deploy excessive attentional resources toward contamination-related stimuli (Foa, Ilai, McCarthy, Shoyer, & Murdock, 1993; Tata, Leibowitz, Prunty, Cameron, & Pickering, 1996). OCD may also be characterized by enhanced memory for threat-related stimuli; after viewing a large number of 'contaminated' and 'clean' objects, patients with contamination-related OCD were more likely to remember which items had been 'contaminated' than were nonclinical control participants, although signal-detection analyses did not reveal a significant difference between the two groups (Radomsky & Rachman, 1999).

EMOTIONAL MODELS

OCD has traditionally been conceptualized as a fear-based disorder, and most current models of the disorder emphasize the role of fear and anxiety. Recent research, however, has begun to explore the potential role of disgust in contamination-related OCD. Disgust is characterized by a set of physiological, behavioral, and cognitive features (Levenson, 1992; Rozin, Haidt, & McCauley, 1993) that may be distinct from fear. The hypothesized evolutionary function of disgust is to prevent contamination and disease (Izard, 1993), in particular the oral incorporation of potential contaminants. Models of anxiety disorders have been developed around the disease-avoidance theory, including specific phobias of small animals (Matchett & Davey, 1991) and of blood, injections, and injuries (Sawchuk, Lohr, Tolin, Lee, & Kleinknecht, 2000; Tolin, Lohr, Sawchuk, & Lee, 1997). OCD patients with washing compulsions show a marked aversion to potential contamination, and many do not report or exhibit feelings of fear (Tallis, 1996), and often describe contaminated objects as 'disgusting' rather than 'frightening'. Emotion ratings before, during, and after exposure therapy indicate that contamination-related OCD patients experience feelings of disgust that are reduced by washing compulsions (Sieg & Scholz, 2001). OCD patients without washing compulsions did not report feelings of disgust. Evidence for the relationship of disgust sensitivity to OCD, however, has been mixed. In some studies, although disgust sensitivity correlated significantly with measures of OCD, the potential mediating role of other factors such as anxiety or depression either was not addressed (Olatunji, Sawchuk, Lohr, & De Jong, 2004; Schienle, Stark, Walter, & Vaitl, 2003), or was found to diminish the relationship between OCD and disgust (Muris, Merckelbach, Schmidt, & Tierney, 1999; Tolin, Woods, & Abramowitz, 2006; Woody & Tolin, 2002). In other studies, however, the relationship between disgust and OCD symptoms remained significant even after controlling for other emotional features

(Mancini, Gragnani, & D'Olimpio, 2001; Olatunji, Lohr, Sawchuk, & Tolin, 2007; Thorpe, Patel, & Simonds, 2003). Furthermore, nonclinical participants with high OCD scores show significantly reduced completion of disgust-related behavioral avoidance tests, and disgust sensitivity appears to mediate the relationship between OCD and avoidance of these tasks.

BIOLOGICAL MODELS

Neuroimaging and neurosurgical evidence suggest that OCD is associated with hyperactivity in frontal-striatal circuits of the brain that include the orbitofrontal cortex (OFC), anterior cingulate cortex (ACC), caudate nucleus, and thalamus (Baxter et al., 1992; Breiter & Rauch, 1996; Maltby, Tolin, Worhunsky, O'Keefe, & Kiehl, 2005; Saxena & Rauch, 2000). A few neuroimaging studies have investigated whether different OCD symptoms are associated with different patterns of neural activation. Among healthy controls, viewing washing-related pictures is associated with activation in dorsal and ventral prefrontal regions; this pattern differed somewhat from activations while viewing checking- and hoarding-related pictures, both of which were associated with more restricted prefrontal activation (Mataix-Cols et al., 2003). A heterogeneous group of OCD patients exhibited significantly greater activation in the ventromedial prefrontal cortex and right caudate than did healthy controls while viewing washing-related pictures; this again was distinct from patterns of activation while viewing other picture categories (Mataix-Cols et al., 2004). These studies did not, however, examine the specific relationship between patterns of neural activation and symptoms of contamination-related OCD. Rauch and colleagues (1998) found a trend toward positive correlations between severity of washing symptoms (in the absence of symptom provocation) and regional cerebral blood flow in the left OFC, bilateral ACC, and right dorsolateral prefrontal cortex. While viewing washing-related pictures, individuals with contamination-related OCD symptoms exhibited activation in the insula and visual regions (Phillips et al., 2000).

To what extent do the neural findings described above resemble those associated with the basic emotion of disgust? Across studies, there appears to be a relationship between disgust and activation of the basal ganglia (Phan, Wager, Taylor, & Liberzon, 2002). The insula has also been frequently cited in studies of disgust; in particular, studies comparing disgust with fear suggest a specific relationship between disgust and insular activation (Phillips et al., 1997; Shapira et al., 2003; Sprengelmeyer, Rausch, Eysel, & Przuntek, 1998; Wright, He, Shapira, Goodman, & Liu, 2004). Other studies, however, have found that the insula may be active during both fear and disgust (Schafer, Schienle, & Vaitl, 2005; Schienle, Schafer, Stark, Walter, & Vaitl, 2005; Schienle et al., 2002; Stark et al., 2003), leading some (e.g., Schienle et al., 2002) to suggest that the insula is part of a common affective circuit that is activated during processing of emotions in general, rather than specifically related to disgust. Several studies have found a relationship between activation of the amygdala and the processing of disgust-inducing stimuli; however, this relationship co-occurred with activation of the insula (Schafer et al., 2005; Schienle et al., 2002; Stark et al., 2003).

To date, only two fMRI studies have investigated the specific relationship between contamination-related OCD and the emotion of disgust. Phillips and colleagues (2000) examined differences between OCD patients who were primarily washers or checkers and healthy controls while viewing disgust-relevant and washing-relevant pictures. For all participants, viewing disgust-relevant pictures was associated with activation in the insula and visual regions. When viewing washing-relevant pictures, only patients who were primarily washers demonstrated similar activation in the insula and visual regions. Shapira and colleagues (2003) investigated differences between OCD patients who were primarily washers and healthy controls while viewing disgust-inducing and threat-inducing pictures. Washers demonstrated greater activation in the right insula, parahippocampal region, and inferior frontal regions while viewing disgust-inducing pictures compared to healthy controls. The groups did not differ significantly while viewing threat-inducing pictures. These findings highlight the relationship between washing symptoms and the emotion of disgust.

RELATIONSHIP TO OBSESSIVE–COMPULSIVE DISORDER

STUDIES OF OCD PATIENT SUBTYPES

In many respects, contamination fears and washing/cleaning compulsions represent prototypical symptoms of OCD. Traditionally, subtype models of OCD have been employed, in which patients are categorized as 'washers', 'checkers', 'hoarders', etc. Studies using cluster analysis of responses to the symptom checklist of the Yale–Brown Obsessive Compulsive Scale (Y–BOCS; Goodman et al., 1989) have identified distinct groups of patients who could be described as primarily contamination-fearful (Abramowitz, Franklin, Schwartz, & Furr, 2003; Calamari, Wiegartz, & Janeck, 1999; Calamari et al., 2004). In two studies that used a 5-cluster solution, the contamination/washing group represented 25% of treatment-seeking OCD patients (Abramowitz et al., 2003; Calamari et al., 1999). In a study that used a 7-cluster solution, the contamination/washing group represented 18% of the total sample (Calamari et al., 2004).

STUDIES OF OCD SYMPTOM DIMENSIONS

Analyses of OCD subtypes have been criticized for two main reasons (see Taylor, 2005, for a review). First, OCD symptoms appear to exist on a continuum from subclinical to severe, therefore discrete subtypes (e.g., in which a patient is designated as being a 'washer' or not) may be inadequate to describe this continuum. Second (and perhaps more problematic for categorical models), most OCD patients do not fit neatly into specific symptom categories. Rather, the majority of patients report multiple symptoms of different kinds (Foa et al., 1995). Therefore, examination of OCD symptom dimensions, rather than symptom subtypes, may be preferable. Dimensional models allow each participant to be rated on the severity, rather than mere presence, of a symptom; they also allow participants to be rated on several different symptoms rather than being restricted to one subtype. Factor analyses of the Y–BOCS symptom checklist have generally yielded a contamination/ washing factor that is distinct from the other symptoms (Leckman et al., 1997; Mataix-Cols, Marks, Greist, Kobak, & Baer, 2002; Mataix-Cols, Rauch, Manzo, Jenike, & Baer, 1999; Summerfeldt, Richter, Antony, & Swinson, 1999), although in three studies, contamination and harming-related symptoms were part of the same factor (Baer, 1994; Feinstein, Fallon, Petkova, & Liebowitz, 2003; Hantouche & Lancrenon, 1996), possibly consistent with the common fear that one will spread harmful contamination to others. Consistent with the hypothesized role of disgust in contamination-related OCD, in one study the contamination-related items on the Y–BOCS checklist could be divided into those that focused on disgust or revulsion toward contaminants, vs. those that focused on harm resulting from contaminants. The harm-related items loaded onto an 'aggressive obsessions' factor, whereas the disgust-related items loaded onto their own unique factor (Feinstein, Fallon, Petkova, & Liebowitz, 2003).

The dichotomous scoring of the Y–BOCS symptom checklist, however, does not lend itself particularly well to factor analysis. Some authors have altered the scoring of the measure; for example, employing a numeric system that 'weighted' a symptom more heavily if patients endorsed it as their primary concern (Baer, 1994), or summing the number of positive lifetime symptoms within each hypothesized symptom dimension (Leckman et al., 1997). It is not clear whether these unique scoring methods clarify or obscure the true dimensions of OCD symptoms; we note that in the latter study (Leckman et al., 1997) there could be an advantage for hypothesized dimensions that had more items. Other studies have employed measures that use ordinal scaling of symptom severity, rather than nominal scaling of the presence or absence of symptoms. In one such study using the self-report Padua Inventory (Sanavio, 1988), Van Oppen, Hoekstra, & Emmelkamp (1995) found a distinct factor of contamination-related OCD symptoms. Recently, Rosario-Campos and colleagues (2006) developed the Dimensional Yale–Brown Obsessive Compulsive Scale (DY–BOCS), a semi-structured interview that examines the severity of multiple symptom dimensions for each participant. Sixty-one percent of a pediatric sample, and 69% of an adult sample, reported a lifetime history of contamination-related symptoms. Note that these proportions are much higher than are those in the previous 'subtype' studies (Abramowitz et al., 2003; Calamari et al., 1999; Calamari, Weigartz, & Janeck, 2004), suggesting that many OCD patients who would otherwise be categorized in different subtypes still report clinically relevant contamination-related symptoms. The contamination dimension on the DY–BOCS correlated significantly with sexual/religious and hoarding-related dimensions in the pediatric sample, but not in the adult sample.

EXTERNAL VALIDATION OF SUBTYPES AND DIMENSIONS

Cluster-analytic studies (Abramowitz et al., 2003; Calamari, Wiegartz, & Janeck, 1999; Calamari et al., 2004) have revealed no significant differences between contamination-related OCD patients and those in other subtypes in terms of age, gender, or overall OCD severity. In one study, contamination-related patients showed less depression and trait anxiety than did patients in a 'certainty' subgroup (Calamari et al., 1999), although in another study there was no difference across subtypes in terms of the frequency of comorbid depressive or anxiety disorders (Abramowitz et al., 2003). Few of the dimensional studies examined external validators of the obtained symptom dimensions; in the DY–BOCS study, the contamination dimension did not correlate significantly with measures of depression or general anxiety (Rosario-Campos et al., 2006). Contamination-related symptoms were not predictive of the presence of personality disorders (Mataix-Cols, Baer, Rauch, & Jenike, 2000).

TREATMENT

PHARMACOTHERAPY

Serotonin reuptake inhibitors (SRIs) are the first-line pharmacological treatment for OCD (Rasmussen & Eisen, 1997). Across studies, 30–60% of OCD patients respond to SRI monotherapy, although some earlier studies employed a fairly liberal definition of 'treatment response' (for a review see Tolin, Abramowitz, & Diefenbach, 2005). Meta-analytic studies suggest that the SRI clomipramine may yield higher rates of responding than do the selective SRIs (SSRIs), but that no SSRI is superior to any other (Greist, Jefferson, Kobak, Katzelnick, & Serlin, 1995; Stein, Spadaccini, & Hollander, 1995).

To date, the relationship between OCD symptom dimensions/subtypes and response to SRI medication has received little empirical attention. In a large sample of OCD patients who had received a variety of SRI medications, patients reporting symptoms of compulsive hoarding showed a less favorable response to medications than did patients with other symptom dimensions (including contamination). Contamination-related OCD did not predict treatment response to a greater extent than did other symptom dimensions (Mataix-Cols et al., 1999).

COGNITIVE–BEHAVIORAL THERAPY (CBT)

The most widely studied variant of CBT for OCD is exposure and response prevention (ERP), which consists of graded, prolonged exposure to fear-eliciting stimuli or situations, combined with instructions for strict abstinence from compulsive behaviors. Numerous controlled studies attest to the efficacy of ERP for patients with OCD (Cottraux, Mollard, Bouvard, & Marks, 1993; Fals-Stewart,

Marks, & Schafer, 1993; Foa et al., 2005; Lindsay, Crino, & Andrews, 1997; van Balkom et al., 1998). In addition, open trials suggest that ERP is also at least moderately effective for patients who have not responded adequately to medications for OCD (Kampman, Keijsers, Hoogduin, & Verbraak, 2002; Tolin, Maltby, Diefenbach, Hannan, & Worhunsky, 2004).

In an early study, OCD symptom subtype was unrelated to outcome of ERP (Foa & Goldstein, 1978). In two larger studies, poorer response to ERP was found among patients with compulsive hoarding symptoms (Abramowitz et al., 2003; Mataix-Cols et al., 2002); one of these also found a decreased treatment response among patients with sexual and religious obsessions (Mataix-Cols et al., 2002). Patients with contamination-related OCD, on the other hand, fared about as well as did patients with other symptom subtypes. Mataix-Cols et al. (2002) reported a 14% dropout rate and 64% responder rate (defined as a 40% or greater Y–BOCS decrease) among contamination-related OCD patients; these figures did not differ significantly from those of other subtypes. Abramowitz et al. (2003) reported a 9% dropout rate and 70% rate of clinically significant change (Jacobson & Truax, 1991), which again did not differ from other subtypes. However, in a study of group CBT, McLean and colleagues (2001) found that only 9% of patients classified as 'washers,' compared to 20% of primarily 'obsessional' patients, 33% of 'checkers,' and 58% of patients with 'miscellaneous' OCD symptoms, were classified as having recovered.

Cognitive therapy (CT), another variant of CBT, aims to teach patients to identify and correct dysfunctional beliefs about feared situations (e.g., Wilhelm & Steketee, 2006). Although CT has received less empirical attention to date than has ERP, the existing data appear encouraging (Cottraux et al., 2001; Emmelkamp, Visser, & Hoekstra, 1988; van Balkom et al., 1998; van Oppen et al., 1995; Whittal, Thordarson, & McLean, 2005). At this time it is not clear whether ERP and CT operate via different mechanisms of action, as the 'behavioral experiments' in CT resemble exposure, and thus may facilitate habituation as well as the 'indirect' cognitive change that is as evident among ERP patients as it is among CT patients (McLean et al., 2001; Whittal et al., 2005). One novel and intense variant of CT for contamination-related OCD patients ('Danger Ideation Reduction Therapy,' or DIRT), however, did not employ direct exposure to possible contaminants (Jones & Menzies, 1997). In addition to traditional cognitive restructuring dialogue, this treatment also incorporated experiences designed to alter threat appraisals, such as watching filmed interviews with various workers who regularly contact contamination-related stimuli and did not become ill, discussion of the results of a series of microbiological experiments showing a lack of transfer of pathogenic microorganisms when contacting avoided stimuli, and discussion aimed at generating realistic probability estimates. The DIRT intervention appeared effective in reducing symptoms of contamination-related OCD in a small controlled trial (Jones & Menzies, 1998) as well as in an open pilot study of five adult patients who had previously failed to respond to pharmacotherapy and ERP (Krochmalik, Jones, & Menzies, 2001).

The potential role of disgust in contamination-related OCD may have implications for CBT. In studies of patients with specific phobia of spiders, exposure-based therapy led to reductions in both self-reported fear and disgust toward spiders, although it did not appear to influence more general disgust sensitivity (de Jong, Andrea, & Muris, 1997; de Jong, Vorage, & van den Hout, 2000; Merckelbach, de Jong, Arntz, & Schouten, 1993; Smits, Telch, & Randall, 2002). Self-reported disgust appeared to habituate more slowly than did self-reported fear, suggesting that disgust-based reactions may require longer exposure sessions. Changes in fear and disgust appeared to be at least partially independent of each other, suggesting two distinct emotional processes (Smits, Telch, & Randall, 2002). In a study of analogue spider phobic participants, Edwards and Salkovskis (2006) presented one of three stimuli during a session of prolonged video exposure to spiders: neutral (teddy bear), disgust (fake vomit), or fear (a tarantula). When the tarantula, but not the teddy bear or fake vomit, was presented, participants reported an increase in fear and disgust. When the fake vomit was presented, participants reported an increase in disgust, but not fear. The study authors concluded that the experience of fear enhances the disgust response, but not vice versa. In the absence of a 'pure' fear-eliciting stimulus, however, one cannot be certain whether fear, or a combined fear and disgust reaction, is the more important determinant of response to exposure. We note as well that the 'fear' stimulus, a spider, was much more closely aligned with the participants' concerns (spider phobia) and the ongoing exposure exercise (watching a video of spiders) than was the 'disgust' stimulus (fake vomit). It is perhaps not surprising that exposure to vomit does not substantially impact reports of spider phobia; the relevance of this finding is unclear.

Few studies have investigated the role of disgust in exposure-based treatment for OCD. McKay (2006) exposed patients with contamination-related vs. contamination-unrelated OCD symptoms to disgust (but not fear)-eliciting stimuli, as well as to fear-eliciting stimuli. No differences were detected between the groups in terms of habituation to fear-eliciting stimuli. However, the contamination-related OCD group showed less, and slower, habituation to the disgust-eliciting stimuli than did the group with other forms of OCD. Thus, some individuals with contamination-related OCD may show a particularly strong disgust reaction that is slow to habituate.

CONCLUSIONS

Regardless of whether a subtype or dimensional perspective is taken, contamination fears and washing/cleaning compulsions represent a distinct and robust variant of OCD. As illustrated by the two patients described at the beginning of this chapter, some individuals with contamination fear express a concern that they or others will be harmed by disease, whereas others report a more vague sense of distress, revulsion, and 'dirtiness' without specific fears of harm. Contamination-related OCD symptoms might be characterized not only by fear but also by the emotional process of disgust, as well as the sympathetic magic beliefs thought to be characteristic of disgust processes. Sympathetic magic beliefs are evident in patients with contamination-related OCD (e.g., a belief that contagion lasts forever and that mere physical similarity can render an object contaminated). Although most treatment outcome studies have indicated that contamination-related OCD responds to treatment about as well as do other forms of OCD, one study of group CBT found that these patients were less likely to show a strong response than were patients with other forms of OCD. One factor that may affect treatment response is the role of disgust in the habituation response; disgust, as compared to fear, may show a slower, and attenuated, response to exposure-based treatment.

REFERENCES

Abramowitz, J. S., Franklin, M. E., Schwartz, S. A., & Furr, J. M. (2003). Symptom presentation and outcome of cognitive–behavioral therapy for obsessive–compulsive disorder. *Journal of Consulting and Clinical Psychology, 71*, 1049–1057.

Baer, L. (1994). Factor analysis of symptom subtypes of obsessive compulsive disorder and their relation to personality and tic disorders. *Journal of Clinical Psychiatry, 55 Suppl*, 18–23.

Baxter, L. R., Jr., Schwartz, J. M., Bergman, K. S., Szuba, M. P., Guze, B. H., Mazziotta, J. C., Alazraki, A., Selin, C. E., Ferng, H. K., Munford, P., et al. (1992). Caudate glucose metabolic rate changes with both drug and behavior therapy for obsessive–compulsive disorder. *Archives of General Psychiatry, 49*, 681–689.

Beck, A. T., Emery, G., & Greenberg, R. L. (1985). *Anxiety disorders and phobias: A cognitive perspective*. New York: Basic Books.

Breiter, H. C., & Rauch, S. L. (1996). Functional MRI and the study of OCD: from symptom provocation to cognitive–behavioral probes of cortico-striatal systems and the amygdala. *NeuroImage, 4*, S127–138.

Calamari, J. E., Wiegartz, P. S., & Janeck, A. S. (1999). Obsessive–compulsive disorder subgroups: a symptom-based clustering approach. *Behaviour Research and Therapy, 37*, 113–125.

Calamari, J. E., Wiegartz, P. S., Riemann, B. C., Cohen, R. J., Greer, A., Jacobi, D. M., Jahn, S. C., & Carmin, C. (2004). Obsessive–compulsive disorder subtypes: an attempted replication and extension of a symptom-based taxonomy. *Behaviour Research and Therapy, 42*, 647–670.

Cottraux, J., Mollard, E., Bouvard, M., & Marks, I. (1993). Exposure therapy, fluvoxamine, or combination treatment in obsessive–compulsive disorder: one-year followup. *Psychiatry Research, 49*, 63–75.

Cottraux, J., Note, I., Yao, S. N., Lafont, S., Note, B., Mollard, E., Bouvard, M., Sauteraud, A., Bourgeois, M., & Dartigues, J. F. (2001). A randomized controlled trial of cognitive therapy versus intensive behavior therapy in obsessive compulsive disorder. *Psychotherapy and Psychosomatics, 70*, 288–297.

de Jong, P. J., Andrea, H., & Muris, P. (1997). Spider phobia in children: Disgust and fear before and after treatment. *Behaviour Research and Therapy, 35*, 559–562.

de Jong, P. J., Vorage, I., & van den Hout, M. A. (2000). Counterconditioning in the treatment of spider phobia: Effects on disgust, fear and valence. *Behaviour Research and Therapy, 38*, 1055–1069.

Edwards, S., & Salkovskis, P. M. (2006). An experimental demonstration that fear, but not disgust, is associated with return of fear in phobias. *Journal of Anxiety Disorders, 20*, 58–71.

Emmelkamp, P. M., Visser, S., & Hoekstra, R. J. (1988). Cognitive therapy vs exposure in vivo in the treatment of obsessive–compulsives. *Cognitive Therapy and Research, 12*, 103–144.

Fairbrother, N., Newth, S. J., & Rachman, S. (2005). Mental pollution: Feelings of dirtiness without physical contact. *Behaviour Research and Therapy, 43*, 121–130.

Fairbrother, N., & Rachman, S. (2004). Feelings of mental pollution subsequent to sexual assault. *Behaviour Research and Therapy, 42*, 173–189.

Fals-Stewart, W., Marks, A. P., & Schafer, J. (1993). A comparison of behavioral group therapy and individual behavior therapy in treating obsessive–compulsive disorder. *Journal of Nervous and Mental Disease, 181*, 189–193.

Feinstein, S. B., Fallon, B. A., Petkova, E., & Liebowitz, M. R. (2003). Item-by-item factor analysis of the Yale–Brown Obsessive Compulsive Scale Symptom Checklist. *Journal of Neuropsychiatry and Clinical Neuroscience, 15*, 187–193.

Foa, E. B., & Goldstein, A. (1978). Continuous exposure and complete response prevention in the treatment of obsessive–compulsive neurosis. *Behavior Therapy, 9*, 821–829.

Foa, E. B., Ilai, D., McCarthy, P. R., Shoyer, B., & Murdock, T. (1993). Information processing in obsessive–compulsive disorder. *Cognitve Therapy and Research, 17*, 173–189.

Foa, E. B., Kozak, M. J., Goodman, W. K., Hollander, E., Jenike, M. A., & Rasmussen, S. A. (1995). DSM-IV field trial: Obsessive–compulsive disorder. *American Journal of Psychiatry, 152*, 90–96.

Foa, E. B., Liebowitz, M. R., Kozak, M. J., Davies, S., Campeas, R., Franklin, M. E., Huppert, J. D., Kjernisted, K., Rowan, V., Schmidt, A. B., Simpson, H. B., & Tu, X. (2005). Randomized, placebo-controlled trial of exposure and ritual prevention, clomipramine, and their combination in the treatment of obsessive–compulsive disorder. *American Journal of Psychiatry, 162*, 151–161.

Goodman, W. K., Price, L. H., Rasmussen, S. A., Mazure, C., Fleischmann, R. L., Hill, C. L., Heninger, G. R., & Charney, D. S. (1989). The Yale–Brown Obsessive Compulsive Scale. I. Development, use, and reliability. *Archives of General Psychiatry, 46*, 1006–1011.

Greist, J. H., Jefferson, J. W., Kobak, K. A., Katzelnick, D. J., & Serlin, R. C. (1995). Efficacy and tolerability of serotonin transport inhibitors in obsessive–compulsive disorder. A meta-analysis. *Archives of General Psychiatry, 52*, 53–60.

Hantouche, E. G., & Lancrenon, S. (1996). [Modern typology of symptoms and obsessive–compulsive syndromes: results of a large French study of 615 patients]. *Encephale, 22 Spec No. 1*, 9–21.

Hodgson, R. J., & Rachman, S. (1972). The effects of contamination and washing in obsessional patients. *Behaviour Research and Therapy, 10*, 111–117.

Izard, C. E. (1993). Organizational and motivational functions of discrete emotions. In M. Lewis & J. M. Haviland (Eds.), *Handbook of emotions*. New York: Guilford Press.

Jacobson, N. S., & Truax, P. (1991). Clinical significance: A statistical approach to defining meaningful change in psychotherapy research. *Journal of Consulting and Clinical Psychology, 59*, 12–19.

Jones, M. K., & Menzies, R. G. (1997). Danger ideation reduction therapy (DIRT): preliminary findings with three obsessive–compulsive washers. *Behaviour Research and Therapy, 35*, 955–960.

Jones, M. K., & Menzies, R. G. (1998). Danger ideation reduction therapy (DIRT) for obsessive–compulsive washers: A controlled trial. *Behaviour Research and Therapy, 36*, 959–970.

Kampman, M., Keijsers, G. P., Hoogduin, C. A., & Verbraak, M. J. (2002). Addition of cognitive–behaviour therapy for obsessive–compulsive disorder patients non-responding to fluoxetine. *Acta Psychiatrica Scandinavica, 106*, 314–319.

Kozak, M. J., & Foa, E. B. (1997). *Mastery of obsessive–compulsive disorder: A cognitive–behavioral approach*. San Antonio, TX: The Psychological Corporation.

Krochmalik, A., Jones, M. K., & Menzies, R. G. (2001). Danger Ideation Reduction Therapy (DIRT) for treatment-resistant compulsive washing. *Behaviour Research and Therapy, 39*, 897–912.

Leckman, J. F., Grice, D. E., Boardman, J., Zhang, H., Vitale, A., Bondi, C., Alsobrook, J., Peterson, B. S., Cohen, D. J., Rasmussen, S. A., Goodman, W. K., McDougle, C. J., & Pauls, D. L. (1997). Symptoms of obsessive–compulsive disorder. *American Journal of Psychiatry, 154*, 911–917.

Levenson, R. W. (1992). Autonomic nervous system differences among emotions. *Psychological Science, 3*, 23–27.

Lindsay, M., Crino, R., & Andrews, G. (1997). Controlled trial of exposure and response prevention in obsessive–compulsive disorder. *British Journal of Psychiatry, 171*, 135–139.

Maltby, N., Tolin, D. F., Worhunsky, P., O'Keefe, T. M., & Kiehl, K. A. (2005). Dysfunctional action monitoring hyperactivates frontal-striatal circuits in obsessive–compulsive disorder: an event-related fMRI study. *NeuroImage, 24*, 495–503.

Mancini, F., Gragnani, A., & D'Olimpio, F. (2001). The connection between disgust and obsessions and compulsions in a non-clinical sample. *Personality and Individual Differences, 31*, 1173–1180.

Mataix-Cols, D., Baer, L., Rauch, S. L., & Jenike, M. A. (2000). Relation of factor-analyzed symptom dimensions of obsessive–compulsive disorder to personality disorders. *Acta Psychiatrica Scandinavica, 102*, 199–202.

Mataix-Cols, D., Cullen, S., Lange, K., Zelaya, F., Andrew, C., Amaro, E., Brammer, M. J., Williams, S. C., Speckens, A., & Phillips, M. L. (2003). Neural correlates of anxiety associated with obsessive–compulsive symptom dimensions in normal volunteers. *Biological Psychiatry, 53*, 482–493.

Mataix-Cols, D., Marks, I. M., Greist, J. H., Kobak, K. A., & Baer, L. (2002). Obsessive–compulsive symptom dimensions as predictors of compliance with and response to behaviour therapy: results from a controlled trial. *Psychotherapy and Psychosomatics, 71*, 255–262.

Mataix-Cols, D., Rauch, S. L., Manzo, P. A., Jenike, M. A., & Baer, L. (1999). Use of factor-analyzed symptom dimensions to predict outcome with serotonin reuptake inhibitors and placebo in the treatment of obsessive–compulsive disorder. *American Journal of Psychiatry, 156*, 1409–1416.

Mataix-Cols, D., Wooderson, S., Lawrence, N., Brammer, M. J., Speckens, A., & Phillips, M. L. (2004). Distinct neural correlates of washing, checking, and hoarding symptom dimensions in obsessive–compulsive disorder. *Archives of General Psychiatry, 61*, 564–576.

Matchett, G., & Davey, G. C. (1991). A test of a disease-avoidance model of animal phobias. *Behaviour Research and Therapy, 29*, 91–94.

McKay, D. (2006). Treating disgust reactions in contamination-based obsessive–compulsive disorder. *Journal of Behavior Therapy and Experimental Psychiatry, 37*, 53–59.

McLean, P. D., Whittal, M. L., Thordarson, D. S., Taylor, S., Sochting, I., Koch, W. J., Paterson, R., & Anderson, K. W. (2001). Cognitive versus behavior therapy in the group treatment of obsessive–compulsive disorder. *Journal of Consulting and Clinical Psychology, 69*, 205–214.

Merckelbach, H., De Jong, P. J., Arntz, A., & Schouten, E. (1993). The role of evaluative learning and disgust sensitivity in the etiology and treatment of spider phobia. *Advances in Behaviour Research and Therapy, 15*, 243–255.

Muris, P., Merckelbach, H., Schmidt, H., & Tierney, S. (1999). Disgust sensitivity, trait anxiety and anxiety disorder symptoms in normal children. *Behaviour Research and Therapy, 37*, 953–961.

OCCWG (Obsessive Compulsive Cognitions Working Group) (1997). Cognitive assessment of obsessive–compulsive disorder. *Behaviour Research and Therapy, 35*, 667–681.

OCCWG (Obsessive Compulsive Cognitions Working Group) (2005). Psychometric validation of the Obsessive Beliefs Questionnaire and the Interpretation of Intrusions Inventory: Part 2, factor analyses and testing of a brief version. *Behaviour Research and Therapy, 43*, 1527–1542.

Olatunji, B. O., Lohr, J. M., Sawchuk, C. N., & Tolin, D. F. (2007). Multimodal assessment of disgust in contamination-related obsessive–compulsive disorder. *Behaviour Research and Therapy, 45*, 263–276.

Olatunji, B. O., Sawchuk, C. N., Lohr, J. M., & De Jong, P. J. (2004). Disgust domains in the prediction of contamination fear. *Behaviour Research and Therapy, 42*, 93–104.

Phan, K. L., Wager, T., Taylor, S. F., & Liberzon, I. (2002). Functional neuroanatomy of emotion: a meta-analysis of emotion activation studies in PET and fMRI. *NeuroImage, 16*, 331–348.

Phillips, M. L., Marks, I. M., Senior, C., Lythgoe, D., O'Dwyer, A. M., Meehan, O., Williams, S. C., Brammer, M. J., Bullmore, E. T., & McGuire, P. K. (2000). A differential neural response in obsessive–compulsive disorder patients with washing compared with checking symptoms to disgust. *Psychological Medicine, 30*, 1037–1050.

Phillips, M. L., Young, A. W., Senior, C., Brammer, M., Andrew, C., Calder, A. J., Bullmore, E. T., Perrett, D. I., Rowland, D., Williams, S. C., Gray, J. A., & David, A. S. (1997). A specific neural substrate for perceiving facial expressions of disgust. *Nature, 389*, 495–498.

Rachman, S. (1994). Pollution of the mind. *Behaviour Research and Therapy, 32*, 311–314.

Rachman, S. (1998). A cognitive theory of obsessions: elaborations. *Behaviour Research and Therapy, 36*, 385–401.

Radomsky, A. S., & Rachman, S. (1999). Memory bias in obsessive–compulsive disorder (OCD). *Behaviour Research and Therapy, 37*, 605–618.

Rasmussen, S. A., & Eisen, J. L. (1997). Treatment strategies for chronic and refractory obsessive–compulsive disorder. *Journal of Clinical Psychiatry, 58 Suppl 13*, 9–13.

Rauch, S. L., Dougherty, D. D., Shin, L. M., Baer, L., Breiter, H. C. R., Savage, C. R., & Jenike, M. A. (1998). Neural correlates of factor-analyzed OCD symptom dimension: A PET study. *CNS Spectrums, 3*.

Rosario-Campos, M. C., Miguel, E. C., Quatrano, P. C., Ferrao, Y., Findley, D., Scahill, L., King, R., Woody, S., Tolin, D. F., Hollander, E., Kano, Y., Goodman, W. K., & Leckman, J. F. (2006). The Dimensional Yale–Brown Obsessive Compulsive Scale (DY–BOCS): An instrument for assessing obsessive–compulsive symptom dimensions. *Molecular Psychiatry, 11*, 495–504.

Rozin, P., Haidt, J., & McCauley, C. R. (1993). Disgust. In M. Lewis & J. M. Haviland (Eds.), *Handbook of Emotions*. New York: Guilford Press.

Rozin, P., Millman, L., & Nemeroff, C. (1986). Operations of the laws of sympathetic magic in disgust and other domains. *Journal of Personality and Social Psychology, 50*, 703–712.

Salkovskis, P. M. (1985). Obsessional–compulsive problems: A cognitive–behavioural analysis. *Behaviour Research and Therapy, 23*, 571–583.

Sanavio, E. (1988). Obsessions and compulsions: The Padua Inventory. *Behaviour Research and Therapy, 26*, 169–177.

Sawchuk, C. N., Lohr, J. M., Tolin, D. F., Lee, T. C., & Kleinknecht, R. A. (2000). Disgust sensitivity and contamination fears in spider and blood-injection-injury phobias. *Behaviour Research and Therapy, 38*, 753–762.

Saxena, S., & Rauch, S. L. (2000). Functional neuroimaging and the neuroanatomy of obsessive–compulsive disorder. *Psychiatric Clinics of North America, 23*, 563–586.

Schafer, A., Schienle, A., & Vaitl, D. (2005). Stimulus type and design influence hemodynamic responses towards visual disgust and fear elicitors. *International Journal of Psychophysiology, 57*, 53–59.

Schienle, A., Schafer, A., Stark, R., Walter, B., & Vaitl, D. (2005). Neural responses of OCD patients towards disorder-relevant, generally disgust-inducing and fear-inducing pictures. *International Journal of Psychophysiology, 57*, 69–77.

Schienle, A., Stark, R., Walter, B., Blecker, C., Ott, U., Kirsch, P., Sammer, G., & Vaitl, D. (2002). The insula is not specifically involved in disgust processing: an fMRI study. *Neuroreport, 13*, 2023–2026.

Schienle, A., Stark, R., Walter, B., & Vaitl, D. (2003). The connection between disgust sensitivity and blood-related fears, faintness symptoms, and obsessive–compulsiveness in a non-clinical sample. *Anxiety, Stress, and Coping, 16*, 185–193.

Shapira, N. A., Liu, Y., He, A. G., Bradley, M. M., Lessig, M. C., James, G. A., Stein, D. J., Lang, P. J., & Goodman, W. K. (2003). Brain activation by disgust-inducing pictures in obsessive–compulsive disorder. *Biological Psychiatry, 54*, 751–756.

Sieg, J., & Scholz, O. B. (2001). Subjektives Gefühls- und Körpererleben bei Wasch- und Kontrollzwangshandlungen [Subjective emotional and physical experience during compulsive washing and checking]. *Verhaltenstherapie, 11*, 288–296.

Smits, J. A., Telch, M. J., & Randall, P. K. (2002). An examination of the decline in fear and disgust during exposure-based treatment. *Behaviour Research and Therapy, 40*, 1243–1253.

Sprengelmeyer, R., Rausch, M., Eysel, U. T., & Przuntek, H. (1998). Neural structures associated with recognition of facial expressions of basic emotions. *Proceedings: Biological Sciences, 265*, 1927–1931.

Stark, R., Schienle, A., Walter, B., Kirsch, P., Sammer, G., Ott, U., Blecker, C., & Vaitl, D. (2003). Hemodynamic responses to fear and disgust-inducing pictures: an fMRI study. *International Journal of Psychophysiology, 50*, 225–234.

Stein, D. J., Spadaccini, E., & Hollander, E. (1995). Meta-analysis of pharmacotherapy trials for obsessive–compulsive disorder. *International Clinical Psychopharmacology, 10*, 11–18.

Summerfeldt, L. J., Richter, M. A., Antony, M. M., & Swinson, R. P. (1999). Symptom structure in obsessive–compulsive disorder: a confirmatory factor-analytic study. *Behaviour Research and Therapy, 37*, 297–311.

Tallis, F. (1996). Compulsive washing in the absence of phobic and illness anxiety. *Behaviour Research and Therapy, 34*, 361–362.

Tata, P. R., Leibowitz, J. A., Prunty, M. J., Cameron, M., & Pickering, A. D. (1996). Attentional bias in obsessional compulsive disorder. *Behaviour Research and Therapy, 34*, 53–60.

Taylor, S. (2005). Dimensional and subtype models of OCD. In J. S. Abramowitz & A. C. Houts (Eds.), *Concepts and controversies in obsessive–compulsive disorder* (pp. 27–41). New York: Springer.

Thorpe, S. J., Patel, S. P., & Simonds, L. M. (2003). The relationship between disgust sensitivity, anxiety and obsessions. *Behaviour Research and Therapy, 41*, 1397–1409.

Tolin, D. F., Abramowitz, J. S., & Diefenbach, G. J. (2005). Defining 'response' in clinical trials for OCD: A signal detection analysis of the Yale–Brown Obsessive–Compulsive Scale. *Journal of Clinical Psychiatry, 66*, 1549–1557.

Tolin, D. F., Brady, R. E., & Hannan, S. E. (in press). Obsessive beliefs and symptoms of obsessive–compulsive disorder in a clinical sample. *Behaviour Research and Therapy*.

Tolin, D. F., Lohr, J. M., Sawchuk, C. N., & Lee, T. C. (1997). Disgust and disgust sensitivity in blood-injection-injury and spider phobia. *Behaviour Research and Therapy, 35*, 949–953.

Tolin, D. F., Maltby, N., Diefenbach, G. J., Hannan, S. E., & Worhunsky, P. (2004). Cognitive-behavioral therapy for medication nonresponders with obsessive–compulsive disorder: A wait-list-controlled open trial. *Journal of Clinical Psychiatry, 65*, 922–931.

Tolin, D. F., Woods, C. M., & Abramowitz, J. S. (2003). Relationship between obsessive beliefs and obsessive–compulsive symptoms. *Cognitive Therapy and Research, 27*, 657–669.

Tolin, D. F., Woods, C. M., & Abramowitz, J. S. (2006). Disgust sensitivity and obsessive–compulsive symptoms in a nonclinical sample. *Journal of Behavior Therapy and Experimental Psychiatry, 37*, 30–40.

Tolin, D. F., Worhunsky, P., & Maltby, N. (2004). Sympathetic magic in contamination-related OCD. *Journal of Behavior Therapy and Experimental Psychiatry, 35*, 193–205.

Tsao, S. D., & McKay, D. (2004). Behavioral avoidance tests and disgust in contamination fears: distinctions from trait anxiety. *Behaviour Research and Therapy, 42*, 207–216.

van Balkom, A. J., de Haan, E., van Oppen, P., Spinhoven, P., Hoogduin, K. A., & van Dyck, R. (1998). Cognitive and behavioral therapies alone versus in combination with fluvoxamine in the treatment of obsessive compulsive disorder. *Journal of Nervous and Mental Disease, 186*, 492–499.

van Oppen, P., de Haan, E., van Balkom, A. J., Spinhoven, P., Hoogduin, K., & van Dyck, R. (1995). Cognitive therapy and exposure in vivo in the treatment of obsessive compulsive disorder. *Behaviour Research and Therapy, 33*, 379–390.

van Oppen, P., Hoekstra, R. J., & Emmelkamp, P. M. (1995). The structure of obsessive–compulsive symptoms. *Behaviour Research and Therapy, 33*, 15–23.

Whittal, M. L., Thordarson, D. S., & McLean, P. D. (2005). Treatment of obsessive–compulsive disorder: cognitive behavior therapy vs. exposure and response prevention. *Behaviour Research and Therapy, 43*, 1559–1576.

Wilhelm, S., & Steketee, G. (2006). *Cognitive therapy for obsessive–compulsive disorder: A guide for professionals*. Oakland, CA: New Harbinger.

Williams, J. M. G., Watts, F. N., MacLeod, C., & Mathews, A. (1997). *Cognitive psychology and emotional disorders* (2nd ed.). New York: John Wiley & Sons.

Woody, S. R., & Tolin, D. F. (2002). The relationship between disgust sensitivity and avoidant behavior: studies of clinical and nonclinical samples. *Journal of Anxiety Disorders, 16*, 543–559.

Wright, P., He, G., Shapira, N. A., Goodman, W. K., & Liu, Y. (2004). Disgust and the insula: fMRI responses to pictures of mutilation and contamination. *Neuroreport, 15*, 2347–2351.

2

DOUBTING AND COMPULSIVE CHECKING

ADAM S. RADOMSKY, ANDREA R. ASHBAUGH, LAURIE A. GELFAND, AND MICHEL J. DUGAS

Department of Psychology, Concordia University, Montreal

PHENOMENOLOGY AND HISTORY

Compulsive checking is one of the most common, yet most complex symptoms of obsessive–compulsive disorder (OCD); its prevalence among symptoms of OCD is second only to compulsive washing/cleaning (Rachman & Hodgson, 1980). Patients can spend many hours each day checking not only certain objects or places in their homes or other environments, but can also be consumed by mentally checking their recollections of these previous checks in an attempt to ensure that they were performed correctly. Interestingly, as will be described below, checking can become intertwined with other OCD symptoms such as compulsive cleaning or hoarding, as patients will often check to ensure that something has been properly cleaned or that their many belongings are properly ordered and arranged. Checking behavior is paradoxical in nature as people who check repeatedly should presumably experience a subsequent reduction in their urge to check again, yet this does not seem to occur. Importantly, some degree of checking, even repeated checking, is also common in the general population; for example, many people report repeatedly checking for their passports and/or tickets before or during travel, or repeatedly checking that an alarm clock is properly set the night before an important morning appointment. While claims related to this, that checking behavior occurs

Correspondence to: Adam S. Radomsky, Department of Psychology, Concordia University, 7141 Sherbrooke West, Montreal, QC, H4B 1R6, Canada.

19

on a continuum from normative checking to more pathological checking, have been longstanding, a recent taxometric analysis (which assesses the degree to which a particular construct is dimensional or categorical in nature) has shown that, among a number of different beliefs and symptoms, checking behavior clearly does fit best within a dimensional characterization and not a categorical one (Haslam, Williams, Kyrios, McKay, & Taylor, 2005).

Early models of, and treatments for, compulsive checking were psychodynamic in nature and unfortunately did not lead to improvements in the lives of people with OCD (Knight, 1941). The next important development in understanding compulsive checking came from behavioral conceptualizations. Checking (along with other forms of OCD) was presumed to result from conditioning experiences that paired negative events (e.g., fires, burglaries, floods, and other aversive experiences) with previously neutral stimuli (e.g., stoves, door locks, faucets). Compulsive behavior was proposed to be maintained because the behavior served as a negative reinforcement for recurrent urges to check. That is, an urge to check (an unpleasant sensation) that subsided following checking behavior was reinforced by this behavior and therefore likely to recur. This account of compulsive checking is consistent with Mowrer's (1960) two-stage theory, but unfortunately has not received wide support in the literature. This is predominantly because many people who engage in compulsive behavior often deny a previous experience during which a negative event, such as those described above, occurred (see Rachman, 1977). Despite shortcomings in behavioral models of compulsive checking, the main treatment that resulted from them, exposure and response prevention, stands as an effective intervention for compulsive checking (see below for more information about treatments). This is likely at least partially due to the fact the compulsive urges, in this case to check, have been shown to spontaneously decay with time (Rachman, de Silva, & Roper, 1976), supporting the use of response prevention techniques from both behavioral and cognitive–behavioral perspectives.

COGNITIVE MODELS: RESPONSIBILITY/THREAT

The next important advancement in the conceptualization of compulsive checking came in the form of a cognitive approach to understanding OCD. This approach was based on the concept of 'inflated responsibility' (Salkovskis, 1985) and was a significant and productive step forward in our ability to conceptualize obsessions and compulsions generally, and compulsive checking in particular. Salkovskis proposed that rather than thinking about how behavioral mechanisms contribute to the onset and maintenance of OCD, as described above, it was necessary to think about cognitive components of the disorder. Initially, these were broadly construed in terms of 'inflated responsibility', defined as 'the belief that one possesses pivotal power to provoke or prevent subjectively crucial negative outcomes' (Salkovskis, Rachman, Ladouceur, & Freeston, 1992, cited in Salkovskis, 1996, p. 111). While this important cognitive reformulation was applied broadly to all forms of OCD, it has been particularly relevant to compulsive checking.

Intuitively, one would not bother to check something unless one *felt responsible* for preventing some form of harm from occurring. This explains why people who compulsively check only check certain objects – usually their own.

There have been a number of psychometric investigations demonstrating significant relationships (often based on correlations) between inflated responsibility and checking symptomatology (e.g., Rhéaume, Ladouceur, Freeston, & Letarte, 1995; Salkovskis et al., 2000). And, while a number of studies have implicated other cognitive domains, such as the overestimation of threat, as more specific to checking symptomatology (e.g., Emmelkamp & Aardema, 1999; Tolin, Abramowitz, Brigidi, & Foa, 2003), the most convincing evidence of connections between responsibility and checking comes from experimental work. In a novel experimental manipulation of perceived responsibility, participants meeting the diagnostic criteria for OCD with compulsive checking as a primary symptom signed 'responsibility contracts' that either assigned complete responsibility for any harm that may result from an improper check to the participant or to the experimenter (Lopatka & Rachman, 1995). Those participants assigned to the 'high responsibility condition' reported significantly greater urges to check and estimations of threat than those assigned to the 'low responsibility condition'. A second highly novel and informative experimental study of connections between responsibility and checking was conducted by Ladouceur et al. (1995). In this study, non-clinical participants were asked to complete a pill sorting task under one of two conditions. In the high responsibility condition, participants were told that the results of their individual performance would have important implications for the health of inhabitants of a developing country, whereas those in the low responsibility condition were told that the study was designed to assess color perception and that their sorting trials were only for practice. Ladouceur et al. (1995) found that participants in the high responsibility condition showed significantly more compulsive behavior (e.g., hesitations, checking, etc.) than those in the low responsibility condition. Other experiments (e.g., Shafran, 1997) replicated these findings, confirming the critical role that inflated responsibility plays in compulsive checking (and other OCD) symptomatology.

Interestingly, all of the responsibility manipulations described above also involve the manipulation of threat to some extent. This reflects the complicated nature of inflated responsibility, is consistent with its definition (Salkovskis, Rachman, Ladouceur, & Freeston, 1992) and explains why two of the original six OCD belief domains (responsibility and threat overestimation) identified by the Obsessive Compulsive Cognitions Working Group (OCCWG, 1997) have recently been collapsed into one domain, based on a large psychometric investigation (OCCWG, 2005).

NEW DIRECTIONS IN RESEARCH ON RESPONSIBILITY IN CHECKING

Increasingly, research evaluating the relationships between compulsive checking and inflated responsibility has led to the suggestion that inflated responsibility is comprised of several components. Results identifying separate dimensions of inflated responsibility have led to some new questions about its homogeneity, and about how achieving a better understanding of its complex structure may contribute to a greater understanding of obsessive–compulsive (OC) symptoms in general, and of compulsive checking in particular. This may require revisions and/or extensions to existing measures of responsibility. Menzies and colleagues (2000) examined perceptions of responsibility for negative outcomes as they occurred for 'the self' versus 'for others' in a non-clinical population. Two groups of participants were asked to rate the severity of 10 different negative outcomes, half of which were related to checking. Participants in the 'personally responsible' condition completed a questionnaire that described them as being responsible for an action that may have led to a negative outcome, whereas those in the 'other responsible' condition completed a questionnaire presenting someone other than the participant as being responsible for the potentially negative outcome. It was found that those in the 'personally responsible' condition rated the severity of negative outcomes as being significantly greater than those in the 'other responsible' condition. This suggests that increasing an individual's *personal* responsibility for a negative outcome leads to increases in their estimates of outcome severity, and that the perception of being *personally* responsible differs from perceptions of others' responsibility. Although there was no significant interaction between responsibility condition and outcome type (checking or otherwise), it is clear from these results that perceptions of *who is responsible* may indeed affect one of the important cognitive components (perceived severity of harm) associated with checking behavior (Rachman, 2002).

One implication is that there may be a facet of responsibility that is affected by interpersonal beliefs, in that beliefs about other people's responsibility for the outcome of an event may have an effect on beliefs about one's own responsibility for the same outcome. In this way, Ashbaugh, Gelfland, & Radomsky (2006) investigated the hypothesis that interpersonal aspects of responsibility are related to OCD symptomatology. They asked participants to complete a questionnaire package that included newly developed measures designed to evaluate different features of interpersonal influences on responsibility. Predictably, the overall results of this study suggest that interpersonal beliefs about responsibility were related to all measured OCD symptom types. However, when examining personal responsibility in comparison with the perceived responsibility of others specifically relating to externally manifested OCD symptoms (such as checking), a different picture emerged. The relationship between the belief that others are responsible and compulsive symptomatology (i.e., checking) disappeared after personal beliefs about responsibility were accounted for, suggesting instead that these beliefs are intertwined with checking symptomatology. Ashbaugh et al. (2006) that this resulted from the fact that for overt, more observable symptoms such as checking, other people may indeed have an impact on the outcome of the event (e.g., by being able to provide reassurance, to check themselves), whereas for an OCD symptom such as experiencing repugnant unwanted intrusive blasphemous images, the responsibility of other people may be irrelevant. After controlling for depression and inflated personal responsibility, it was also found that the belief that one is more responsible than others was significantly related to OCD symptoms where one is attempting to ensure that no harm will come to pass, such as checking. On the contrary, an OCD symptom such as obsessions was found to be least related to this same belief. This suggests that the structure of inflated responsibility may be different depending on the symptom context in which it appears, and that comparative beliefs about responsibility might not be as relevant for some symptom types as they are for others. Finally, when evaluating how high- and low-checking individuals distribute or allocate responsibility, individuals scoring highly on a measure of checking symptoms allocated significantly more responsibility to themselves than to others in general; this was particularly apparent for events that had a neutral or negative valence. That an individual with checking symptoms allocates more responsibility to themselves under negative circumstances is consistent with the current definition of inflated responsibility, and is thus not altogether surprising. However, in terms of neutral events, it may be that individuals who score high on a measure of checking symptoms interpret neutral events as negative, such that the ambiguity of a neutral event may be enough to categorize it as a negative one. Thus, based on this research, it may be possible to develop interventions that help individuals to distinguish their personal beliefs about responsibility from those regarding other people's responsibility.

INTOLERANCE OF UNCERTAINTY IN COMPULSIVE CHECKING

Over the past decade, the relationship between intolerance of uncertainty and clinical forms of anxiety has received increased attention. In particular, research suggests that intolerance of uncertainty plays a key role in both OCD and generalized anxiety disorder (GAD). In the GAD literature, intolerance of uncertainty has typically been assessed using the Intolerance of Uncertainty Scale (IUS; Freeston, Rhéaume, Letarte, Dugas, & Ladouceur, 1994). Studies using the IUS have shown that patients with GAD report higher levels of intolerance of uncertainty than do patients with panic disorder (Dugas, Marchand, & Ladouceur, 2005), patients with various other anxiety disorders (Ladouceur et al., 1999), and non-clinical controls (Dugas, Gagnon, Ladouceur, & Freeston, 1998). In non-clinical samples, studies relying on the IUS suggest that intolerance of uncertainty is more closely related to worry (the cardinal feature of GAD) than to panic and OC symptoms (Dugas, Gosselin, & Ladouceur, 2001).

In the OCD literature, studies have relied either on a subscale of the Obsessive Beliefs Questionnaire (OBQ; OCCWG, 1997) or the IUS to assess intolerance of uncertainty. One study using the OBQ found that a group of patients with OCD had higher levels of intolerance of uncertainty than did a group of patients with various other anxiety disorders (Steketee, Frost, & Cohen, 1998). In a more focused investigation, Tolin, Abramowitz, Brigidi, & Foa (2003), using the IUS, observed that individuals diagnosed with OCD who reported compulsive checking as a primary symptom were more intolerant of uncertainty than were individuals diagnosed with OCD who did not report compulsive checking as problematic and then non-clinical controls (the latter groups had equivalent levels of intolerance of uncertainty). Finally, in a study using the IUS in a sample of non-clinical individuals, Holoway, Heimberg, & Coles (2006) found that checking and doubting compulsions were more highly related to intolerance of uncertainty than were most other forms of compulsive behavior.

Overall, these findings suggest that intolerance of uncertainty plays a particularly important role in GAD and compulsive checking in OCD. It stands to reason that holding negative beliefs about uncertainty and its implications can lead to different types of responses, some of which are more adaptive than others. One such response is worry (as in GAD), where the individual becomes excessively preoccupied by the multiple negative outcomes that may result from the uncertainty-inducing, ambiguous situations of everyday life. Another such response is compulsive checking (as in OCD), where the person repeatedly checks in an attempt to eliminate the uncertainty and anxiety associated with a particular situation and/or a particular future threat. Therefore, it may be that intolerance of uncertainty leads to a variety of responses, two of the most prevalent being excessive worry and checking behavior. Although these two types of responses have mostly been discussed separately in the literature, they are obviously not mutually exclusive phenomena. Clinical observations and empirical data clearly indicate that different forms of checking are prevalent in GAD and that excessive worrying is an associated feature of OCD checking (as well as other OCD symptoms). As such, exposure to an ambiguous situation may trigger a complex pattern of cognitive, emotional, and behavioral responses in those who are intolerant of uncertainty. For some, the primary response may be one of excessive worry, whereas for others, the main response may be one of compulsive checking, while for others, the main response may be the combination of worry and checking (for others still, the primary response may not be worry or checking, but we will restrict our discussion to these two responses for the purposes of this chapter). Although the patterns of worry and checking may fluctuate, they tend to show relatively stable individual differences. As a case in point, patients with GAD clearly favor worry over checking whereas OCD checkers clearly favor checking over worry and while GAD and OCD clearly share some features, most would argue that these two diagnostic categories are reliably and validly distinct.

Given that intolerance of uncertainty can lead to different patterns of responses that show relatively stable individual differences, the next step is to elucidate the personal and situational factors that combine to determine these specific patterns of responses. Simply stated, why does intolerance of uncertainty lead primarily to worry for some individuals and mainly to checking for others? The answer to this question has the potential to make a significant contribution to our understanding of the cognitive processes involved in different forms of clinical and non-clinical anxiety and this work is currently under way.

CHECKING IN OTHER FORMS OF OCD AND IN OTHER
PSYCHOPATHOLOGY: THE CONCEPT OF SUBTYPES

As stated previously, checking can and does occur in the context of other forms of OCD. While the most commonly checked objects are appliances, door locks, and other aspects of an individual's environment from which potential harm could result, people diagnosed with OCD will often check to ensure that certain objects are clean, have been properly counted, or have been properly placed (McKay et al., 2004; Radomsky & Taylor, 2005). Clinical reports reveal that individuals can even check to ensure that certain thoughts or images have left their minds and/or repeatedly check their memories in an attempt to reassure themselves that a compulsion (sometimes checking compulsions, but others as well) has been carried out properly. It can therefore be said that compulsive checking can cut across most, if not all other OCD symptomatology.

Similarly, checking is a feature of a number of other disorders. Compulsive checking has been documented in generalized anxiety disorder (Schut, Castonguay, & Borkovec, 2001); patients with panic disorder will often repeatedly check their pulse (Rachman & de Silva, 2004); patients with health anxiety/hypochondriasis will often repeatedly check a number of different sensations and also repeatedly check with physicians and other health care providers about the status of their health (Salkovskis & Warwick, 1986; Taylor & Asmundson, 2004); individuals with both eating disorders (Fairburn, Cooper, & Shafran, 2003) and body dysmorphic disorder (Rosen, Reiter, & Orosan, 1995) will repeatedly check their bodies for weight- and/or shape-related changes; and depressed patients have been shown to check with others about their self-worth (Joiner, Alfano, & Metalsky, 1992).

Interestingly, some of the 'checking' described in the previous paragraph could also be described as reassurance-seeking. Reassurance-seeking has recently been described as 'checking-by-proxy' (Rachman, 2002) and is probably best construed as a form of compulsive checking, also likely related to responsibility, threat, and metamemory (Parrish & Radomsky, submitted).

Given that compulsive checking in a variety of forms seems to cut across not only multiple manifestations of OCD, but also multiple other mental disorders, it seems unlikely that it would be a good fit with the concept of OCD subtypes, although much debate on this issue continues (McKay et al., 2004; Radomsky & Taylor, 2005).

ATTENTION, MEMORY AND METAMEMORY IN
COMPULSIVE CHECKING

While basic cognitive processes tend to be broadly connected to a number of mood and anxiety disorders, memory (and associated constructs like attention and metamemory – or factors that have to do with memory, such as the vividness of memory or the confidence that one has in one's memory) has an important connection to compulsive checking. When someone who checks compulsively is asked why they are going back to check something again, a common response is, 'Because I'm not sure if I did it correctly before.' This seems to imply the presence of a problem in memory, although as outlined below, the role of memory and other related processes in compulsive checking is quite complex.

There has been considerable debate about whether compulsive checking is characterized by a memory deficit or a memory bias. According to the memory deficit hypothesis, individuals compulsively check objects because of a short-term or long-term memory deficit (Sher, Frost, & Otto, 1983). However, the fact that checking is usually circumscribed (e.g., only a few specific items are checked) argues against a general memory deficit. Building upon models of information processing and emotion (Bower, 1981), other researchers have suggested that compulsive checkers may actually have a *more accurate memory* for stimuli that are consistent with their fears (Radomsky, Rachman, & Hammond, 2001). Both hypotheses have been assessed.

A number of memory processes have been examined in relation to compulsive checking. Clear evidence either for or against a memory deficit has been scarce. Evidence for a memory deficit has been demonstrated in some studies that evaluated for memory for actions, with most studies demonstrating that clinical and non-clinical checkers are less accurate in recalling a series of actions that were performed earlier (Ecker & Engelcamp, 1995; Sher et al., 1983; Sher, Frost, Kushner, Crews, & Alexander, 1989; Sher, Mann, & Frost, 1984). In contrast, there is little evidence that compulsive checking is related to a reality monitoring deficit in which memory for actions that have been carried out is compared with memory for actions that have been imagined (Brown, Kosslyn, Breiter, Baer, & Jenike, 1994; Constans, Foa, Franklin, & Mathews, 1995; Hermans, Martens, De Cort, Pieters, & Eelen, 2003; McNally & Kohlbeck, 1993; Merckelbach & Wessel, 2000; Sher et al., 1983; but see Rubenstein, Peynircioglu, Chambless, & Pigott, 1993).

Evidence for verbal and non-verbal memory deficits are less clear. For example, Sher and colleagues (1984) found that non-clinical checkers performed significantly worse on the Logical Memory subscale of the Weschler Memory Scale, a measure of verbal memory. However, in other studies, no differences between clinical checkers and control participants were found on this same subscale (Sher et al., 1989), nor on other measures of verbal memory (e.g., MacDonald, Antony, MacLeod, & Richter, 1997). Similar inconsistencies have been found in studies that sought to assess non-verbal memory, with some studies finding that checkers are less accurate than non-checkers (Bouvard & Cottraux, 1997; Sher et al., 1989), and others finding checking to be unrelated to such memory processes (Sher et al., 1984; Tallis, Pratt, & Jamani, 1999).

Attempts have recently been made to reconcile these inconsistent findings using meta-analyses and through assessing memory in OCD using large batteries of neuropsychological tests. A recent meta-analysis examining memory in compulsive checking found no evidence for a reality monitoring or verbal recognition deficit, some evidence of a verbal and visual recall deficit, and evidence for a deficit associated with memory for actions (Woods, Vivea, Chambless, & Bayen, 2002). However, because most studies have not included clinical control groups, it is difficult to conclude how specific these memory deficits are to compulsive checking. Moritz and colleagues (2005) demonstrated, using a large battery of neuropsychological tests, that individuals with OCD did not perform significantly differently from an anxious control group on any test, including those assessing memory. Furthermore, several recent studies have failed to find any evidence for a relationship between checking and performance on neuropsychological tests (Moritz et al., 2005; Moritz, Jacobsen, Willenborg, Jelinek, & Fricke, 2006; Simpson et al., in press). In fact, some results suggests that any neuropsychological deficits observed in OCD can be accounted for by elevated levels of depression (Moritz, Kloss, Jahn, Schick, & Head, 2003; Moritz, Kuelz, Jacobsen, Kloss, & Fricke, 2006). Thus, recent evidence suggests that memory deficits observed in compulsive checking, and OCD in general may not be specific to these problems.

In contrast to research examining the possibility of a memory deficit in compulsive checking, research on memory *biases* has been more consistent. One of the first studies to find evidence of a memory bias in compulsive checking was actually intended to examine reality monitoring (Constans et al., 1995). In this study, groups of OC checkers and clinical controls were asked to either perform or imagine a series of actions that were either threat-related (e.g., lighting/blowing out a candle) or non-threat-related (e.g., pushing/pulling in a chair). OC checkers were more accurate in recalling the final state of threat-related objects (e.g., the candle was blown out), but not more accurate in recalling the final state of non-threat-related objects. This study demonstrated the possibility that compulsive checkers might more accurately recall threat-related material. Consistent with these findings, it was recently found that non-clinical checkers were more accurate in recalling which stove knobs they last checked compared to low checkers, after a single trial of turning on, turning off, and checking a random combination of stove burners (Ashbaugh & Radomsky, submitted). At least one study, however, has failed to find a memory bias in individuals with OCD and sub-clinical checkers (Tuna, Tekan, & Topçuoğ, 2005). However, unlike the previous two studies, which assessed memory for previously completed (or imagined) threat-related actions (e.g., checking a stove), this study only assessed memory for threat-related words.

A study by Radomsky, Rachman, & Hammond (2001) may help to explain the discrepant findings associated with memory research in compulsive checking. They had individuals diagnosed with OCD and who reported checking as a primary symptom repeatedly check objects that they normally checked under conditions of high responsibility (e.g., the participant was responsible for the outcome), low responsibility (e.g., the experimenter was responsible for the outcome), and no responsibility (e.g., they watched the actions unfold on a videotape a week later). When asked to recall the information, participants were more accurate in recalling threat-relevant information (e.g., how many times they checked) than threat-irrelevant information (e.g., the color of the experimenter's pen), especially under conditions of high responsibility. This suggests that memory biases may be apparent only under conditions in which inflated responsibility is present. Though replications of these studies are necessary, the few available studies supporting a memory bias suggest that such biases may exist under conditions in which an appropriate threat is perceived by participants. Standardized tests of memory and other cognitive processes may not be well suited to assessments of this nature. That is, it may be that in order to detect positive memory biases for threat, tests must be tailored to provoke these threats in participants. Since people who engage in compulsive checking often feel threatened, traditional tests of memory may underestimate these individuals' true memory abilities. These results and hypotheses support a recent call for research using ecologically valid stimuli and conditions of testing (Radomsky & Rachman, 2004).

Though empirical evidence suggests that compulsive checking is characterized by a memory bias for threat-related stimuli, such findings do not explain why individuals who compulsively check go back to check repeatedly. In fact, if compulsive checkers do have a better memory for threat-related stimuli, it is surprising that they would check at all. Decreased confidence in memory has been reported in several studies examining memory in compulsive checking (Hermans et al., 2003; McDonald, Antony, MacLeod, & Richter, 1997; McNally & Kohlbeck, 1993; Radomsky et al., 2001), though some studies have failed to show this effect (Moritz et al., 2005; Tallis, Pratt, & Jamani, 1999).

A recent series of influential studies have attempted to explore why compulsive checking may be associated with distrust in memory. Van den Hout and Kindt (2003a, 2003b, 2004) argue that repeated checking may result in increased conceptual or top-down processing and decreased perceptual or bottom-up processing of stimuli. This is proposed to lead to a less vivid and detailed memory trace, which in turn leads individuals to have less confidence in their memory. To test this hypothesis, they had undergraduate (non-clinical) participants check a virtual (i.e., on a computer screen) stove. On subsequent trials, participants either repeatedly checked the virtual stove (relevant checks) or a set of virtual light bulbs (irrelevant checks). Finally, all participants checked the stove again. Participants in the relevant checking condition reported a less vivid and detailed memory, and were less confident in their memory compared to participants in the irrelevant checking condition. That is, repeated checking produced memory distrust. These findings have been replicated several times using checks of real objects instead of virtual ones (Ashbaugh & Radomsky, submitted; Coles, Radomsky, & Horng, 2006; Radomsky, Gilchrist, & Dussault, 2006). Though more research demonstrating van den Hout and Kindt's (2003a) hypotheses using more varied designs is warranted, this promising new understanding of reduced memory confidence in association with compulsive checking may help reconcile research demonstrating an objective memory bias with self-reports of poor memory in compulsive checkers. In fact, Rachman (2002) suggests that the effect of repeated checking on memory confidence may be a 'self-perpetuating mechanism' that maintains compulsive checking behavior.

As with the research on memory in compulsive checking, there has been debate in the field about whether OCD is characterized by an attentional bias towards threat-related information or a more general reduction in cognitive inhibition, the process of inhibiting to-be-ignored information in order to selectively attend to other information in the environment. Proponents of the cognitive inhibition theory argue that a deficit in cognitive inhibition may explain the difficulty that individuals with OCD have in disengaging from unwanted thoughts (Enright & Beech, 1993). One way to measure cognitive inhibition is via negative priming. For example, in the Stroop color-naming task, negative priming occurs when an individual is asked to name a color that they had to ignore on the previous trial. On these negative priming trials individuals tend to exhibit slower reaction times compared to normal Stroop trials, which is believed to reflect the cost of cognitive inhibition. Enright and colleagues (1993, 1995) found that individuals with OCD exhibited less negative priming compared to anxious control participants, and that individuals with checking compulsions exhibited even less negative priming compared to individuals without checking compulsions (Enright, Beech, & Claridge, 1995). However, other researchers have been unable to replicate these findings when comparing compulsive checkers, non-checkers, and non-anxious control participants (MacDonald et al., 1999).

Proponents of the attentional bias hypothesis argue that OCD is characterized not by a general attentional deficit, but a selective attentional bias towards threat-related stimuli (Lavy, van Oppen, & van den Hout, 1994). One study found that non-clinical checkers exhibited an attention bias towards threatening information, as demonstrated by slower reaction times on a Stroop colour-naming task when the stimuli were threat-related compared to non-threat-related (Novara & Sanavio, 2001). This has been replicated in diverse samples of individuals with OCD, which included individuals who compulsively check (Cohen, Lachenmeyer, & Springer, 2003; Lavy, van Oppen, & van den Hout, 1994), though this effect has not been consistently demonstrated in all studies (Kyrios & Iob, 1998). Unfortunately, given the inconsistencies of the findings to date, and the fact that few of these studies have specifically examined attention in relation to compulsive checking, it is difficult to draw firm conclusions regarding the role of attention in compulsive checking.

In summary, the debate continues as to whether compulsive checking is characterized by attentional and memorial biases or deficits. The limited research on attention processes prevents us from drawing firm conclusions about whether compulsive checking is characterized by selective attentional biases, or general cognitive inhibition deficits. As far as memory is concerned, research appears to support the presence of a memory bias for threat-related information, though the exact nature of this bias, notably the conditions under which it occurs, would benefit from further investigation. Recent research suggests that decreased memory confidence may well explain self-reports of poor memory in compulsive checkers, as this may best be accounted for by poor memory confidence rather than by poor memory.

NEW COGNITIVE MODEL OF COMPULSIVE CHECKING

A recent cognitive model of compulsive checking has incorporated many of the constructs discussed earlier in this chapter in a comprehensive, integrated fashion (Rachman, 2002). The model can be summarized in three simple statements:

> Compulsive checking occurs when people who believe that they have a special, elevated responsibility for preventing harm feel unsure that a perceived threat has been adequately

reduced or removed. In their attempts to achieve certainty about the absence or the unlikeli-
hood of harm occurring, people with high responsibility repeatedly check for safety.
Paradoxically, these attempts to check for safety can produce adverse affects that turn the
checking behaviour into a self-perpetuating mechanism. (Rachman, 2002, p. 629)

As stated above, the model is essentially comprised of two main features:
'multipliers' and a self-perpetuating checking/doubting mechanism. Rachman
(2002) proposes that the 'multipliers' that operate in compulsive checking include
perceived responsibility, perceived probability of harm and perceived seriousness
of harm. The model states these multipliers interact with each other to produce
checking behavior. When the multipliers are all elevated, intense and prolonged
checking ensues. Similarly, when they are low, checking should be minimal.
Finally, under conditions of no responsibility, no perceived probability or seriousness of harm, checking should be absent. It will be important to determine if the
right combination of these multipliers does indeed increase or decrease checking
behavior and associated phenomena (urges to check, time spent checking, doubt,
anxiety, etc.) through the use of ecologically valid protocols and we are currently
investigating these questions.

The second main feature of the model is the self-perpetuating mechanism. It is
proposed that checking behavior itself produces conditions that promote doubt
and uncertainty. Support for this mechanism comes from several studies described
above (e.g., Coles, Radomsky & Horng, 2006; Radomsky, Gilchrist, & Dussault,
2006; van den Hout & Kindt, 2003a, 2003b, 2004) demonstrating that repeated
checking produces memory distrust. Together, the two main components of the
model both explain the psychopathology of compulsive checking in OCD and
also support the two main psychological treatments for this problem.

TREATMENT

Unfortunately, treatment research related to compulsive checking has not pro-
gressed as much as psychopathology research on checking. The prevailing psychological treatment for OCD, exposure and response prevention (ERP), is
moderately effective, but up to 50% of patients drop out of treatment or decline to
undertake this effective and empirically supported treatment because it is too
demanding or perceived as too threatening (e.g., Foa et al., 2005). The authors of
a recent analysis of the clinical efficacy of this method concluded that although
ERP is the best available treatment, only 50–60% of patients recover (Fisher &
Wells, 2005). Moreover, it is disappointing and troubling that the success rates
achieved when the treatment was introduced early in the 1970s have not increased
(e.g., Foa et al., 2005). Other recent studies appear to replicate earlier findings that
both individual ERP and individual CBT are effective treatments for OCD
(Whittal, Thordarson, & McLean, 2005), although there is some evidence that
group CBT is an inferior treatment, likely due to the complexity of CBT and the
highly heterogeneous nature of OCD (McLean et al., 2001).

While these results are not specific to compulsive checking, they can likely be generalized to compulsive checking, given the prevalence of this behavior in OCD. Despite the fact that research evaluating treatment for specific manifestations of OCD, such as compulsive checking, is scant, it has generally been shown that individuals with checking and washing/cleaning symptoms appear to respond better to behavioral treatments than do those with other compulsions and obsessions (Ball, Baer, & Otto, 1996). It would be surprising if treatments based more on cognitive and/or cognitive–behavioral interventions produced a different set of findings. However, given the relatively high drop-out and refusal rates, as well as the disappointingly low rates of clinically significant improvement, an update of currently effective treatments is warranted. This will likely focus on new cognitively based interventions that incorporate many of the above recent findings. These will likely include a number of interventions, perhaps based on interpersonal aspects of responsibility, changing beliefs about memory, boosting memory confidence, and/or lowering threshold for memory vividness.

It is anticipated that the above new advances in our understanding of compulsive checking, primarily from research that has investigated various aspects of cognition, will lead to cognitive interventions with enhanced effectiveness. Furthermore, treatment research that capitalizes on our ability to assess different OCD symptoms, either under the rubric of subtypes or not, is likely to improve our ability to better match treatments to specific individuals with specific symptoms. Given the current state of understanding of compulsive checking symptomatology, as well as the nature and volume of research in this area that is currently under way, this particular manifestation of OCD stands to benefit perhaps sooner and greater than other forms of this complicated and often debilitating disorder.

REFERENCES

Ashbaugh, A. R., Gelfand, L. A., & Radomsky, A. S. (2006). Interpersonal aspects of responsibility and obsessive compulsive symptoms. *Behavioural and Cognitive Psychotherapy, 34*, 151–163.

Ashbaugh, A.R., & Radomsky, A.S. (submitted). Attentional focus during repeated checking influences memory but not metamemory.

Ball, S.G., Baer, L., & Otto, M. W. (1996). Symptom subtypes of obsessive–compulsive disorder in behavioral treatment studies: A quantitative review. *Behaviour Research & Therapy, 34*, 47–51.

Bouvard, M., & Cottraux, J. D. (1997). Etude de la mémoire de sujets obsessionnels compulsifs laveurs et vérificateurs et de sujets contrôles. *Revue Européenne de Psychologie Appliquée, 47*, 189–195.

Bower, G. H. (1981). Mood and memory. *American Psychologist, 36*, 129–148.

Brown, H. D., Kosslyn, S. M., Breiter, H. C., Baer, L., & Jenike, M. A. (1994). Can patients with obsessive–compulsive disorder discriminate between precepts and mental images? A signal detection analysis. *Journal of Abnormal Psychology, 103*, 445–454.

Cohen, Y., Lachenmeyer, J. R., & Springer, C. (2003). Anxiety and selective attention in obsessive–compulsive disorder. *Behaviour Research & Therapy, 41*, 1311–1323.

Coles, M. E., Radomsky, A. S., & Horng, B. (2006). Exploring the boundaries of memory distrust from repeated checking: Increasing external validity and examining thresholds. *Behaviour Research & Therapy, 44*, 995–1006.

Constans, J. I., Foa, E. B., Franklin, M. E., & Mathews, A. (1995). Memory for actual and imagined events in OC checkers. *Behaviour Research & Therapy, 33*, 665–671.

Dugas, M. J., Gagnon, F., Ladouceur, R., & Freeston, M. H. (1998). Generalized Anxiety Disorder: A preliminary test of a conceptual model. *Behaviour Research & Therapy, 36*, 215–226.

Dugas, M. J., Gosselin, P., & Ladouceur, R. (2001). Intolerance of uncertainty and worry: Investigating narrow specificity in a nonclinical sample. *Cognitive Therapy and Research, 25*, 551–558.

Dugas, M. J., Marchand, A., & Ladouceur, R. (2005). Further validation of a cognitive–behavioral model of generalized anxiety disorder: Diagnostic and symptom specificity. *Journal of Anxiety Disorders, 19*, 329–343.

Ecker, W., & Engelcamp, J. (1995). Memory for actions in obsessive–compulsive disorder. *Behavioural and Cognitive Psychotherapy, 23*, 349–371.

Emmelkamp, P. M. G., & Aardema, F. (1999). Metacognition, specific obsessive–compulsive beliefs and obsessive–compulsive behaviour. *Clinical Psychology and Psychotherapy, 6*, 139–145.

Enright, S. J., & Beech, A. R. (1993). Further evidence of reduced cognitive inhibition in obsessive–compulsive disorder. *Personality and Individual Differences, 14*, 387–395.

Enright, S. J., Beech, A. R., & Claridge, G. S. (1995). A further investigation of cognitive inhibition in obsessive–compulsive disorder and other anxiety disorders. *Personality and Individual Differences, 19*, 535–542.

Fairburn, C. G., Cooper, Z., & Shafran, R. (2003). Cognitive-behaviour therapy for eating disorders: A 'transdiagnostic' theory and treatment. *Behaviour Research & Therapy, 41*, 509–528.

Fisher, P., & Wells, A. (2005). How effective are cognitive and behavioural treatments for OCD? A clinical significance analysis. *Behaviour Research & Therapy, 43*, 1543–1558.

Foa, E. B., Liebowitz, M. R., Kozak, M. J., Davies, S., Campeas, R., Franklin, M. E., et al. (2005). Randomized, placebo-controlled trial of exposure and ritual prevention, clomipramine, and their combination in the treatment of obsessive–compulsive disorder. *American Journal of Psychiatry, 162*, 151–161.

Freeston, M. H., Rhéaume, J., Letarte, H., Dugas, M. J., & Ladouceur, R. (1994). Why do people worry? *Personality and Individual Differences, 17*, 791–802.

Haslam, N., Williams, B. J., Kyrios, M., McKay, D., & Taylor, S. (2005). Subtyping obsessive–compulsive disorder: A taxometric analysis. *Behavior Therapy, 36*, 381–392.

Hermans, D., Martens, K., DeCort, K., Pieters, G., & Eelen, P. (2003). Reality monitoring and metacognitive beliefs related to cognitive confidence in obsessive–compulsive disorder. *Behaviour Research & Therapy, 41*, 383–401.

Holoway, R. M., Heimberg, R. G., Coles, M. E. (2006). A comparison of intolerance of uncertainty in analogue obsessive–compulsive disorder and generalized anxiety disorder. *Journal of Anxiety Disorders, 20*, 158–174.

Joiner, T. E., Alfano, M. S., & Metalsky, G. I. (1992). When depression breeds contempt: Reassurance seeking, self-esteem, and rejection of depressed college students by their roommates. *Journal of Abnormal Psychology, 101*, 165–173.

Knight, R. P. (1941). Evaluation of results of psychoanalytic therapy. *American Journal of Psychiatry, 98*, 434–446.

Kyrios, M., & Iob, M. A. (1998). Automatic and strategic processing in obsessive–compulsive disorder: Attentional bias, cognitive avoidance or more complex phenomena? *Journal of Anxiety Disorders, 21*, 271–292.

Ladouceur, R., Dugas, M. J., Freeston, M. H., Rhéaume, J., Blais, F., Gagnon, F., et al. (1999). Specificity of generalized anxiety disorder symptoms and processes. *Behavior Therapy, 30*, 191–207.

Ladouceur, R., Rhéaume, J., Freeston, M. H., Aublet, F., Jean, K., Lachance, S., et al. (1995). Experimental manipulations of responsibility: An analogue test for models of obsessive–compulsive disorder. *Behaviour Research & Therapy, 33*, 937–946.

Lavy, E., van Oppen, P., & van den Hout, M. (1994). Selective processing of emotional information in obsessive compulsive disorder. *Behaviour Research & Therapy, 32*, 243–246.

Lopatka, C., & Rachman, S. (1995). Perceived responsibility and compulsive checking: An experimental analysis. *Behaviour Research & Therapy, 33*, 673–684.

MacDonald, P. A., Antony, M. M., MacLeod, C. M., & Richter, M. A. (1997). Memory and confidence in memory judgments among individuals with obsessive compulsive disorder and non-clinical controls. *Behaviour Research & Therapy, 35*, 497–505.

MacDonald, P. A., Antony, M. M., MacCleod, C. M., & Swinson, R. P. (1999). Negative priming for obsessive–compulsive checkers and noncheckers. *Journal of Abnormal Psychology, 108*, 679–686.

McKay, D., Abramowitz, J. S., Calamari, J. E., Kyrios, M., Radomsky, A. S., Sookman, D., et al. (2004). A critical evaluation of obsessive–compulsive disorder subtypes: Symptoms versus mechanisms. *Clinical Psychology Review, 24*, 283–313.

McLean, P. D., Whittal, M. L., Thordarson, D. S., Taylor, S., Sochting, I., Koch, W. J., et al. (2001). Cognitive versus behavior therapy in the group treatment of obsessive–compulsive disorder. *Journal of Consulting and Clinical Psychology, 69*, 205–214.

McNally, R. J., & Kohlbeck, P. A. (1993). Reality monitoring in obsessive–compulsive disorder. *Behaviour Research & Therapy, 31*, 249–253.

Menzies, R. G., Harris, L. G., Cumming, S. R., & Einstein, D. A. (2000). The relationship between inflated responsibility and exaggerated danger expectancies in obsessive–compulsive disorder. *Behaviour Research and Therapy, 38*, 1029–1037.

Merckelbach, H., & Wessel, I. (2000). Memory for actions and dissociation in obsessive–compulsive disorder. *Journal of Nervous and Mental Disease, 188*, 846–848.

Moritz, S., Jacobsen, D., Willenborg, B., Jelinek, L., & Fricke, S. (2006). A check on the memory deficit hypothesis of obsessive–compulsive checking. *European Archives of Psychiatry and Clinical Neuroscience, 256*, 82–86.

Moritz, S., Kloss, M., Jacobson, D., Kellner, M., Andresen, B., Fricke, S., et al. (2005). Extent, profile, and specificity of visuospatial impairment in obsessive–compulsive disorder (OCD). *Journal of Clinical and Experimental Neuropsychology, 27*, 795–814.

Moritz, S., Kloss, M., Jahn, H., Schick, M., & Head, I. (2003). Impact of co-morbid depression on nonverbal memory and visuospatial performance in obsessive–compulsive disorder. *Cognitive Neuropsychiatry, 8*, 261–272.

Moritz, S., Kuelz, A. K., Jacobsen, D., Kloss, M., & Fricke, S. (2006). Severity of subjective cognitive impairment in patients with obsessive–compulsive disorder and depression. *Journal of Anxiety Disorders, 20*, 427–443.

Mowrer, O. H. (1960). *Learning theory and behavior*. New York: Wiley.

Novara, C., & Sanavio, E. (2001). Compulsive checking and selective processing of threatening information. *Psychological Reports, 88*, 1171–1181.

OCCWG (Obsessive Compulsive Cognitions Working Group) (1997). Cognitive assessment of obsessive–compulsive disorder. *Behaviour Research & Therapy, 35*, 667–681.

OCCWG (Obsessive Compulsive Cognitions Working Group) (2005). Psychometric validation of the obsessive belief questionnaire and interpretation of intrusions inventory – Part 2: Factor analyses and testing of a brief version. *Behaviour Research & Therapy, 43*, 1527–1542.

Parrish, C. L., & Radomsky, A. S. (submitted). An experimental investigation of responsibility and reassurance: Relationships with compulsive checking. Manuscript submitted for publication.

Rachman, S. (1977). The conditioning theory of fear acquisition: A critical examination. *Behaviour Research & Therapy, 15*, 375–387.

Rachman, S. (2002). A cognitive theory of compulsive checking. *Behaviour Research & Therapy, 40*, 625–639.

Rachman, S., & de Silva, P. (2004). *Panic disorder: The facts*. Oxford: Oxford University Press.

Rachman, S., de Silva, P., & Roper, G. (1976). The spontaneous decay of compulsive urges. *Behaviour Research & Therapy, 14*, 445–453.

Rachman, S., & Hodgson, R. J. (1980). *Obsessions and compulsions*. Englewood Cliffs, NJ: Prentice Hall.

Radomsky, A. S., & Rachman, S. (2004). The importance of importance in OCD memory research. *Journal of Behavior Therapy and Experimental Psychiatry, 35*, 137–151.

Radomsky, A. S., & Taylor, S. (2005). Subtyping OCD: Prospects and problems. *Behavior Therapy, 36*, 371–379.

Radomsky, A. S., Gilchrist, P. T., & Dussault, D. (2006). Repeated checking really does cause memory distrust. *Behaviour Research & Therapy, 44*, 305–316.

Radomsky, A. S., Rachman, S., & Hammond, D. (2001). Memory bias, confidence and responsibility in compulsive checking. *Behaviour Research & Therapy, 39*, 813–822.

Rhéaume, J., Ladouceur, R., Freeston, M. H., & Letarte, H. (1995). Inflated responsibility in obsessive–compulsive disorder: Validation of an operational definition. *Behaviour Research & Therapy, 33*, 159–169.

Rosen, J. C., Reiter, J., & Orosan, P. (1995). Cognitive–behavioral body image therapy for body dysmorphic disorder. *Journal of Consulting and Clinical Psychology, 63*, 263–269.

Rubenstein, C. S., Peynircioglu, Z. F., Chambless, D. L., & Pigott, T. A. (1993). Memory in sub-clinical obsessive compulsive checkers. *Behaviour Research & Therapy, 31*, 759–765.

Salkovskis, P. M. (1985). Obsessional–compulsive problems: A cognitive-behavioural analysis. *Behaviour Research & Therapy, 23*, 571–583.

Salkovskis, P. M. (1996). Cognitive-behavioural approaches to understanding Obsessional problems. In R. M. Rapee (Ed.), *Current controversies in the anxiety disorders* (pp. 103–133). New York: Guilford.

Salkovskis, P. M., Rachman, S., Ladouceur, R., & Freeston, M. (1992). *The definition of 'responsibility'.* Paper presented at the World Congress of Behavioural and Cognitive Psychotherapies, Toronto, Canada.

Salkovskis, P. M., & Warwick, H. M. (1986). Morbid preoccupations, health anxiety and reassurance: A cognitive-behavioural approach to hypochondriasis. *Behaviour Research & Therapy, 24*, 597–602.

Salkovskis, P. M., Wroe, A. L., Gledhill, A., Morrison, N., Forrester, R., Richards, C., et al. (2000). Responsibility attitudes and interpretations are characteristic of obsessive–compulsive disorder. *Behaviour Research & Therapy, 38*, 347–372.

Schut, A. J., Castonguay, L. G., & Borkovec, T. D. (2001). Compulsive checking behaviors in generalized anxiety disorder. *Journal of Clinical Psychology, 57*, 705–715.

Shafran, R. (1997). The manipulation of responsibility in obsessive–compulsive disorder. *British Journal of Clinical Psychology, 36*, 397–407.

Sher, K. J., Frost, R. O., Kushner, M., Crews, T. M., & Alexander, J. E. (1989). Memory deficits in compulsive checkers: Replication and extension in a clinical sample. *Behaviour Research & Therapy, 27*, 65–69.

Sher, K. J., Frost, R. O., & Otto, R. (1983). Cognitive deficits in compulsive checkers: An exploratory study. *Behaviour Research & Therapy, 21*, 357–363.

Sher, K. J., Mann, B., & Frost, R. O. (1984). Cognitive dysfunction in compulsive checkers: Further explorations. *Behaviour Research & Therapy, 22*, 493–502.

Simpson, H. B., Rosen, W., Huppert, J. D., Lin, S-H., Foa, E. B., & Liebowitz, M. R. (in press). Are there reliable neuropsychological deficits in obsessive–compulsive disorder? *Journal of Psychiatric Research.*

Steketee, G., Frost, R. O., & Cohen, I. (1998). Beliefs in obsessive–compulsive disorder. *Journal of Anxiety Disorders, 12*, 525–537.

Tallis, F., Pratt, P., & Jamani, N. (1999). Obsessive compulsive disorder, checking, and non-verbal memory: A neuropsychological investigation. *Behaviour Research & Therapy, 37*, 161–166.

Taylor, S., & Asmundson, G. J. G. (2004). *Treating health anxiety: A cognitive–behavioral approach.* New York: Guilford.

Tolin, D. F., Abramowitz, J. S., Brigidi, B. D., & Foa, E. B. (2003). Intolerance of uncertainty in obsessive–compulsive disorder. *Journal of Anxiety Disorders, 17*, 233–242.

Tolin, D. F., Woods, C. M., & Abramowitz, J. S. (2003). Relationship between obsessive beliefs and obsessive–compulsive symptoms. *Cognitive Therapy and Research, 27*, 657–669.

Tuna, S., Tekan, A. İ, & Topçuoğ, V. (2005). Memory and metamemory in obsessive–compulsive disorder. *Behaviour Research & Therapy, 43*, 15–27.

van den Hout, M., & Kindt, M. (2003a). Repeated checking causes memory distrust. *Behaviour Research & Therapy, 41*, 301–316.

van den Hout, M., & Kindt, M. (2003b). Phenomenological validity of an OCD-memory model and the remember/know distinction. *Behaviour Research & Therapy, 41*, 369–378.

van den Hout, M., & Kindt, M. (2004). Obsessive–compulsive disorder and the paradoxical effects of perseverative behaviour on experienced uncertainty. *Journal of Behavior Therapy and Experimental Psychiatry, 35*, 165–181.

Whittal, M. L., Thordarson, D. S., & McLean, P. D. (2005). Treatment of obsessive–compulsive disorder: Cognitive-behaviour therapy vs. exposure and response prevention. *Behaviour Research & Therapy, 43*, 1559–1576.

Woods, C. M., Vivea, J. L., Chambless, D. L., & Bayen, U. J. (2002). Are compulsive checkers impaired in memory? A meta-analytic review. *Clinical Psychological Science and Practice, 9*, 353–366.

3

SYMMETRY, ORDERING, AND ARRANGING

MEREDITH E. COLES AND ASHLEY S. PIETREFESA

Binghamton University, New York

PHENOMENOLOGY

Current data indicate that symmetry, ordering, and arranging is one of the more common presentations of obsessive–compulsive disorder (OCD) among individuals seeking treatment for this condition. Rasmussen and Eisen (1992) reported that in a large treatment sample of OCD patients, symmetry obsessions were present in 32% of individuals, while compulsions aimed at achieving symmetry and precision occurred in 28% of the sample. Symmetry, ordering, and arranging symptoms were also documented in the *DSM-IV* field trial for OCD (Foa et al., 1995). Across outpatient sites, symmetry obsessions were reported by 10% of over 400 patients, while ordering compulsions occurred at a rate of 6%. In addition to these data collected in the United States, data support the cross-cultural prevalence of symmetry, ordering, and arranging symptoms among treatment-seeking individuals. For example, a study of 90 Egyptian treatment-seeking patients with OCD revealed that symmetry/exactness obsessions occurred in 43% of these individuals, while ordering and arranging compulsions were reported by just over 50% of the sample (Okasha, Saad, Khalil, Dawla, & Yehia, 1994). Although there is variability in the precise prevalence rates for symmetry, ordering, and arranging across studies (lower estimates from the *DSM-IV* field trial than other papers), even the most

Correspondence to: Meredith E. Coles, Assistant Professor, Department of Psychology, Binghamton University (SUNY), Binghamton, NY 13902–6000.

modest estimates suggest that symmetry, ordering, and arranging symptoms occur in a notable portion of adults with OCD.

Epidemiological studies have also indicated that symmetry, ordering, and arranging is common in children and adolescents with OCD. In a study of non-referred high school students, straightening was the third most common ritual among 20 adolescents found to have OCD, reported by 35% of clinical cases. Three (15%) of these 20 adolescents with OCD also reported having to do things 'just right' (Flament et al., 1988), a likely correlate of symmetry, ordering and arranging symptoms. Another epidemiological study of a community sample of over 3000 young adolescents revealed that among the 26 adolescents identified as having OCD, arranging was the most frequently reported compulsion, reported by 56% of those with the disorder (Valleni-Basile et al., 1994).

One commonly noted feature of individuals with symmetry and ordering rituals is that their affective experiences are often devoid of the fear and anxiety typically seen in individuals with other OCD phenomenological profiles. In contrast to individuals whose OCD symptoms are aimed at preventing or avoiding harm (e.g., washing compulsions accompanied by contamination obsessions), those with symmetry, ordering, and arranging behaviors often do not report feared consequences of not engaging in their rituals. A number of clinicians have documented that these patients frequently describe their behavior as being exclusively aimed at reducing feelings of dissatisfaction, discomfort, or insufficiency associated with the perception that things are not just right (Rasmussen & Eisen, 1991, 1992; Summerfeldt, 2004; Summerfeldt, Kloosterman, Antony, Richter, & Swinson, 2004; Tallis, 1996). The occurrence of tension preceding, and relief following, the performance of a compulsive act has been noted to be more similar to the sensory experiences and premonitory sensory urges of individuals with tic disorders than to the anxiety experienced by OCD patients with harm-avoidant symptoms (Leckman, Walker, Goodman, Pauls, & Cohen, 1994; Rasmussen & Eisen, 1991). Indeed, contrasting patients with symmetry, ordering, and arranging to patients with other OCD symptom profiles, Rasmussen and Eisen (1991, 1992) noted that patients whose symptoms were characterized by a need for symmetry, order, and precision exhibited lower levels of anxiety and experienced their symptoms as more ego-syntonic.

Therefore, in addition to OCD symptoms being variable in their content, as is often noted, it appears that there is also variability in the motivations underlying symptoms. To date, categorization of OCD symptoms has typically relied on overt content, such as washing versus checking versus hoarding. Although this symptom content approach to classification has advantages and is pervasive, another approach to creating subgroups is to emphasize the underlying motivation behind symptoms – either to avoid harm or to achieve a sensation of things being 'just right' or complete. Instead of being motivated by a desire to prevent harm, some OCD symptoms may be motivated by a desire to get things 'just right' or to correct sensations of things being incomplete, independent of a separate feared consequence. Incompleteness has been described as a tormenting sensation arising from the perception that one's actions or experiences are insufficient or incomplete

(Summerfeldt, 2004). We propose that symmetry, ordering, and arranging symptoms represent a subtype of OCD symptoms that are frequently motivated by this desire to get things 'just right'.

Both clinical observations and available data suggest a link between symmetry, ordering, and arranging, and feelings of incompleteness or things not being 'just right'. Indeed, over a century ago Pierre Janet described individuals plagued by feelings of incompleteness as having a strong need for uniformity and order (in Pitman, 1987), alluding to a relationship with symmetry, ordering, and arranging symptoms. Consistent with Janet's view, recent writings also suggest a link between symmetry, ordering, and arranging and a desire to get things 'just right' or achieve a sense of completeness. For example, Rasmussen and Eisen (1991, 1992) noted that individuals exhibiting a need for things to be symmetrical or in a certain order experienced a subjective feeling of discontent or tension when objects were not perfectly even. These authors described several individuals with a pronounced desire for symmetry and precision, including a 26-year-old woman who felt unable to answer the telephone until she heard a ring that was exactly the right pitch, which often did not occur until after thirty or forty rings (Rasmussen & Eisen, 1991). Finally, in addition to these clinical observations, available data support a link between symmetry, ordering, and arranging and not just right experiences. In large undergraduate samples, symmetry, ordering, and arranging behavior has been significantly associated with reports of not just right experiences on screening questionnaires (Coles, Frost, Heimberg, & Rhéaume, 2003), and with the intensity of urges to react in response to not just right experiences elicited both in the lab and in naturally occurring situations (Coles, Heimberg, Frost, & Steketee, 2005). Thus, preliminary research and clinical observations converge to suggest that feelings of things being incomplete or not just right are a primary factor underlying preoccupations with symmetry and compulsive ordering and arranging.

In summary, available data suggest that symmetry, ordering and arranging symptoms are common in both adolescents and adults with OCD. These symptoms are unique in that individuals exhibiting symmetry, ordering and arranging behaviors frequently deny the anxiety and feared consequences characteristic of individuals with many other OCD symptom profiles. Therefore, we argue herein that instead of an exclusive reliance on overt symptom content in creating OCD subtypes, distinguishing the motivations underlying the symptoms may be important. Indeed, it appears that symmetry, ordering, and arranging symptoms are likely to be motivated by desires to get things 'just right' as opposed to the more commonly considered desire to prevent harm. Attention to this somewhat unique motivational basis may provide a more comprehensive framework for understanding the nature and treatment of symmetry, ordering, and arranging.

ETIOLOGY AND CONCEPTUALIZATION

Although symmetry, ordering, and arranging symptoms are frequently clustered together as being unique from other domains of OCD symptoms, very little work has addressed the etiology of these symptoms specifically. At the current time, very little is known about the phenomenology of symmetry, ordering, and arranging (Radomsky & Rachman, 2004). However, available data suggest that symmetry, ordering, and arranging behaviors have their roots in normal phenomena. Indeed, such behaviors are prevalent among healthy children (Evans, Leckman, Carter, & Reznick, 1997), and common in the social rituals of many cultures (Fiske & Haslam, 1997). In addition, research has shown that non-clinical samples demonstrate a preference for order and symmetry (Radomsky & Rachman, 2004). Therefore, it is possible that the disruptive levels of symmetry, ordering, and arranging observed in clinical OCD samples may represent a failure to extinguish normal childhood habits or an exacerbation of culturally prescribed patterns of behavior.

The disruptive levels of symmetry, ordering, and arranging observed in clinical OCD samples may represent a continuation of childhood behaviors and habits that typically decrease over time. It has been speculated that there is continuity between childhood rituals and OCD (Leonard, Goldberger, Rapoport, Cheslow, & Swedo, 1990). Casual observation and controlled research have both shown that symmetry, ordering, and arranging behaviors are common in non-clinical children. Young children frequently show a preference for balance, symmetry and wholeness, and often exhibit 'just right' phenomena by arranging favored objects in relatively strict and circumscribed ways (Evans et al., 1997; Leonard et al., 1990). Consistent with these observations, Evans and colleagues (1997) found that approximately 60% of parents of 2-, 3-, and 4-year-olds reported that their child engaged in 'just right' behaviors. They also found that 'just right' behaviors had a mean age of onset of slightly less than 2 years (22 months), suggesting that these rituals involving symmetry are common at a very young age.

Additional data from Evans et al. (1997), in combination with other findings, suggest that the prevalence of symmetry, ordering and arranging behaviors typically decreases as children mature, but that these behaviors continue to be common. Evans et al. (1997) found the highest rates of 'just right' behaviors in children aged 2, 3, and 4 years, and that rates decreased in a sample of 5- and 6-year-old children. However, it is important to note that 'just right' behaviors continued beyond age 4. Approximately 45% of parents of 5-year-olds reported that their child engaged in this type of behavior (Evans et al., 1997). Consistent with these findings, Leonard and colleagues (1990) noted that numerous OCD-like behaviors, such as games with elaborate rules and prohibitions, collecting of objects, etc., continue throughout childhood and into adolescence.

Moving beyond early childhood, some additional research suggests that symmetry, ordering, and arranging behaviors are common in both adolescents and adults, although the prevalence of such behaviors seems to decrease with increasing age. Using a sample of non-clinical control children between the ages of 9 and 18, Leonard et al. (1990) found that 27% engaged in at least one marked ritualized behavior. Further, the majority of examples provided by Leonard and colleagues (1990) represent symmetry, ordering, and arranging (e.g., arranging a collection, arranging possessions). Studying a slightly older sample, Rassin, Merckelbach, Muris, & Stapert (1999) found that of the 99 college students that reported a clear ritual, 11% endorsed behaviors including washing, cleaning, and ordering. Finally, moving beyond overt ordering and arranging symptoms, Radomsky and Rachman (2004, study 2) found that unselected college students demonstrated a preference for order. Using a novel paradigm in which subjects rated how comfortable they would likely feel in rooms varying in orderliness, as depicted in pictures of different scenes, they found that young adults reported that they would feel significantly more comfortable in orderly than disorderly environments. Strikingly, an overwhelming majority of subjects (72 out of 74) showed this preference for order (Radomsky & Rachman, 2004).

In summary, data gathered at different points of development suggest that symmetry, ordering, and arranging behaviors are common in young children and that the frequency of these behaviors may decrease (but do not disappear) as individuals enter adulthood. Indeed, previous authors have argued that the dominance of symmetry, ordering, and arranging behaviors appears to gradually wane in adulthood (Radomsky & Rachman, 2004). It is notable that when formal OCD symptoms are controlled for, adolescents with OCD have been shown to be comparable to adolescents without OCD on levels of normative childhood rituals (Leonard et al., 1990). This is consistent with developmental continuity between children that do, and do not, develop OCD (see Leonard et al., 1990, for further discussion and additional interpretations). In addition to considering the behaviors of ordering and arranging, it is worthwhile to consider the cognitions associated with such behaviors, such as a preference for order. It is notable that a preference for order appears to frequently remain into adulthood, despite the gradual tapering-off of symmetry, ordering, and arranging behaviors beyond early childhood (Radomsky & Rachman, 2004).

Another possible explanation for the disruptive levels of symmetry, ordering, and arranging observed in individuals with OCD is that the behaviors may represent an exacerbation of culturally prescribed patterns of behavior. Research has shown that OCD symptoms are phenomenologically similar to socially prescribed rituals, sharing similar patterns of thought and action (Fiske & Haslam, 1997). In addition, ordering and arranging appears to be one of the most common forms of rituals. For example, in their study of 52 cultures, Fiske and Haslam (1997) found that ordering or arranging was the fifth most common feature of cultural rituals, occurring in approximately 65% of the sample. Socially prescribed rituals are common in society and are viewed by the larger group as having meaning and value. The performance of these behaviors typically connects the individual with the larger social group. However, individuals with OCD frequently also perform rituals that are only valued by the person him- or herself (i.e., individually meaningful rituals). Therefore, these individual rituals have lost their social linkage (Fiske & Haslam, 1997) and serve to isolate the individual (Leonard et al., 1990). Fiske and Haslam (1997) propose that because the rituals of individuals with OCD do not serve a social function, they are associated with feelings that the task is not done properly or completely.

Additional research is needed to study the etiology of symmetry, ordering, and arranging behaviors. Research should examine the prevalence of symmetry, ordering, and arranging behaviors and associated preference for order across different age groups. Longitudinal studies tracking unselected samples prospectively would likely be of great use. These studies could seek to identify developmental points at which there are typically notable changes in the frequency of such behaviors or beliefs. Such studies could also examine whether decreases in the expression of preferences for symmetry (i.e., ordering or arranging behaviors) covary with the cognitive preference for order, or whether a decrease in ordering and arranging behaviors typically occurs during development even though the cognitive preference for order remains. Finally, arguably the most important question for these studies would be what variables predict changes in the behaviors and beliefs. If the data continue to suggest that most individuals show decreases in ordering and arranging behaviors after early childhood, what markers can be identified that would predict which children would not show this natural decrease, or that would show an increase in ordering and arranging behaviors over time? A myriad of potential variables are worthy of investigation. Perhaps children with a genetic vulnerability to OCD or anxiety do not show the natural decrease in ordering and arranging over time (see Alsobrook, Leckman, Goodman, Rasmussen, & Pauls, 1999, for evidence of a role of genetics in symmetry and ordering; see also Radomsky & Rachman, 2004). Alternatively, or perhaps additionally, children who are exposed to psychosocial risk factors for anxiety, such as overprotective parents or experiences with severe negative life events, may not show the natural decrease in ordering and arranging over time. Finally, ordering and arranging behaviors may represent emotion-control strategies (Kopp, 1989) and be maintained in children who fail to develop other emotion-control strategies.

The view of ordering and arranging as an exacerbation of culturally prescribed rituals is consistent with the notion that extreme levels of such behaviors represent a failure of these behaviors to naturally decrease across development. Again, the question remains, what are the variables that predict which individuals will develop individually meaningful rituals around symmetry, ordering, and arranging? Fiske and Haslam (1997) speculate regarding mechanisms that would maintain personal rituals, such as cognitive, neurochemical, and social processes. However, research is needed to address the development of individualized behaviors, such as ordering and arranging, and to test these predictions.

RELATIONSHIP TO OBSESSIVE–COMPULSIVE DISORDER

Given that symmetry, ordering, and arranging symptoms are only one example of the many diverse forms that OCD symptoms can take, researchers have sought to develop an organizational scheme for classifying OCD symptoms. As noted above, most efforts have been focused on developing a symptom-based typology in which patients are classified according to the content of their obsessions and compulsions. Following this content approach, clinical observation has pointed to the existence of a subgroup of patients characterized by symmetry, ordering, and arranging. For example, based on clinical experience with over 500 individuals with OCD, Rasmussen and Eisen (1991, 1992) described the phenomenological profiles of seven patient subtypes, including a group characterized by a need for symmetry, order, and precision.

A number of empirical studies have been undertaken in the past decade with the aim of establishing a symptom-based taxonomy of OCD (for a review see McKay et al., 2004). While statistical analyses of symptom inventories have generated varying sets of symptom subgroups, symmetry, ordering, and arranging has consistently emerged as a discrete symptom category. The most commonly used symptom inventory measure is the Yale–Brown Obsessive Compulsive Scale Symptom Checklist (Y–BOCS; Goodman et al., 1989a, b), containing more than 50 specific OCD symptoms organized into rationally derived domains of obsessions and compulsions.

In an early study evaluating the structure of OC symptoms, Baer (1994) conducted a principal components analysis of Y–BOCS symptom checklist data from 107 OCD patients and identified three factors, the largest of which was termed symmetry/hoarding. This factor had high factor loadings from items assessing symmetry and saving obsessions, ordering, hoarding, repeating, and counting. Baer noted that, based on Janet's early descriptions of OCD, the common theme of this factor was a sensation of incompleteness and imperfection. Consistent with Baer's observation linking symmetry and incompleteness, the symmetry/hoarding factor was the only factor found to be related to comorbid obsessive–compulsive personality disorder (OCPD) or to a lifetime history of Tourette's syndrome/chronic tic disorder. Indeed, incompleteness and imperfection also frequently characterize individuals with these other disorders – OCPD and tic disorders with comorbid OCD (Eisen et al., in press; Leckman et al., 1994; Miguel et al., 2000).

Since Baer's (1994) initial investigation, a number of additional factor analytic studies have yielded further support for symmetry, ordering, and arranging as a distinct set of OCD symptoms. Leckman and colleagues (1997) found that four factors accounted for most of the variance in the Y–BOCS symptom checklist, with the second factor reflecting a need for symmetry or exactness, repeating rituals, counting compulsions, and ordering/arranging compulsions. Similarly, results of a principal components analysis conducted by Mataix-Cols, Rauch, Manzo, Jenike, & Baer (1999) identified a symmetry/ordering dimension that had high factor loadings from symmetry obsessions and ordering, counting, and repeating compulsions. As in the two previous studies (Baer, 1994, Leckman et al., 1997), patients with comorbid tic disorders scored significantly higher on this symptom dimension than a group of individuals without a lifetime history of tic disorders (Mataix-Cols, Rauch, Manzo, Jenike, & Baer, 1999). Replicating their earlier findings in a new sample of 153 OCD patients, Mataix-Cols, Marks, Greist, Kobak, & Baer (2002) again found support for a five-factor model in which symmetry/ordering formed a singular dimension. Finally, a more recent attempt to identify symptom dimensions involved a principal components analysis of both the Y–BOCS symptom checklist and the Padua Inventory revised (a self-report questionnaire), which were administered to 150 outpatients with OCD. A stable factor consisting of symmetry and exactness obsessions combined with ordering, arranging, counting, and repeating compulsions again emerged (Denys, de Gues, van Megen, & Westenberg, 2004). Therefore, although the precise details of these exploratory factor analyses differ (e.g., number of factors derived, etc.), they converge on the finding that symmetry, ordering, and arranging symptoms tend to cluster together and be separate from most other OCD symptoms.

While the majority of factor analytic studies of the Y–BOCS symptom checklist have been exploratory in nature, Summerfeldt, Richter, Antony, & Swinson (1999) used confirmatory factor analysis to test existing models of OCD symptom structure. Using a large sample of individuals with OCD and data from the rationally derived subscales of the Y–BOCS symptom checklist, Summerfeldt and colleagues (1999) found the best support for a four-factor model composed of obsessions/checking, symmetry/ordering, contamination/cleaning, and hoarding (the model previously identified by Leckman et al., 1997). In this model the symmetry/ordering factor was specified by symmetry obsessions, ordering/arranging compulsions, repeating rituals, and counting compulsions. All paths were found to be significant except for counting compulsions. Notably, the intercorrelations between the symmetry and ordering factor and the other three factors were low (parameter estimates from 11 to .19), suggesting that symmetry, ordering, and arranging represented a relatively distinct symptom dimension.

In addition to the analyses using the rationally derived Y–BOCS subscales, Summerfeldt et al. (1999) repeated the analyses using the individual checklist items. Of most relevance herein, results for the symmetry/ordering factor showed that items assessing ordering/arranging compulsions and obsessions with a need for symmetry/exactness *not* accompanied by magical thinking had the strongest loadings. In contrast, repeating compulsions, counting rituals and symmetry/exactness obsessions that *were* accompanied by magical thinking showed weak factor-to-item parameter estimates. This is consistent with a model of symmetry and ordering behaviors and thoughts that are motivated not by feared consequences or magical thinking, but by a desire to get things 'just right'. In summary, both exploratory and confirmatory factor analytic studies of the Y–BOCS symptom checklist have yielded evidence for a unique symmetry, ordering, and arranging factor and are consistent with the possibility of this factor being associated with incompleteness/not-just-right experiences.

More recently, researchers have used cluster analysis to identify symptom-based OCD subgroups of patients. Cluster analysis groups individuals into discrete clusters and allows one to examine the degree to which symptoms are present across different patient subgroups (Abramowitz, Franklin, Schwartz, & Furr, 2003). Three studies have conducted cluster analyses of the Y–BOCS symptom checklist in large samples of OCD patients (over 100 subjects). The first study (Calamari, Wiegartz, & Janeck, 1999) found five clusters: harming, hoarding, contamination, certainty, and obsessionals. Although this study did not find a distinct symmetry subtype, it is noteworthy that members of the certainty subgroup had elevated scores for symmetry obsessions and ordering compulsions, and exhibited a need to achieve a 'just right' feeling (Calamari et al., 1999). In the second study, combining their original sample with another large patient sample, Calamari and colleagues (2004) found support for a seven-subgroup taxonomy, in which a distinct symmetry subgroup emerged separate from the certainty subgroup. The symmetry subgroup had high levels of symmetry obsessions, along with ordering and checking compulsions, whereas the certainty subgroup desired certainty regarding harm-related concerns. Finally, Abramowitz and colleagues (2003) identified five clusters including a symmetry cluster. Patients in the symmetry cluster had significantly higher scores for symmetry obsessions and ordering compulsions, than for the other symptom domains, and in comparison to members of the other clusters. In summary, results of cluster analyses have generally been compatible with those of factor analytic studies in generating support for symmetry, ordering, and arranging as a distinct symptom category.

Given that a symmetry factor or cluster has consistently been identified in OCD subtyping studies, symmetry, ordering, and arranging appears to represent a distinct subset of OCD symptoms. However, it should be noted that all of the studies reviewed above used adult samples. One study using a youth sample (McKay et al., 2006) suggests that OCD symptom categories may be less distinct in children. Additional research is needed to address the structure of OCD symptoms at various points in development. However, a large body of adult data currently suggests that symmetry, ordering, and arranging represents a unique symptom constellation.

It is also important to note that in addition to the support for the separability of symmetry, ordering, and arranging symptoms from factor analyses and cluster analyses of symptom lists, there is also some evidence for the external validity of this symptom cluster. First, there is preliminary data suggesting that symmetry, ordering, and arranging symptoms may be implemented in a different neural system than checking and washing symptoms. For example, using positron emission tomography (PET) with 14 OCD patients, Rauch et al. (1998) found that symmetry and ordering symptoms tended to be *negatively* related to regional cerebral blood flow in the right striatum, whereas checking symptoms were *positively* correlated with increased activation in the bilateral striatum. In addition, washing symptoms appeared to be implemented in separate brain regions, being positively correlated with increased regional cerebral blood flow in the bilateral anterior cingulate cortex and the left orbitofrontal cortex. Although replication is clearly warranted, these findings suggest symmetry and ordering symptoms are implemented within unique neural processes.

A second line of support for the external validity of a symmetry, ordering, and arranging cluster of symptoms comes from three studies with student samples showing that these symptoms are related to particular domains of OCD-related beliefs. Based on theoretical conceptualizations it would be anticipated that ordering and arranging symptoms would be strongly associated with beliefs regarding perfectionism and a need for certainty (see Radomsky & Rachman, 2004). Consistent with these predictions, empirical studies have shown that perfectionism and intolerance of uncertainty beliefs significantly (and robustly) predict ordering symptoms (Tolin, Woods & Abramowitz, 2003) and scores on the Symmetry, Ordering, and Arranging Questionnaire (Ouimet et al., 2004). Further, these symptoms were not predicted from beliefs associated with overestimates of threat and the importance (and control) of intrusive thoughts (Ouimet et al., 2004, Tolin et al., 2003). Finally, a study by Woods, Tolin, & Abramowitz (2004) revealed that ordering symptoms significantly predicted perfectionism and responsibility beliefs, but not beliefs regarding the importance and control of thoughts.

A third and final line of support for the external validity of symmetry, ordering and arranging comes from research indicating that patients characterized by early onset of their OCD symptoms frequently demonstrate incompleteness and a need for symmetry. Both symmetry and exactness obsessions (Sobin, Blundell, & Karayiorgou, 2000; Tükel et al., 2005) and sensory phenomena (i.e., incompleteness and not-just-right experiences; Rosario-Campos et al., 2001) occur more frequently among individuals with onset of symptoms of OCD prior to age 18 than in those with onset in adulthood. Furthermore, the rate of symmetry and exactness obsessions in a sample of 116 outpatients with a primary diagnosis of OCD was found to significantly predict early-onset OCD (Tükel et al., 2005). Thus, symmetry, ordering, and arranging symptoms appear to represent a separable symptom grouping that may have unique neural substrates, cognitive correlates, and age of onset.

TREATMENT

Treatment of symmetry, ordering, and arranging has largely been consistent with the treatment of OCD in general, focusing on the use of cognitive–behavioral therapy (CBT) and pharmacotherapy. We are not aware of any therapy programs specifically designed for the treatment of symmetry, ordering, and arranging. Existing treatment studies have included individuals with this symptom presentation together with patients characterized by washing, checking, doubting, and hoarding. Therefore, a review of treatment approaches for symmetry, ordering, and arranging represents a review of the treatment of OCD in general. Whereas a complete review of the OCD treatment literature is beyond the scope of this chapter, we will briefly review the two primary forms of treatment for OCD and their theoretical bases in order to provide a context for interpreting data on the efficacy of such treatments for symmetry, ordering, and arranging in particular.

Cognitive–behavioral therapy for OCD includes numerous related treatment procedures that vary in the extent to which they emphasize behavioral techniques, cognitive techniques, and their integration. By far the most widely utilized and studied approach is exposure and response (ritual) prevention (ERP), which seeks to weaken associations between obsessional thoughts and anxiety, and between ritualistic behaviors and anxiety reduction (see Abramowitz et al., 2003). As implied by its name, the two core components of the intervention are (a) systematic confrontation with fear-evoking situations and stimuli (therapeutic exposure), and (b) abstinence from compulsive rituals that serve to immediately reduce obsessional anxiety. Exposure can take one of two forms, either *in vivo* exposure in which the patient directly confronts the feared situation in real life, or *imaginal* exposure in which the patient vividly imagines the feared situation or consequence. For example, a patient with ordering and arranging compulsions would purposely place his or her objects in the 'wrong' order or location, or vividly imagine doing so, and any related feared consequences if they are present. Response prevention involves abstinence from efforts to reduce anxiety during exposures and throughout the day. For example, a patient may be advised to not rearrange the papers on her desk if they become disordered. Abstinence from rituals in the presence of fear teaches the patient two primary lessons: (a) that anxiety decreases naturally over time, even without compulsions, and (b) that feared consequences are unlikely to occur even when rituals are not performed. The techniques of ERP are hypothesized to reduce symptoms by altering pathological fear structures (see Foa and Kozak, 1985, 1986; Kozak & Coles, 2005 for additional detail).

Pharmacological approaches to the treatment of OCD primarily utilize serotonin reuptake inhibitors, although monoamine oxidase inhibitors (MAOIs), neuroleptics, and other medications are sometimes used adjunctively. Use of serotonin reuptake inhibitors was spawned by observations that clomipramine, a tricyclic agent, relieved OCD symptoms while other medications in the same class did not. It was noted that clompiramine is unique among the tricyclic antidepressants, which block the uptake of monoamines by nerve terminals, in its strong blockage of serotonin reuptake (Goodman, 2002). Since this initial discovery, evidence has accumulated showing that medications that alter serotonin levels preferentially change OCD symptoms (see Pigott, 1996). Therefore, treatment with serotonin reuptake inhibitors such as sertraline, paroxetine and fluvoxamine are the current first-line approach to pharmacotherapy for OCD.

Although there are large literatures supporting the efficacy of ERP and serotonin reuptake inhibitors for OCD, as alluded to previously, very little research has focused on outcomes for symmetry, ordering, and arranging in particular. Clinical lore holds that the treatment of ordering and arranging is difficult (see Radomsky & Rachman, 2004). However, this hypothesis has not been thoroughly tested. At the current time, it remains unclear whether patients characterized by symmetry, ordering, and arranging symptoms respond better or worse than patients with other presentations of OCD to behavioral interventions. Very few studies have directly addressed this issue, and the existing data do not provide a clear take-home message. In one of the few behavioral treatment studies to examine the efficacy of ERP according to symptom domain, Mataix-Cols, Marks, Greist, Kobak, & Baer (2002) found that patients with symmetry and ordering symptoms showed response rates similar to patients with contamination/cleaning symptoms, aggressive/checking symptoms, somatic symptoms, and mental rituals. Specifically, 36% of patients with symmetry and ordering symptoms experienced a decrease of at least 40% in their Y–BOCS scores following ERP. Therefore, Mataix-Cols et al. (2002) concluded that patients with symmetry and ordering symptoms are among the groups for which ERP is advisable.

Using data from a sample of 132 individuals that received open-treatment with ERP for OCD, Abramowitz and colleagues (2003) also investigated the impact of symptom presentation on outcomes of ERP. Patients characterized by symmetry symptoms showed significant reductions in Y–BOCS scores from pre- to post-treatment (as was true for all symptom groups). Specifically, at post-treatment, Y–BOCS scores of patients characterized by symmetry symptoms were higher (more severe) than the scores for individuals with harming, contamination; and unacceptable thoughts symptoms, and lower (less severe) than the scores of individuals with hoarding symptoms. In contrast, results using a *clinical* significance criterion (i.e., high endstate functioning and reliable change) showed that 76% of patients with symmetry symptoms achieved these criteria, the highest percentage of any OCD symptom group. However, only the hoarding group differed significantly from the other groups, with the lowest percentage of patients attaining clinical significance (31%). It seems somewhat surprising that the symmetry group had the highest proportion of individuals attain clinical significance given that their changes in Y–BOCS scores were relatively modest compared to individuals in the harming, contamination, and unacceptable thoughts groups. However, these results show that individuals with symmetry symptoms experienced statistically significant reductions in their Y–BOCS scores from pre- to post-treatment, and that approximately 75% obtained clinically significant change. Therefore, although replication and additional research are needed, existing data (Abramowitz et al., 2003; Mataix-Cols et al., 2002) suggest that the responses of patients characterized by symmetry, ordering, and arranging to ERP are generally similar to those of patients with other types of OCD symptoms (e.g., washing, checking, harming, unacceptable thoughts).

At the current time, it also remains unclear whether pharmacological interventions produce similar outcomes for patients characterized by symmetry, ordering, and arranging symptoms in comparison to patients with other forms of OCD. In one study examining the impact of symptom presentation on outcomes from pharmacotherapy with serotonin reuptake inhibitors (clomipramine, fluvoxamine, fluoxetine, sertraline, paroxetine), Mataix-Cols et al. (1999) found that the presence of symmetry/ordering symptoms at baseline did not significantly predict outcome. Only the presence of hoarding symptoms was found to predict outcomes (predicting poorer response). In another study, Jenike, Baer, Minichiello, Rauch, & Buttolph (1997) examined the efficacy of fluoxetine (a serotonin reuptake inhibitor) and phenelzine (a monoamine oxidase inhibitor). Only fluoxetine was found to produce significantly better outcomes than placebo. However, 7 of the 20 patients receiving phenelzine were classified as responders, leading the authors to examine the characteristics of these individuals. Results showed that the presence of symmetry obsessions was significantly more common in responders to phenelzine than responders to fluoxetine. On the basis of these findings, Jenike et al. (1997) called for replication and suggested that although serotonin reuptake inhibitors are the first-line treatment for OCD, trials of monoamine oxidase inhibitors such as phenelzine may be warranted for patients with particular obsessions and compulsions, such as those involving symmetry, ordering, and arranging. The authors also noted that these results were consistent with their findings from a previous study in which potential predictors of outcome from cingulotomy were explored (Baer, Rauch, Ballantine, & Martuza, 1995). In that study, the presence of symmetry obsessions, ordering compulsions, and hoarding compulsions significantly predicted better outcomes (lower OCD symptom levels at the final follow-up assessment) following cingulotomy.

In addition to considering the extent of treatment response for symmetry, ordering, and arranging, it is also worth briefly considering whether patients with this symptom presentation show a unique pattern of treatment-seeking behaviors. One study investigating rates of talking with a medical professional regarding OCD symptoms (Mayerovitch et al., 2003) showed that of the OCD symptom domains assessed, symmetry and precision compulsions were associated with the lowest rates of seeking professional consultation. Only 9.5% of individuals with symmetry and precision had consulted a professional, whereas 76.2% of patients with violent/unpleasant obsessions and 30.2% with hand washing/checking had talked to a provider about their symptoms. Consistent with these findings, Ball, Baer, & Otto (1996) found that when reviewing the nature of OCD symptoms reported in behavioral outcome trials, the majority of patients' primary symptoms were cleaning or checking compulsions (75% of the sample). They noted that only 12% of the sample had 'multiple' compulsions, or 'other' compulsions (e.g., ordering, exactness, repeating, slowness, hoarding). Therefore, it is reasonable to question whether symptom manifestations characterized by incompleteness/not-just-right experiences (e.g., symmetry, ordering, arranging, or hoarding) are underrepresented in behavioral treatment trials. It is possible that patients with symptoms characterized by incompleteness may be less likely to enter treatment or more likely to drop out of treatment. These observations are also consistent with a potential link between symmetry, ordering, and arranging and OCPD (see Eisen et al., 2006), as Axis II disorders are typically viewed as more ego-syntonic and therefore less likely to prompt individuals to seek professional assistance. More research is needed examining whether individuals with symmetry, ordering, and arranging seek treatment and their response to treatment when they engage it.

In summary, the limited existing data suggest that individuals with symmetry, ordering, and arranging respond similarly to patients with other OCD symptoms when treated behaviorally, but there is some modest suggestion that they may show different medication response profiles. One issue that has been understudied is the motivation underlying the ordering and arranging symptoms. As discussed earlier, we propose that symmetry, ordering, and arranging symptoms may typically be motivated by a need to get things 'just right' or to achieve a sense of completeness. Differentiating motivations behind the symptoms may be particularly important for predicting treatment response, as there is some evidence to suggest that symptoms that are not associated with a feared consequence (i.e., harm avoidance) may be less amenable to current behavioral interventions. For example, Foa, Abramowitz, Franklin, & Kozak (1999) found that OCD patients who did not articulate feared consequences tended to have more severe post-treatment scores following ERP than patients who had articulated feared consequences. One possibility is that the patients who did not articulate feared consequences were distressed by feelings of incompleteness or not-just-right experiences. Therefore, distinguishing between harm avoidance and incompleteness may be important for improving treatments for OCD, including symmetry, ordering, and arranging symptoms. One notable effort along these lines is a recent article on treating incompleteness by Summerfeldt (2004), which highlights ways to adapt existing cognitive–behavioral treatments for OCD to patients characterized by incompleteness and not-just-right experiences. For example, Summerfeldt notes that affective/sensory experiences may be more dominant than cognitive appraisals in such patients, and that behavioral exercises targeting the affective/sensory experiences may therefore warrant greater attention.

CONCLUSIONS

Symmetry obsessions and ordering and arranging compulsions are common among individuals with OCD. Numerous empirical studies seeking to create symptom-based subgroups support the clustering of these symptoms and indicate that they are separable from many other manifestations of OCD (e.g., washing, checking). Limited available data suggest that individuals with symmetry, ordering, and arranging are likely to have acceptable outcomes to existing treatment via ERP or serotonin reuptake inhibitors. However, there are still large gaps in our understanding of this symptom profile. First, research is needed to clarify the etiology of symmetry, ordering, and arranging, as very little is known at this time. It is possible that these symptoms may represent a failure of behaviors often observed in childhood to decrease in frequency, or an exacerbation of cultural rituals; however, data are sorely lacking with regard to these hypotheses. Second, research testing the utility of distinguishing the motivation underlying symmetry, ordering, and arranging symptoms is warranted. We have proposed herein that these symptoms are often different from other forms of OCD in that they are more likely to be motivated by a sense of incompleteness or of things not being 'just right', in contrast to the more commonly acknowledged motivation to prevent harm. Distinguishing these unique motivations may have important implications for the conceptualization and treatment of symmetry, ordering, and arranging.

REFERENCES

Abramowitz, J. S., Franklin, M. E., Schwartz, S. A., & Furr, J. M. (2003). Symptom presentation and outcome of cognitive–behavioral therapy for obsessive–compulsive disorder. *Journal of Consulting and Clinical Psychology, 71*, 1049–1057.

Alsobrook, J. P., Leckman, J. F., Goodman, W. K., Rasmussen, S. A., & Pauls, D. L. (1999). Segregation analysis of obsessive compulsive disorder using symptom based factor scores. *American Journal of Medical Genetics (Neuropsychiatric Genetics), 88,* 669–675.

Baer, L. (1994). Factor analysis of symptom subtypes of obsessive compulsive disorder and their relation to personality and tic disorders. *Journal of Clinical Psychiatry, 55,* 18–23.

Baer, L., Rauch, S. L., Ballantine, T., & Martuza, R. (1995). Cingulotomy for intractable obsessive–compulsive disorder: Prospective long-term follow-up of 18 patients. *Archives of General Psychiatry, 52,* 384–392.

Ball, S. G., Baer, L., & Otto, M. W. (1996). Symptom subtypes of obsessive–compulsive disorder in behavioral treatment studies: A quantitative review. *Behaviour Research and Therapy, 34,* 47–51.

Calamari, J. E., Wiegartz, P. S., & Janeck, A. S. (1999). Obsessive–compulsive disorder subgroups: A symptom-based clustering approach. *Behaviour Research and Therapy, 37,* 113–125.

Calamari, J. E., Wiegartz, P. S., Riemann, B. C., Cohen, R. J., Greer, A., Jacobi, D. M., Jahn, S. C., & Carmin, C. (2004). Obsessive–compulsive disorder subtypes: An attempted replication and extension of a symptom-based taxonomy. *Behaviour Research and Therapy, 42,* 647–670.

Coles, M. E., Frost, R. O., Heimberg, R. G., & Rhéaume, J. (2003). 'Not just right experiences': Perfectionism, obsessive–compulsive features and general psychopathology. *Behaviour Research and Therapy, 41,* 681–700.

Coles, M. E., Heimberg, R. G., Frost, R. O., & Steketee, G. (2005). Not just right experiences and obsessive–compulsive features: Experimental, self-monitoring perspectives. *Behaviour Research and Therapy, 43,* 153–167.

Denys, D., de Gues, F., van Megen, H. J. G. M., & Westenberg, H. G. M. (2004). Symptom dimensions in obsessive–compulsive disorder: Factor analysis on a clinician-rated scale and a self-report measure. *Psychopathology, 37,* 181–189.

Eisen, J. L., Coles, M. E., Shea, T. T., Pagano, M. E., Stout, R. L., Yen, S., & Rasmussen, S. A. (2006). Clarifying the convergence between Obsessive Compulsive Personality Disorder criteria and Obsessive Compulsive Disorder. *Journal of Personality Disorders, 20,* 294–305.

Evans, D. W., Leckman, J. F., Carter, A., & Reznick, J. S. (1997). Ritual, habit, and perfectionism: The prevalence and development of compulsive-like behavior in normal young children. *Child Development, 68*(1), 58–68.

Fiske, A. P., & Haslam, N. (1997). Is obsessive–compulsive disorder a pathology of the human disposition to perform socially meaningful rituals? Evidence of similar content. *Journal of Nervous and Mental Disease, 185*(4), 211–222.

Flament, M. F., Whitaker, A., Rapoport, J. L., Davies, M., Berg, C., Kalikow, K., Sceery, W., & Shaffer, D. (1988). Obsessive compulsive disorder in adolescence: An epidemiological study. *Journal of the American Academy of Child and Adolescent Psychiatry, 27,* 764–771.

Foa, E. B., Abramowitz, J. S., Franklin, M. E., & Kozak, M. J. (1999). Feared consequences, fixity of belief, and treatment outcome in patients with obsessive–compulsive disorder. *Behavior Therapy, 30,* 717–724.

Foa, E. B., & Kozak, M. J. (1985). Treatment of anxiety disorders: Implications for psychopathology. In A. H. Tuma & J. D. Maser (Eds.), *Anxiety and the anxiety disorders* (pp. 421–454). Hillsdale, NY: Lawrence Erlbaum Associates.

Foa, E. B., & Kozak, M. S. (1986). Emotional processing of fear: Exposure to corrective information. *Psychology Bulletin, 99,* 20–35.

Foa, E. B., Kozak, M. J., Goodman, W. K., Hollander, E., Jenike, M. A., & Rasmussen, S. (1995). DSM-IV field trial: Obsessive–compulsive disorder. *American Journal of Psychiatry, 152,* 90–96.

Goodman, W. K. (2002). Pharmacotherapy for obsessive–compulsive disorder. In D. J. Stein & E. Hollander (Eds.), *Textbook of anxiety disorders* (pp. 207–220). Washington, DC: American Psychiatric Publishing.

Goodman, W. K., Price, L. H., Rasmussen, S. A., Mazure, C., Delgado, P., Heninger, G. R., & Charney, D. S. (1989a). The Yale–Brown obsessive compulsive scale (Y–BOCS): Validity. *Archives of General Psychiatry, 46,* 1012–1016.

Goodman, W. K., Price, L. H., Rasmussen, S. A., Mazure, C., Fleischmann, R. L., Hill, C. L., Heninger, G. R., & Charney, D. S. (1989b). The Yale–Brown obsessive–compulsive scale (Y–BOCS): Development, use, reliability. *Archives of General Psychiatry, 46,* 1006–1011.

Jenike, M. A., Baer, L., Minichiello, W. E., Rauch, S. L., & Buttolph, M. L. (1997). Placebo-controlled trial of fluoxetine and phenelzine for obsessive–compulsive disorder. *American Journal of Psychiatry, 154,* 1261–1264.

Kopp, C. B. (1989). Regulation of distress and negative emotions: A developmental view. *Developmental Psychology, 25*(3), 343–354.

Kozak, M. J., & Coles, M. E. (2005). Treatment for obsessive compulsive disorder: unleashing the power of exposure. In J. S. Abramowitz & Arthur C. Houts (Eds.), *Handbook of controversial issues in obsessive–compulsive disorder* (pp. 283–304). New York: Kluwer.

Leckman, J. F., Grice, D. E., Boardman, J., Zhang, H., Vitale, A., Bondi, C., Alsobroook, J., Peterson, B. S., Cohen, D. J., Rasmussen, S. A., Goodman, W. K., McDougle, C. J., & Pauls, D. L. (1997). Symptoms of obsessive–compulsive disorder. *American Journal of Psychiatry, 154,* 911–917.

Leckman, J. F., Walker, D. E., Goodman, W. K., Pauls, D. L., & Cohen, D. J. (1994). 'Just right' perceptions associated with compulsive behavior in Tourette's syndrome. *American Journal of Psychiatry, 151,* 675–680.

Leonard, H. L., Goldberger, E. L., Rapoport, J. L., Cheslow, D. L., & Swedo, S.E. (1990). Childhood rituals: Normal development or obsessive–compulsive symptoms? *Journal of the American Academy of Child & Adolescent Psychiatry, 29*(1), 17–23.

Mataix-Cols, D., Marks, I. M., Greist, J. H., Kobak, K. A., & Baer, L. (2002). Obsessive–compulsive symptom dimensions as predictors of compliance with and response to behaviour therapy: Results from a controlled trial. *Psychotherapy & Psychosomatics, 71,* 255–262.

Mataix-Cols, D., Rauch, S. L., Manzo, P. A., Jenike, M. A., & Baer, L. (1999). Use of factor-analyzed symptom dimensions to predict outcome with serotonin reuptake inhibitors and placebo in the treatment of obsessive–compulsive disorder. *American Journal of Psychiatry, 156,* 1409–1416.

Mayerovitch, J. I., du Fort, G. G., Kakuma, R., Bland, R. C., Newman, S. C., & Pinard, G. (2003). Treatment seeking for obsessive–compulsive disorder: Role of obsessive–compulsive disorder symptoms and comorbid psychiatric diagnoses. *Comprehensive Psychiatry, 44*(2), 162–168.

McKay, D., Abramowitz, J. S., Calamari, J. E., Kyrios, M., Radomsky, A., Sookman, D., Taylor, S., & Wilhelm, S. (2004). A critical evaluation of obsessive–compulsive disorder subtypes: Symptoms versus mechanisms. *Clinical Psychology Review, 24,* 283–313.

McKay, D., Piacentini, J., Greisberg, S., Graae, F., Jaffer, M., & Miller, J. (2006). The structure of childhood obsessions and compulsions: Dimensions in an outpatient sample. *Behaviour Research and Therapy, 44,* 137–146.

Miguel, E. C., Rosario-Campos, M. C., Prado, H. S., Valle, R., Rauch, S. L., Coffey, B. J., Baer, L., Savage, C. R., O'Sullivan, R. L., Jenike, M. A., & Leckman, J. F. (2000). Sensory phenomena in obsessive–compulsive disorder and Tourette's disorder. *Journal of Clinical Psychiatry, 61,* 150–156.

Okasha, A., Saad, A. H., Khalil, A., Dawla, S. E., & Yehia, N. (1994). Phenomenology of obsessive–compulsive disorder: A transcultural study. *Comprehensive Psychiatry, 35,* 191–197.

Ouimet, A. J., Ashbaugh, A. R., Paradis, M. R., Lahoud, M., Radomsky, A. S., & O'Connor, K. P. (2004, November). *Relationships between OCD symptoms and belief domains.* Poster presented at the 38th annual convention of the Association for the Advancement of Behavior Therapy, New Orleans, Louisiana.

Pigott, T. (1996). OCD: Where the serotonin selectivity story begins. *Journal of Clinical Psychiatry, 57,* 11–20.

Pitman, R. K. (1987). Pierre Janet on obsessive–compulsive disorder (1903). *Archives of General Psychiatry, 44,* 226–232.

Radomsky, A. S., & Rachman, S. (2004). Symmetry, ordering and arranging compulsive behavior. *Behavior Research and Therapy, 42,* 893–913.

Rasmussen, S., & Eisen, J. L. (1991). Phenomenology of OCD: Clinical subtypes, heterogeneity and coexistence. In J. Zohar, T. Insel & S. Rasmussen (Eds.), *The psychobiology of obsessive–compulsive disorder* (pp. 13–43). New York: Springer.

Rasmussen, S. A., & Eisen, J. L. (1992). The epidemiology and clinical features of obsessive compulsive disorder. *Psychiatric Clinics of North America, 15*, 743–758.

Rassin, E., Merckelbach, H., Muris, P., & Stapert, S. (1999). Suppression and ritualistic behaviour in normal participants. *British Journal of Clinical Psychology, 38*, 195–201.

Rauch, S. L., Dougherty, D. D., Shin, L. M., Alpert, N. M., Manzo, P., Leahy, L., Fischman, A. J., Jenike, M. A., & Baer, L. (1998). Neural correlates of factor-analyzed OCD symptom dimensions: A PET study. *CNS Spectrums, 3*, 37–43.

Rosario-Campos, M. C., Leckman, J. F., Mercadante, M. T., Shavitt, R. G., Prado, H. S., Sada, P., Zamignani, D., & Miguel, E. C. (2001). Adults with early-onset obsessive–compulsive disorder. *American Journal of Psychiatry, 158*, 1899–1903.

Sobin, C., Blundell, M. L., & Karayiorgou, M. (2000). Phenotypic differences in early- and late-onset obsessive–compulsive disorder. *Comprehensive Psychiatry, 41*, 373–379.

Summerfeldt, L. J. (2004). Understanding and treating incompleteness in obsessive–compulsive disorder. *Journal of Clinical Psychology, 60*, 1155–1168.

Summerfeldt, L. J., Kloosterman, P. H., Antony, M. M., Richter, M. A., & Swinson, R. P. (2004). The relationship between miscellaneous symptoms and major symptom factors in obsessive–compulsive disorder. *Behavior Research and Therapy, 42*, 1453–1467.

Summerfeldt, L. J., Richter, M. A., Antony, M. M., & Swinson, R. P. (1999). Symptom structure in obsessive–compulsive disorder: A confirmatory factor analysis. *Behaviour Research and Therapy, 37*, 297–311.

Tallis, F. (1996). Compulsive washing in the absence of phobic and illness anxiety. *Behaviour Research and Therapy, 34*, 361–362.

Tolin, D. F., Woods, C. M., & Abramowitz, J. S. (2003). Relationship between obsessive beliefs and obsessive–compulsive symptoms. *Cognitive Therapy and Research, 27*, 657–669.

Tükel, R., Ertekin, E., Batmaz, S., Alyanak, F., Sözen, A., Aslantas, B., Atli, H., & Özyildirim, İ. (2005). Influence of age of onset on clinical features in obsessive–compulsive disorder. *Depression and Anxiety, 21*, 112–117.

Valleni-Basile, L. A., Garrison, C. Z., Jackson, K. L., Waller, J. L., McKeown, R. E., Addy, C. L., & Cuffe, S. P. (1994). Frequency of obsessive–compulsive disorder in a community sample of young adolescents. *Journal of the American Academy of Child and Adolescent Psychiatry, 33*, 782–791.

Woods, C. M., Tolin, D. F., & Abramowitz, J. S. (2004). Dimensionality of the obsessive beliefs questionnaire (OBQ). *Journal of Psychopathology and Behavioral Assessment, 26*, 113–125.

4

PURE OBSESSIONS: CONCEPTUAL MISNOMER OR CLINICAL ANOMALY?

DAVID A. CLARK AND BRENDAN D. GUYITT

Department of Psychology, University of New Brunswick

Over the decades obsessive–compulsive disorder (OCD) has proven to be one of the most difficult of the anxiety disorders to understand and treat. This conundrum is due largely to its heterogeneous symptom presentation and failure to exhibit a single key psychological process that binds obsessive and compulsive phenomena into a single coherent diagnostic entity. Many clinical researchers, including the authors of this chapter and editors of the present volume, are now considering whether OCD should be conceptualized as a syndrome consisting of distinct subtypes with their own unique pathogenic course and treatment regimen.

Even when considering the most fundamental diagnostic feature of OCD, such as the required presence of obsessions and/or compulsions (*DSM-IV-TR*; American Psychiatric Association [APA], 2000), typological differences can be found. Obsessions are unwanted, unacceptable, and repetitive intrusive thoughts, images or impulses of dirt/contamination, doubt, aggression/harm/injury, unacceptable sex, religion, orderliness/symmetry, and other miscellaneous concerns that are disturbing, subjectively resisted, but difficult to control (Rachman, 1983). Most individuals recognize that the obsession is senseless or at least highly exaggerated. Compulsions are repetitive, stereotyped behaviors, such as washing, checking,

Correspondence to: A. Clark, Department of Psychology, University of New Brunswick, Bag Service #45444, Fredericton, New Brunswick, Canada E3B 6E4.

repeating and redoing, that are usually performed in response to the obsession in order to reduce anxiety/distress or prevent some imagined dreaded outcome (APA, 2000). A strong urge to carry out the compulsion often accompanies the ritual, leading the person to perceive a loss of control (Rachman & Hodgson, 1980).

The early behavioral theories of OCD emphasized the functional relation between obsessions and compulsions. Obsessions were viewed as noxious stimuli that elicit a state of heightened anxiety, whereas the compulsive ritual was seen as an active avoidance response (Rachman, 1971). The cornerstone of the behavioral model was the *anxiety reduction hypothesis*, which asserted that compulsive rituals persist because they engender an immediate, albeit temporary, reduction in anxiety caused by the obsession (Carr, 1974; Rachman & Hodgson, 1980). However the anxiety reduction hypothesis had difficulty explaining compulsions that led to no change or even an increase in anxiety/discomfort.

Another finding of great difficulty for the anxiety reduction hypothesis was the existence of a small group of patients who experienced severe obsessions without the expected overt compulsive response (i.e., Carr, 1974). Labeled '*pure obsessions*', '*obsessional rumination*', or simply '*obsessional*', individuals with this symptom presentation exhibited frequent and intense obsessions but no overt anxiety-reducing or corrective compulsive rituals. Salkovskis and Westbrook (1989) articulated the problem most clearly in their critique of traditional behavior therapy for OCD. The behavioral theory predicts that obsessions without overt compulsions should be easy to treat because the phenomena are not strengthened by avoidance learning (i.e., the overt compulsive ritual). In reality obsessions without overt compulsions are more difficult to treat than obsessions with overt compulsions (Likierman & Rachman, 1982; Rachman, 1983), and so the development of effective behavioral interventions for obsessions lagged behind treatment for obsessions accompanied by compulsive rituals (Beech & Vaughan, 1978; Rachman, 1983). This led Salkovskis (1988) to conclude that the standard behavioral model cannot account for the findings of obsessions alone and he argued for a formulation of OCD that placed greater emphasis on cognition. Thus the existence of 'pure obsessions' was an important factor in the evolution of behavioral therapy into the current cognitive–behavioral perspectives on OCD.

Despite the theoretical and clinical significance of pure obsessions, there remains much controversy over the legitimacy of this OCD subtype. We begin by considering the historical basis, definition, and prevalence of pure obsessions, obsessional rumination, and covert compulsions. This is followed by a critical review of empirical evidence for obsessions without overt compulsions based on symptom presentation and distinct psychological processes. We then discuss treatment approaches that are specific for pure obsessionality, OCD rumination, and covert compulsions, with a particular focus on their effectiveness. The chapter concludes with a statement on the current status of the pure obsession subtype and outstanding questions that must be addressed in order to validate this OCD subtype.

HISTORICAL PRECEDENCE, DEFINITION AND PREVALENCE

It has long been recognized that not all patients with OCD present with obsessions and associated overt rituals such as compulsive cleaning, checking or repeating. In 1971 Rachman presented a behavioral account of obsessional ruminations, recognizing that obsessions without overt compulsions represent a challenge for behavioral treatment of OCD. He also noted that although obsessional ruminations are similar to other phobic stimuli, they are more closely associated with depression than anxiety even though they involve extensive avoidance. Other early behaviorists recognized the special nature and treatment of pure obsessions and obsessional rumination (e.g., Hallam, 1974).

Early psychiatric accounts of OCD also recognized that obsessions without overt compulsions might represent a special characterization of the disorder. Sir Aubrey Lewis acknowledged the existence of obsessional ruminations as a subtype of obsessional phenomena that takes the form of endless questioning or search (Lewis, 1966). Ingram (1960) described a diagnostic category distinct from OCD called *phobic-ruminative states*, which involved predominantly phobic or ruminative symptoms without motor symptoms. A number of early psychiatric descriptive studies recognized a subgroup of OCD patients with minimal or no compulsive rituals and predominantly obsessions alone or phobic ruminative symptoms (e.g., Akhtar, Wig, Varma, Pershad, & Verma, 1975; Lo, 1967; Welner, Reich, Robins, Fishman, & Van Doren, 1976). It is evident from this early clinical literature that diagnosticians identified a small subset of OCD patients who had a presenting symptomatology in which overt compulsions were relatively absent and repetitive thought was dominant.

DEFINITIONAL ISSUES

Over the years there has been much confusion in our use of the terms 'pure obsessions', 'obsessional rumination' and 'covert compulsions'. Some writers refer to 'pure obsessions' when overt or behavioral compulsions are absent, whereas others suggest a more restrictive definition in which the term 'pure obsessions' is reserved for individuals with obsessions and no overt or covert (mentalistic) compulsions (de Silva, 2003). The term 'obsessional rumination' has also had a messy legacy in the OCD literature. De Silva (2003) made a convincing argument that the term 'obsessional rumination' be more precisely defined as 'a compulsive cognitive activity that is carried out in response to an obsessional thought' (p. 198). However this point has often been lost to clinical researchers and practitioners who have assumed that obsessional rumination maps onto obsessional rather than compulsive phenomena. For example, Salkovskis, Richards, & Richards (1998) defined obsessional ruminations as 'obsessions where there is no overt compulsive behaviour' (p. 54).

A perusal of contemporary work on OCD indicates that most researchers use the term 'pure obsessions' in reference to repeated intrusive thoughts, images or impulses, often of an aggressive or sexual nature, that are distressing, difficult to control but *not* accompanied by overt (behavioral) compulsive rituals (Insel, 1990; Rachman, 1971; Salkovskis & Westbrook, 1989). Salkovskis (1998, 1999), however, noted that most cases of pure obsessions involve some form of covert compulsion and avoidance. Moreover these covert compulsions are functionally indistinguishable from overt rituals (i.e., they are neutralizing responses to obsessional fear). If we extend our understanding of 'compulsion' to include any form of neutralization, then occurrences of obsessions without some form of compulsive or neutralizing response (overt or covert) would be exceedingly rare (i.e., the strict definition of pure obsessions). In the present discussion neutralization is a broader category than compulsions, referring to any voluntary, effortful response directed at removing, preventing, or canceling the immediate or anticipated consequences of the obsession (Clark, 2004; Freeston & Ladouceur, 1997; Rachman & Shafran, 1998). Examples of neutralization include thought/image substitution or replacement, distraction, rationalization, self-reassurance, or the like. Some authors subsume overt and covert compulsions under the concept of neutralization (Salkovskis, 1998, 1999; Salkovskis & Westbrook, 1989). In this chapter, then, *pure obsessions will refer to obsessional thoughts, images or impulses that are not accompanied by overt compulsions but can be associated with cognitive compulsions or other forms of neutralization.*

De Silva (2003) provided a number of reasons why rumination in the context of OCD should be viewed as a covert or internal compulsion triggered by an obsession. First, rumination specifically involves engagement in directed self-focused thinking and is not the mere occurrence of a negative thought. Obsessions, on the other hand, are experienced as distinct, involuntary thought intrusions. Second, obsessional ruminations often involve persistent questioning about the nature of the universe, metaphysical topics or the possibility of future calamity (e.g., 'what is the purpose of my existence?', 'why does the world exist?', 'will something bad happen to me?'). Third, like a compulsion, the individual feels a strong urge to engage in the ruminative process. And yet rumination is different from a standard compulsion because there can be considerable variability in the thought content and sequence between ruminative episodes on a particular obsessional theme. In sum, de Silva (2003) suggested that obsessional rumination be considered a distinct type of compulsive thinking. Based on de Silva's (2003) description, we reserve the term *obsessional rumination* for *compulsive cognitive activity that is purposefully and effortfully directed toward the neutralization of a particular obsessional concern.*

The final term we consider in this section, *covert (mentalistic) compulsions,* has been more clearly articulated in the literature. Examples of covert compulsions include having to form a certain image (e.g., the Virgin Mary), mentally rehearsing a particular sequence of numbers, staring at an object and forming its exact mental representation, ritualistic prayers, mental replay of conversations, or mentally checking or patterning objects (de Silva & Rachman, 1992; Einstein & Menzies, 2003). Covert compulsions are functionally similar to their overt counterparts as their aim is to reduce anxiety or prevent (neutralize) the possibility of some imagined dreaded outcome (Salkovskis, 1999; Salkovskis et al., 1998). Although they are less accessible and more difficult to control, Salkovskis (1999) contends that the same therapeutic approach used with overt compulsions can be applied to their mentalistic form, albeit with slight modifications.

PREVALENCE RATES

How prevalent are pure obsessions, obsessional rumination, and covert compulsions? In their unpublished treatment manual of cognitive–behavioral therapy for obsessions, Freeston and Ladouceur (1997) reviewed 12 studies that reported on the proportion of their OCD sample that had obsessions with no overt compulsions. The percentage ranged from 1.5% to 44%, with a median percent across studies estimated at 20%. The *DSM-IV* field trial involving 454 patients with OCD drawn from five health care sites provides the best description of symptom presentation in OCD. Based on a stringent definition of symptom dominance, Foa et al. (1995) found that only 2% of the sample had predominantly obsessions, a group that probably fits with de Silva's (2003) strict definition of 'pure obsessions' as the presence of obsessions without overt or covert compulsions. If a more inclusive criterion of 'pure obsessions' is adopted, approximately 30% of the sample fell into this category. Another small group of patients (2%) had predominantly compulsions. It is likely that obsessional ruminators, as defined by de Silva (2003), might be represented in this group. Foa et al. (1995) also conducted a thorough assessment of mental compulsions (i.e., words or images used for neutralization, special prayers, counting, mental list making and mental reviewing) and discovered that approximately 80% of the sample reported mental compulsions.

At this point a number of conclusions can be drawn about the prevalence of the pure obsessional subtype. A number of studies have reported on the prevalence of obsessions without overt compulsions (pure obsessions) and the best estimate is that they represent approximately 20% of OCD samples. There are no accurate figures on the occurrence of obsessional rumination but it is likely to be relatively rare (possibly under 5% of OCD samples). Although few studies have specifically reported on covert (mental) compulsions, the findings of the *DSM-IV* field trial suggest that this form of ritualistic response is much more common than previously recognized in the literature.

THE PURE OBSESSIONAL SUBTYPE: EMPIRICAL EVIDENCE

Whether the distinction *pure obsessions* is a valid subtype of OCD does not rest entirely on its conceptualization and description in the clinical literature. It is also necessary to determine whether the subtype represents an internally consistent symptom cluster that can be distinguished from other patterns of obsessive–compulsive symptom presentation. Two key questions are: (a) is there an identifiable and relatively homogenous symptom presentation that we can label 'pure obsessions', and (b) is there a 'pure obsessions' subgroup of OCD patients who share a similar clinical presentation that distinguishes them from individuals with OCD who have a different symptom profile?

The existing research on OCD taxonomy is dominated by studies that seek to distinguish subtypes of patients by their overt symptom presentation. As compulsions are the most obvious feature of OCD symptomatology, subtyping attempts have focused on patients' major presenting compulsion (Abramowitz, Franklin, Schwartz, & Furr, 2003; Calamari, Weigartz, & Janeck, 1999; McKay et al., 2004). Thus research on classic compulsive distinctions such as 'washers' versus 'checkers' has flourished while research on less obvious symptom distinctions is scarce (Mataix-Cols, Rosario-Campos, & Leckman, 2005). Such is the case with research on pure obsessionals who display no overt compulsions and thus are most often overlooked by symptom-based studies. In this section we examine the validity of the pure obsessions subtype based on four research approaches: factor and cluster analysis of symptom measures, taxometric analysis of symptoms, neuropsychological investigations, and neuroimaging research.

DISTINCT SYMPTOM PROFILE

Factor analytic studies

Most factor analytic studies have reported a distinct symptom dimension that is primarily characterized by obsessions rather than compulsions (Mataix-Cols, 2006; Mataix-Cols et al., 2002; McKay et al., 2004), although the exact composition of this factor has differed significantly between studies. In the first factor analysis of OCD symptoms, Baer (1994) found a factor that included religious, sexual, and aggressive obsessions without significant loadings from the overt compulsive categories. This result would be entirely consistent with a pure obsessional subtype. Subsequent studies, however, found that overt compulsive categories also loaded significantly on this same predominantly obsessional factor. In addition to aggressive, sexual, religious, and sometimes somatic obsessions, overt checking compulsions were almost always present (Denys, de Geus, van Megen, & Westenberg, 2004a; Leckman, Grice, Boardman, Zhang, Vitale, & Bondi, 1997; Mataix-Cols, 2006; Summerfeldt, Richter, Antony, & Swinson, 1999). The picture is further complicated by findings reported by Mataix-Cols, Rauch, Manzo, Jenike, & Baer (1999) that sexual and religious obsessions formed a separate factor from aggressive obsessions and checking compulsions.[1] In a subsequent analysis Mataix-Cols et al. (2002) found that the sexual/religious obsessions and hoarding factors remained

---

[1] A table of factor loadings was not reported in the article to allow verification of this claim.

largely unchanged over a two-year period while significant variability was evident in the other three factors. Together this suggests that a pure obsessional subtype consisting of sexual and religious obsessions may exist, however, only one subsequent study has confirmed that finding. Denys, de Geus, van Megen, & Westenberg (2004b) found five factors, one of which contained only aggressive, sexual, and religious obsessions without a significant loading from checking compulsions.

Overall the factor analytic studies of symptom measures like the Yale–Brown Obsessive Compulsive Scale (Y–BOCS; Goodman et al., 1989) have consistently found a distinct symptom profile defined predominantly by religious, sexual, and, to a lesser extent, aggressive obsessions. However, two problems emerge from this literature. First there are important differences across studies in the exact obsessional content that loads on this factor. Second, it is clear that overt compulsions are present in this symptom dimension thus providing weak empirical support for a pure obsessions distinction. Too many studies found that checking compulsions also had high loadings on the 'pure obsessions' factor making these solutions problematic for an obsessional subtype.

Cluster analytic studies

Since factor analysis partitions variance from individual subjects across all the identified factors, the results can often be unclear (Borgen & Weiss, 1971). Considerable overlap between symptom dimensions occurred in the previously discussed studies (Mataix-Cols, 2006). This led Calamari et al. (1999) to propose that cluster analysis may be a more appropriate statistical tool for identifying symptom subtypes. Cluster analysis assigns individuals to groups by maximizing between group differences and minimizing within group variability. Boundaries are drawn around individuals in which subject variance is only assigned to one cluster, thus making the final clusters less heterogeneous (Calamari et al., 1999, 2004).

Three studies employed cluster analysis in an attempt to delineate OCD subtypes. As in the studies utilizing factor analysis, patient symptoms were assessed using the symptom checklist section of the Y–BOCS. The studies using cluster analysis, however, also included the Y–BOCS miscellaneous obsessions and compulsions categories.[2] All three studies identified an obsessional (i.e., pure obsessional) group; however, the use of cluster analysis did little to simplify the heterogeneous nature of the subtype. In the first study, Calamari et al. (1999) noted that the obtained subgroups represented dominant symptom patterns but also had significant secondary concerns reflecting symptom heterogeneity. The authors commented that the obsessional cluster suffered most from the psychometric limitations of the Y–BOCS as evidenced by the significant presence of overt compulsions like symmetry, checking, and repeating. Calamari et al. (2004) conducted a

[2]Only one OCD factor analysis study included the Y–BOCS miscellaneous categories (Hantouche & Lancrenon, 1996). An initial factor analysis on the 15 item categories revealed that miscellaneous compulsions loaded significantly onto an obsessional factor. In a second factor analysis based on the 58 Y–BOCS symptom items an excessive number of factors were extracted resulting in a virtually unusable factor solution.

second cluster analysis based on an expanded sample of 220 OCD patients. Although significant changes occurred in the composition of the obsessional cluster, overt compulsions were again prominent. Thus both Calamari studies that included the Y–BOCS miscellaneous categories did little to clarify the existence of a pure obsessional subtype.

Abramowitz et al. (2003) attempted to better delineate the obsessional cluster by providing a more thorough assessment of mental compulsions. It was hypothesized that the presence of mental compulsions might help clarify a pure obsession subtype. They employed a revised version of the Y–BOCS symptom checklist from the *DSM-IV* OCD field trial (Foa et al., 1995). This version was identical to the original Y–BOCS except for the addition of a new symptom checklist category that assessed mental compulsions. A five cluster solution was obtained that included an obsessional group. Named *unacceptable thoughts*, it was characterized by elevated levels of sexual, religious, and aggressive obsessions. As expected, mental compulsions were significantly more prevalent in this cluster, thereby enabling a better differentiation from the other subtypes. The composition of the cluster, however, remained just as diverse as in previous research as the obsessional group did not differ significantly from the other clusters on the Y–BOCS Compulsion Scale. Miscellaneous and overt checking compulsions had a significant presence in this cluster.

Abramowitz et al. (2003) concluded that covert mental compulsions are a significant part of the pure obsessional subtype. These findings need replication but the presence of differing levels of mental compulsions might help distinguish between pure obsessionals and other OCD subtypes.

Summary

Findings from the factor and cluster analytic studies indicate that all patients with OCD, even pure obsessionals, have co-occurring overt compulsions. Overall these studies did not find a pure obsessions dimension or patient cluster with no overt compulsive symptoms. Instead the 'pure obsessions' factor or cluster was quantitatively distinguished from other subtypes, with overt compulsions playing a less prominent role and obsessions predominating, although this conclusion was not as consistently supported in the studies using cluster analysis. Although three factor analytic studies did find evidence of obsessional symptoms without any overt compulsions (e.g., Baer, 1994; Denys et al., 2004b; Mataix-Cols et al., 1999), at the very least the findings have been sufficiently equivocal to call into question the existence of a reliable and significant subgroup of OCD patients with pure obsessions and no overt compulsions. Instead any differences between OCD patients in the presence or absence of overt compulsions appear to be quantitative rather than qualitative in nature.

Methodological issues

All but one of the studies previously reviewed based their factor or cluster analysis of OCD symptoms on the Y–BOCS symptom checklist. This 58 item checklist assesses 15 different categories of obsessive and compulsive symptoms and is considered the gold standard in OCD research (Deacon & Abramowitz, 2005). However, its suitability for subtype research is questionable because of limits in its content validity. More common obsessions and compulsions (e.g., contamination and cleaning) are overrepresented in the Y–BOCS symptom checklist whereas other symptoms that may be related to more complex OCD subtypes are under-represented (McKay et al., 2004). This biased representation is particularly problematic for research on the pure obsessional subtype as the symptom checklist includes few, if any, items that may help to differentiate such individuals. For example, the checklist has only one question that assesses mental compulsions which is found in the miscellaneous compulsions category, a section of the checklist often excluded in symptom-based analyses. Furthermore, Calamari et al. (2004) note that even though the miscellaneous categories may assess important OCD symptoms the categories have no logical coherence or empirical support. It is also difficult to include the miscellaneous categories in subtype analyses because these items are rare and so infrequently endorsed by OCD patients (Abramowitz et al., 2003). In short, not including the miscellaneous categories severely undermines the comprehensiveness of the Y–BOCS, especially with regard to a pure obsessional subtype, while including them often makes the solution too heterogeneous and unstable (e.g., Calamari et al., 1999, 2004; Hantouche & Lancrenon, 1996). As a result, symptoms considered important to the pure obsession subtype, such as mental or covert compulsions, have not been adequately assessed or accounted for in OCD taxonomies (Abramowitz et al., 2003; McKay et al., 2004).

Researchers have also debated over the best method for quantifying endorsements on the Y–BOCS checklist so that patients' primary symptoms are weighted more heavily than symptoms of secondary importance (Calamari et al., 2004; McKay et al., 2004). The biased representation of high base rate symptoms on the Y–BOCS checklist means that individuals have a greater chance of endorsing these items even when they may not be their primary obsessive or compulsive symptoms. To overcome this unequal distribution of item content, the symptom checklist is typically scored so that all categories 'have equal representation [in a factor or cluster analysis], regardless of how many specific symptom examples were provided under each [category]' (Mataix-Cols et al., 1999, p. 1411). This equal categorical weighting may artificially elevate the relationship between symptom categories resulting in less distinction between factors or clusters (Calamari et al., 2004). It may be that the presence of overt compulsions in the pure obsessional factors and clusters is a product of this measurement artefact rather than reflecting the true nature of this subtype.

Finally, one additional methodological shortcoming of these studies is their reliance on coded category data rather than specific symptom items. With the exception of the factor analyses by Hantouche and Lancrenon (1996), Leckman et al. (1997), Summerfeldt et al. (1999), and Denys et al. (2004b), researchers have utilized categorical data in their factor and cluster analyses. Individuals are given a value of 0, 1, or 2 for each category that is intended to reflect the primacy of the symptom presentation in that category. Unfortunately this restricts the range of the checklist variance by dividing each data set into category values instead of using each of the individual checklist items. Although some researchers argue the benefits of this technique (e.g., Calamari et al., 2004), the amount of variance entered into the factor or cluster analysis is severely restricted as compared to the original data set. This reduces the power of the analysis, accentuates the impact of common symptoms (Denys et al., 2004b) and constrains the ability to find less common subtypes, such as pure obsessionals. In addition, Summerfeldt et al. (1999) performed a confirmatory factor analysis at the item level and found that the Y–BOCS checklist categories are not empirically supported. As a result, Denys et al. (2004b) concluded that subtypes emerging from factor and cluster analysis conducted at the categorical level are biased. It is interesting to note that Denys et al. (2004b), one of only three studies to find a pure obsessional factor without overt compulsions, was also one of only four studies that conducted an item-level analysis. Clearly, more research is needed that utilizes individual items from symptom measures.

Taxometric analysis

Factors analysis has been criticized as being biased towards the dimensional perspective (Meehl, 1992). Taxometric statistical methods have been advocated as a better alternative for testing between categorical and dimensional distributions (Haslam, Williams, Kyrios, McKay, & Taylor, 2005). Taxometric methods test between taxonic (categorical) and nontaxonic (dimensional) models of the latent structure of a phenomenon. Taxometric methodology demands that several independent procedures yield convergent evidence, thus providing highly reliable judgments of taxonicity (Meehl & Yonce, 1994). Only one known OCD subtyping study has used taxometric methods. Haslam et al. (2005) used the Padua Inventory – Washington State University Revision (Burns, Keortge, Formea, & Sternberger, 1996) to measure three symptom-based subtypes of OCD (contamination, checking, obsessional) and the Obsessive Beliefs Questionnaire developed by the Obsessive Compulsive Cognitions Working Group (OCCWG, 2003) to measure three cognitive subtypes of obsessive thinking (responsibility/threat estimation, perfectionism/certainty, importance/control). These data were then entered into two taxometric procedures (MAXEIG and MAMBAC). Overall, the plots produced by the MAXEIG procedure more closely matched a dimensional view of the contamination and checking subtypes, but a taxonic or categorical view of the obsessional subtype. The MAMBAC procedure, however, was inconclusive with regard to the checking subtype but favored a dimensional model of the contamination and obsessional subtypes. With respect to cognitive subtypes, the MAXEIG plots were largely inconclusive, while the MAMBAC plots provided some support for a cognitive subtype based upon elevated concerns about the importance of controlling intrusive thoughts.

While this study requires replication, the results provide some very tentative support for two OCD subtypes; an obsessional symptom group and an importance of control cognitive subtype. Given that these two subtypes emerged on different measures, it may be that these symptoms represent different aspects of the same taxon (Haslam et al., 2005).

NEUROPSYCHOLOGICAL EVIDENCE FOR PURE
OBSESSIONS

Neuropsychological testing of patients with OCD has generally shown a pattern of neurocognitive deficits that are most often related to the orbitofrontal cortex region of the brain (Abbruzzese, Ferri, & Scarone, 1997; Harris & Dinn, 2003), although some studies have found no differences when compared to non-clinical controls (e.g., Simpson et al., 2006). The vast majority of these studies have treated OCD as a homogeneous diagnostic group (e.g., Purcell, Maruff, Kyrios, & Pantelis, 1998) and so have not compared OCD subtypes on neuropsychological measures.

A small number of studies have investigated neuropsychological differences in OCD symptom dimensions defined by prior factor or cluster analysis. Generally few differences have emerged on the neuropsychological measures (Mataix-Cols et al., 2005). Khanna and Vijaykumar (2000) compared OCD patients grouped as obsessionals, checkers, washers, and washers and checkers on five different neuropsychological measures. No significant group differences were found on these measures. Across the groups, however, increased severity of obsessions was related to greater basal ganglia, orbitofrontal, and anterior cingulate dysfunction. Deckersbach et al. (1999) examined performance on the California Verbal Learning Test between five different OCD symptom dimensions and found no significant differences between the groups. Abbruzzese, Ferri, & Scarone (1995) found no differences between four OCD subtypes (checkers, washers, mental checkers, and mixed cohorts) on the Wisconsin Card Sorting Test and Abbruzzese, Bellodi, Ferri, & Scarone (1993) found no difference between subtypes on the revised Wechsler Memory Scale. Kyrios, Wainwright, Purcell, Pantelis, & Maruff (1999) found that obsessional symptoms in a clinical group were correlated significantly with spatial working memory and movement time on a planning task although, surprisingly, severity of symptoms was associated with better neuropsychological performance. When comparing between groups of washers, checkers, and pure obsessionals, however, the weak neuropsychological differences that were found (mainly that washers performed better than checkers and obsessionals on a pattern recognition task) were eliminated when differences in symptom severity were controlled.

Overall, neuropsychological studies of OCD have found little support for a distinction between OCD symptom subtypes and no support for neuropsychological differences underlying a pure obsessional subtype. It may be that existing neuropsychological measures are not sufficiently sensitive to distinguish between the proposed subtypes (Mataix-Cols et al., 2005).

NEUROIMAGING RESEARCH ON PURE OBSESSIONS

In the past decade, advances in brain imaging techniques have led to a greater understanding of the neural correlates of OCD (Rosenberg, MacMillan, & Moore, 2001). Patients with OCD, as compared to baseline healthy controls, typically show differences in the orbitofrontal and medial and/or dorsolateral prefrontal cortex. Differences in the caudate nucleus have also been consistently observed (Friedlander & Desrocher, 2006). Like neuropsychology, neuroimaging has yet to distinguish between possible subtypes of OCD and instead collapses over different symptom presentations (Mataix-Cols et al., 2005). Only two studies have used patients with one predominant type of symptom presentation (Cottraux et al., 1996; Phillips et al., 2000) and compared individuals with washing or checking compulsions versus non-clinical controls. Only one study has measured and compared neuroimaging profiles from OCD subtypes derived from prior factor or cluster analysis (see review by Friedlander & Desrocher, 2006). In this study Rauch et al. (1998) obtained a significant positive correlation between scores on a factor that contained religious, aggressive, and sexual obsessions, along with checking compulsions, and regional cerebral blood flow (rCBF) in the bilateral striatum. Severity scores on the other two factors failed to correlate significantly with rCBF. The authors concluded that the commonly found checking/obsessions factor may be associated with hyperactivity in the direct striato-pallido thalamic pathway.

While existing neuropsychiatric research does not provide evidence for a pure obsessional subtype of OCD, findings such as Rauch et al. (1998) illustrate the potential that neuroimaging research holds for refining how clinical phenotypes are characterized (Miguel et al., 2005). Quantifiable neural differences provide a high degree of specification which one day may allow for a separation of pure obsessions from the heterogeneous obsessional factors and clusters that exist today.

PSYCHOLOGICAL TREATMENT OF PURE OBSESSIONS

Even if the empirical evidence for a distinct, homogeneous subtype of pure obsessions is equivocal at best, it may be that individuals with predominantly obsessional symptoms and no overt compulsions require special treatment considerations. In fact it has been repeatedly noted in the literature that individuals with obsessions and no behavioral compulsions show a poor response to standard behavioral treatment for OCD involving exposure and response prevention, or to psychopharmacotherapy (e.g., Griest, 1990; Jenike & Rauch, 1994; Rasmussen & Eisen, 1989; Salkovskis & Westbrook, 1989). So why are pure obsessions so difficult to treat?

A number of factors may make obsessions without overt compulsions especially challenging for therapy (for discussion see McKay et al., 2004). A high proportion of this OCD subtype has repugnant obsessions involving themes of sex, religion and harm/aggression (see Rachman, 1997, 1998). Because repugnant obsessions often involve feared consequences with catastrophic outcomes that are a violation of moral standards (e.g., 'what if I molested a child'), the individual is strongly motivated to avoid anything that might increase perceived risk of the horrific outcome (see Purdon & Clark, 2005, for further discussion). Thus an intervention that calls for increased exposure to the 'child molestation' obsession would be resisted if the individual believes that with greater frequency the obsession might increase the chance of actually molesting a child. As well, shame and embarrass-ment might cause individuals to be very reluctant to admit they experience such repulsive thinking (Newth & Rachman, 2001). Finally, individuals with repugnant obsessions often rely on a variety of mental rituals, other cognitive neutralization strategies, and extensive avoidance in a desperate effort to control their obsessions. They may be very reluctant to abandon such strategies for fear of making matters worse. Thus the phrase 'better the devil you know than the devil you don't know' becomes a guiding principle for those with pure obsessions that can be a significant impediment for treatment.

Despite these difficulties, individuals with pure obsessions often present for treatment because of their intense anxiety and their inability to function in daily living. As mental health practitioners, it is important that we address the special challenges of obsessions without overt compulsions and offer the most efficacious empirically supported intervention for these individuals. In this section we briefly examine the outcome literature for behavioural and cognitive–behavioral inter-ventions for pure obsessions.

BEHAVIOR THERAPY APPROACHES

Thought-stopping

The early behavioral approaches employed thought-stopping as a direct inter-vention to reduce obsessional thinking. Strongly advocated by Wolpe (1958, 1988), thought-stopping involved the repeated deliberate evocation of the obsession fol-lowed by a 'stop command' that was at first vocalized and than eventually pro-duced sub-vocally. In some versions of the treatment, the stop command was accompanied by an aversive stimulus such as snapping an elastic wrist band or delivering a faradic shock.

The efficacy of thought-stopping for obsessions proved to be modest even under the best circumstances. Salkovskis and Westbrook (1989) calculated treatment effects across studies and concluded that only 46% of patients (13/28) showed improvement in the frequency of their obsessions and only 12% (2/17) were improved on ratings of the distress of obsessions. In addition, Rachman (1976) noted that thought-stopping is an *ad hoc* technique that lacks a psychological rationale. This led many to conclude that thought-stopping had limited treatment effect and so the technique has been largely abandoned as a credible intervention for obsessions. Moreover, it would appear from the clinical descriptions that thought-stopping was no more or less effective for those with pure obsessions (e.g., Emmelkamp & van der Heyden, 1980; Likierman & Rachman, 1982; Stern, Lipsedge, & Marks, 1973; see Emmelkamp & Kwee, 1977, for more favorable results).

There is one exception to this fairly negative conclusion about thought-stopping. This intervention may be an appropriate and even effective form of treatment for covert compulsions and obsessional rumination, where it is employed as a thought blocking or response prevention strategy (for discussion see Clark, 2004; de Silva,

2003). De Silva and Rachman (1992) described the use of thought-stopping to reduce a mental compulsion in a patient who felt compelled to correct any asymmetrical pattern by imagining a perfect symmetrical form. Treatment involved exposure to various asymmetrical forms with instructions to block the mental compulsion with self-administered thought-stopping. In this context thought-stopping has a more solid conceptual basis as a form of response prevention or thought blocking. Except for a very few case examples reported in the literature (e.g., Albert & Hayward, 2002; Yamagami, 1971), there is no empirical evidence to verify the effectiveness of thought-stopping for covert compulsions or obsessional rumination.

Audiotaped habituation training

Habituation training initially seemed more promising than thought-stopping. It was based on the same behavioral rationale as standard exposure and response prevention (ERP) used for obsessions with overt compulsions. Rachman (1976) first suggested that prolonged exposure to the obsession with instructions to refrain from any overt or covert neutralization might be an effective intervention for obsessional phenomena. In a later study, Likierman and Rachman (1982) compared the effectiveness of habituation training and thought-stopping in 12 patients, some who may have had obsessions with no overt compulsions, but this is not clear from the short clinical descriptions provided in the article. Both forms of treatment produced weak and inconsistent results, especially on the inter-session measures. Other attempts to demonstrate the effectiveness of habituation training or prolonged exposure on reduction in obsessional thinking led to weak and inconclusive findings (Emmelkamp & Kwee, 1977; Emmelkamp & Giesselbach, 1981; Hackman & McLean, 1975; Gurnani & Vaughan, 1981; Vogel, Peterson & Broverman, 1982).

A procedural problem may account for the relatively discouraging findings with habituation training. Because of the private nature of obsessions, it is difficult to ensure that individuals are engaged in prolonged attentive focus on the obsession during the exposure sessions. If individuals exhibited cognitive avoidance of the distressing obsession, this would undermine the effectiveness of exposure. To overcome this limitation, Salkovskis (1988) introduced an audiotaped version of habituation training. The obsessional rumination was recorded on a loop tape and individuals were instructed to listen to the tape for daily 20–90 minute exposure sessions. Again they were asked to refrain from any form of overt or covert neutralization while listening to the tape. In the original case study, significant reductions were achieved in the daily frequency of a harming obsession with overt compulsions (Salkovskis, 1988). In addition, other single case studies have reported significant treatment effects on obsessions with audiotaped habituation (Headland & McDonald, 1987; Martin & Tarrier, 1992; Salkovskis & Westbrook, 1989; Thyer, 1985), but it is unclear how many involved pure obsessions without overt compulsions. In a more recent single case study that clearly involved a harming obsession with no overt compulsion, an audiotaped habituation component of treatment produced reductions in the subjective distress associated with the obsession

(Dunne, 2000). Although there is a dearth of empirical research on the specific effects of audiotaped habituation training for pure obsessions, it has been incorporated into more recent cognitive–behavioral treatment packages designed specifically for the pure obsession subtype (e.g., Freeston et al., 1997).

COGNITIVE–BEHAVIORAL THERAPY (CBT) FOR PURE OBSESSIONS

Cognitive–behavioral therapy for OCD is a 'psychological treatment that utilizes both cognitive and behavioral therapeutic change strategies to achieve reductions in obsessive and compulsive symptoms by modifying the faulty appraisals, specific core beliefs, and dysfunctional neutralization responses that are implicated in the etiology and persistence of obsessional symptoms' (Clark, 2004, p. 187). CBT is based on the cognitive–behavioral model of OCD in which obsessions are derived from faulty appraisals of normal unwanted intrusive thoughts, images or impulses. The faulty appraisals and beliefs of inflated responsibility ('I must ensure that I don't accidentally contaminate others'), overimportance of thought ('The obsession must be significant because it repeatedly enters my mind'), perceived need to control ('If I don't get better control over this terrible thought, I won't be able to stand the anxiety'), overestimated threat ('If I touch that doorknob, I might possibly get a terrible life-threatening disease'), intolerance of uncertainty ('I must be certain I haven't made a mistake on the form'), and perfectionism ('I can't complete the task until I know it is done flawlessly') lead to erroneous conclusions that an unwanted distressing intrusive thought is highly significant because it could lead to a perceived dreaded outcome (Freeston, Rhéaume & Ladouceur, 1996; OCCWG, 1997; Rachman, 1997, 1998; Salkovskis, 1985, 1989, 1999). Once the intrusive thought is perceived in this highly exaggerated but personally threatening manner, the individual feels compelled to engage in escape, avoidance, compulsions or other forms of control responses that will neutralize the anxiety associated with the mental intrusion and/or prevent the imagined negative outcome. These two processes, faulty appraisals and neutralization responses, are considered the key psychological processes responsible for the escalation of unwanted intrusive thoughts into obsessions. Accordingly, the CBT therapist utilizes cognitive and behavioral interventions to modify appraisals of the obsession and eliminate neutralization responses. It is expected that this will lead to a reduction in the frequency and distress of obsessive and compulsive symptoms.

It is interesting that Salkovskis (1985) first proposed an approach to OCD that placed greater emphasis on cognition in response to the weak effects of behavioral interventions that focused directly on the modification of obsessions. As noted at the beginning of this chapter, the relatively poor outcome for behavioral treatments of obsessions without overt compulsions led to a more cognitive treatment approach. Exposure and response prevention in the form of audio loop tapes, disconfirmatory behavioral experiments, and cognitive restructuring are used to challenge beliefs about the personally threatening nature of the obsession and the need for neutralization. Rachman (1997, 1998) offered a cognitive–behavioral theory specific to obsessions and then a cognitive–behavioral treatment protocol for pure obsessions (Rachman, 2003). So has CBT offered new hope for the treatment of pure obsessions or obsessional rumination?

The critical treatment outcome studies of CBT for obsessions without compulsions are only now beginning to emerge. Probably the most important clinical trial of CBT for pure obsessions was reported by Freeston and colleagues at Laval University in Quebec (Freeston et al., 1997). Twenty-nine individuals with obsessions and no overt compulsions were randomly assigned to approximately 25 sessions of CBT or a wait-list control condition that crossed over into treatment after 16 weeks. CBT consisted of (a) a detailed educational component on the cognitive explanation for obsessions and the rationale for ERP; (b) audio loop tape exposure training; (c) cognitive restructuring of overimportance, overestimated threat, inflated responsibility and perfectionistic expectations; and (d) relapse prevention. At posttreatment the CBT group showed significant improvement on obsessional symptoms compared with the wait-list controls. Overall, 67% of the total treated sample showed clinically significant change on the Y–BOCS but this dropped to 53% at 6 month follow-up. These findings are most encouraging when compared to the rather dismal results obtained with other interventions for pure obsessions. However, it is not clear how many patients in the Freeston et al. (1997) study would meet our criteria of 'pure obsession' subtype. Patients with overt compulsions were included if 'the overt compulsions were not functionally related to the target obsession and much less severe than the obsession' (Freeston et al., 1997, p. 407). It would be interesting to know if a higher proportion of those with truly pure obsessions were overrepresented in the treatment nonresponder group.

In a more recent study, O'Connor et al. (2005) compared a group and individualized format of CBT in 26 patients with predominantly obsessions and few or no overt compulsions. Both treatment formats produced significant improvement but the effect was greater for those in the individualized (68% improved) than in the group (38% improved) condition. These improvements were maintained at 6 month follow-up. However, the relation between change in beliefs and symptom outcome was not striking. Abramowitz et al. (2003) examined changes in Y–BOCS scores following a trial of ERP with a cognitive emphasis for five OCD subtypes derived from a hierarchical cluster analysis. Patients assigned to the 'unacceptable thoughts cluster', which could be construed as a pure obsessions group, showed as favorable a treatment response as other types of OCD patients.

There have been a few case studies of CBT for pure obsessions. Simos and Dimitriou (1994) treated a woman with a pure harming obsession by targeting her exaggerated probability of threat through audio loop tape exposure. Significant symptomatic improvement was evident within five weeks of treatment and was maintained at 2.5 and 4 month follow-up. O'Kearney (1993) describes use of audio loop tape exposure as well as cognitive decatastrophizing and re-attribution to treat a woman with harm and aggression obsessions and no overt compulsions. Significant improvement in obsessional symptoms was obtained but a relapse did occur at 2.5 months that required additional intervention. However, treatment gains were maintained at 9 month follow-up. Abramowitz (2002) used a CBT treatment that primarily emphasized in vivo exposure to successfully treat a 19-year-old male with obsessional sex and aggressive thoughts and impulses but no overt compulsions. Significant reductions in obsessional symptoms were obtained after approximately 8 weeks of treatment and were maintained at 3 and 6 month follow-up. Wilhelm (2003) reported significant symptom reduction with 14 sessions of CBT offered to a man with severe sexual and violent obsessions and no overt compulsions. Freeston, Léger, & Ladouceur (2001) treated six individuals with obsessions and no overt compulsions with an average of 16 weekly sessions of cognitive therapy without instructions to engage in exposure or response prevention. The faulty appraisals and beliefs considered key to the persistence of obsessions was the focus of treatment. Based on a multiple-baseline, experimental case design, four patients were improved on the Y–BOCS by posttreatment (66%) and 5 were improved at 6 and 12 month follow-up (83%).

Although the treatment outcome data on the effectiveness of CBT for pure obsessions is only preliminary, these initial findings are encouraging. It would appear that at last we have a psychological intervention that might be particularly well-suited to change pure obsessions and obsessional rumination. However, there are a number of key issues that must be addressed before CBT can be considered efficacious for obsessions. First, controlled comparative outcome studies are needed, especially between CBT and medication alone in order to determine if CBT has any treatment-specific benefits for pure obsessionals. Second, randomized treatment studies have not used 'pure' samples of obsessionals. Individuals with overt compulsions have been allowed to participate as long as the compulsion is not related to the primary obsession. Although these broader inclusion criteria may be necessary to generate a sufficient sample size over a reasonable time period, it nevertheless clouds the interpretation of the findings for obsessions without any overt compulsions. And third, dismantling studies are needed to determine if cognitive interventions add any therapeutic effects beyond exposure-based interventions such as the audio loop tape approach. Until these critical questions are addressed, the efficacy of CBT for pure obsessions must be considered tentative.

SUMMARY AND CONCLUSION

We began this chapter with a question: does the label 'pure obsessions' represent an artificial distinction arising from our attempts to bring nosological order to a clinically diverse diagnostic group or does it define a symptomatically distinct type of OCD? As we have seen from a brief review of the clinical literature, it has long been recognized that a significant minority of OCD patients suffer primarily from repugnant obsessions of violence, sex or immorality but without the expected overt compulsive ritual. Until recently research on this clinical phenomenon has been hampered by confusion and inconsistencies in the use of terms such as 'pure obsessions' or 'obsessional rumination'. As well, early behavioral treatment protocols were developed and tested on OCD with overt compulsions and so not surprisingly these protocols did not generalize well to that subgroup of obsessional patients with no behavioral compulsions.

In recent years much progress has been made in understanding and treating individuals with obsessions and no overt behavioral compulsions. We now have more precise definitions of the terms 'pure obsessions', 'obsessional rumination' and 'covert compulsions'. It is now clear that the vast majority of individuals with pure obsessions have mental compulsions or other forms of neutralization that are functionally equivalent to overt compulsions. Rachman (1997, 1998) has offered a specific theory of obsessions and a cognitive–behavioral treatment protocol specific to pure obsessions. The few clinical trials and case studies that have been published indicate much improved treatment effectiveness for pure obsessions when cognitive interventions are combined with modified ERP such as audio loop tape habituation training.

Despite this progress, there are still fundamental issues about the distinctiveness of a pure obsessions subtype of OCD. Symptom-based factor and cluster analytic studies have failed to find a reliable and consistent subtype of OCD that represents obsessions without overt compulsions. At best, symptom dimensions or groups have been identified that approximate a 'pure obsessions' subtype but in most studies these dimensions are contaminated with the presence of overt compulsive symptoms. The most parsimonious conclusion that can be drawn is that this 'obsessional subtype' differs mainly in degree rather than in kind from other OCD patients. In other words, they show a greater predominance of obsessions and less predominance of compulsions than other OCD patients but there is rarely a complete absence of even overt compulsive behavior. Even the increased presence of mental compulsions and relative absence of overt rituals may be less important if overt and covert compulsions are considered functionally equivalent. Finally, the clinical utility of defining OCD subtypes might be questioned if practitioners embrace an individualized case formulation approach to each patient rather than rely solely on manualized treatment approaches for each OCD subtype.

So what must be done to advance progress on pure obsessions? Radomsky and Taylor (2005) discuss a number of issues that must be addressed in order to validate OCD subtypes. When considering pure obsessions, four issues are particularly germane to this process. First, the existing symptom-based research has not adequately investigated the existence of pure obsessions because standardized measures such as the Y–BOCS or Padua Inventory do not assess important symptom features of pure obsessions or obsessional rumination. Symptoms like mental compulsions, reassurance seeking, and presence of repugnant obsessions are either absent or poorly represented in these measures. As a result, pure obsessions fail to emerge as a distinct dimension. What is needed are broader and more precise symptom measures that capture the unique clinical presentation of pure obsessionality, obsessional rumination, and covert compulsions.

A second issue raised by Radomsky and Taylor (2005) is the need to take into account the functional characteristics of symptoms. For example, it is important to know whether a person repeatedly asks for reassurance on whether 'God has forgiven me' because of an irresistible urge (i.e., an obsessional rumination), or as a form of neutralization in response to a religious obsession about committing the 'unforgivable sin'. This is particularly critical for identifying pure obsessions where overt, observable compulsions are absent. Again, a refined assessment strategy that included the functional nature of symptoms would help elucidate differences between subtypes.

Third, it may be that a dimensional rather than categorical approach will prove more helpful in understanding the heterogeneity of OCD. Subtype research has been based on the premise that there are distinct defining boundaries between these different types of OCD. However, the empirical research reviewed in this chapter suggests that symptom differences occur along a continuum. It is not that individuals with pure obsessions have no overt compulsions but rather that severe obsessions play a more prominent role and overt compulsions a relatively minor role in their symptom presentation. It may be that some form of profile analysis that recognizes the dimensional nature of OCD symptoms might be a more fruitful basis for defining pure obsessionality than the current categorical approaches (e.g., Taylor et al., 2006).

Finally, more treatment studies are needed that specifically target individuals with pure obsessions. Comparative treatment studies are required in which, for example, CBT is compared to pharmacotherapy in its effectiveness for pure obsessions. As well, dismantling studies would elucidate the precise treatment processes that are most effective in dealing with severe obsessions. Until we see progress on these issues, questions about the validity of the pure obsessions subtype and whether a specialized treatment approach is required will remain unanswered.

ACKNOWLEDGEMENTS

Preparation of this chapter was partially supported by a grant from the Social Sciences and Humanities Research Council of Canada (No. 410-2001-0084) awarded to the first author and a Social Sciences and Humanities Research Council of Canada Doctoral Fellowship awarded to the second author.

REFERENCES

Abbruzzese, M., Bellodi, L., Ferri, S., & Scarone, S. (1993). Memory functioning in obsessive-compulsive disorder. *Behavioural Neurology, 6,* 112–119.

Abbruzzese, M., Ferri, S., & Scarone, S. (1995). Wisconsin Card Sorting Test performance in obsessive–compulsive disorder: No evidence for involvement of the dorsolateral prefrontal cortex. *Psychiatry Research, 58,* 37–43.

Abbruzzese, M., Ferri, S., & Scarone, S. (1997). The selective breakdown of frontal functions in patients with obsessive–compulsive disorder and in patients with schizophrenia: A double dissociation experimental finding. *Neuropsychologia, 35,* 907–912.

Abramowitz, J. S. (2002). Treatment of obsessive thoughts and cognitive rituals using exposure and response prevention. *Clinical Case Studies, 1,* 6–24.

Abramowitz, J. S., Franklin, M. E., Schwartz, S. A., & Furr, J. M. (2003). Symptom presentation and outcome of cognitive-behavioural therapy for obsessive–compulsive disorder. *Journal of Consulting and Clinical Psychology, 71*, 1049–1057.

Akhtar, S., Wig, N. N., Varma, V. K., Pershad, D., & Verma, S. K. (1975). A phenomenological analysis of symptoms in obsessive-compulsive neurosis. *British Journal of Psychiatry, 127*, 342–348.

Albert, I., & Hayward, P. (2002). Treatment of intrusive ruminations about mathematics. *Behavioural and Cognitive Psychotherapy, 30*, 223–226.

American Psychiatric Association (2000). *Diagnostic and statistical manual of mental disorders* (4th ed., text rev.) (*DSM-IV-TR*). Washington, DC: APA.

Baer, L. (1994). Factor analysis of symptom subtypes of obsessive compulsive disorder and their relation to personality and tic disorders. *Journal of Clinical Psychiatry, 55* (Suppl. 3), 18–23.

Beech, H. R., & Vaughan, M. (1978). *Behavioural treatment of obsessional states*. Chichester: Wiley.

Borgen, F. H., & Weiss, D. J. (1971). Cluster analysis and counselling research. *Journal of Counselling Psychology, 18*, 583–591.

Burns, G. L., Keortge, S. G., Formea, G. M., & Sternberger, L. G. (1996). Revision of the Padua Inventory for obsessive–compulsive disorder symptoms: Distinctions between worry, obsessions, and compulsions. *Behaviour Research and Therapy, 34*, 163–173.

Calamari, J. E., Wiegartz, P. S., & Janeck, A. S. (1999). Obsessive–compulsive disorder subgroups: A symptom-based clustering approach. *Behaviour Research and Therapy, 37*, 113–125.

Calamari, J. E., Weigartz, P. S., Riemann, B. C., Cohen, R. J., Greer, A., Jacobi, D. M., et al. (2004). Obsessive–compulsive disorder subtypes: An attempted replication and extension of a symptom-based taxonomy. *Behaviour Research and Therapy, 42*, 647–670.

Carr, A. T. (1974). Compulsive neurosis: A review of the literature. *Psychological Bulletin, 81*, 311–318.

Clark, D. A. (2004). *Cognitive–behavioral therapy for OCD*. New York: Guilford Press.

Cottraux, J., Gerard, D., Cinotti, L., Froment, J. C., Deiber, M., Le Bars, D., et al. (1996). A controlled positron emission tomography study of obsessive and neutral auditory stimulation in obsessive–compulsive disorder with checking rituals. *Psychiatry Research, 60*, 101–112.

Deacon, B. J., & Abramowitz, J. S. (2005). The Yale–Brown Obsessive Compulsive Scale: Factor analysis, construct validity, and suggestions for refinement. *Journal of Anxiety Disorders, 19*, 573–585.

Deckersbach, T., Savage, C. R., Mataix-Cols, D., Wilhelm, S., Baer, L., & Jenike, M. A. (1999). *Verbal memory in OCD subtypes*. Poster presented at the Annual Conference of the Association for Advancement of Behaviour Therapy, Toronto, ON.

Denys, D., de Geus, F., van Megen, H. J., & Westenberg, H. G. (2004a). Symptom dimensions in obsessive–compulsive disorder: Factor analysis on a clinician-rated scale and a self-report measure. *Psychopathology, 37*, 181–189.

Denys, D., de Geus, F., van Megen, H. J., & Westenberg, H. G. (2004b). Use of factor analysis to detect potential phenotypes in obsessive–compulsive disorder. *Psychiatry Research, 128*, 273–280.

De Silva, P. (2003). Obsessions, ruminations and covert compulsions. In R. G. Menzies & P. de Silva (Eds.), *Obsessive–compulsive disorder: Theory, research and treatment* (pp. 195–208). Chichester: Wiley.

De Silva, P., & Rachman, S. (1992). *Obsessive compulsive disorder: The facts*. Oxford: Oxford University Press.

Dunne, P. (2000). Overvalued ideas and obsessions: Some clinical considerations. *Behaviour Change, 17*, 265–274.

Einstein, D., & Menzies, R. G. (2003). Atypical representations. In R. G. Menzies & P. de Silva (Eds.), *Obsessive–compulsive disorder: Theory, research and treatment* (pp. 209–220). Chichester: Wiley.

Emmelkamp, P. M. G., & Giesselbach, P. (1981). Treatment of obsessions: Relevant v. irrelevant exposure. *Behavioural Psychotherapy, 9*, 322–329.

Emmelkamp, P. M. G., & Kwee, K. G. (1977). Obsessional ruminations: A comparison between thought-stopping and prolonged exposure in imagination. *Behaviour Research and Therapy, 15*, 441–444.

Emmelkamp, P. M. G., & van der Heyden, H. (1980). Treatment of harming obsessions. *Behavioural Analysis and Modification, 4*, 28–35.

Foa, E. B., Kozak, M. J., Goodman, W. K., Hollander, E., Jenike, M. A., & Rasmussen, S. A. (1995). DSM-IV field trial: Obsessive–compulsive disorder. *American Journal of Psychiatry, 152*, 90–96.

Freeston, M. H., & Ladouceur, R. (1997). *The cognitive behavioral treatment of obsessions: A treatment manual.* Unpublished manuscript, École de psychologie, Université Laval, Québec, Canada.

Freeston, M. H., Ladouceur, R., Gagnon, F., Thibodeau, N., Rhéaume, J., Letarte, H., et al. (1997). Cognitive–behavioral treatment of obsessive thoughts: A controlled study. *Journal of Consulting and Clinical Psychology, 65,* 405–413.

Freeston, M. H., Léger, E., & Ladouceur, R. (2001). Cognitive therapy of obsessive thoughts. *Cognitive and Behavioral Practice, 8,* 61–78.

Freeston, M. H., Rhéaume, J., & Ladouceur, R. (1996). Correcting faulty appraisals of obsessional thoughts. *Behaviour Research and Therapy, 34,* 433–446.

Friedlander, L., & Desrocher, M. (2006). Neuroimaging studies of obsessive–compulsive disorder in adults and children. *Clinical Psychology Review, 26,* 32–49.

Goodman, W. K., Price, L. H., Rasmussen, S. A., Mazure, C., Delgado, P., Heninger, G. R., et al. (1989). The Yale–Brown Obsessive–Compulsive Scale: Development, use, reliability, and validity. *Archives of General Psychiatry, 46,* 1006–1011.

Greist, J. H. (1990). Treatment of obsessive–compulsive disorder: Psychotherapies, drugs, and other somatic treatment. *Journal of Clinical Psychiatry, 51,* 44–50.

Gurnani, P. D., & Vaughan, M. (1981). Changes in frequency and distress during prolonged repetition of obsessional thoughts. *British Journal of Clinical Psychology, 20,* 79–81.

Hackman, A., & McLean, C. (1975). A comparison of flooding and thought stopping in the treatment of obsessional neurosis. *Behaviour Research and Therapy, 13,* 263–269.

Hallam, R. S. (1974). Extinction of ruminations: A case study. *Behavior Therapy, 5,* 565–568.

Hantouche, E. G., & Lancrenon, S. (1996). Modern typology of symptoms and obsessive–compulsive syndromes: Results of a large French study of 615 patients. *Encephale, 22,* 9–21.

Harris, C. L., & Dinn, W. M. (2003). Subtyping obsessive–compulsive disorder: Neuropsychological correlates. *Behavioural Neurology, 14,* 75–87.

Haslam, N., Williams, B. J., Kyrios, M., McKay, D., & Taylor, S. (2005). Subtyping obsessive–compulsive disorder: A taxometric analysis. *Behavior Therapy, 36,* 381–391.

Headland, K., & McDonald, B. (1987). Rapid audio-tape treatment of obsessional ruminations: A case report. *Behavioural Psychotherapy, 15,* 188–192.

Ingram, I. M. (1960). Obsessional illness in mental hospital patients. *Journal of Mental Science, 197,* 382–402.

Insel, T. R. (1990). Phenomenology of obsessive compulsive disorder. *Journal of Clinical Psychiatry, 51* (Suppl.), 4–8.

Jenike, M. A., & Rauch, S. L. (1994). Managing the patient with treatment-resistant obsessive–compulsive disorder: Current strategies. *Journal of Clinical Psychiatry, 55,* 11–17.

Khanna, S., & Vijaykumar, D. R. (2000). Neuropsychology of obsessive–compulsive disorder. *Biological Psychiatry, 47,* 127S.

Kyrios, M., Wainwright, K., Purcell, R., Pantelis, C., Maruff, P. (1999). *Neuropsychological performance in subtypes of obsessive–compulsive disorder.* Paper presented at the Annual Conference of the Association for Advancement of Behavior Therapy, Toronto, ON.

Leckman, J. F., Grice, D. E., Boardman, J., Zhang, H., Vitale, A., & Bondi, C. (1997). Symptoms of obsessive–compulsive disorder. *American Journal of Psychiatry, 154,* 911–917.

Lewis, A. J. (1966). Obsessional disorder. In R. Scott (Ed.), *Price's textbook of the practice of medicine* (10th ed.). Oxford: Oxford University Press.

Likierman, H., & Rachman, S. (1982). Obsessions: An experimental investigation of thought-stopping and habituation training. *Behavioural Psychotherapy, 10,* 324–338.

Lo, W. H. (1967). A follow-up of obsessional neurosis in Hong Kong Chinese. *British Journal of Psychiatry, 113,* 823–832.

Martin, C., & Tarrier, N. (1992). The importance of cultural factors in the exposure to obsessional ruminations: A case example. *Behavioural Psychotherapy, 20,* 181–184.

Mataix-Cols, D. (2006). Deconstructing obsessive–compulsive disorder: A multidimensional perspective. *Current Opinion in Psychiatry, 19,* 84–89.

Mataix-Cols, D., Rauch, S. L., Baer, L., Eisen, J. L., Shera, D. M., Goodman, W. K., et al. (2002). Symptom stability in adult obsessive–compulsive disorder: Data from a naturalistic two-year follow-up study. *American Journal of Psychiatry, 159,* 263–268.

Mataix-Cols, D., Rauch, S. L., Manzo, P. A., Jenike, M. A., & Baer, L. (1999). Use of factor-analysed symptom dimensions to predict outcome with serotonin reuptake inhibitors and placebo in the treatment of obsessive–compulsive disorder. *American Journal of Psychiatry, 156,* 1409–1416.

Mataix-Cols, D., Rosario-Campos, M. C., & Leckman, J. F. (2005). A multidimensional model of obsessive–compulsive disorder. *American Journal of Psychiatry, 162,* 228–238.

McKay, D., Abramowitz, J. S., Calamari, J. E., Kyrios, M., Radomsky, A., Sookman, D., et al. (2004). A critical evaluation of obsessive–compulsive disorder subtypes: Symptoms versus mechanisms. *Clinical Psychology Review, 24,* 283–313.

Meehl, P. E. (1992). Factors and taxa, traits and types, differences of degree and differences in kind. *Journal of Personality, 60,* 117–174.

Meehl, P. E., & Yonce, L. J. (1994). Taxometric analysis: I. Detecting taxonicity with two quantitative indicators using means above and below a sliding cut (MAMBAC procedure). *Psychological Reports, 74,* 1059–1274.

Miguel, E. C., Leckman, J. F., Rauch, S., Rosario-Campos, M. C., Hounie, A. G., Mercadante, M. T., et al. (2005). Obsessive–compulsive disorder phenotypes: Implications for genetic studies. *Molecular Psychiatry, 10,* 258–275.

Newth, S., & Rachman, S. (2001). The concealment of obsessions. *Behaviour Research and Therapy, 39,* 457–464.

OCCWG (Obsessive Compulsive Cognitions Working Group) (1997). Cognitive assessment of obsessive–compulsive disorder. *Behaviour Research and Therapy, 35,* 667–681.

OCCWG (Obsessive Compulsive Cognitions Working Group) (2003). Psychometric validation of the Obsessive Beliefs Questionnaire and the Interpretation of Intrusions Inventory: Part I. *Behaviour Research and Therapy, 41,* 863–878.

O'Connor, K., Freeston, M. H., Gareau, D., Careua, Y., Dufour, M. J., Aardema, F., et al. (2005). Group versus individual treatment in obsessions without compulsions. *Clinical Psychology and Psychotherapy, 12,* 87–96.

O'Kearney, R. (1993). Additional considerations in the cognitive–behavioral treatment of obsessional ruminations – a case study. *Journal of Behavior Therapy and Experimental Psychiatry, 24,* 357–365.

Phillips, M. L., Marks, I. M., Senior, C., Lythgoe, D., O'Dweyer, A.-M., Meehan, O., et al. (2000). A differential neural response in obsessive–compulsive disorder patients with washing compared with checking symptoms to disgust. *Psychological Medicine, 30,* 1037–1050.

Purcell, R., Maruff, P., Kyrios, M., & Pantelis, C. (1998). Neuropsychological deficits in obsessive–compulsive disorder: A comparison with unipolar depression, panic disorder, and normal controls. *Archives of General Psychiatry, 55,* 415–423.

Purdon, C., & Clark, D. A. (2005). *Overcoming obsessive thoughts: How to gain control of your OCD.* Oakland, CA: New Harbinger.

Rachman, S. J. (1971). Obsessional ruminations. *Behaviour Research and Therapy, 9,* 229–235.

Rachman, S. J. (1976). The modification of obsessions: A new formulation. *Behaviour Research and Therapy, 14,* 437–443.

Rachman, S. J. (1983). Obstacles to the successful treatment of obsessions. In E. B. Foa & P. M. G. Emmelkamp (Eds.), *Failures in behavior therapy* (pp. 35–57). New York: Wiley.

Rachman, S. J. (1997). A cognitive theory of obsessions. *Behaviour Research and Therapy, 35,* 793–802.

Rachman, S. J. (1998). A cognitive theory of obsessions: Elaborations. *Behaviour Research and Therapy, 36,* 385–401.

Rachman, S. J. (2003). *The treatment of obsessions.* Oxford: Oxford University Press.

Rachman, S. J., & Hodgson, R. J. (1980). *Obsessions and compulsions.* Englewood Cliffs, NJ: Prentice-Hall.

Rachman, S. J., & Shafran, R. (1998). Cognitive and behavioral features of obsessive–compulsive disorder. In R. P. Swinson, M. M. Antony, S. Rachman, & M.A. Richter (Eds.), *Obsessive–compulsive disorder: theory, research and treatment* (pp. 51–78). New York: Guilford Press.

Radomsky, A. S., & Taylor, S. (2005). Subtyping OCD: Prospects and problems. *Behavior Therapy, 36*, 371–379.

Rasmussen, S. A., & Eisen, J. L. (1989). Clinical features and phenomenology of obsessive compulsive disorder. *Psychiatric Annals, 19*, 67–73.

Rauch, S. L., Dougherty, D. D., Shin, L. M., Alpert, N. M., Manzo, P., & Leahy, L., et al. (1998). Neural correlates of factor-analyzed OCD symptom dimensions: A PET study. *CNS Spectrums, 3*, 37–43.

Rosenberg, D. R., MacMillan, S. N., & Moore, G. J. (2001). Brain anatomy and chemistry may predict treatment response in paediatric obsessive–compulsive disorder. *International Journal of Neuropsychopharmacology, 4*, 179–190.

Salkovskis, P. M. (1985). Obsessional–compulsive problems: A cognitive–behavioural analysis. *Behaviour Research and Therapy, 23*, 571–583.

Salkovskis, P. M. (1988). Intrusive thoughts and obsessional disorders. In D. Glasgow & N. Eisenberg (Eds.), *Current Issues in Clinical Psychology*, vol. 4. London: Gower.

Salkovskis, P. M. (1989). Cognitive–behavioural factors and the persistence of intrusive thoughts in obsessional problems. *Behaviour Research and Therapy, 27*, 677–682.

Salkovskis, P. M. (1998). Cognitive–behavioral approach to understanding obsessional thinking. *British Journal of Psychiatry, 173* (Suppl. 35), 53–63.

Salkovskis, P. M. (1999). Understanding and treating obsessive–compulsive disorder. *Behaviour Research and Therapy, 37*, S29–S52.

Salkovskis, P., Richards, E., & Richards, C. (1998). A cognitive–behavioural approach to understanding obsessional thinking. *British Journal of Psychiatry, 35* (Suppl.), 53–63.

Salkovskis, P. M., & Westbrook, D. (1989). Behaviour therapy and obsessional ruminations: Can failure be turned into success? *Behaviour Research and Therapy, 27*, 149–160.

Simos, G., & Dimitriou, E. (1994). Cognitive–behavioural treatment of culturally bound obsessional ruminations: A case report. *Behavioural and Cognitive Psychotherapy, 22*, 325–330.

Simpson, H. B., Rosen, W., Huppert, J. D., Lin, S. H., Foa, E. B., & Liebowitz, M. R. (2006). Are there reliable neuropsychological deficits in obsessive–compulsive disorder? *Journal of Psychiatric Research, 40*, 247–257.

Stern, R. S., Lipsedge, M. S., & Marks, I. M. (1973). Obsessive ruminations: A controlled trial of thought stopping. *Behaviour Research and Therapy, 11*, 659–662.

Summerfeldt, L. J., Richter, M. A., Antony, M. M., & Swinson, R. P. (1999). Symptom structure in obsessive–compulsive disorder: A confirmatory factor analytic study. *Behaviour Research and Therapy, 37*, 297–311.

Taylor, S., Abramowitz, J. S., McKay, D., Calamari, J. E., Sookman, D., Kyrios, M. et al. (2006). Do dysfunctional beliefs play a role in all types of obsessive–compulsive disorder? *Journal of Anxiety Disorders, 20*, 85–97.

Thyer, B. A. (1985). Audio-taped exposure therapy in a case of obsessional neurosis. *Journal of Behavior Therapy and Experimental Psychiatry, 16*, 271–273.

Vogel, W., Peterson, L. E., & Broverman, I. K. (1982). A modification of Rachman's habituation technique for treatment of the obsessive–compulsive disorder. *Behaviour Research and Therapy, 20*, 101–104.

Welner, A., Reich, T., Robins, E., Fishman, R., & Van Doren, T. (1976). Obsessive–compulsive neurosis: Record, follow-up, and family studies. I. Inpatient Record Study. *Comprehensive Psychiatry, 17*, 527–539.

Wilhelm, S. (2003). Cognitive treatment of obsessions. *Brief Treatment and Crisis Intervention, 3*, 187–199.

Wolpe, J. R. (1958). *Psychotherapy by Reciprocal Inhibition*. Stanford, CA: Stanford University Press.

Wolpe J. R. (with Wolpe, D.) (1988). *Life without fear: anxiety and its cure*. Oakland, CA: New Harbinger Publications.

Yamagami, T. (1971). The treatment of an obsession by thought stopping. *Journal of Behavior Therapy and Experimental Psychiatry, 2*, 133–135.

5

COMPULSIVE HOARDING

RANDY O. FROST[1] AND GAIL STEKETEE[2]

[1]Department of Psychology, Smith College, Massachusetts;
[2]School of Social Work, Boston University, Massachusetts

DEFINITION AND SEVERITY

Until very recently little attention was paid to the hoarding of possessions as a clinical disorder. At most, it was thought of as an eccentricity rather than a serious symptom, and a quirk of older people who had lived through the depression (Warren & Ostrom, 1988). Several early theorists mention hoarding. Fromm (1947) described a 'hoarding orientation', in which security was dependent on collecting and saving things. Salzman (1973) tied hoarding to the striving for perfect control over one's personal environment. This together with uncertainty about what might be needed in the future leads some people to take the safest course and save everything. The early research literature on hoarding was limited to case studies describing hoarding behaviors and related pathology. Greenberg (1987), for instance, described four cases in which clients collected masses of junk, broken items, clothes, and paper. Frankenburg (1984) reported a case of hoarding in a woman with anorexia nervosa who collected pieces of paper, Styrofoam, toothpaste caps, screws, nails, and other small items. Greenberg, Witztum, and Levy (1990) detailed a series of eight cases with a wide variety of associated psychopathology.

Since 1993, the research on hoarding has been more systematic. Frost and Gross (1993) defined hoarding as 'the acquisition of and failure to discard possessions

Correspondence to: Randy O. Frost, Department of Psychology, Smith College, Northampton, Massachusetts 01063.

that appear to be useless or of limited value'. Frost and Hartl (1996) suggested two additional features that are necessary for the hoarding to pose a clinically significant problem. First, the living spaces must be so cluttered that the normal activities are not possible. Second, the behaviors must cause significant distress or impairment in functioning.

The impairment caused by hoarding behavior can be extreme and endanger not only the health and safety of the individual, but also those living nearby. In a survey of health officers across Massachusetts, we (Frost, Steketee, & Williams, 2000) found that over 60% had received complaints within the past 5 years about hoarding, mostly from neighbors. Complaints typically involved more than one agency and often resulted in significant costs to the community. The hoarding behaviors found in the investigated cases were judged to seriously jeopardize the health of the individual. In several cases health officers reported that hoarding led directly to the person's death from fire or being crushed by objects in the home. Subsequent studies have found high levels of disability, depression, and anxiety among hoarding patients (Frost, Steketee, Williams, & Warren, 2000; Samuels et al., 2002; Saxena et al., 2002).

The definition of hoarding provided above outlines three major manifestations: difficulty discarding, clutter, and acquisition. The hallmark of hoarding is inability to discard possessions, even those that would appear worthless. This behavior can look delusional, as when someone insists on keeping something that would seem obviously worthless like rotten food or nail clippings and other trash. For the most part, however, the types of things saved by people who hoard are the same as those things saved by most of us (Frost & Gross, 1993). Even more interesting, however, is that the reasons people who hoard give for saving them are the same ones most of us would give. These reasons fall into one or more of three categories (Frost & Hartl, 1996). Instrumental reasons reflect the value given to objects because of their potential utility. Sentimental value is assigned to objects that have emotional meaning, usually because of an association with a particular person, place, or event. Intrinsic value is sometimes given to possessions that have little or no emotional or functional significance, but the person simply likes them. Though the reasons for saving don't differ for people who hoard and those who don't, the extent to which items are infused with these kinds of value do. People who hoard assign greater instrumental, sentimental, and intrinsic value to almost everything they own, reflecting the beliefs they hold about these possessions. We will explore these beliefs later in this chapter.

Acquisition and failure to discard possessions are relatively common behaviors and typically are not pathological. The pathological nature of hoarding most often derives from the inability to keep the possessions organized. It is the extreme clutter and disorganization that interferes with the ability to use living space and to carry out necessary daily routines (e.g., daily hygiene) and frequently results in threats to health and safety. Though the acquisition and saving are major components of hoarding, the disorganization and resulting clutter are often the most troublesome part of the disorder.

From our first investigations into hoarding behavior it was apparent that hoarding involved not only difficulty discarding, but also a tendency to acquire in excess of normal. In our first study hoarders reported that they bought extra things to a significantly greater extent than did non-hoarders (Frost & Gross, 1993). In a subsequent study we found our early hoarding measure correlated highly with compulsive buying and with the tendency to collect free things, such as items from other people's trash (Frost et al., 1998; Kyrios, Frost, & Steketee, 2004). Moreover, in a series of studies we have found high levels of hoarding among compulsive buyers (Frost, Steketee, & Williams, 2002) and compulsive gamblers (Frost, Meagher, & Riskind, 2001). In fact, the tendency to compulsively acquire and save possessions may be a larger construct that encompasses a variety of acquisitive behaviors, including compulsive buying, acquisition of free things, pathological gambling, and perhaps even kleptomania. While there are no studies of kleptomania and hoarding, we have seen a number of cases where the acquisition and hoarding involved stealing.

These findings suggest that compulsive acquiring is an integral aspect of compulsive hoarding. A recent analysis of pilot data from one of our projects (Frost, Steketee, Tolin, & Brown, 2006) indicated that nearly 85% of hoarding participants who met criteria for clinically significant clutter and difficulty discarding had scores that were more than one standard deviation above the mean for a non-clinical population on the Acquisition subscale of the Saving Inventory-Revised (see below for discussion of this measure). Conversely, a re-analysis of data from our compulsive buying study (Frost et al., 2002) revealed that more than 75% of compulsive buyers had hoarding scores more than one standard deviation above the mean from a normal sample. We have seen some cases with serious clutter where the individuals described more passive than active acquisition. In these cases the clutter consisted mostly of items that entered the home at a normal rate, but were never discarded. However, many of these individuals reported acquisition problems at an earlier time during their lives.

There are no epidemiological studies of hoarding. Even basic demographic and clinical course information is confusing or absent. For instance, in our studies, primarily drawn from community samples, most of the hoarding participants are women (Frost & Gross, 1993; Frost, Hartl, Christian, & Williams, 1995; Frost, Krause, & Steketee, 1996; Frost et al., 1998, 2000). In studies drawn from samples of people with obsessive–compulsive disorder (OCD), the gender ratio for hoarding varies from being more frequent in women (Saxena et al., 2002), roughly even (Black, Monahan, Gabel, Blum, Clancy, & Baker, 1998), or more frequent in men (Samuels et al., 2002). People with hoarding problems appear to divorce or remain single more often than those without hoarding problems (Frost & Gross, 1993; Steketee, Frost, & Kim, 2001; Samuels et al., 2002).

Hoarding has been viewed as a disorder of the elderly (Frost et al., 2000). However, when we ask our elderly participants how long they have been struggling with clutter, they typically admit that it has been a lifelong course. Several studies suggest the onset of hoarding occurs between ages 11 and 15, though the reporting procedures leave questions about the reliability of these numbers (Fontenelle, Mendlowicz, Soares, & Versiani, 2004; Samuels et al., 2002; Seedat & Stein, 2002). Grisham, Frost, Steketee, Kim, & Hood (2006) conducted an interview-based time-line study of the course of hoarding symptoms among 51 people solicited from the community for hoarding problems. Onset of mild hoarding behavior occurred at approximately 13 years of age, though acquisition began significantly later than difficulty discarding or clutter. Hoarding problems did not reach moderate intensity until at least a decade later, and did not become severe until a decade after that. Though symptoms fluctuated for a few participants, full remission was rare. Hoarding was a lifelong pattern for some, while for others it appeared to have been precipitated by stress or loss (Grisham et al., 2006).

HOARDING AND OCD

Research examining symptom-based OCD subtypes derived from the Yale–Brown Obsessive Compulsive Scale (Y–BOCS) have identified anywhere from three to seven distinct subtypes using factor and cluster analyses (see McKay et al., 2004). In eight of the 10 studies reviewed by McKay et al. (2004) hoarding emerged as a distinct subtype and in two, it was combined with symmetry or ordering symptoms. In reviewing the OCD subtype research, Mataix-Cols, Rosario-Campos, & Leckman (2005) concluded that the evidence for a distinct dimension of OCD was strongest for the hoarding factor.

These studies all suffer measurement problems using the Y–BOCS symptom checklist since there are only two hoarding items on the checklist (hoarding obsessions, hoarding compulsions), and their definition is somewhat ambiguous. For example, Y–BOCS interviewers are asked to identify hoarding obsessions, but it is not clear whether intrusive thoughts about hoarding actually occur or whether such thoughts are unwanted and recognized as senseless. Furthermore, these dichotomous items from the Y–BOCS checklist have never been validated against observations made in patients' homes. Attempts at validating these subtypes using other OCD measures have also identified hoarding as a distinct subtype (Foa et al., 2002; Watson, Wu, & Cutshall, 2004). Unfortunately, these studies also suffer from the use of unvalidated measures of hoarding, though they appear to be better psychometrically supported than the Y–BOCS checklist for hoarding.

Aside from the question of whether hoarding is a distinct subtype or dimension of OCD, there are growing questions about whether hoarding is a distinct disorder completely separate from OCD (Mataix-Cols et al., 2005; Wu & Watson, 2005). Why hoarding became classed as an OCD symptom is not clear. Hoarding first appeared in the *DSM-III-R* where it was listed as a symptom of obsessive–compulsive personality disorder (OCPD). Description of the symptoms suggests that it may result from problems with decision making, also a symptom of OCPD according to the *DSM-III-R* (American Psychiatric Association, 1987). No mention was made of its association with OCD. In the *DSM-IV* (American Psychiatric Association, 1994) and *DSM-IV-TR* (American Psychiatric Association, 2000), again, no mention of hoarding was made in the OCD section, but hoarding was again listed as a symptom of OCPD. Interestingly, decision-making problems were no longer listed for OCPD. In the differential diagnosis section of OCPD, the *DSM-IV* states 'A diagnosis of Obsessive–Compulsive Disorder should be considered especially when hoarding is extreme (e.g., accumulated stacks of worthless objects present a fire hazard and make it difficult for others to walk through the house)' (p. 671). Hoarding is mentioned in the field trials for the *DSM-IV*, but primarily as one among many OCD symptoms captured on the Y–BOCS. It may be that inclusion of hoarding on the Y–BOCS symptom checklist eventually led to assumptions that it was an OCD symptom. Development of the Y–BOCS checklist items resulted from a combination of the clinical experience of the authors and item content from existing OCD scales.

Although hoarding is usually associated with OCD, it occurs in the context of a number of other axis I and II disorders as well. Greenberg et al. (1990) found that six of eight hoarding clients had combinations of delusional disorder, schizophrenia, and organic mental disorder. Luchins, Goldman, Lieb, & Hanrahan (1992) reported hoarding as one of the repetitive dysfunctional behaviors in schizophrenic patients. Frankenberg (1984) described hoarding in an anorexic patient. Hoarding is a frequent behavior in what has been variously called Diogenes or Squalor Syndrome (Clark, Mankikar, & Gray, 1975; Macmillan & Shaw, 1966), characterized by self-neglect, domestic squalor, and the hoarding of trash. Hwang, Tsai, Yang, Liu, & Lirng (1998) reported that approximately 20% of dementia patients hoard objects. An even higher percentage of hoarding occurs in developmental disorders like Prader Willi Syndrome (Stein, Keating, Zar, & Hollander, 1994). Anderson, Domasio, & Domasio (2005) found hoarding behavior in 14% of brain injury patients with focal brain lesions acquired in adulthood.

Almost no research has examined the frequency of hoarding behavior among people with anxiety disorders other than OCD. Recently, however, Meunier, Tolin, Frost, Steketee, & Brady (2006) studied the frequency of clinically significant hoarding across 139 consecutive patients at an anxiety disorder clinic. Surprisingly, the frequency of hoarding was higher among patients with generalized anxiety disorder (27%) than OCD (11%). A smaller percentage of hoarding cases were found among those diagnosed with social phobia (14%), and virtually no hoarding occurred in panic or simple phobia cases.

The variety of disorders in which hoarding has been found led Greenberg et al. (1990) to conclude that 'hoarding is a final common pathway for a variety of processes' (p. 417) and argues for not limiting the definition of hoarding to OCD. A resolution of the issue will require studies of hoarding cases that are not drawn from OCD samples, but instead from unselected community and clinical samples.

Nonetheless, at present, hoarding remains identified most closely with OCD and a number of research studies have examined the relationship of these two conditions. In nearly 20 studies reporting data, the frequency with which hoarding symptoms occurred in OCD patients ranged from a low of 7% (Alonso et al., 2001) to a high of 54% (Friedman et al., 2003), with a median figure among these studies of 29%. The frequency of hoarding as a primary symptom has varied from 3.5% (Foa & Kozak, 1995; *DSM-IV* trials) to 11% (Saxena et al., 2002) of OCD cases. In general, studies using the Y–BOCS checklist suggest that hoarding is less common than classic OCD symptoms like cleaning or checking and roughly equivalent in frequency to symmetry and ordering symptoms.

Correlational research is of some value in determining the association of hoarding and OCD symptoms. Frost and Gross (1993) found hoarding symptoms to be significantly correlated with OCD symptoms in student, community, and OCD clinical populations, with the association with checking and doubting being consistently the strongest. Frost et al. (1998) found hoarding to be associated with impaired mental control on the Padua Inventory, but not with contamination or checking. These studies suggest some variability in the types of OCD symptoms with which hoarding is associated. Checking and impaired mental control appear most consistently associated with hoarding (Frost & Gross, 1993). Wu and Watson (2005) found hoarding was moderately correlated with checking measured by three different OCD scales, while correlations with other subscales were less consistent. Several clinical studies suggest higher levels of symmetry, ordering, and counting among OCD hoarding samples (Baer, 1994; Fontenelle et al., 2004; Samuels et al., 2002).

Frost, Krause, & Steketee (1996) found the hoarding scale was moderately correlated with the Y–BOCS compulsion subscale ($r = .50$), but not the obsession subscale among student volunteers. Those scoring higher on the Y–BOCS also were more likely to indicate the presence of hoarding symptoms than those who scored lower. A similar finding occurred using the Maudsley Obsessive Compulsive Inventory (MOCI). In a comparison with community controls, people solicited for hoarding behavior had higher scores on all Y–BOCS measures. Furthermore, the Y–BOCS mean total score for the hoarding group was above that normally considered clinically significant in treatment studies. In addition, hoarding subjects listed a higher number of non-hoarding OCD symptoms as targets and endorsed significantly more of these symptoms on the Y–BOCS checklist.

Hoarders in the Frost et al. (1996) study also had more general distress and psychopathology, so elevated OCD symptoms could reflect greater overall pathology rather than specific OCD. In the same study, Frost et al. (1996) measured hoarding symptoms among a sample of OCD patients. Using the Y–BOCS checklist, comparisons across these three studies indicate comparable levels of hoarding across the different samples with hoarding frequencies ranging from 30–33% for students, 26–37% for unselected community controls, and 26–31% for OCD patients. These figures suggest that hoarding may occur outside the context of OCD with equal frequency. Further research is needed here.

Consistent with the possibility that hoarding may not be an OCD symptom, Wu and Watson (2005) found that hoarding symptoms correlated less strongly with non-hoarding OCD symptoms than those symptoms inter-correlated among themselves. Some caution is warranted here since the sample may have under-represented people with hoarding problems. In the same vein, one of our recent studies (Frost,

Steketee, & Grisham, 2004) found significant but small correlations between Difficulty Discarding and Compulsive Acquisition (subscales of the Saving Inventory-Revised) and the Y–BOCS (modified to remove the hoarding items from the checklist) among a sample of 70 hoarders (r's from .26 to .29). The Y–BOCS correlation with the Clutter subscale was not significant. The magnitude of these correlations may have been reduced by including only significant hoarding cases thus restricting the range of scores. In contrast to the Frost et al. (1996) and Samuels et al. (2002) studies, a large number of subjects in this sample had no other OCD symptoms. This study also suggested that the relationship between hoarding and OCD measures is not uniform, but varies with the dimension of hoarding being measured (e.g., acquisition, difficulty discarding, or clutter), and may vary as a function of sampling procedures and sizes.

Several studies that have drawn samples from those seeking treatment from OCD clinics have compared patients who hoard to those with OCD and no hoarding. As noted below, this may bias samples in specific ways, but the findings are nonetheless of interest in understanding whether and how hoarding and OCD are related. In the first of these, Frost, Steketee, Williams, & Warren (2000) found equivalent levels of Y–BOCS scores, but the hoarding patients had significantly higher levels of depression, anxiety, and disability, as well as elevated levels of dependent and schizotypal personality disorder symptoms. Samuels et al. (2002) reported a younger age of onset, more decision-making problems, and fewer aggressive obsessions among the hoarding patients compared to non-hoarding OCD patients. Their total Y–BOCS scores were also significantly higher, suggesting more severe symptoms. Fontenelle et al. (2004) found hoarding patients had more education, earlier onset, and higher rates of bipolar II and eating disorders than non-hoarding OCD patients. Saxena et al. (2002) reported higher anxiety and poorer overall functioning (GAS) among OCD hoarding patients compared to OCD non-hoarding patients. Lochner, Kinnear, & Hemmings (2005) found greater severity and disability, as well as higher levels of depression, dysthymia, specific phobia, generalized anxiety disorder, and obsessive–compulsive personality disorder among OCD hoarders. In contrast with other research, however, they failed to find differences in social anxiety, avoidant personality disorder, and compulsive shopping.

The pattern of association between hoarding and other OCD symptoms suggests that hoarding is related to some OCD symptoms, in particular checking, impaired mental control, symmetry, counting, and ordering, but not other OCD symptoms. Further, recent evidence suggests that some aspects of hoarding are more strongly associated with OCD than others; compulsive acquisition and difficulty discarding showed stronger relationships to OCD than clutter (Frost et al., 2002, 2004).

Complicating the research on hoarding and OCD is the possibility that hoarding with OCD is different than hoarding without OCD. Grisham, Brown, Liverant, & Campbell-Sills (2005) found than hoarders without other OCD symptoms had significantly lower anxiety, worry, stress, and negative affect scores than hoarders with other OCD symptoms. They suggest that hoarding without OCD may be a distinct condition. Another possibility is that hoarding combined with OCD simply confers more pathology, as do most comorbid conditions; two disorders increase the psychopathology load.

Until recently no studies have examined diagnostic comorbidity in samples with clinically significant hoarding who are not drawn from OCD clinics. Frost et al. (2006) examined diagnostic comorbidity in 75 cases of hoarding solicited from the general population. Only 31% of these cases had significant OCD symptoms other than hoarding. Surprisingly, but consistent with Meunier et al. (2006), 25% received generalized anxiety disorder (GAD) diagnoses, and 16% received social phobia diagnoses. Findings from this study together with those from Meunier et al. (2006), though preliminary, suggest that hoarding may be as frequent or more so in GAD than in OCD, and conversely, that self-identified hoarding clients may suffer symptoms of GAD or other mood and anxiety disorders as often as they do symptoms of OCD.

COGNITIVE BEHAVIORAL MODEL OF COMPULSIVE HOARDING

Elsewhere we have proposed a cognitive behavioral model of compulsive hoarding (Frost & Hartl, 1996; Frost & Steketee, 1998; Steketee & Frost, 2003). Here we will update this model of the development and maintenance of compulsive hoarding. We posit that hoarding results from four types of deficits: (1) core beliefs and vulnerabilities; (2) information processing deficits; (3) beliefs about and meaning of possessions; and (4) emotions and their role in reinforcing hoarding behavior.

CORE BELIEFS AND VULNERABILITIES

Preliminary evidence suggests that both genetic and neurobiological factors play a role in hoarding. Frost and Gross (1993) observed a high percentage of hoarding in first degree relatives of people who hoard. This finding has been replicated in several studies (Cullen et al., submitted; Winsberg, Cassic, & Koran, 1999; Samuels et al., 2007). Other evidence for a genetic linkage exists as well in Alsobrook, Leckman, Goodman, Rasmussen, & Pauls (1999), and Leckman et al.'s (2003) evidence for a recessive mode of transmission in families with two affected siblings with Tourette's syndrome. Zhang et al. (2002) and Feng, Leckman, & Zhang (2004) reported evidence of linkage to hoarding on chromosomes 4q, 5q, and 17q in subsamples of Tourette's patients.

In addition to suggestive genetic evidence, several fMRI findings suggest differences in functioning between people with hoarding problems and those with OCD. Mataix-Cols et al. (2004) found distinct patterns of neural activation for OCD subtypes with hoarding associated with activation of the left precentral gyrus and right orbitofrontal cortex. Saxena et al. (2004) found lower glucose metabolization, compared to non-hoarding OCD patients, in the dorsal anterior and posterior cingulated gyrus and cuneus. While the exact nature of these findings is uncertain, it would appear that there may be underlying brain activity associated with hoarding. Furthermore, Anderson et al. (2005) reported a high frequency of hoarding among patients with focal brain lesions in the mesial frontal region and suggest that this 'disrupts a mechanism which normally modulates subcortically driven predispositions to acquire and collect' (p. 201).

In addition to genetic and neurobiological vulnerabilities, comorbidity with other disorders may affect the development or manifestation of hoarding problems. The most frequent comorbid conditions include depression, OCD, social phobia, and GAD (Meunier, Tolin, Frost, Steketee, & Brady, 2006; Steketee & Frost, 2003). In addition, people with hoarding problems score higher on measures of ADHD (Hartl, Duffany, Allen, Steketee, & Frost, 2005). Several studies have suggested that the experience of traumatic or stressful events is associated with compulsive hoarding (Grisham et al., 2005, Hartl et al., 2005), especially witnessing a crime, childhood abuse, and sexual assault (Cromer, Schmidt, & Murphy, 2006). In our own treatment research, we have encountered several clinical cases in which loss and/or trauma directly precipitated hoarding behavior.

Anecdotally, we have found a high frequency of certain kinds of core beliefs, specifically beliefs about self-worth, vulnerability, helplessness, and lovability. Some of these may be associated with problems forming attachments among hoarders (Alonso et al., 2004; Kryios, Frost, & Steketee, in preparation). Early family histories of people suffering from hoarding have yet to be studied in depth.

INFORMATION PROCESSING DEFICITS

Our model posits that hoarding is associated with several deficits in the ability to process information, including attention, categorization, memory, and decision making. Hoarding clients appear to have difficulties staying focused on sorting tasks even when a therapist is present (Steketee, Frost, Wincze, Greene, & Douglass, 2000). Hartl et al. (2005) found hoarding patients to have significantly higher scores on measures of adult attention deficit/hyperactivity disorder (ADHD), childhood symptoms of ADHD, and current cognitive failures in perception, memory, and motor function. Such deficits might be associated with the circuitry problems in the frontal-striatal areas of the brain, as well as help to explain the organizing problems and resulting clutter observed in hoarding. Deficits in attention seem to present as ADHD-like distractibility, especially caused by the sight of possessions of interest. Beyond this, hoarding clients may have a 'creative attentional bias', in which their focus on non-essential details of possessions make it difficult to judge the importance of these items.

Categorization problems appear as a tendency to view each possession as so unique that it cannot be grouped with other similar objects. Our research suggests that the tendency to have difficulty categorizing objects is specific to things the person owns rather than to general objects (Wincze, Steketee, & Frost, 2007). Perhaps these apparent problems classifying objects derive in part from the creative bias just mentioned in which people who hoard attend to too many features of items rather than constraining their focus to essential elements.

Memory function also seems to be impaired in people with hoarding problems. Hartl et al. (2004) found that hoarding participants displayed problems with the organization and delayed recall of visual information and short and long-delayed recall of verbal information. However, we suspect that hoarding itself derives more from fears about having a poor memory rather than actual memory deficits. The differences in memory function between hoarding and non-hoarding cases were significant but small, while the relationship between hoarding and poor memory confidence was strong.

Finally, decision making has been regarded as a hallmark of compulsive hoarding and was found to be associated in a number of studies (Frost & Gross, 1993; Frost & Shows, 1993; Samuels et al., 2007). People who hoard seem to have a great deal of difficulty processing a set of facts and drawing a conclusion. This may reflect, in part, the need (or wish) for a large amount of information before a decision can be made, or a tendency to focus on and ascribe importance to non-essential details of a possession. The process appears to be not only difficult, but painful as well (Steketee & Frost, 2003).

BELIEFS ABOUT AND MEANINGS OF POSSESSIONS

The third component of the model involves beliefs about and meanings of possessions (Steketee, Frost, & Kyrios, 2003). A number of these beliefs reflect an exaggeration of certain features of possessions, including their esthetic value, usefulness, uniqueness, sentimental value, and ability to provide a source of identity and safety. In addition, general beliefs about hoarded items focus on concerns about responsibility and waste, memory, the importance of maintaining control over possessions, and perfectionism.

EMOTIONS AND THEIR ROLE IN REINFORCING HOARDING BEHAVIOR

These three features of the model (vulnerabilities, information processing deficits, and beliefs about possessions) provoke strong emotional states, both positive and negative. Positive emotional states are associated with the acquisition of new possessions (at least temporarily) and the finding of a cherished possession while sorting through the clutter. Negative emotions take various forms, including anxiety at the prospect of losing a valued object, sadness or grief at the loss of an important possession, anger about losing something of value, frustration about not being able to make decisions, or guilt over violating a moral code (e.g., being wasteful).

We propose that these features form the backdrop for the development of hoarding, causing people who hoard to experience distress at the thought of discarding or not acquiring an item, thereby causing them to avoid both. In this way hoarding beliefs and attachments play a role similar to obsessive thoughts that provoke strong negative emotions like anxiety and guilt. However, these feelings only occur in certain situations, such as when trying not to acquire something or when trying to get rid of something. Hoarding behaviors (acquiring, saving) allow the person to avoid feelings of anxiety, grief, loss, guilt, etc. and are therefore part of an avoidance conditioning paradigm. Avoidance conditioning may be exacerbated by a high sensitivity to punishment (Fullana, Mataix-Cols, & Caseras, 2004) or high anxiety sensitivity (Steketee & Frost, 2003).

In addition, certain types of attachments may positively reinforce saving behavior. For most people possessions are reinforcing because they are used for something. However, for most hoarders the possessions are never used. For example, one of our former clients saved cookbooks (over 300 of them). In addition she saved every recipe that appeared in the newspaper and in any of the hundreds of magazines she collected. Yet she almost never cooked. Her difficulty in not collecting and getting rid of any of these was the thought that if she didn't do so, she would not have the opportunity to be the kind of cook she wanted to be. Saving the cookbooks and recipes allowed her to believe that she would someday be the wonderful cook she would like to be. Thus, the cookbooks offered her a potential identity, one she would not have if she got rid of them. Acquiring and keeping them were both positively and negatively reinforced.

In addition to the reinforcement process just described, the absence of discarding behavior also prevents people who hoard from receiving any corrective feedback about what is appropriate to keep and what is appropriate to discard. Many of our clients seem to have almost no idea how to make decisions about discarding because they have done so little of it.

ASSESSMENT

Early research on hoarding suffered from inadequate measurement instruments. The Y–BOCS checklist items, for example, provide little information about the severity of clutter because hoarding is rated in combination with other OCD symptoms that may also be present. Newer self-report OCD measures that contain hoarding subscales improve upon the Y–BOCS, but are as yet unvalidated and fail to distinguish between the manifestations of hoarding (clutter, difficulty discarding, compulsive acquisition). To remedy this problem, we currently use several self-report and observational measures of hoarding behaviors. These include the Saving Inventory-Revised, Activities of Daily Living, and Clutter Image Rating.

The Saving Inventory-Revised (SI-R, Frost, Steketee, & Grisham, 2004) is a 23-item self-report measure containing three subscales; clutter, difficulty discarding, and compulsive acquisition. Both internal and test–retest correlations are good for all three subscales. Each of the subscales distinguishes people with hoarding problems from non-hoarding OCD patients and non-clinical controls. The SI-R subscales correlate highly with other indices of hoarding, and show weaker correlations with non-hoarding constructs. The subscales are also sensitive to treatment effects (Frost, Steketee, Tolin, & Brown, 2006).

The Activities of Daily Living scale (ADL), revised from an earlier version (Frost et al., 2004), measures the extent to which clutter interferes with people's ability to function. Though it was designed as an observational measure, it can also be used as a self-report instrument. The ADL contains three sections: activities of daily living, condition of the home, and safety-related issues. Items refer to activities of daily living (cooking, cleaning, etc.) that may be impeded by clutter, deteriorating conditions in the home, or conditions that threaten the individual's health or safety. Our ongoing research suggests that this is a reliable and valid measure (Steketee, Frost, & Tolin, in preparation).

The Clutter Image Rating (CIR; Frost, Steketee, Tolin, & Renaud, in preparation) is an observational measure that consists of three sets of nine pictures depicting a bedroom, living room, and kitchen with increasing levels of clutter. Respondents are asked to select the photo that most resembles their living room, bedroom, or kitchen. In a study of 85 people suffering from hoarding problems, the CIR has shown excellent inter-rater, test–retest, and cross-context (in clinic vs. in home) reliability, as well as both concurrent and discriminant validity (Frost et al., in preparation), and treatment sensitivity (Frost et al., 2006).

TREATMENT OF COMPULSIVE HOARDING

INITIAL TREATMENT OUTCOME RESEARCH

Initial research on treatment outcomes using treatments that work for OCD have shown limited promise for treating hoarding (Steketee & Frost, 2003). These studies were largely anecdotal case studies or small group studies done within the context of general OCD treatment and included both medication and cognitive behavior therapy (CBT). Black et al. (1998) reported that only 18% of those with hoarding symptoms responded to treatment (medication and/or CBT) compared to 67% of OCD patients who did not hoard. Mataix-Cols, Rauch, Manzo, Jenike, & Baer (1999) reported similar findings among a sample treated with serotonergic reuptake inhibitors (SRIs). Only the hoarding symptom dimension of OCD was associated with poor outcomes. In a subsequent study Mataix-Cols, Marks, Greist, Kobak, & Baer (2002) found that hoarding predicted poor compliance and response to behavior therapy. Winsberg et al. (1999) also reported poor outcomes following SSRI treatments among 20 patients treated for hoarding problems. Finally, Abramowitz, Franklin, Schwartz, & Furr (2003) reported a poorer response to exposure and response prevention among hoarding participants compared to other OCD symptom subtypes. The findings from these studies were disappointing enough to lead several investigators to suggest that hoarding should be labeled a predictor of poor outcome (Black et al., 1998; Christensen & Greist, 2001; Mataix-Cols et al., 1999).

Several themes were apparent in this early literature on treatments for compulsive hoarding. Poor insight and limited symptom recognition characterized most participants in these trials, along with low motivation and treatment compliance. Patients were frequently forced into treatment by significant others in their lives (Christensen & Greist, 2001) and displayed considerable ambivalence and indecision. Furthermore, this early research was methodologically flawed in lacking an adequate definition of compulsive hoarding and reliable and valid measures of this behavior. Subsequent research has been based on a more systematic definition and conceptualization of compulsive hoarding and its treatment.

TREATMENT DESCRIPTION

Our own initial attempts to treat hoarding (Hartl & Frost, 1999; Steketee et al., 2000) were based on early versions of the cognitive behavioral model described above. Since then our treatment program has evolved from what we have learned in our research and clinical experiences during treatment. Difficulties with motivation and treatment compliance and the poor outcomes using standard OCD treatments led us to incorporate motivational interviewing into the treatment. People with hoarding problems are frequently ambivalent about getting help. Even after making the decision to seek help, their motivation waxes and wanes as treatment progresses, leading to homework assignments not done and sometimes to missed appointments. Rigid beliefs about control over possessions also dictate the need for motivational enhancement methods to avoid endless arguments over what to discard. Our current therapy methods include: (1) learning skills for attention focusing, organizing, decision making, and problem solving; (2) cognitive therapy to examine and correct faulty thinking and beliefs; and (3) exposure to induce habituation of emotions and reduce avoidance behavior. Clinicians usually begin with skills training for organizing and apply these during the sorting process. Following this, clinicians generally apply cognitive therapy methods, often in the context of exposure strategies. Other skills training methods are applied depending on the client's need and progress in treatment. Motivational interviewing methods are used whenever ambivalence is evident.

Treatment is delivered individually in the clinic, at home, and at locations where the client has trouble controlling acquisition. The cognitive and behavioral activities of therapy occur during attempts to sort/organize, discard, or not acquire possessions. Much of the treatment relies on the therapist's and client's design and completion of behavioral experiments. These are focused exposures developed to test hypotheses generated from the case conceptualization and the client's day-to-day struggles with hoarding problems. A complete guide to the treatment can be found in Steketee and Frost (2006).

Hartl and Frost (1999) reported a multiple baseline experimental case study of a specialized hoarding treatment based on the early cognitive behavioral model (Frost & Hartl, 1996). The therapy consisted of work on decision making and categorizing along with exposure to discarding and cognitive restructuring. Clutter was virtually eliminated from the client's home after 18 months of treatment. In a similar case, Cermele, Melendex-Pallitto, & Pandina (2001) reported a good outcome in a case study also based on a treatment derived from the cognitive behavioral model.

Several single-group pre–post comparisons have also reported promising outcomes with early forms of cognitive behavioral therapy (CBT) for hoarding. Steketee et al. (2000) reported positive, but modest, outcomes after 15 sessions among a group of seven clients. Likewise, Saxena et al. (2002) reported significant improvement among a sample of 20 hoarding clients with OCD. Clients in this study were treated with a combination of medication (SSRIs) and specialized cognitive behavioral therapy for hoarding in a day treatment program.

In a follow-up to the Steketee et al. (2000) study, we tested a revised version of the treatment program in an open trial with nine hoarding clients. The longer 26-session individual treatment resulted in significant reductions (25–34%) in global measures of hoarding severity. Observational measures of clutter (CIR) also showed 25–33% improvement, and compulsive acquisition improved by 33%. Among treatment completers, 57% were rated by both the client and therapist as 'much' or 'very much' improved. Despite these improvements, full remission of hoarding symptoms was infrequent (Frost, Steketee, & Tolin, 2005).

Following the open trial (Frost et al., 2006), we revised the treatment manual (Steketee & Frost, 2006) and implemented a wait-list-controlled study in which hoarding clients were randomly assigned to a cognitive behavioral treatment or a 12-week wait-list followed by treatment. Treatment duration for the 26 sessions varied from 7 to 12 months. Forty-three clients were enrolled in the treatment and six (14%) dropped out. Clients averaged 56.2 years of age and ranged from 42 to 66. To date 10 clients have completed the wait-list period and 13 have completed 12 weeks of treatment. Samples did not show pretreatment differences on measures of hoarding. The treatment resulted in significant reductions in hoarding symptoms among the treated group (26% reduction) compared to the wait-list group (11% reduction). The effect size (Cohen's d) for the comparison of treated and wait-listed clients after 12 weeks was 1.26. Among these clients, 17 have so far completed the full 26-session treatment; they showed a 45% reduction in hoarding symptoms with a very large effect size (Cohen's d) of 2.04.

SUMMARY

Compulsive hoarding problems pose a challenge for many sectors of society, including public health, housing, elder services and clinical health and mental health providers. Though we still know relatively little about hoarding, the research to date has given us a clearer picture of its manifestations, comorbidities, and possible causes. The current conceptual model incorporates biological and psychological vulnerabilities, cognitive processing problems, problematic beliefs, and both positive and negative emotional states. Treatment based on this model shows considerable promise for improving the lives of individuals with this difficult condition.

ACKNOWLEDGEMENTS

Preparation of this chapter was supported by grants from the National Institute of Mental Health to both authors (R21 MH 068539-01; R01 MH068007-01; R01 MH068008-01).

REFERENCES

Abramowitz, J. S., Franklin, M. E., Schwartz, S. A., & Furr, J. M. (2003). Symptom presentation and outcome of cognitive–behavioral therapy for obsessive-compulsive disorder. *Journal of Consulting and Clinical Psychology, 71*, 1049–1057.

Alonso, P., Menchón, J. M., Mataix-Cols, D., Pifarré, J., Urretavizcaya, M. N., Crespo, J. M., Jiménez, S., Vallejo, G., & Vallejo, J. (2004). Perceived parental rearing style in obsessive-compulsive disorder: Relation to symptom dimensions. *Psychiatry Research, 127*, 267–278.

Alonso, P., Menchon, J. M., Pifarre, J., Mataix-Cols, D., Torres, L., Salgado, P., & Vallejo, J. (2001). Long-term follow-up and predictors of clinical outcome in obsessive-compulsive patients treated with serotonin reuptake inhibitors and behavior therapy. *Journal of Clinical Psychiatry, 62*, 535–540.

Alsobrook II, J. P., Leckman, J. F., Goodman, W. K., Rasmussen, S. A., & Pauls, D. L. (1999). Segregation analysis of obsessive-compulsive disorder using symptom-based factor scores. *American Journal of Medical Genetics, 88*, 669–675.

American Psychiatric Association (1987). *Diagnostic and satistical manual of mental disorders* (3rd ed. rev.) (*DSM-III-R*). Washington, DC: APA.

American Psychiatric Association (1994). *Diagnostic and statistical manual of mental disorders* (4th ed.) (*DSM-IV*). Washington, DC: APA.

American Psychiatric Association (2000). Diagnostic and Statistical Manual of Mental Disorders (4th ed. text rev.) (*DSM-IV-TR*). Washington, DC: APA.

Anderson, S. W., Domasio, H., & Domasio, A. R. (2005). A neural basis for collecting behaviour in humans. *Brain, 128*, 201–212.

Baer, L. (1994). Factor analysis of symptom subtypes of obsessive-compulsive disorder and their relation to personality and tic disorders. *Journal of Clinical Psychiatry, 55*, 18–23.

Black, D., Monahan, W. P., Gabel, J., Blum, N., Clancy, P., & Baker, P. (1998). Hoarding and treatment response in 38 nondepressed subjects with obsessive-compulsive disorder. *Journal of Clinical Psychiatry, 59*, 420–425.

Calamari, J. E., Wiegartz, P. S., Riemann, B. C., Cohen, R. J., Greer, A., Jacobi, D. M., Jahn, S. C., & Carmin, C. (2004). Obsessive-compulsive disorder subtypes, an attempted replication and extension of a symptom-based taxonomy. *Behaviour Research and Therapy, 42*, 647–670.

Cermele, J. A., Melendez-Pallitto, L., & Pandina, G. J. (2001). Intervention in compulsive hoarding. *Behavior Modification, 25*, 214–232.

Christensen, D. D., & Greist, J. H. (2001). The challenge of obsessive-compulsive disorder hoarding. *Primary Psychiatry, 8*, 79–86.

Clark, A., Mankikar, G. D., & Gray, I. (1975). Diogenes's syndrome: a clinical study of self neglect in old age. *The Lancet, 1*, 366–368.

Cromer, K., Schmidt, N. B., & Murphy, D. L. (2006). *Elucidating the relationship between hoarding and traumatic life events*. Paper presented at the Anxiety Disorders Association of America, Miami, FL.

Cullen, B., Brown, C. H., Grados, M., Riddle, M. A., Bienvenu, O. J., Willour, V. L., et al. (submitted). Factor analysis of the Yale–Brown Obsessive Compulsive Scale in a family study of obsessive compulsive disorder anxiety and depression.

Feng, R., Leckman, J. F., & Zhang, H. (2004). Linkage analysis of ordinal traits for pedigree data. *Proceedings of the National Academy of Science USA, 101*, 16739–16744.

Foa, E. B., Huppert, J. D., Leiberg, S., Langner, R., Kichic, R., Hajcak, G., & Salkovskis, P. M. (2002). The Obsessive–Compulsive Inventory: development and validation of a short version. *Psychological Assessment, 14*, 485–495.

Foa, E. B., & Kozak, M. J. (1995). DSM-IV field trial: Obsessive–compulsive disorder. *American Journal of Psychiatry, 152*, 90–96.

Fontenelle, L. F., Mendlowicz, M. V., Soares, I. D., & Versiani, M. (2004). Patients with obsessive–compulsive disorder and hoarding symptoms: A distinctive clinical subtype? *Comprehensive Psychiatry, 45*, 375–383.

Frankenburg, F. R. (1984). Hoarding in anorexia nervosa. *British Journal of Medical Psychology, 57*, 57–60.

Friedman, S., Smith, L. C., Halpern, B., Levine, C., Paradis, C., Viswanathan, R., Trappler, B., & Ackerman, R. (2003). Obsessive–compulsive disorder in a multi-ethnic urban outpatient clinic: Initial presentation and treatment outcome with exposure and ritual prevention. *Behavior Therapy, 34*, 397–410.

Fromm, E. (1947). *Man against himself: An inquiry into the psychology of ethics.* New York: Rinehart.

Frost, R., & Gross, R. (1993). The hoarding of possessions. *Behaviour Research and Therapy, 31*, 367–382.

Frost, R. O., & Hartl, T. L. (1996). A cognitive–behavioral model of compulsive hoarding. *Behavior Research and Therapy, 14*, 341–350.

Frost, R., Hartl, T., Christian, R., & Williams, N. (1995). The value of possessions in compulsive hoarding: Patterns of use and attachment. *Behaviour Research and Therapy, 33*, 897–902.

Frost, R. O., Kim, H.-J., Morris, C., Bloss, C., Murray-Close, M., & Steketee, G. (1998). Hoarding, compulsive buying and reasons for saving. *Behaviour Research and Therapy, 36*, 657–664.

Frost, R. O., Krause, M. S., & Steketee, G. (1996). Hoarding and obsessive–compulsive symptoms. *Behavior Modification, 20*, 116–132.

Frost, R. O., Meagher, B. M., & Riskind, J. H. (2001). Obsessive–compulsive features in pathological lottery and scratch ticket gamblers. *Journal of Gambling Studies, 17*, 5–19.

Frost, R. O., & Shows, D. (1993). The nature and measurement of compulsive indecisiveness. *Behaviour Research and Therapy, 31*, 683–692.

Frost, R. O., & Steketee, G. (1998). Hoarding: Clinical aspects and treatment strategies. In M. Jenike, L. Baer, & J. Minnichelo, *Obsessive compulsive disorder: practical management* (3rd ed.). St Louis, MO: Mosby Inc.

Frost, R. O., Steketee, G., & Grisham, J. R. (2004). Measurement of compulsive hoarding. Saving inventory-revised. *Behaviour Research and Therapy, 42*, 1163–1182.

Frost, R. O., Steketee, G., & Tolin, D. (2005). *Cognitive changes in the treatment of hoarding.* Paper presented at the European Association of Behavioural and Cognitive Therapies, Thessaloniki, Greece.

Frost, R. O., Steketee, G., Tolin, D., & Brown, T. (2006). *Co-morbidity and diagnostic issues in compulsive hoarding.* Paper presented at the Anxiety Disorders Association of America, Miami, FL.

Frost, R. O., Steketee, G., Tolin, D., & Renaud, S. (in preparation). Development of an observational measure of hoarding: The clutter image rating.

Frost, R. O., Steketee, G., & Williams, L. (2000). Hoarding: A community health problem. *Health and Social Care in the Community, 8*, 229–234.

Frost, R. O., Steketee, G., & Williams, L. (2002). Compulsive buying, compulsive hoarding, and obsessive-compulsive disorder. *Behavior Therapy, 33*, 201–214.

Frost, R. O., Steketee, G., Williams, L., & Warren, R. (2000). Mood, disability, and personality disorder symptoms in hoarding, obsessive compulsive disorder, and control subjects. *Behaviour Research and Therapy, 38*, 1071–1082.

Fullana, M. A., Mataix-Cols, D., & Caseras, X. (2004). High sensitivity to punishment and low impulsivity in obsessive–compulsive patients with hoarding symptoms. *Psychiatry Research, 129*, 21–27.

Greenberg, D. (1987). Compulsive hoarding. *American Journal of Psychotherapy, 41*, 409–416.

Greenberg, D., Witztum, E., & Levy, A. (1990). Hoarding as a psychiatric symptom. *Journal of Clinical Psychiatry, 51*, 417–421.

Grisham, J. R., Brown, T. A., Liverant, G., & Campbell-Sills, L. (2005). The distinctiveness of compulsive hoarding from obsessive-compulsive disorder. *Journal of Anxiety Disorders, 19*, 767–779.

Grisham, J. R., Frost, R. O., Steketee, G., Kim, H.-J., & Hood, S. (2006). Age of onset in compulsive hoarding. *Journal of Anxiety Disorders, 20*, 675–686.

Hartl, T. L., Duffany, S. R., Allen, G. J., Steketee, G., & Frost, R.O. (2005). Relationships among compulsive hoarding, trauma, and attention-deficit/hyperactivity disorder. *Behaviour Research and Therapy, 43*, 269–276.

Hartl, T. L., & Frost, R. O. (1999). Cognitive–behavioral treatment of compulsive hoarding: a multiple baseline experimental case study. *Behaviour Research and Therapy, 37*, 451–461.

Hartl, T. L., Frost, R. O., Allen, G. J., Deckersbach, T., Steketee, G., Duffany, S. R., & Savage, C. R. (2004). Actual and perceived memory deficits in individuals with compulsive hoarding. *Depression and Anxiety, 20*, 59–69.

Hwang, J.-P., Tsai, S.-J., Yang, C.-H., Liu, K.-M., & Lirng, J.-F. (1998). Hoarding behavior in dementia: A preliminary report. *American Journal of Geriatric Psychiatry, 6*, 285–289.

Kyrios, M., Frost, R. O., & Steketee, G. (2004). Cognitions in compulsive buying and acquisition. *Cognitive Therapy and Research, 28*, 241–258.

Kyrios, M., Frost, R. O., & Steketee, G. (in preparation) Hoarding and attachment.

Leckman, J .F., Pauls, D. L., Zhang, H., Rosario-Campos, M. C., Katsovich, L., Kidd, K. K., Pakstis, A. J., Alsobrook, J. P., Robertson, M. M., McMahon, W. M., Walkup, J. T., van de Wetering, B. J., King, R. A., & Cohen, D. J. (2003). Obsessive–compulsive symptom dimensions in affected sibling pairs diagnosed with Gilles de la Tourette syndrome. *American Journal of Medical Genetics, 116B*, 60–68.

Lochner, C., Kinnear, C., & Hemmings, S. (2005). Hoarding in obsessive–compulsive disorder: Clinical and genetic correlates. *Journal of Clinical Psychiatry, 66*, 1155–1160.

Luchins, D. J., Goldman, M. B., Lieb, M., & Hanrahan, P. (1992). Repetitive behaviors in chronically institutionalized schizophrenic patients. *Schizophrenia Research, 8*, 119–123.

Macmillan, D., & Shaw, P. (1966). Senile breakdown in standard of personal and environmental cleanliness. *British Medical Journal, ii*, 1032–1037.

Mataix-Cols, D., Marks, I. M., Greist, J. H., Kobak, K. A., & Baer, L. (2002). Obsessive–compulsive symptom dimensions as predictors of compliance with and response to behaviour therapy: Results from a controlled trial. *Psychotherapy and Psychosomatics, 71*, 255–262.

Mataix-Cols, D., Rauch, S. L., Manzo, P. A., Jenike, M. A., & Baer, L. (1999). Use of Factor-analyzed symptom dimensions to predict outcome with serotonin reuptake inhibitors and placebo in the treatment of obsessive–compulsive disorder. *American Journal of Psychiatry, 156*, 1409–1416.

Mataix-Cols, D., Rosario-Campos, M. C., & Leckman, J. F. (2005). A multidimensional model of obsessive–compulsive disorder. *American Journal of Psychiatry, 162*, 228–238.

Mataix-Cols, D., Wooderson, S., Lawrence, N., Brammer, M. J., Speckens, A., Phillips, M. L. (2004). Distinct neural correlates of washing, checking, and hoarding symptom dimensions in obsessive-compulsive disorder. *Archives of General Psychiatry, 61*, 564–576.

McKay, D., Abramowitz, J. S., Calamari, J. E., Kyrios, M., Radomsky, A., Sookman, D., Taylor, S., & Wilhelm, S. (2004). A critical evaluation of obsessive–compulsive disorder subtypes: Symptoms versus mechanisms. *Clinical Psychology Review, 24*, 283–313.

Meunier, S. A., Tolin, D. F., Frost, R. O., Steketee, G., & Brady, R. E. (2006). *Prevalence of hoarding symptoms across the anxiety disorders.* Paper presented at the Anxiety Disorders Association of America, Miami, FL.

Salzman, L. (1973). *The obsessive personality: origins, dynamics and therapy.* New York: Jaso Aronson., Inc.

Samuels, J., Bienvenu, O. J., Riddle, M. A., Cullen, B. A. M., Grados, M. A., Liang, K. Y., Hoehn-Saric, R., & Nestadt, G. (2002). Hoarding in obsessive–compulsive disorder, results from a case-control study. *Behaviour Research and Therapy, 40*, 517–528.

Samuels, J. O., Bienvenu, J., Pinto, A., Fyer, A., McCracken, J. T., Rauch, S. et al. (2007). Hoarding in obsessive compulsive disorder: Results from the OCD Collaborative Genetics Study. *Behaviour Research and Therapy, 45*, 673–686.

Saxena, S., & Maidment, K. M. (2004). Treatment of compulsive hoarding. *Journal of Clinical Psychology, 60*(11), 1143–1154.

Saxena, S., Brody, A. L., Maidment, K. M., Smith, E., Zohrabi, N., Katz, E., Baker, S. K., & Baxter, L. R. (2004). Cerebral glucose metabolism in obsessive–compulsive hoarding. *American Journal of Psychiatry, 161*, 1038–1048.

Saxena, S., Maidment, K. M., Vapnik, T., Golden, G., Rishwain, T., Rosen, R. M., Tarlow, G., & Bystritsky, A. (2002). Obsessive–compulsive hoarding, symptom severity and response to multi-modal treatment. *Journal of Clinical Psychiatry, 63*, 21–27.

Seedat, S., & Stein, D. J. (2002). Hoarding in obsessive-compulsive disorder and related disorders: A preliminary report of 15 cases. *Psychiatry and Clinical Neurosciences, 56*, 17–23.

Stein, D. J., Keating, B. S., Zar, H. J., & Hollander, M. D. (1994). A survey of the phenomenology and pharmacology of compulsive and impulsive-aggressive symptoms in Prader–Willi syndrome. *Journal of Neuropsychiatry and Clinical Neurosciences, 6*, 23–29.

Steketee, G., & Frost, R. O. (2003). Compulsive hoarding: Current status of the research. *Clinical Psychology Review, 23*, 905–927.

Steketee, G., & Frost, R. O. (2006). *Compulsive hoarding and acquiring: therapist guide.* Oxford: Oxford University Press.

Steketee, G., Frost, R. O., & Kim, H-J. (2001). Hoarding by elderly people. *Health & Social Work, 26*, 176–184.

Steketee, G., Frost, R. O., & Kyrios, M. (2003). Cognitive aspects of compulsive hoarding. *Cognitive Therapy and Research, 27*, 467–479.

Steketee, G., Frost, R. O., & Tolin, D. (in preparation). Measurement of dysfunction in compulsive hoarding: activities of daily living.

Steketee, G., Frost, R. O., Wincze, J., Greene, K., & Douglass, H. (2000). Group and individual treatment of compulsive hoarding: A pilot study. *Behavioural and Cognitive Psychotherapy, 28*, 259–268.

Warren, L. W., & Ostrom, J. C. (1988). Pack rats: World class savers. *Psychology Today.* Retrieved March 13, 2007 from www.findarticles.com/p/articles/mi_m1175/is_n2_v22/ai_6306685.

Watson, D., Wu, K. D., & Cutshall, C. (2004). Symptom subtypes of obsessive–compulsive disorder and their relation to dissociation. *Anxiety Disorders, 18*, 435–458.

Wincze, J. P., Steketee, G., & Frost, R. O. (2007). Categorization in compulsive hoarding. *Behaviour Research and Therapy, 45*, 63–72.

Winsberg, M. E., Cassic, K. S., & Koran, L. M. (1999). Hoarding in obsessive–compulsive disorder: A report of 20 cases. *Journal of Clinical Psychiatry, 60*, 591–597.

Wu, K. D., & Watson, D. (2004). Hoarding and its relation to obsessive–compulsive disorder. *Behaviour Research and Therapy, 43*, 897–921.

Zhang, H., Leckman, J. F., Pauls, D. L., Tsai, C. P., Kidd, K. K., Campos, M. R. (2002). Genomewide scan of hoarding in sib pairs in which both sibs have Gilles de la Tourette syndrome. *American Journal of Human Genetics, 70*, 896–904.

6

TIC-RELATED OBSESSIVE–COMPULSIVE DISORDER

BUNMI O. OLATUNJI[1], SABINE WILHELM[2], AND THILO DECKERSBACH[2]

[1]*Vanderbilt University;* [2]*Massachusetts General Hospital, Harvard Medical School*

PHENOMENOLOGY

Factor- and cluster-analytic approaches to symptoms of obsessive–compulsive disorder (OCD) suggest that this disorder can be subdivided into distinct symptom dimensions or subtypes (Baer, 1994; Leckman, Grice et al., 1997; Mataix-Cols, Rosario-Campos, & Leckman, 2005; McKay et al., 2004). Over the past two decades evidence supporting the distinctiveness of tic-related OCD as a potentially unique presentation of obsessive–compulsive pathology has emerged (Miguel, Rauch, & Jenike, 1997). Below we review the evidence for a subtype of OCD related to tic disorders.

TIC DISORDERS

Studies have consistently documented elevated rates of OCD in patients with Tourette syndrome or chronic motor tic disorder (e.g., Cardona, Romano, Bollea, & Chiarotti, 2004; Eapen, Trimble, & Robertson, 1996; Leckman, Walker, Goodman, Pauls, & Cohen, 1994). Tic disorders are characterized by the presence of tics that

Correspondence to: Thilo Deckersbach, Department of Psychiatry, Massachusetts General Hospital/Harvard Medical School, Bldg 149, 2611, 13th Street, Charlestown, MA 02129.

cause significant distress or interfere with psychosocial functioning. Tics are recurrent, non-rhythmic, stereotyped motor movements or vocalizations that typically involve the head, torso, and upper and lower limbs (American Psychiatric Association, 1994). Common motor tics include eye blinking, touching, squatting or knee bends. Vocal tics often include uttering sounds or words such as grunts, yelps, sniffs, or throat clearing (Leckman, Peterson, King, Scahill, & Cohen, 2001).

The *Diagnostic and Statistical Manual of Mental Disorders* (*DSM-IV*) (American Psychiatric Association, 1994) recognizes three distinct tic disorders: (1) transient tic disorder, (2) chronic tic disorder, and (3) Tourette syndrome (TS). Transient tic disorder usually consists of one or more simple motor tics, which fluctuate in severity over weeks to months but occur for fewer than 12 consecutive months. Chronic tic disorder is characterized by either motor or vocal tics, but not both. The tics occur many times a day nearly every day, or intermittently for a period of more than 1 year. During that time, the patient is never without symptoms for more than 3 consecutive months. The majority of the tics typically involve the eyes, face, head, and upper extremities. TS involves multiple tics including at least one phonic tic (e.g., throat clearing, grunting, squeaks) occurring several times a day, every day, throughout a period of more than 1 year and the onset occurring before the age of 18 (American Psychiatric Association, 1994). Tics are often preceded by unpleasant sensory sensations or urges (Leckman, Walker, & Cohen, 1993). Sensory phenomena (sensations, urges), as generalized or focal uncomfortable feelings or sensations preceding tics, are usually reported as being relieved by the tic (Leckman et al., 1993; Mink, 2001, 2006). Although tics have traditionally been conceptualized as involuntary responses, many patients describe their tics as a response to such premonitory urges (Leckman et al., 1993). For example, a cross-sectional study of 135 patients with tic disorder found that 93% reported premonitory urges, located mostly in the palms, shoulders, midline abdomen, and throat. Eighty-four percent reported that tics were associated with a feeling of relief. Ninety-two percent indicated that their tics were either fully or partially a voluntary response to the premonitory urges (Leckman et al., 1993).

Tics typically develop in childhood (Cohen et al., 1992) and in TS generally fluctuate in severity throughout the lifetime (Nomoto, 1989). Community estimates indicate that 1–13% of both boys and girls experience tics (Zahner, Clubb, Leckman, & Pauls, 1988). Tic disorders often negatively impact self-esteem, family life, peer relations, and academic and occupational functioning (Leckman, Peterson, Pauls, & Cohen, 1997). Although the impact of tic disorders on the quality of life is well established, there is no conclusive evidence that the different tic disorders have different etiologies or that they respond differently to treatment (Carr & Chong, 2005).

THE OVERLAP BETWEEN OCD AND TIC DISORDERS

Data from the Epidemiological Catchment Area Study (ECA) suggest that OCD has a 6-month prevalence of 1.6% (Myers et al., 1984) and a lifetime prevalence of 2.5% (Robins et al., 1984). Although the reported comorbidity of tic disorders and

OCD varies considerably across studies, there is consistent evidence of elevated rates of OCD in cohorts of patients with tic disorders (e.g., Cardona et al., 2004; Eapen et al., 1996; Leckman et al., 1994) compared to prevalence estimates of OCD in the general population (Myers et al., 1984). For example, in a sample of 134 TS patients, 23% were found to meet full criteria for OCD (Leckman et al., 1994). Likewise, Cardona et al. (2004) documented that in a sample of 125 children and adolescents affected by any tic disorder, 19% had OCD and another 46% showed symptoms of OCD. In a sample of 30 TS patients, OCD symptoms were observed in more than 50% of the patients (Eapen et al., 1996). Conversely, studies in individuals with OCD have also yielded high rates of comorbid tic conditions ranging from 7% to 37% (King, Leckman, Scahill, & Cohen, 1999; Pitman, Green, Jenike, & Mesulam, 1987; Rasmussen & Eisen, 1992). As estimated by Swedo, Rapoport et al. (1989), the lifetime occurrence of tics in patients with OCD is approximately 7–20% in children.

Family studies also support a relation between OCD and TS (Pitman et al., 1987). OCD is found in 20–60% of TS patients (Apter et al., 1993), and a greater prevalence of OCD is reported in first-degree relatives of TS probands, compared to controls, independent of concurrent OCD (Pauls et al., 1991). Leonard et al. (1992) conducted a 2–7-year follow-up on 54 children (aged 7–19 yrs) who had participated in treatment protocols for OCD and also investigated 171 of their first-degree relatives. At baseline, 31 patients had lifetime histories of tics but did not meet criteria for TS. At follow-up, 32 study participants had lifetime histories of tics; 8 of these (all males) met the criteria for TS. Of the relatives, 3 had TS, and 24 had a tic disorder. Hebebrand et al. (1997) also found that OCD and obsessive–compulsive symptoms were frequently associated with TS in families that had children and adolescents with TS. Similarly, Grados (2001) found that relatives of patients with OCD had a greater lifetime prevalence of tic disorders compared to controls.

Other studies have shown that early onset OCD tends to be more frequently associated with tics (George, Trimble, Ring, Sallee & Robertson, 1993; Grados, 2001; Riddle, Scahill, & King, 1990; Rosario-Campos et al., 2001). For example, in a study of 42 adult outpatients with OCD, those with early onset (symptom onset before the age of 10) reported a higher frequency of tics and a higher rate of comorbid tic disorders (Rosario-Campos et al., 2001). Some evidence suggests that when OCD co-occurs with TS, associated tics and obsessions seem to develop independently of one another (Swedo & Leonard, 1994). For example, it has been reported that for approximately 30–60% of TS patients, obsessions and compulsions emerge several years after the onset of tics (Leckman, Peterson et al., 1997). However, overall, the higher prevalence rates of OCD in tic disorders and vice versa suggest a link between OCD and tic disorders for patients who meet criteria for both.

OCD SYMPTOMS IN TIC-RELATED OCD

Studies investigating differences in the symptom profile of OCD patients with and without tic disorders suggest that the severity of OCD does not seem to differ between the two groups. The distribution of obsessive–compulsive symptoms differs between individuals with OCD and tics and those with OCD alone (e.g., George et al., 1993; Leckman et al., 1995; Miguel, Rauch et al., 1997). For example, contamination obsessions and washing compulsions have been found more frequently in OCD patients without tics, whereas patients with tics are more likely to present with intrusive violent thoughts, sexual obsessions, and counting rituals (George et al., 1993). Similarly, Leckman et al. (1995) found that tic-related OCD may be characterized by more frequent aggressive and symmetry obsessions.

Factor analytic studies have highlighted OCD symptom dimensions that may be related to tics. For example, Baer (1994) administered the Yale–Brown Obsessive Compulsive Scale Symptom Checklist to 107 patients with OCD and applied principal components analysis to identify OCD symptom dimensions. Three factors, named 'symmetry/hoarding', 'contamination/cleaning', and 'pure obsessions', best explained the variance in OCD symptoms. Only the symmetry/hoarding factor was significantly related to a lifetime history of TS or chronic tic disorder. Leckman, Grice et al. (1997) identified four OCD symptom dimensions: (1) harmful, sexual, somatic, and religious obsessions and related compulsions; (2) symmetry, ordering, counting, and arranging obsessions and compulsions; (3) contamination obsessions and cleaning compulsions; and (4) hoarding and collecting obsessions and compulsions. Patients with tic-related OCD scored higher on dimensions one, two and four than OCD patients without tics. Holzer et al. (1994) reported that ritualistic touching, tapping, rubbing, blinking, or staring, as well as intrusive images, sounds, words or music were more frequently exhibited by OCD patients with tics compared to OCD patients without tics. Similarly, Leonard et al. (1992) found that the compulsive need to touch, tap or rub items was present in 70–80% of OCD patients with comorbid TS and 20–40% of patients with chronic tics, compared to 5–25% of patients with non-tic-related OCD.

There is mounting evidence for differences in the antecedents and functions of certain types of compulsions between groups of patients with OCD and tics and those without tics. For example, Miguel, Baer et al. (1997) reported that in individuals with non tic-related OCD cognitions, autonomic anxiety (i.e., dry mouth, sweating, or accelerated heart rate) precede repetitive behaviors whereas for patients with OCD and TS, sensory phenomena (i.e., generalized or focal uncomfortable feelings or sensations) more often precede repetitive behaviors (Miguel, Baer et al., 1997). Summerfeldt (2004) highlighted the distinction between compulsions that serve to prevent harm ('harm avoidance') and compulsions that serve to restore an inner balance ('incompleteness'). Compulsions associated with harm avoidance are typically associated with intrusive thoughts (obsessions) and functionally serve to reduce fears about potential harm. For example, repetitive checking of electrical equipment may serve to prevent fire and harm of significant others. Likewise, excessive washing (or avoidance of 'contaminated' objects) may serve to reduce the likelihood of contamination, infection and illness.

Compulsions associated with feelings of incompleteness, on the other hand, are motivated by the subjective experience of things not being right (Summerfeldt, 2004) and functionally serve to restore a sense of inner balance, but do not appear to be motivated by fear of harm. For example, patients may trace the outline of objects, count up to certain numbers until it 'feels right', or may strive for symmetry and order in their environment. Taken together, studies comparing symptom profiles of OCD patients with and without comorbid tic disorders suggest that patients with OCD and tics, compared to those without tics, are characterized by higher rates of compulsions associated with these feelings of incompleteness.

Various names have been employed for this type of compulsion that is aimed at restoring some form of an inner balance. These include 'feeling of incompleteness' (Janet, 1903 cited in Pitman, 1987; Rasmussen & Eisen, 1992; Summerfeldt, Antony, & Swinson, 2002), 'not just right' perceptions (Coles, Frost, Heimberg, & Rhéaume, 2003; Leckman et al., 1994), 'sensory phenomena' (Miguel et al., 2000), and 'sensitivity of perception' (Veale et al., 1996). As described by Summerfeldt (2004), the experience of things not being right can be manifested through various sensory modalities, including the visual (e.g., appearance of belongings or documents), auditory (e.g., preference for the sameness in ambient noise), tactile (e.g., checking textures by touching or tapping), and proprioceptive (e.g., having to 'even up' actions; Summerfeldt, 2004). Behaviorally similar compulsions may be associated with either harm avoidance or feelings of incompleteness, thereby cutting across factor-analytically derived symptom dimensions of OCD. For example, a patient may engage in compulsive counting to prevent 'bad luck' or to achieve a feeling of completeness. Likewise, Tallis (1996) described washing compulsions in the absence of fears of contamination leading to illness.

While compulsions associated with harm avoidance in patients with OCD and tics can be distinguished from complex tics due to the preceding obsessions as well as their function (prevention of harm), diagnostically the distinction between compulsions associated with feelings of incompleteness and certain types of complex tics represents a challenge. Some complex tics consist of a combination of simple tics (e.g., a series or combination of rapid jerk-like muscle movements forming a complex tic). Other complex tics are slower and involve more complex movements (e.g., resuming certain postures). Like compulsions associated with incompleteness, such slower complex tics are often preceded by a deviation from an inner balance (i.e., the premonitory urge), and this deviation is reduced following the execution of the tic (Leckman et al., 1993). Findings by Miguel et al. (2000) suggest that the type of mental sensation associated with tics or incompleteness compulsions may be of utility to distinguish such complex tics from compulsions associated with feelings of incompleteness. Miguel et al. (2000) reported that repetitive behaviors in patients with OCD and TS were more frequently preceded or accompanied by feelings of incompleteness or a need for things to be 'just right' than in patients with TS or OCD alone. Both patients with OCD plus TS and patients with TS alone also experienced urges or nonfocal feelings of mental energy that needed to be discharged preceding repetitive behaviors (Miguel et al., 2000). Slower complex tics may be differentiated from compulsions associated with incompleteness based on the presence of an urge or need for mental energy release, whereas the need for 'just-right'-perceptions and feelings of incompleteness may be specific to compulsions not associated with harm avoidance. Further support for the distinctiveness of the two types of repetitive behaviors comes from our work with patients who met *DSM-IV* criteria for both OCD and TS who reported an urge preceding a complex motor tic (e.g., rub one's eye). Execution of the tic was associated with a reduction of that urge yet it increased a need to repeat the eye-rubbing until it felt 'right' (T. Deckersbach, personal communication, April 10, 2006).

NEUROBIOLOGY OF TIC-RELATED OCD

The basal ganglia and related cortical and thalamic structures have been implicated in the neurobiology of both OCD and tics (Leckman, Grice et al., 1997; Rauch et al., 1995). Functionally, the basal ganglia are composed of pathways that are part of the multiple parallel cortico-striato-thalamo-cortical circuits that subserve a wide variety of sensorimotor, motor, cognitive, and limbic processes (Goldman-Rakic & Selemon, 1990). Several parallel segregated cortico-striatal pathways, each one subserving different types of function, have been described (Alexander, Crutcher, & Delong, 1990). Structural and functional neuroimaging studies most consistently implicate the striatum, orbitofrontal cortex (OFC), and the anterior cingulate (ACC) in the pathophysiology of OCD. For example, studies using positron emission tomography (PET) and single photon emission computed tomography (SPECT) in OCD patients at rest found increased regional brain activity within the OFC, ACC (Baxter et al., 1987, 1988, 1992; Machlin et al., 1991; Nordahl et al., 1989; Rubin, Villaneuva-Myer, Ananth, Trajmar & Mena, 1992; Swedo, Shapiro et al., 1989), and the striatum (specifically, caudate nucleus; Baxter et al., 1987, 1988). Increased brain activity or activation within the anterior/lateral OFC, ACC, as well as in the caudate nucleus, has been observed using PET and functional magnetic resonance imaging (fMRI) when OCD-related obsessions were provoked using OCD-related stimuli (Adler et al., 2000; Breiter et al., 1996; Rauch et al., 1994). In addition, abnormal regional brain activity within the OFC, ACC and caudate nucleus is attenuated in responders to behavioral or pharmacological treatments in OCD (Baxter et al., 1992; Benkelfat et al., 1990; Hoehn-Saric, Pearlson, Harris, Machlin, & Camargo, 1991; Perani et al., 1995; Schwartz, Stoessel, Baxter, Martin & Phelps, 1996). These findings have been incorporated into the cortico-striatal model of OCD (Rauch, Whalen, Dougherty & Jenike, 1998) according to which abnormal striatal function leads to inefficient gating at the level of the thalamus, which results in hyperactivity within the OFC and ACC. In this model, compulsions are conceptualized as repetitive, ritualistic behaviors that are performed to recruit the inefficient striatum to achieve thalamic gating, and hence, neutralize unwanted thoughts and anxiety.

More recently, studies have begun to explore associations between OCD subtypes or OCD symptom dimensions and patterns of brain activity or activation (e.g., Crespo-Facorro et al., 1999; Mataix-Cols et al., 2004; Rauch, Dougherty et al., 1998; Saxena et al., 2004). For example, Crespo-Facorro et al. (1999) using SPECT reported abnormal regional blood flow (rCBF) in the OFC in patients with

OCD but failed to find differences in the patterns of rCBF between OCD patients with and without comorbid chronic motor tic disorder. However, it is possible that the small sample size of OCD patients with tics (n = 7) accounts for this non-significant finding. Although, to our knowledge, in OCD, patterns of brain activity (or activation) associated with harm avoidance or incompleteness have not yet been compared directly, findings by Rauch and colleagues (Rauch, Dougherty et al., 1998) suggest that different types of striatal activation may be associated with compulsions reflecting primarily harm avoidance compared to those more closely associated with feelings of incompleteness (Rauch, Dougherty et al., 1998). Specifically, rCBF in the striatum in individuals with OCD during a continuous performance task was negatively correlated with the severity of symmetry and ordering compulsions (Rauch, Dougherty et al., 1998), whereas the combined sever-ity of checking compulsions, aggressive, religious, and sexual obsessions corre-lated positively with rCBF within the striatum (Rauch, Dougherty et al., 1998). In addition, only the combined severity of checking compulsions, and aggressive, religious and sexual obsessions was correlated with rCBF in the OFC (Rauch et al., 1988). As suggested by Mink (2001, 2006), tics occur when specific sets of striatal neurons become overactive in discrete repeated episodes resulting in stereo-typed, unwanted movements. These neurons normally contribute to the inhibition of unwanted, and facilitation of desired, movements (Mink, 2001, 2006). Thus, both the pattern of compulsions associated with feelings of incompleteness, as well as the type and topography of tics may depend on the pattern of striatal dysregulation, whereas compulsions associated with harm avoidance may be more closely associated with OFC abnormalities within cortico-striato-thalamo-cortical circuits. Functionally, both tics and compulsions associated with incompleteness reduce premonitory urges or sensations (tics) or feelings of incompleteness which may negatively reinforce neural activity patterns associated with stereotyped behaviors (Mink, 2001, 2006; Woods & Miltenberger, 1995), thereby contributing to the maintenance of tics or compulsions associated with feelings of incompleteness. Recently, Maltby et al. (2005) suggested that increased dorsal ACC activation in OCD reflects exaggerated or false error signals (even when actions were performed correctly) that contribute to compulsive behaviors including 'just-right' compulsions (i.e., compulsions associ-ated with the feeling of incompleteness). However, in a recent symptom provocation fMRI study (Mataix-Cols et al., 2004), both the provocation of contamination obses-sions, as well as the provocation of aggressive obsessions, yielded increased activa-tion in the dorsal ACC, suggesting that abnormal ACC activation may not be specific to compulsions associated with the feeling of incompleteness.

TREATMENT OF TIC-RELATED OCD

Pharmacotherapy has been considered the treatment of choice in tic-related conditions (Piacentini & Chang, 2001) with demonstrated efficacy in placebo-controlled studies (e.g., Peterson & Azrin, 1993). For OCD, serotonin reuptake inhibitors (SRIs) have become the first-line pharmacotherapy (Dougherty, Rauch, & Jenike, 2004). Patients with tic-related OCD tend to respond less favorably to SRI medication (McDougle et al., 1993, 1994) and response can be improved by augmenting SRI montherapy with antipsychotic medication (Bloch et al., in press; McDougle et al.,1994; McDougle, Epperson, Pelton, Wasylink, & Price, 2000).

Although the overall efficacy of behavioral treatments for OCD (e.g., exposure and response prevention) is well documented (e.g., Foa et al., 2005), little is known about the efficacy of behavioral treatments for compulsions associated with feelings of incompleteness. Patients with these compulsions appear to be underrepresented in behavioral outcome studies (for a review see Ball, Baer & Otto, 1996). Clinically, these compulsions appear to respond less favorably to exposure and response prevention, compared to washing or checking compulsions associated with harm avoidance (Tallis, 1996; Wilhelm, personal communication, March 30, 2006). For tics a behavioral treatment called habit reversal has become a nonpharmacological treatment alternative (Piacentini & Chang, 2001). The efficacy of habit reversal has been demonstrated for tics but has not been applied to compulsions in tic-related OCD. Briefly, within habit reversal, patients learn to apply antagonistic, competing movements to inhibit the occurrence of tics (Azrin & Nunn, 1973). The initial stages of habit reversal consist of awareness training and self-monitoring (detection of tics and preceding sensations). Patients then learn to implement movements that are incompatible with the tic. For example, to prevent a bending of the arm, the patient would rotate the arm slightly inward so that the tic cannot occur and maintain that position until the urge to perform the tic has subsided. This competing movement is then consistently applied upon early sensations or urges to perform the tic.

Randomized clinical trials have demonstrated the efficacy of habit reversal in reducing tic severity in patients with TS. For instance, Azrin and Peterson (1990) reported a 93% tic reduction in a group of patients treated with habit reversal compared with no improvement in patients on a wait-list. In two separate studies, Wilhelm et al. (2003) and Deckersbach, Rauch, Buhlmann & Wilhelm (in press) conducted randomized controlled trials comparing the efficacy of habit reversal with supportive psychotherapy in patients with TS. They found that habit reversal, but not supportive psychotherapy, significantly reduced tic severity following 14 individual sessions. These effects were maintained at a 10-month follow-up assessment (Wilhelm et al., 2003). Verdellen, Keijers, Cath, & Hoogduin (2004) recently found that 10 sessions of individual habit reversal treatment was effective in reducing tic severity. However, it should be noted that exposure and response prevention (i.e., exposure to premonitory urges) also used by Verdellen et al. (2004), was as effective as habit reversal in reducing tic severity, suggesting a common mode of action for both treatments. Finally, the role of cognitive interventions for tic-related OCD has gained interest. For example, distraction techniques may help patients resist sensory urges and restore the patient's sense of control over the tic. In addition, cognitive restructuring may be useful for reducing stress-inducing thoughts, which in turn may decrease tic frequency.

SUMMARY AND CONCLUSIONS

There is mounting evidence that OCD is a heterogeneous disorder comprised of distinct subtypes or symptom dimensions. Elevated rates of OCD in patients with tic disorders and vice versa suggest that patients who experience both OCD and tics may constitute a distinct subtype. Compared to patients with OCD alone, patients with OCD and tics have an earlier age of onset and tend to respond better when SRI pharmacotherapy is augmented with antipsychotic medication. OCD patients with tics, compared to OCD alone, also seem to have higher rates of compulsions associated with feelings of incompleteness. It should be emphasized, however, that in our experience OCD patients with tics often present with a mixture of both compulsions associated with harm avoidance, as well as compulsions associated with feelings of incompleteness. Few empirical data are available regarding how compulsions associated with incompleteness respond to behavioral treatments. Our clinical impression is that they respond less favorably to exposure and response prevention than other types of OCD symptoms (e.g., washing or checking associated with harm avoidance). Habit reversal, a behavioral treatment, has received empirical support for its efficacy in treating tics but its efficacy for compulsions associated with incompleteness remains to be demonstrated. It is possible that patients with OCD and tics require a multi-modal treatment approach combining various behavioral treatment techniques, including exposure and response prevention, habit reversal and cognitive techniques for treating obsessions, compulsions and tics. Findings from functional neuroimaging studies focusing on symptom dimensions relevant for tic-related OCD (symmetry and order) challenge the generic cognitive neuroscience model of OCD, although further studies are needed to support the finding of distinct neural correlates associated with such symptom dimensions. However, it is possible that tic-related OCD might be better conceptualized as consisting of separate symptom dimensions that result in a subtype of OCD associated with tics.

REFERENCES

Adler, C. M., McDonough-Ryan, P., Sax, K. W., Holland, S. K., Arndt, S., & Strakowski, S. M. (2000). fMRI of neuronal activation with symptom provocation in unmedicated patients with obsessive compulsive disorder. *Psychiatry Research, 34*, 317–324.

Alexander, G. E., Crutcher, M. D., & Delong, M. R. (1990). Basal ganglia-thalamocortical circuits: Parallel substrates for motor, oculomotor, 'prefrontal' and 'limbic' functions. *Progress in Brain Research, 85*, 119–146.

American Psychiatric Association (1994). *Diagnostic and statistical manual of mental disorders* (4th ed.) (*DSM-IV*). Washington, DC: APA.

Apter, A., Pauls, D. L., Bleich, A., Zohar, A. H., Kron, S., Ratzoni, G., et al. (1993). An epidemiological study of Gilles de la Tourette's syndrome in Israel. *Archives of General Psychiatry, 50*, 734–738.

Azrin, N. H., & Nunn, R. G. (1973). Habit reversal: A method for eliminating nervous habits and tics. *Behaviour Research and Therapy, 11*, 619–628.

Baer, L. (1994). Factor analysis of symptom subtypes of obsessive compulsive disorder and their relation to personality and tic disorders. *Journal of Clinical Psychiatry, 55* (3, Suppl), 18–23.

Ball, S., Baer, L., & Otto, M. (1996). Symptom subtypes of obsessive–compulsive disorder in behavioural treatment studies: A quantitative review. *Behaviour Research and Therapy, 34,* 47–51.

Baxter, L. R. Jr., Schwartz, J. M., Bergman, K. S., Szuba, M. P., Guze, B. H., Mazziotta, J. C., et al. (1992). Caudate glucose metabolic rate changes with both drug and behavior therapy for obsessive–compulsive disorder. *Archives of General Psychiatry, 49,* 681–689.

Baxter, L. R., Phelps, M. E., Mazziotta, J. C., Guze, B. H., Schwartz, J. M., & Selin, C. E. (1987). Local cerebral glucose metabolic rates in obsessive compulsive disorder: A comparison with rates in unipolar depression and in normal controls. *Archives of General Psychiatry, 44,* 211–218.

Baxter, L., Schwartz, J., Mazziotta, J., Phelps, M. E., Pahl, J. J., Guze, B. H., et al. (1988). Cerebral glucose metabolic rates in nondepressed patients with obsessive–compulsive disorder. *American Journal of Psychiatry, 145,* 1560–1563.

Benkelfat, C., Nordahl, T. E., Semple, W. E., King, A. C., Murphy, D. L., & Cohen, R. M. (1990). Local cerebral glucose metabolic rates in obsessive–compulsive disorder: Patients treated with clomipramine. *Archives of General Psychiatry, 47,* 840–848.

Bloch, M. H., Landeros-Weisenberger, A., Kelmendi, B., Coric, V., Bracken, M. B., & Leckman, J. F. (2006). A systematic review: Antipsychotic augmentation with treatment refractory obsessive–compulsive disorder. *Molecular Psychiatry, 11,* 622–632.

Breiter, H. C., Rauch, S. L., Kwong, K. K., Baker, J. R., Weisskoff, R. M., Kennedy, D. N., et al. (1996). Functional magnetic resonance imaging of symptom provocation in obsessive compulsive disorder. *Archives of General Psychiatry, 53,* 595–606.

Cardona, F., Romano, A., Bollea, L., & Chiarotti, F. (2004). Psychopathological problems in children affected by tic disorders: Study on a large Italian population. *European Child and Adolescent Psychiatry, 13,* 166–171.

Carr, J. E., & Chong, I. M. (2005). Habit reversal treatment of tic disorders: A methodological critique of the literature. *Behavior Modification, 29,* 858–875.

Cohen, D. J., Leckman, J. F., & Shaywitz, B. A. (1992). The Tourette syndrome and other tics. In J. F. Cohen & D. J. Cohen (Eds.), *Clinician guide to child psychiatry* (pp. 3–26). New York: Raven Press.

Coles, M. E., Frost, R. O., Heimberg, R. G., & Rhéaume, J. (2003). 'Not just right experiences': Perfectionism, obsessive–compulsive features and general psychopathology. *Behaviour Research and Therapy, 41,* 681–700.

Crespo-Facorro, B., Cabranes, J. A., Alcocer, M. I., Paya, B., Perez, C. F., Encinas, M., Ayuso Mateos, J. L., et al. (1999). Regional cerebral blood flow in obsessive–compulsive patients with and without a chronic tic disorder: A SPECT study. *European Archives of Psychiatry and Clinical Neuroscience, 249,* 156–161.

Deckersbach, T., Rauch, S. L., Buhlmann, U., & Wilhelm, S. (2006). Habit reversal versus supportive psychotherapy in Tourette's disorder: A randomized controlled trial and predictors of treatment response. *Behaviour Research and Therapy, 44,* 1079–1090.

Dougherty, D. D., Rauch, S. L., & Jenike, M. A. (2004). Pharmacotherapy for obsessive–compulsive disorder. *Journal of Clinical Psychology, 60,* 1195–1202.

Eapen, V., Trimble, M. R., & Robertson, M. M. (1996). The use of fluoxetine in Gilles de la Tourette syndrome and obsessive compulsive behaviors: Preliminary clinical experience. *Progress in Neuro-Psychopharmacology and Biological Psychiatry, 20,* 737–746.

Foa, E. B., Liebowitz, M. R., Kozak, M. J., Davies, S., Campeas, R., Franklin, M. E., et al. (2005). Randomized, placebo-controlled trial of exposure and ritual prevention, clomipramine, and their combination in the treatment of obsessive–compulsive disorder. *American Journal of Psychiatry, 162,* 151–161.

George, M. S., Trimble, M. R., Ring, H. A., Sallee F. R., & Robertson, M. M. (1993). Obsessions in obsessive compulsive disorder with and without Gilles de la Tourette's syndrome. *American Journal of Psychiatry, 150,* 93–97.

Goldman-Rakic, P. S., & Selemon, L. D. (1990). New frontiers in basal ganglia research. *Trends in Neurosciences, 13*, 244–245.

Grados, M. A. (2001). The familial phenotype of obsessive–compulsive disorder in relation to tic: The Hopkins OCD family study. *Biological Psychiatry, 50*, 559–565.

Hebebrand, J., Klug, B., Fimmers, R., Seuchter, S., Wettke-Schäfer, R., Deget, F., et al. (1997). Rates for tic disorders and obsessive compulsive symptomatology in families of children and adolescents with Gilles de la Tourette syndrome. *Journal of Psychiatric Research, 31*, 519–530.

Hoehn-Saric, R., Pearlson, G. D., Harris, G. J., Machlin, S. R., & Camargo, E. E. (1991). Effects of fluoxetine on regional cerebral blood flow in obsessive–compulsive patients. *American Journal of Psychiatry, 148*, 1243–1245.

Holzer, J. C., Goodman, W. K., McDougle, C. J., Baer, L., Boyarsky, B. K., Leckman, J. F., et al. (1994). Obsessive compulsive disorder with and without a chronic tic disorder. *British Journal of Psychiatry, 164*, 469–473.

King, R. A., Leckman, J. F., Scahill, L., & Cohen, D. J. (1999). Obsessive–compulsive disorder, anxiety, and depression. In J. F. Leckman & D. J. Cohen (Eds.), *Tourette's syndrome – tics, obsessions, compulsions: Developmental psychopathology and clinical care* (pp. 43–62). New York: Wiley.

Leckman, J. F., Grice, D. E., Barr, L. C., de Vries, A. L. C., Martic, C., Cohen, D. J., et al. (1995). Tic-related vs. non-tic related obsessive compulsive disorder. *Anxiety, 1*, 208–215.

Leckman, J. F., Grice, D. E., Boardman, J., Zhang, H., Vitale, A., Bondi, C., et al. (1997). Symptoms of obsessive–compulsive disorder. *American Journal of Psychiatry, 154*, 911–917.

Leckman, J. F., Peterson, B. S., King, R. A., Scahill, L., & Cohen, D. J. (2001). Phenomenology of tics and natural history of tic disorders. *Advances in Neurology, 85*, 1–14.

Leckman, J. F., Peterson, B. S., Pauls, D. L., & Cohen, D. J. (1997). Tic disorders. *Psychiatric Clinics of North America, 20*, 839–861.

Leckman, J. F., Walker, D. E., & Cohen, D. J. (1993). Premonitory urges in Tourette's syndrome. *American Journal of Psychiatry, 150*, 98–102.

Leckman, J. F., Walker, D. E., Goodman, W. K., Pauls, D. L., & Cohen, D. J. (1994). 'Just right' perceptions associated with compulsive behavior in Tourette's syndrome. *American Journal of Psychiatry, 151*, 675–680.

Leonard, H. L., Lenane, M. C., Swedo, S. E., Rettew, D. C., Gershon, E. S., & Rapoport, J. L. (1992). Tic and Tourette's disorder: A 2- to 7-year follow-up of 54 obsessive–compulsive children. *American Journal of Psychiatry, 149*, 1244–1251.

Machlin, S. R., Harris, G. J., Pearlson, G. D., Hoehn-Saric, R., Jeffery, P., & Camargo, E. E. (1991). Elevated medial-frontal cerebral blood flow in obsessive–compulsive patients: A SPECT study. *American Journal of Psychiatry, 148*, 1240–1242.

Maltby, N., Tolin, D. F., Worhunsky, P., O'Keefe, T. M., & Kiehl, K. A. (2005). Dysfunctional action monitoring hyperactivates frontal-striatal circuits in obsessive–compulsive disorder: An event-related fMRI study. *Neuroimage, 24*, 495–503.

Mataix-Cols, D., Rosario-Campos, M. C., & Leckman, J. F. (2005). A multidimensional model of obsessive–compulsive disorder. *American Journal of Psychiatry, 162*, 228–238.

Mataix-Cols, D., Wooderson, S., Lawrence, N., Brammer, M. J., Speckens, A., & Phillips, M. L. (2004). Distinct neural correlates of washing, checking, and hoarding symptom dimensions in obsessive–compulsive disorder. *Archives of General Psychiatry, 61*, 564–576.

McDougle, C. J., Epperson, C. N., Pelton, G. H., Wasylink, S., & Price, L. H. (2000). A double-blind, placebo-controlled study of risperidone addition in serotonin reuptake inhibitor-refractory obsessive–compulsive disorder. *Archives of General Psychiatry, 57*, 794–801.

McDougle, C. J., Goodman, W. K., Leckman, J. F., Barr, L. C., Heninger, G. R., & Price, L. H. (1993). The efficacy of fluvoxamine in obsessive–compulsive disorder: Effects of comorbid chronic tic disorder. *Journal of Clinical Psychopharmacology, 13*, 354–358.

McDougle, C. J., Goodman, W. K., Leckman, J. F., Lee, N. C., Heninger, G. R., & Price, L. H. (1994). Haloperidol addition in fluvoxamine-refractory obsessive–compulsive disorder. A double-blind, placebo-controlled study in patients with and without tics. *Archives of General Psychiatry, 51*, 302–308.

McKay, D., Abramowitz, J. S., Calamari, J. E., Kyrios, M., Radomsky, A., Sookman, D., et al. (2004). A critical evaluation of obsessive–compulsive disorder subtypes: Symptoms versus mechanisms. *Clinical Psychology Review, 24*, 283–313.

Miguel, E. C., Baer, L., Coffey, B. J., Rauch, S. L., Savage, C. R., O'Sullivan R. L., et al. (1997). Phenomenological differences appearing with repetitive behaviours in obsessive–compulsive disorder and Gilles de la Tourette's syndrome. *British Journal of Psychiatry, 170*, 140–145.

Miguel, E. C., do Rosario-Campos, M. C., da Silva, P. H., do Valle, R., Rauch, S. L., Coffey, B. J., et al. (2000). Sensory phenomena in obsessive–compulsive disorder and Tourette's disorder. *Journal of Clinical Psychiatry, 61*, 150–156.

Miguel, E. C., Rauch, S. L., & Jenike, M. A. (1997). Obsessive–compulsive disorder. *Psychiatric Clinics of North America, 20*, 863–883.

Mink, J. W. (2001). Basal ganglia dysfunction in Tourette's Syndrome: A new hypothesis. *Pediatric Neurology, 25*, 190–198.

Mink, J. W. (2006). Neurobiology of basal ganglia and Tourette syndrome: Basal ganglia circuits and thalamortical outputs. *Advances in Neurology, 99*, 89–98.

Myers, J. K., Weissman, N. M., Tischler, G. L., Holzer, C. E., Leaf, P. J., Orvaschel, H., et al. (1984). Six-month prevalence of psychiatric disorders in three communities, 1980–1982. *Archives of General Psychiatry, 41*, 959–967.

Nomoto, F. (1989). Tourette's syndrome. *Journal of Mental Health, 35*, 63–70.

Nordahl, T. E., Benkelfat, C., Semple, W., Gross, M., King, A. C., & Cohen, R. M. (1989). Cerebral glucose metabolic rates in obsessive–compulsive disorder. *Neuropsychopharmacology, 2*, 23–28.

Perani, D., Colombo, C., Bressi, S., Bonfanti, A., Grassi, F., Scarone, S., et al. (1995). FDG PET study in obsessive–compulsive disorder: A clinical metabolic correlation study after treatment. *British Journal of Psychiatry, 166*, 244–250.

Peterson, A. L., & Azrin, N. H. (1993). Behavioral and pharmacological treatment for Tourette syndrome: A review. *Applied and Preventive Psychology, 2*, 231–242.

Piacentini, J., & Chang, S. (2001). Behavioral treatments for Tourette syndrome and tic disorders: State of the art. In D. J. Cohen, C. G. Goetz, & J. Jankovic (Eds.), *Tourette syndrome (Advances in Neurology)* (Vol. 85, pp. 319–331). Philadelphia, PA: Lippincott, Williams & Wilkins.

Pitman, R. K. (1987). Pierre Janet on obsessive–compulsive disorder (1903). *Archives of General Psychiatry, 44*, 226–232.

Pitman, R. K., Green, R. C., Jenike, M. A., & Mesulam, M. M. (1987). Clinical comparison of Tourette's disorder and obsessive–compulsive disorder. *American Journal of Psychiatry, 144*, 1166–1171.

Rasmussen, S. A., & Eisen, J. L. (1992). The epidemiology and clinical features of obsessive compulsive disorder. *Psychiatric Clinics of North America, 15*, 743–758.

Rauch, S. L., Baer, L., Cosgrove, G. R., & Jenike, M. A. (1995). Neurosurgical treatment of Tourette's syndrome: A critical review. *Comprehensive Psychiatry, 36*, 141–156.

Rauch, S. L., Dougherty, D. D., Shin, L. M., Alpert, N. M., Manzo, P., Leahy, L., et al. (1998). Neural correlates of factor-analyzed OCD symptom dimensions: a PET study. *CNS Spectrums, 3*, 37–43.

Rauch, S. L., Jenike, M. A., Alpert, N. M., Baer, L., Breiter, H. C., Savage, C. R., et al. (1994). Regional cerebral blood flow measured during symptom provocation in obsessive–compulsive disorder using ^{15}O-labeled CO_2 and positron emission tomography. *Archives of General Psychiatry, 51*, 62–70.

Rauch, S. L., Whalen, P. J., Dougherty, D. D., & Jenike, M. A. (1998). Neurobiological models of obsessive compulsive disorders. In M. A. Jenike, L. Baer, & W. E. Minichiello (Eds.), *Obsessive–compulsive disorders: Practical management* (3rd Ed.) (pp. 222–). St Louis, MO: Mosby.

Riddle, M. A., Scahill, L., & King, R. (1990). Obsessive–compulsive disorder in children and adolescents: Phenomenology and family history. *Journal of the American Academy of Child & Adolescent, 29*, 766–772.

Robins, L. N., Helzer, J. E., Weissman, M. M., Orvaschel, H., Gruenberg, E., Burke, J. D., et al. (1984). Life-time prevalence of specific psychiatric disorders in three sites. *Archives of General Psychiatry, 41*, 949–958.

Rosario-Campos, M. C., Leckman, J. F., Mercadante, M. T., Shavitt, R. G., Prado, H. S., Sada, P., et al. (2001). Adults with early-onset obsessive–compulsive disorder. *American Journal of Psychiatry, 158*, 1899–1903.

Rubin, R. T., Villaneuva-Myer, J., Ananth, J., Trajmar, P. G., & Mena, I. (1992). Regional xenon-133 cerebral blood flow and cerebral Technetium 99 m HMPAO uptake in unmedicated patients with obsessive–compulsive disorder and matched normal control subjects. *Archives of General Psychiatry, 49*, 695–702.

Saxena, S., Brody, A. L., Maidment, K. M., Smith, E. C., Zohrabi, N., Katz, E., et al. (2004). Cerebral glucose metabolism in obsessive–compulsive hoarding. *American Journal of Psychiatry, 161*, 1038–1048.

Schwartz, J. M., Stoessel, P. W., Baxter, L. R. Jr., Martin, K. M., & Phelps, M. E. (1996). Systematic changes in cerebral glucose metabolic rate after successful behavior modification. *Archives of General Psychiatry, 53*, 109–113.

Summerfeldt, L. J. (2004). Understanding and treating incompleteness in obsessive–compulsive disorder. *Journal of Clinical Psychology, 60*, 1155–1168.

Summerfeldt, L. J., Antony, M. M., & Swinson, R. P. (2002). Reply to Bilsbury and others. More on the phenomenology of perfectionism: 'Incompleteness' [Letter to the editor]. *Canadian Journal of Psychiatry, 47*, 977–978.

Swedo, S. E., & Leonard, H. L. (1994). Childhood movement disorders and obsessive–compulsive disorder. *Journal of Clinical Psychiatry, 55*, 32–37.

Swedo, S. E., Rapoport, J. L., Cheslow, D. L., Leonard, H. L., Ayoub, E. M., Hosier, D. M., et al. (1989). High prevalence of obsessive–compulsive symptoms in patients with Sydenham's chorea. *American Journal of Psychiatry, 146*, 246–249.

Swedo, S. E., Shapiro, M. B., Grady, C. L., Cheslow, D. L., Leonard, H. L., Kumar, A., et al. (1989). Cerebral glucose metabolism in childhood-onset obsessive–compulsive disorder. *Archives of General Psychiatry, 46*, 518–523.

Tallis, F. (1996). Compulsive washing in the absence of phobic and illness anxiety. *Behaviour Research and Therapy, 34*, 361–362.

Veale, D., Gournay, K., Dryden, W., Boocock, A., Shah, F., Wilson, R., et al. (1996). Body dysmorphic disorder: A cognitive behavioural model and pilot randomised controlled trial. *Behaviour Research and Therapy, 34*, 717–729.

Verdellen, C. W. J., Keijsers, G. P. J., Cath, D. C., & Hoogduin, C. A. L. (2004). Exposure with response prevention versus habit reversal in Tourette's syndrome: A controlled study. *Behaviour Research and Therapy, 42*, 501–511.

Wilhelm, S., Deckersbach, T., Coffey, B. J., Bohne, A., Peterson, A. L., & Baer, L. (2003). Habit reversal versus supportive psychotherapy for Tourette's disorder: A randomized controlled trial. *American Journal of Psychiatry, 160*, 1175–1177.

Woods, D. W., & Miltenberger, R. G (1995). Habit reversal: A review of applications and variations. *Journal of Behavior Therapy and Experimental Psychiatry, 26*, 123–131.

Zahner, G. E. P., Clubb, M. M., Leckman, J. F., & Pauls, D. L. (1988). The epidemiology of Tourette's syndrome. In D. J. Cohen, R. D. Bruun, & J. F. Leckman (Eds.), *Tourette's Syndrome and Tic Disorders* (pp. 79–89). New York: Wiley.

7

AUTOGENOUS OBSESSIONS AND REACTIVE OBSESSIONS

HAN-JOO LEE AND MICHAEL J. TELCH

University of Texas at Austin

Obsessions are persistent ideas, thoughts, impulses, or images that are experienced as intrusive or inappropriate. They are generally accompanied by some compulsions the individual feels driven to perform in order to reduce distress or prevent some dreaded event (*DSM-IV*; American Psychiatric Association, 1994). Examples of common obsessions include recurrent thoughts about becoming contaminated, doubts about having made some terrible mistakes, aggressive or horrific impulses, perverted sexual or sacrilegious imagery, a need for symmetry, and so forth. Although they are all anxiety-provoking mental intrusions that occur against one's will, noticeable heterogeneity exists in numerous aspects. Let us consider the following cases of obsessive–compulsive disorder (OCD) sufferers.

Matt, a man in his late twenties, suffered recurrent guilt-provoking obsessional thoughts involving sacrilege and obscene sexual acts for several years. The most torturous obsession involved thoughts of blurting out blasphemous ideas, such as 'The Virgin Mary slept with God,' in public. As much as he treasured piety as his prime life goal, this thought was experienced as devastating. Matt also experienced sexual obsessions, which included repeated images of brutally raping women in public. These left him fraught with extreme

Correspondence to: Laboratory for the Study of Anxiety Disorders, Department of Psychology, University of Texas at Austin, 1 University Station A8000.

guilt and shame. Consequently, he invented a number of mental strategies in order to dispel or neutralize the thoughts, including inwardly saying 'stop' five times inwardly, thinking 'safe' images to counter the obsessional thoughts, praying, repeating verses from the Bible, singing a part of a hymn five times, and so forth. In his effort to prevent his blasphemous thoughts, Matt remained on the lookout for objects or places that he associated with these thoughts, such as crosses, churches, dogs ('dog' is 'God' spelled backward), female statues, and so forth. He also constantly avoided situations where he might be alone with a woman for fear that his obsessions would be triggered or intensified. However, the harder he tried to push the obsessional thoughts away, the more intense they became.

Sheila, a middle-aged woman, had obsessions about making mistakes in the home that would endanger her two young children. One of her main concerns was that she would do something negligent that would result in harm (e.g., mistakenly poisoning the children). She was also obsessed with the idea that a broken piece of glass or metal would be brought into her home via someone's shoes or clothes, and that this would harm her children in some way. A very time-consuming ritual developed of excessive vacuuming whenever someone would enter the house. Moreover, she constantly checked her vacuum cleaner to ensure it was in perfect working condition. Sheila also had other recurrent thoughts of harm coming to her children resulting from her leaving the oven on or the doors to the house unlocked. Her obsessions were always followed by reassurance-seeking from her family and ritualistic checking of all locks, windows, electronic appliances, the fire alarm, and water taps.

These two cases illustrate how obsessions can have varying foci of perceived threat and how patients' subsequent reactions to them can vary. In some instances the individual becomes distressed about the mere presence of the obsessional thought itself, and strives to remove or 'neutralize' the thought. In other cases, the person becomes concerned about potentially harmful consequences associated with the thought, and thus engages in a preventative or corrective action that he or she believes will reduce the probability of such consequences.

THE AUTOGENOUS AND REACTIVE SUBTYPE MODEL OF OBSESSIONS

KEY FEATURES: THREATENING THOUGHTS VS. THREATENING THOUGHT TRIGGERS

Lee and Kwon (2003) proposed two subtypes of obsessions: *autogenous* and *reactive* obsessions. *Autogenous obsessions* are highly aversive and unrealistic thoughts, images, or impulses that tend to be perceived as threatening in their own right. In other words, perceived threat is focused on the thoughts themselves. Autogenous obsessions usually take the form of thoughts, images, urges, or impulses with repulsive themes concerning unacceptable sexual behavior, violence and aggression, sacrilege and blasphemy, horrific scenes, and the like. Accordingly, such obsessions tend to be perceived as irrational and unacceptable (i.e., ego-dystonic). Autogenous obsessions might occur from 'out of the blue' without clear antecedents, or be triggered by stimuli that are symbolically, unrealistically, or remotely associated with the thoughts. In the first case described above, Matt's blasphemous obsession worsened and became associated with various symbolic cues of God and Mary. Another example is a woman who desperately attempts to avoid touching any objects beginning with the fourth letter in the alphabet, 'd', or its corresponding number '4' in order to cope with the obsession of harming her 'Dad' (e.g., not touching doors, touching things 5 times or not to end up being 4 times).

Reactive obsessions, in contrast, are somewhat realistic aversive thoughts, doubts, or concerns, in which the perceived threat is not the obsession itself, but rather some associated negative consequence that is *possible* but improbable. Reactive obsessions include thoughts, concerns, or doubts about contamination, mistakes, accidents, asymmetry, or disarray. They tend to be perceived as relatively realistic and likely to come true, thereby eliciting some corrective (usually overt) actions aimed at putting the associated uncomfortable situation back to a safe or desired state. For example, in the case of Sheila described above, her perceived threat was not the obsessional thoughts *per se*, but rather the potential negative consequences associated with the thoughts. Consequently, her checking and cleaning rituals were aimed at rectifying the thought-triggering situation and preventing anticipated catastrophes rather than neutralizing the thought. Relative to autogenous obsessions, reactive obsessions are more likely to occur in reaction to explicit cues, which also correspond to specific core threats (e.g., potential contaminants, disarrayed/unsymmetrical objects, ordinary surroundings/activities potentially involving bad mistakes or accidents). Relative to autogenous obsessions, reactive obsessions typically evidence a more realistic link with their triggers. For instance, believing that one has been exposed to germs may serve as an invariable trigger for obsessions concerning contamination, and lead the person to strive to correct the triggering situation through cleaning or washing.

DIFFERENT COGNITIVE APPRAISALS AND CONTROL STRATEGIES

Obsessions, according to cognitive–behavioral formulations (Rachman, 1997; Salkovskis, 1985), persist due to (a) catastrophic misinterpretations of normally occurring mental intrusions and (b) ensuing neutralization and avoidance behavior. The autogenous–reactive model posits that these two types of obsessions are characterized by distinct threat foci (i.e., thoughts themselves vs. explicit thought triggers); and that each type is associated with a different pattern of appraisals and

TABLE 7.1   Comparison of autogenous obsessions and reactive obsessions

	Autogenous obsessions	Reactive obsessions
Perceived threat	Thoughts themselves	External triggers
Nature of triggers	Unclear/symbolic/remote	Explicit/clear
Focus of cognitive appraisals	Presence and content of thoughts	Anticipated negative consequences of triggering situation
Aim of neutralizations	Removing/neutralizing the thoughts themselves	Reducing the probability of feared consequences
Thought form	Impulses/urges/images	Doubts/concerns/strong needs to have things in a certain state
Common themes	Sexual/blasphemous/ aggressive/horrific	Contamination/mistakes/accidents/ order and symmetry
Perceived unacceptability (ego dystonicity)	High	Low

neutralizations. Autogenous obsessions are perceived as threatening in their own right and are thus associated with appraisals of exaggerated significance regarding their occurrence and context. Neutralization strategies (sometimes referred to as 'control strategies') are typically aimed at reducing the perceived threats associated with the presence of the thought itself. These typically take the form of mental strategies designed to suppress, avoid, or neutralize the mental intrusion itself. Overt rituals performed in response to autogenous obsessions are more likely to be somewhat magical, superstitious, or unrealistic.

In contrast, reactive obsessions are associated with threatening external situations and stimuli which tend to evoke the obsessional anxiety. Accordingly, cognitive appraisals often center on the probability and severity of the threat associated with such triggers. Neutralization is focused on rectifying the unsafe and distressing aspects of the triggering situations or stimuli and typically involves ritualistic behavior such as checking to ensure no mistakes or accidents, and washing to remove suspected germs or to prevent disease. Thus, overt rituals performed in response to reactive obsessions are likely to take the form of problem-solving behaviors in an attempt to change (i.e., reduce the threat value of) the distressing situation rather than divert attention away from the obsessional thoughts themselves. Table 7.1 summarizes the major distinctions between the two subtypes.

VALIDITY OF THE AUTOGENOUS–REACTIVE TAXONOMY

In this section, we provide research evidence supporting the proposed distinction between autogenous and reactive obsessions. This work, conducted primarily by Lee and colleagues, includes a series of studies designed to test the hypothe-sized differences between the two proposed obsession subtypes.

DIFFERENCES IN THREAT FOCUS, APPRAISALS, AND NEUTRALIZATION STRATEGIES

Lee and Kwon (2003) conducted two independent studies with large nonclinical student samples. In Study 1, 370 college students were administered the Revised Obsessional Intrusion Inventory (ROII) (Purdon & Clark, 1993), which evaluates the frequencies of a variety of obsessional thoughts. Exploratory and confirmatory factor analyses on the 52 items of the ROII yielded two distinct factors that highly corresponded to autogenous (e.g., thoughts of stabbing a family member, thoughts of having sex in a public place, etc.) and reactive (e.g., thoughts of leaving the water taps running in the house, thoughts of contracting a fatal disease from touching things strangers have touched, etc.) obsessions. Participants were also asked to select their primary (most significant) obsessional thought from the 52 items of the ROII. The subtype of this primary (nonclinical) obsession was deter-mined on the basis of the demonstrated autogenous–reactive factor structure. Next, participants with primary autogenous obsessions were compared to those reporting reactive obsessions with respect to emotional responses and cognitive appraisals of these types of intrusive thoughts. Results revealed that participants with the autogenous subtype found their intrusions more unacceptable, experi-enced more associated feelings of guilt, and felt it was more important that they control these thoughts, compared to participants with the reactive subtype. In con-trast, those with the reactive subtype scored higher on worry and probability that the thought may come true.

In Study 2, 244 college students were administered a revised version of the ROII designed to more thoroughly examine appraisals and control strategies in response to their primary obsession (Lee & Kwon, 2003). Consistent with the autogenous–reactive distinction, results revealed that (a) in response to autogenous obsessions, participants' distress and threat perception were more focused on the presence of the thoughts themselves, and they reported using more thought control strategies that served to divert attention away from the thoughts (e.g., thought-stopping, dis-traction), and (b) in response to reactive obsessions, participants' perceived threat was more focused on anticipated harm or uncomfortable external conditions asso-ciated with the thoughts, and they reported using more confrontational control strategies designed to change these external conditions (e.g., checking, washing).

These findings suggest that the conceptually driven taxonomy was supported by the latent structure of obsessional experiences reported from college students. Differences in appraisals and control strategies also suggest that the two obsession subtypes have different threat foci (i.e., thoughts themselves vs. external situations).

Lee and his colleagues sought to replicate the findings from Lee and Kwon (2003) with clinical samples of OCD patients (Lee, Kwon, Kwon, & Telch, 2005). Thirty OCD patients were interviewed to identify their primary obsessions, which were then independently classified into either the autogenous (n = 14) or reactive (n = 16) subtype by three doctoral students in clinical psychology. The raters showed excellent inter-rater agreement in making such classifications (Kappa coefficient = .96). Patients' emotional reactions, cognitive appraisals, and control strategies in response to their primary obsessions were also compared between those displaying the autogenous subtype and those displaying the reactive subtype as their primary obsession. Results revealed that autogenous obsessions triggered more guilty feelings, and that the occurrence of the thoughts themselves was perceived as highly threatening as compared to reactive obsessions. Participants with autogenous obsessions also placed greater importance on eliminating (suppressing) their obsessional thoughts and were more likely to employ strategies of thought control in which the primary focus centered on diverting attention away from the thoughts (e.g., thought-stopping, distraction).

In contrast, patients with primary reactive obsessions reported that their obsessions elicited more worries and greater concerns that the thought might come true relative to patients with the autogenous subtype of obsessions. Moreover, patients with reactive obsessions reported a greater sense of responsibility to prevent harm and were more likely to engage in overt rituals such as checking or washing that aimed to correct the situations associated with the thoughts, or checking the rationality of the thoughts. Overall, these findings from a clinical sample of OCD patients are highly consistent with those reported from Lee and Kwon's (2003) student samples. Taken together, these studies suggest that the two proposed subtypes of obsessions differ with respect to (a) the foci of perceived threat, and (b) how the individual responds to such thoughts (appraisals and neutralization strategies).

PHENOMENOLOGICAL DIFFERENCES BETWEEN AUTOGENOUS OBSESSIONS, REACTIVE OBSESSIONS, AND WORRIES

Lee and colleagues hypothesized a continuum in which reactive obsessions fall between autogenous obsessions and worry with respect to several characteristics (Lee, Lee et al., 2005; see Figure 7.1). To test these predictions, nonclinical college students (n = 435) were administered a battery of instruments, including the ROII, the short form of the Worry Domain Questionnaire (WDQ; Stöber & Joormann, 2001), the Thought Control Questionnaire (TCQ; Wells & Davies, 1994), and the Penn State Worry Questionnaire (PSWQ; Meyer, Miller, Metzger, & Borkovec, 1990). Participants were asked to select a primary mental intrusion from the autogenous or reactive factor of the ROII, or from the WDQ. This primary mental intrusion was then identified as falling into one of the following three categories: (a) autogenous obsession, (b) reactive obsession, or (c) worry. Participants were also administered the Thought Examination Scale (TES) constructed by the authors to examine several characteristics of the primary mental intrusions, including the form of the thought, the appraisal of its content, perceptions of how the thought is triggered, and the thought's persistence.

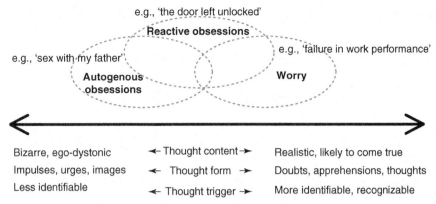

FIGURE 7.1   The continuum hypothesis of obsessions and worry. (From Lee, Lee et al., *Behaviour Research and Therapy, 43*, 999–1010 (2005). Reprinted with permission)

Overall, results were consistent with predictions arising from the autogenous–reactive model. First, a markedly different pattern of correlations emerged between autogenous and reactive obsessions. Compared to autogenous obsessions, reactive obsessions were more strongly associated with worries. Moreover, after controlling for depression and trait anxiety, only reactive obsessions were significantly associated with both of the worry indices. Between-group comparisons on the TES also provided support for the continuum hypothesis: (a) relative to worries, autogenous obsessions were perceived as more bizarre, more unacceptable, and less likely to come true; (b) autogenous obsessions were more likely to take the form of impulses, urges, or images, whereas worries were more likely to take the form of doubts, apprehensions, or thoughts; (c) worries were characterized more by awareness and identifiability of thought triggers; and (d) worries lasted longer than autogenous obsessions, with reactive obsessions falling in between. Finally, those participants reporting reactive obsessions or worries as their primary intrusion were found to use the Worrying thought control strategy, as measured by the TCQ, more often than those reporting autogenous obsessions as their primary mental intrusion. This suggests that compared to autogenous obsessions, reactive obsessions are more similar to worries with respect to several thought characteristics.

Taken together, the data reviewed above support the hypothesis that the three types of mental intrusions fall on a continuum with respect to the various characteristics examined. The differences between worries and autogenous obsessions seem to be more striking than the differences between worries and reactive obsessions. These data provide further support for the proposed taxonomy. Moreover, they are in line with previous findings that have highlighted the differences between obsessions and worries (Langlois, Freeston, & Ladouceur, 2000a, 2000b; Turner, Beidel, & Stanley, 1992; Wells & Davies, 1994), replicating previous findings that worry is perceived as more realistic, less ego-dystonic, more persistent, and more verbally oriented than are obsessions. The continuum hypothesis proposed by Lee, Lee et al. (2005), however, has yet to be examined with samples reporting clinical levels of obsessional and worry symptoms.

THE AUTOGENOUS–REACTIVE TAXONOMY AND FEATURES OF OCD

In the preceding sections, we described key features of autogenous and reactive obsessions, along with supporting research evidence. As an extension of this model, Lee and colleagues have provided preliminary evidence suggesting that the autogenous–reactive distinction could serve to identify two subgroups of OCD patients differing with respect to several OCD-related domains, including symptom profiles, dysfunctional beliefs, and associated personality features. Research evidence for each of these domains will be briefly reviewed in this section.

DIFFERENTIAL ASSOCIATIONS WITH OCD SYMPTOMS

Based on the earlier findings that the two obsession subtypes differ with regard to their threat foci and associated neutralizations (Lee & Kwon, 2003; Lee, Lee et al., 2005), Lee and colleagues hypothesized that the autogenous subtype is most strongly associated with covert or ideational symptoms of OCD (i.e., obsessions) and that the reactive subtype is most strongly associated with overt, behavioral OCD symptoms (i.e., compulsive rituals). To test this hypothesis, Lee & Telch (2005a) examined the association between the autogenous/reactive subtype and OCD symptoms in a large sample of undergraduate students (n = 932) who were administered a packet of instruments, including the ROII, Beck Depresson Inventory (BDI; Beck, Ward, Mendelsohn, Mock, & Erlbaugh, 1961), State-Trait Anxiety Inventory–Trait version (STAI-T; Spielberger, Gorsuch, Luchene, Vagg, & Jacobs, 1983), and the Obsessive–Compulsive Inventory–Revised (OCI–R; Foa et al., 2002). The OCI–R taps six empirically derived dimensions of OCD symptoms: Checking, Hoarding, Neutralizing, Obsessing, Ordering, and Washing. Autogenous and reactive obsession scores were computed from the ROII based on the factor structure previously demonstrated (Lee & Kwon, 2003). Hierarchical regression analyses revealed that, in predicting autogenous obsessions, the six subscales of the OCI–R explained an additional 3.9% of the variance after controlling for the effects of general depression and anxiety. Of the six subscales, Obsessing emerged as the only significant predictor of autogenous obsessions. In contrast, in predicting reactive obsession scores after controlling for depression and anxiety, the six OCI–R subscales explained an additional 21.3% of the variance. Of the six subscales, Checking, Ordering, and Washing emerged as significant predictors of reactive obsessions. These findings support the predictions derived from the autogenous–reactive taxonomy. Moreover, given that most of the OCI–R items (and subscales) assess overt rituals, it is no wonder that the OCI–R subscales explained greater variance in reactive obsessions than in autogenous obsessions.

In a related study (Lee & Telch, 2005b), 460 college students were administered a battery of instruments tapping a wider range of OCD symptoms. Measures included the Symmetry Ordering and Arrangement Questionnaire (SOAQ; Radomsky & Rachman, 2004), the Vancouver Obsessive Compulsive Inventory (VOCI; Thordarson et al., 2004), the ROII, and the Yale–Brown Obsessive Compulsive Scale (Y–BOCS) symptom checklist of obsessions. The SOAQ is a 20-item self-report measure assessing ordering, arranging, and the need for symmetry and exactness in the placement of objects. The VOCI is a 55-item OCD symptom measure consisting of six subscales: Contamination, Checking, Obsessions, Hoarding, Just Right, and Indecisiveness.

Autogenous and reactive obsessions scores computed from the ROII were separately regressed on the subscales of the VOCI and the total scores of the SOAQ. Results revealed that the Obsessions subscale of the VOCI emerged as the only significant predictor of autogenous obsessions, whereas the Contamination, Checking, and Just Right subscales of the VOCI and the total score of the SOAQ emerged as significant predictors of reactive obsessions. In order to rule out the possibility that these findings were limited to the use of a particular instrument (i.e., the ROII), the authors sought to replicate these findings based on autogenous/reactive obsessions scores computed from the Y–BOCS obsession checklist. Four doctoral students were provided a one-page description of the autogenous–reactive model of obsessions. They were then asked to rate each item in the Y–BOCS obsession checklist as either 'autogenous', 'reactive', or 'unclassifiable'. Results demonstrated that the large majority (92%, 34 out of 37) of these obsessions were reliably classified as either autogenous or reactive with good inter-rater reliability (Kappa = .85; 20 autogenous obsessions and 14 reactive obsessions). The types of obsessions deemed 'unclassifiable' were included in the miscellaneous or somatic categories of the Y–BOCS checklist. Hierarchical regression analyses similar to those based on the ROII were then performed to predict autogenous/reactive scores derived from the Y–BOCS. Again, the Obsessions subscale of the VOCI emerged as the only significant predictor of autogenous obsessions, whereas the Contamination and Hoarding subscales of the VOCI, and the total score of the SOAQ were predictive of the reactive obsessions.

Lee, Lee and colleagues (2005) also examined the association between autogenous and reactive obsessions and different OCD symptoms in a clinical sample of OCD patients. Twenty-seven OCD patients were classified as either having primary obsessions of the autogenous subtype (AOs, n = 13) or primary obsessions of the reactive subtype (ROs, n = 14). They were then administered a packet of instruments, including the ROII, the Padua Inventory (PI: Sanavio, 1988), and the Maudsley Obsessional–Compulsive Inventory (MOCI: Hodgson & Rachman, 1977). The ROII was used to reflect the overall severity of obsessional symptoms by its total scores. The PI presents four subscales: (a) Impaired Control over Mental Activities (i.e., lower ability to remove undesirable thoughts, difficulties in simple decisions and doubts, ruminative thinking about low-probability danger, etc.); (b) Becoming Contaminated (i.e., excessive hand washing, stereotyped cleaning, overconcern with dirt, worries about unrealistic contaminations, etc.);

(c) Checking Behavior (i.e., repeatedly checking doors, gas, water taps, letters, money, numbers, etc.); and (d) Urges and Worries of Losing Control of Motor Behavior (i.e., urges of violence against animals or things, impulses to kill oneself or others without reason, fear of losing control over sexual impulse, etc.). The MOCI also taps five different dimensions of OCD symptoms (i.e., Checking, Washing, Slowness, Doubting, and Rumination).

Results revealed that compared to patients with primary reactive obsessions, those with primary autogenous obsessions displayed significantly higher total scores on the ROII, which indicates greater severity of obsessional ideation. In contrast, patients with reactive obsessions scored significantly higher on the MOCI, a measure that mainly taps overt compulsions. The PI, however, which measures both ideational and behavioral symptoms of OCD, yielded no significant group differences. Another multivariate analysis on the subscales from the MOCI and the PI revealed that patients with reactive obsessions displayed more overt behavioral symptoms of OCD than did patients with primarily autogenous obsessions as indicated by their higher scores on the Checking and Washing subscales of the MOCI, as well as the Checking Behaviors subscale of the PI. In contrast, patients with primary autogenous obsessions scored significantly higher on the Urges and Worries of Losing Control subscale of the PI.

Taken together, these findings suggest that reactive obsessions are more likely to be associated with overt OCD symptoms, whereas autogenous obsessions are more likely to be associated with obsessional, ideational OCD symptoms.

DIFFERENTIAL ASSOCIATIONS WITH DYSFUNCTIONAL BELIEFS

Lee, Lee and colleagues (2005) also examined the hypothesis that OCD patients with primary autogenous and reactive obsessions would evidence differential patterns of obsessional (dysfunctional) beliefs, as measured by the Obsessional Belief Questionnaire (OBQ; OCCWG, 2001, 2003, 2005). Specifically, they predicted that compared to patients whose primary obsession was autogenous, those with reactive obsessions would score higher on the belief domains of Inflated Responsibility (i.e., dysfunctional beliefs about one's power to cause or prevent harm), Threat Overestimation (i.e., exaggerations of the probability or severity of harm), Perfectionism (i.e., beliefs that a perfect solution to every problem is possible), and Intolerance of Uncertainty (i.e., the perception of being unable to cope with unpredictable or ambiguous situations). In contrast, it was hypothesized that patients with primary autogenous obsessions would score higher than those with primary reactive obsessions on the belief domains of Control of Thoughts (i.e., dysfunctional beliefs about the ability and importance of controlling intrusive thoughts) and Importance of Thoughts (i.e., dysfunctional beliefs about the meaning of intrusive thoughts) since these beliefs may make the person more likely to perceive one's unwanted thoughts to be threatening and engage in an ineffective struggle with the thoughts.

To this end, Lee and colleagues administered the OBQ to 27 OCD patients, 13 of whom reported autogenous obsessions and 14 of whom reported reactive obsessions as primary symptoms (Lee, Kwon et al., 2005). Consistent with predictions, multivariate analyses demonstrated that those with reactive obsessions were more likely to endorse beliefs indicating intolerance for uncertainty, inflated sense of responsibility, and perfectionism. However, those with autogenous obsessions did not differ from those with reactive obsessions on Control of Thoughts and Importance of Thoughts. It may be that patients with primary reactive obsessions also consider such mental intrusions troublesome even though their perceived threat is more focused on external situations than on the thoughts themselves. OCD patients may generally consider it *desirable* to exert complete control over their mental intrusions. Overall, these data suggest that the two subgroups of OCD patients classified based on the autogenous–reactive taxonomy differ with respect to dysfunctional beliefs related to OCD. These findings, however, need to be replicated with larger samples of OCD patients using a more psychometrically sound instrument.

ASSOCIATIONS WITH DIFFERENT PERSONALITY FEATURES

Lee and colleagues also hypothesized that autogenous/reactive obsessions are associated with different personality features.

Reactive obsessions and perfectionistic personality features

A number of studies have demonstrated the relationship between perfectionistic personality features and OCD (e.g., Bouchard, Rhéaume, & Ladouceur, 1998; Frost and Steketee, 1997). Lee and colleagues hypothesized that compared to autogenous obsessions, reactive obsessions would be more strongly associated with perfectionistic personality features, suspecting that individuals with primary reactive obsessions would display exceedingly high and rigid standards, and strive harder to organize and control their environments to ensure that they are not in unsafe or undesired situations. To test this hypothesis, Lee and colleagues (Lee, Lee et al., 2005) compared 13 patients with primary autogenous obsessions and 14 with primary reactive obsessions on the Multidimensional Perfectionism Scale (MPQ; Frost, Marten, Lahart, & Rosenblate, 1990) administered as a part of the instrument battery (Lee, Lee et al., 2005). This measure consists of six subscales: (a) Concern Over Mistakes (i.e., negative reactions to mistakes and a tendency to interpret mistakes as equivalent to failure), Personal Standards (i.e., a tendency to set excessively high standards and place extreme importance on these high standards for self-evaluation), Parental Expectations (i.e., a tendency to believe one's parents set very high goals), Parental Criticism (i.e., the perception that one's parents were or are overly critical), Doubts about Actions (i.e., a general dissatisfaction with or uncertainty about the quality of one's effort or that one has chosen the right course of action), and Organization (i.e., a tendency to emphasize orderliness and precision in daily tasks).

Consistent with prediction, patients with primary reactive obsessions reported significantly higher scores on Concern over Mistakes, and Personal Standards relative to those with primary autogenous obsessions and also scored higher on Organization, which was marginally significant. These findings suggest that OCD patients whose primary obsession is the reactive type are more likely to interpret mistakes as equivalent to failure, believe that one will lose others' respect contingent on failure, set very high standards for self-evaluation and excessively adhere to orderliness and precision in daily tasks (Lee, Lee et al., 2005).

Autogenous obsessions and schizotypal personality features

Lee and colleagues also hypothesized that compared to reactive obsessions, autogenous obsessions would be more strongly linked to schizotypal personality features such as magical thinking and unusual perceptions. They postulated that autogenous obsessions are more strongly associated with aberrational thinking/perception given the bizarre thought content involving inappropriate sexual, aggressive, or religious thoughts, images, urges, or impulses that appear similar to schizotypal thinking.

To test this hypothesis, a large number of college students (n = 932) were administered a packet of instruments consisting of the ROII, BDI, STAI–T, OCI–R and the Schizotypal Personality Scale (STA; Claridge & Broks, 1984) – a widely used 37-item self-report measure designed to identify a general psychosis-proneness by assessing a multidimensional set of schizotypal traits. In accordance with the current multidimensional conceptualization of schizotypy (Lenzenweger, 1999; Rossi & Daneluzzo, 2002), the STA assesses three robust factors: (a) Magical Thinking; particularly the belief in psychic phenomena, (b) Unusual Perceptual Experiences, and (c) Paranoid Suspiciousness. In particular, we predicted that Magical Thinking and Unusual Perceptual Experiences would be significantly associated with autogenous obsessions, but not with reactive obsessions.

Consistent with our predictions, hierarchical regression analyses revealed that nonclinical obsessions of the autogenous subtype were more strongly associated with schizotypal personality features than with OCD symptom severity, general anxiety, or depression. This association remained significant even after controlling for the effects of depression, general anxiety, and OCD symptoms. In contrast, the relationship between reactive obsessions and schizotypal personality traits was found to be negligible. Autogenous obsessions were best predicted by schizotypal personality traits, whereas reactive obsessions were best predicted by OCD symptom severity. In particular, as predicted, the Magical Thinking and Unusual Perceptual Experiences subscales of the STA emerged as the most potent predictors of autogenous obsessions.

Lee and colleagues conducted another study to further investigate the association between autogenous obsessions and schizotypal traits, particularly anomalous perception and thinking (Lee, Kim, & Kwon, 2005). To this end, the Rorschach Inkblot test (Rorschach, 1942) was administered to 32 schizophrenia patients (SPRs), 15 OCD patients displaying the autogenous subtype as their

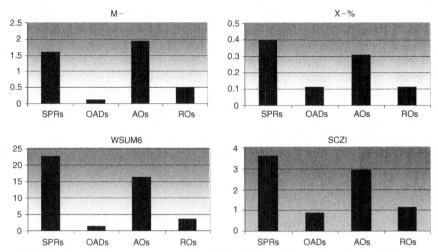

FIGURE 7.2   Differences between SPRs, OADs, AOs, and ROs on M−, X−%, WSUM6, and SCZI. M− (>1) indicates a maladaptive impairment of social perception; X−% (>.29) indicates severe unrealistic perceptions; WSUM6 (>15) reflects a tendency of a formal thought disorder suggesting problems in coherent and logical thinking; SCZI (>3) usually identifies serious adjustment problems attributable to ideational dysfunction (Weiner, 1998)

primary obsession (AOs), 14 OCD patients displaying the reactive subtype as their primary obsession (ROs), and 28 non-psychotic patients with other anxiety disorders (OADs). Rorschach responses were scored based on the Comprehensive System (Exner, 1993), and three domains relevant to the study hypotheses were composed: (a) Perceptual Distortions (X+%, X−%, F+%, S−%, and p), (b) Illogical Ideations (M−, and WSum6), and (c) Schizophrenia Index (SCZI). We hypothesized that AOs and SPRs would display a greater degree of disturbances in these domains than would ROs or OADs. We also expected that AOs and SPRs, and ROs and OADs would not differ from one another. Consistent with our predictions, results revealed that AOs displayed more severely disordered thinking and perception compared to ROs or OADs, whereas ROs and OADs did not differ on most of the indices in the three domains. Both ROs and OADs exhibited adequate levels of perceptual accuracy and ideational logicality. In contrast, AOs displayed severely disordered thinking and perception comparable to those shown by SPRs (i.e., similarly elevated scores on X−>%, M−, and WSum6). Even the Schizophrenia Index did not significantly discriminate SPRs from AOs (see Figure 7.2).

Overall, these findings suggest that of the two obsession subtypes, autogenous obsessions are more strongly associated with schizotypal personality features, particularly deviational thinking and perception. These data are also in line with the earlier finding that OCD patients who reported their primary obsession on the Y–BOCS checklist as aggressive or religious in nature had poorer insight and more perceptual distortions and magical ideation compared to OCD patients with other types of obsessions such as contamination, hoarding, symmetry/order, etc. (Tolin, Abramowitz, Kozak, & Foa, 2001). Moreover, our findings are consistent with the diagnostic criteria for schizotypal personality disorder in *ICD-10* (World Health Organization, 1993), which include ruminations without inner resistance, often with dysmorphophobic, *sexual or aggressive* content, that bear a striking resemblance to the themes of obsessional ruminations reported by OCD patients with autogenous obsessions.

Taken together, it appears that OCD patients with primary autogenous obsessions are more likely to display schizotypal personality features, whereas OCD patients with primary reactive obsessions appear to have greater perfectionistic personality features. Prospective longitudinal studies are needed to examine whether these personality backgrounds would pose a differential developmental risk leading to different types of obsessions.

TWO ACTION TENDENCIES IN OCD

The heterogeneity of clinical manifestations in OCD has led a number of researchers to examine possible underlying subtype structures of its phenomenology. Most authors have attempted to delineate the latent structure of OCD symptoms via factor analysis or classify patients into distinct symptom-based subgroups via cluster analysis (e.g., Baer, 1994; Leckman et al., 1997; Mataix-Cols, Rauch, Manzo, Jenike, & Baer, 1999; Abramowitz, Franklin, Schwartz, & Furr, 2003). However, there are a few limitations worthy of note in these subtyping approaches. First, no consensus has been reached concerning the exact structure of OCD symptoms. Three to seven factors/clusters have been suggested across different studies. Second, the existing literature purporting to identify subtypes relies almost exclusively on overt symptoms such as washing, checking, or hoarding as a basis for subtyping schemes (McKay et al., 2004). Accordingly, washing, checking, hoarding, and ordering have been repeatedly demonstrated as symptom subtypes, whereas pure obsessional, sexual/religious obsessions, and harming obsessions have received mixed empirical support (McKay et al., 2004). Third, these statistical methods have relied on symptom measures without a guiding conceptual model. Consequently, the conceptualization of latent subtypes of OCD has been limited to the manifest items available, and it is clear that this approach systematically under-represents certain subtypes (e.g., mental rituals; McKay et al., 2004).

Unlike factor/cluster analytic approaches based on overt symptom presentation, Lee and his colleagues have investigated two obsession subtypes systematically differing with respect to the functional relationship between thought triggers and obsessions, thought characteristics, associated threat foci, and ensuing cognitive appraisals and compulsive behaviors (Lee & Kwon, 2003; Lee, Lee et al., 2005; Lee & Telch, 2005a, 2005b; Lee, Kwon et al., 2005; Lee, Kim, & Kwon, 2005). Most importantly, the autogenous–reactive taxonomy of obsessions proposes that heterogeneous clinical manifestations of OCD may be reducible to two broad action tendencies. One involves *a struggle with the thoughts themselves*, in which cognitive appraisals are centered on the perceived threats of the thoughts and/or their associated discomfort; the corresponding control strategies are also focused on neutralizing/removing the thoughts themselves. The other action tendency involves *a struggle with the triggering situations* and their perceived threat (i.e., anticipated negative consequences or existing undesired states); the corresponding control strategies are focused on correcting/neutralizing the triggering situations. Autogenous obsessions are more likely to evoke a struggle with the thoughts themselves, whereas reactive obsessions are more likely to evoke a struggle with the thought-triggering situations.

IMPLICATIONS FOR TREATMENT

To our knowledge, the autogenous–reactive taxonomy has yet to be investigated in the context of treatment. We suspect that the proposed taxonomy may have utility in predicting treatment response to both pharmacotherapy and psychosocial treatment. The therapeutic implications of the model are addressed in this next section.

The autogenous–reactive obsessions taxonomy may help to explain why exposure and response prevention (ERP) techniques have been unsuccessful for obsessional ruminators who exhibit obsessions in the absence of overt compulsions (Marks, 1981; Rachman, 1997; Salkovskis & Westbrook, 1989). ERP has been shown to be successful almost exclusively in certain types of OCD patients with explicit and overt compulsions, such as washing and checking (Ball et al., 1996). We presume that OCD patients who most benefit from ERP are those primarily displaying reactive obsessions. One principal reason for proposing poorer treatment response of patients displaying autogenous obsessions is the difficulty of identifying explicit target threats for exposure and identifying target behaviors to block for response prevention. Foa, Abramowitz, Franklin, & Kozak (1999) proposed that patients who articulate a specific feared consequence, relative to patients who do not, may respond better to ERP because their fear allows for threat disconfirmation. Consistently they reported a greater symptom reduction in patients who articulated feared consequences relative to patients who did not (69% vs. 45%). In the same vein, it has also been suggested that compared to reducing subjective distress, preventing harm is a more facilitative motivation leading to a more favorable therapeutic response (Coles, Heimberg, Frost, & Steketee, 2005). From these considerations, ERP is expected to be more applicable for patients classified within the reactive subtype because (a) their fear cues are more explicit and more easily identifiable, (b) their rituals are likely to be more overt, and (c) underlying motivation for rituals is likely to involve harm avoidance, which constitutes favorable conditions for creating potent threat disconfirmation through ERP.

In contrast, for patients with primary autogenous obsessions, intrusive thoughts are perceived as threatening in their own right and lead the person to engage in various avoidant control strategies designed to divert attention away from such stimuli. Thus, applied exposure based on a looped audiotape may prove more effective (Salkovskis & Westbrook, 1989; Freeston et al., 1997). These patients might also profit from a cognitive approach targeting anomalous ideation and perception (e.g., magical thinking). However, considering the evidence suggesting that the presence of schizotypal personality disorder (SPD) predicts poor response to standard pharmacological (SSRIs) and behavioral treatments for OCD (Baer et al., 1992; Jenike et al., 1986; Mundo, Erzegovesi, & Bellodi, 1995; Moritz et al., 2004), it may be that, overall, patients presenting with autogenous obsessions may be less responsive to CBT or pharmacotherapy compared to those primarily displaying reactive obsessions. Randomized controlled trials are required to test these treatment-matching hypotheses.

We are currently working on a project aimed at testing the hypothesized moderation of the autogenous–reactive taxonomy in therapeutic response to psychological and pharmacological treatments for OCD. This will be an important step to demonstrate the clinical utility of the autogenous–reactive obsessions model. Given that approximately 40 to 60% of OCD patients still either drop-out of treatment or fail to respond to either pharmacotherapy or ERP (Baer & Minichiello, 1998; Stanley & Turner, 1995) despite their demonstrated efficacy, indicating large treatment effect sizes (see Abramowitz, 1997), is of great significance to examine putative moderators of treatment for OCD.

FUTURE DIRECTIONS

The autogenous–reactive subtype model has undergone considerable validation work, but more work remains to be done, including treatment outcome studies mentioned in the preceding section. Some future research questions deserve note.

The linkage between autogenous obsessions and schizotypal personality features needs to be replicated using various modes of assessment, including cognitive-perceptual experiment paradigms. For instance, it would be worthwhile to examine using a negative priming paradigm (Enright, Beech, & Claridge, 1995) whether OCD patients displaying the autogenous subtype show deficits in cognitive inhibition similar to those observed among patients with schizophrenia (Beech, Powell, McWilliam, & Claridge, 1989). This line of research may also contribute to the existing literature suggesting a possible linkage between OCD and schizotypy (e.g., Lee, Cougle, & Telch, 2005; Rossi & Daneluzzo, 2002).

On a related note, future research should address patients' reactions associated with their autogenous obsessions. Although the model posits that reactive obsessions tend to be more strongly associated with overt rituals, autogenous obsessions can also be accompanied by overt rituals. However, the overt rituals performed in response to autogenous obsessions tend to be more magical, superstitious or unrealistic (e.g., compulsively touch things beginning with the letter M five times to neutralize the obsession of having sex with one's Mother), whereas those performed in response to reactive obsessions are more likely to be characterized by a more realistic and functional linkage to the triggering situations (e.g., engaging in a washing ritual to remove germs, or checking in order to prevent a terrible mistake). In the case of autogenous obsessions, inexplicit thought triggers and neutralization strategies and their illogical relationship with intrusive thoughts, may contribute to the magical nature of these rituals.

Future work should also be devoted to developing a reliable instrument (e.g., a structured interview) for classifying obsessions into the two subtypes. Some obsessions may require careful consideration of the associated threat focus (beyond the apparent theme of the thoughts) for such classification. For instance, some patients may develop aggressive thoughts into repulsive obsessions in the form of *urges* or *impulses*; whereas others may develop realistic *concerns* or *doubts* that they will harm or have harmed someone. In the former case (typical of the autogenous subtype), the individual may attempt to neutralize the thought itself to reduce the associated anxiety, whereas in the latter case (typical of the reactive subtype), he or she might either physically check to see if harm has been committed, or seek reassurance from others that future harm is not likely. Thus, although both obsessions involve a similar theme, they represent different subtypes because they are associated with different thought forms, threat foci, appraisals, and neutralization strategies.

CONCLUSIONS

The autogenous–reactive obsession model suggests two different subtypes of obsessions differing systematically in several aspects, including focus of perceived threat, types of associated appraisals, and types of neutralization strategies used in response to the obsession. We propose that OCD may be represented by two broad action tendencies based on this subtyping scheme: a struggle with thoughts themselves and a struggle with situations and stimuli that trigger obsessional thoughts. We expect that continued research on this taxonomy will contribute to clarifying the heterogeneity underlying the multifaceted clinical manifestations of OCD.

REFERENCES

Abramowitz, J. S. (1997). Effectiveness of psychological and pharmacological treatments for obsessive–compulsive disorder: A quantitative review. *Journal of Consulting and Clinical Psychology, 65*, 44–52.

Abramowitz, J. S., Franklin, M. E., Schwartz, S. A., & Furr, J. M. (2003). Symptom presentation and outcome of cognitive–behavioral therapy for obsessive–compulsive disorder. *Journal of Consulting and Clinical Psychology, 71*, 1049–1057.

American Psychiatric Association (1994). *Diagnostic and statistical manual of mental disorders* (4th ed.) *(DSM-IV)*. Washington: APA.

Baer, L. (1994). Factor-analysis of symptom subtypes of obsessive–compulsive disorder and their relation to personality and tic disorders. *Journal of Clinical Psychiatry, 55*, 18–23.

Baer, L., & Minichiello, W. E. (1998). Behavior therapy for obsessive–compulsive disorder. In M. A. Jenike, L. Baer, & W. E. Minichiello (Eds.), *Obsessive–compulsive disorder: practical management*. St Louis, MO: Mosby.

Baer, L., Jenike, M. A., Black, D. W., Treece, C., Rosenfeld, R., & Griest, J. (1992). Effect of axis-II diagnoses on treatment outcome with clomipramine in 55 patients with obsessive–compulsive disorder. *Archives of General Psychiatry, 49*, 862–866.

Ball, S., Baer, L., & Otto, M. (1996). Symptom subtypes of obsessive–compulsive disorder in behavioural treatment studies: A quantitative review. *Behaviour Research and Therapy, 34*, 47–51.

Beck, A.T., Ward, C.H., Mendelsohn, M., Mock, J., & Erlbaugh, J. (1961). An inventory for measuring depression. *Archives of General Psychiatry, 4*, 561–571.

Beech, A. R., Powell, T. J., McWilliam, J., & Claridge, G. S. (1989). Evidence of reduced cognitive inhibition in schizophrenia. *British Journal of Clinical Psychology, 28*, 109–116.

Bouchard, C., Rhéaume, J., & Ladouceur, R. (1998). Responsibility and perfectionism in OCD: An experimental study. *Behaviour Research & Therapy, 37*, 239–248.

Claridge, G., & Broks, P. (1984). Schizotypy and hemisphere function. I. Theoretical considerations and the measurement of schizotypy. *Personality and Individual Differences, 5*, 633–648.

Coles, M. E., Heimberg, R. G., Frost, R. O., & Steketee, G. (2005). Not just right experiences and obsessive–compulsive features: Experimental and self-monitoring perspectives. *Behaviour Research and Therapy, 43*, 153–167.

Enright, S. J., Beech, A. R., & Claridge, G. S. (1995). A further investigation of cognitive inhibition in obsessive–compulsive disorder and other anxiety disorders. *Personality and individual differences, 19*, 535–542.

Exner, J. E. (1993). *The Rorschach: A comprehensive system*. Volume I. *Basic Foundations* (3rd ed.). New York: Wilec.

Foa, E. B., Abramowitz, J. S., Franklin, M. E., & Kozak, M. J. (1999). Feared consequences, fixity of belief, and treatment outcome in patients with obsessive–compulsive disorder. *Behavior Therapy, 30*, 717–724.

Foa, E. B., Huppert, J. D., Leiberg, S., Langner, R., Kichic, R., Hajcak, G., & Salkovskis, P. M. (2002). The obsessive–compulsive inventory: development and validation of a short version. *Psychological Assessment, 14*, 485–496.

Freeston, M. H., Ladouceur, R., Gagnon, F., Thibodeau, N., Rhéaume, J., Letarte, H. et al. (1997). Cognitive–behavioral treatment of obsessive thoughts: A controlled study. *Journal of Consulting and Clinical Psychology, 65*, 405–413.

Frost, R. O., & Steketee, G. (1997). Perfectionism in obsessive–compulsive disorder patients. *Behaviour Research and Therapy, 35*, 291–296.

Frost, R. O., Marten, P. A., Lahart, C., & Rosenblate, R. (1990). The dimensions of perfectionism. *Cognitive Therapy and Research, 14*, 449–468.

Hodgson, R. J., & Rachman, S. (1977). Obsessional–compulsive complaints. *Behaviour Research and Therapy, 15*, 389–395.

Jenike, M. A., Baer, L., Minichiello, W. E., Schwartz, C. E., & Carey, R. J. (1986). Concomitant obsessive–compulsive disorder and schizotypal personality-disorder. *American Journal of Psychiatry, 143*, 530–532.

Langlois, F., Freeston, M. H., & Ladouceur, R. (2000a). Differences and similarities between obsessive intrusive thoughts and worry in nonclinical population: study 1. *Behaviour Research and Therapy, 38*, 157–173.

Langlois, F., Freeston, M. H., & Ladouceur, R. (2000b). Differences and similarities between obsessive intrusive thoughts and worry in nonclinical population: study 2. *Behaviour Research and Therapy, 38*, 175–189.

Leckman, J. F., Grice, D. E., Boardman, J., Zhang, H. P., Vitale, A., Bondi, C., Alsobrook, J., Peterson, B. S., Cohen, D. J., Rasmussen, S. A., Goodman, W. K., McDougle, C. J., & Pauls, D. L. (1997). Symptoms of obsessive–compulsive disorder. *American Journal of Psychiatry, 154*, 911–917.

Lee, H.-J., & Telch, M. J. (2005a). Autogenous/reactive obsessions and their relationship with schizotypal personality features and OCD symptoms. *Journal of Anxiety Disorders, 19*, 793–805.

Lee, H.-J., & Telch, M. J. (2005b). Further validation of the autogenous–reactive obsession model. Poster presented at the annual meeting of the Association for Behavioral and Cognitive Therapies, Washington, DC.

Lee, H.-J., Cougle, R. J., & Telch, M. J. (2005). Thought–action fusion and its relationship to schizotypy and OCD symptoms. *Behaviour Research and Therapy, 43*, 29–41.

Lee, H.-J., Kim, Z.-S., & Kwon, S.-M. (2005). Thought disorder in patients with obsessive–compulsive disorder. *Journal of Clinical Psychology, 61*, 401–413.

Lee, H.-J., & Kwon, S.-M. (2003). Two different types of obsession: Autogenous obsessions and reactive obsessions. *Behaviour Research and Therapy, 41*, 11–29.

Lee, H.-J., Kwon, S.-M., Kwon, J.-S., & Telch, M. J. (2005). Testing the autogenous–reactive model of obsessions. *Depression and Anxiety, 21*, 118–129.

Lee, H.-J., Lee, S.-H., Kim, H.-S., Kwon, S.-M., & Telch, M. J. (2005). A comparison of autogenous/reactive obsessions and worry in a non-clinical population: A test of the continuum hypothesis. *Behaviour Research and Therapy, 43*, 999–1010.

Lenzenweger, M. F. (1999). Schizophrenia: refining the phenotype, resolving endophenotypes. *Behaviour Research and Therapy, 37*, 281–295.

Marks, I. M. (1981). Review of behavioral psychotherapy: I. Obsessive–compulsive disorders. *American Journal of Psychiatry, 138*, 584–592.

Mataix-Cols, D., Rauch, S. L., Manzo, P. A., Jenike, M. A., & Baer, L. (1999). Use of factor-analysed symptom dimensions to predict outcome with serotonin reuptake inhibitors and placebo in the treatment of obsessive–compulsive disorder. *American Journal of Psychiatry, 156*, 1409–1416.

McKay, D., Abramowitz, J. S., Calamari, J. E., Kyrios, M., Radomsky, A., Sookman, D., Taylor, S., & Wilhelm, S. (2004). A critical evaluation of obsessive–compulsive disorder subtypes: Symptoms versus mechanisms. *Clinical Psychology Review, 24*, 283–313.

Meyer, T. J., Miller, M. L., Metzger, R. L., & Borkovec, T. D. (1990). Development and validation of the Penn state worry questionnaire. *Behaviour Research and Therapy, 28*, 487–495.

Moritz, S., Fricke, S., Jacobsen, D., Kloss, M., Wein, C., Rufer, M., Katenkamp, B., Farhumand, R., & Hand, I. (2004). Positive schizotypal symptoms predict treatment outcome in obsessive–compulsive disorder. *Behaviour Research and Therapy, 42*, 217–227.

Mundo, E., Erzegovesi, S., & Bellodi, L. (1995). Follow-up of obsessive–compulsive patients treated with proserotonergic agents. *Journal of Clinical Psychopharmacology, 15*, 288–289.

OCCWG (Obsessive Compulsive Cognitions Working Group) (2001). Development and initial validation of the obsessive beliefs questionnaire and the interpretation of intrusions inventory. *Behaviour Research and Therapy, 39*, 987–1006.

OCCWG (Obsessive Compulsive Cognitions Working Group) (2003). Psychometric validation of the obsessive belief questionnaire and the interpretation of intrusion inventory: Part 1. *Behaviour Research and Therapy, 41*, 863–878.

OCCWG (Obsessive Compulsive Cognitions Working Group) (2005). Psychometric validation of the obsessive belief questionnaire and the interpretation of intrusion inventory: Part 2. Factor analyses and testing of a brief version. *Behaviour Research and Therapy, 43*, 1527–1542.

Purdon, C. L., & Clark, D. A. (1993). Obsessive intrusive thoughts in nonclinical subjects. Part I. Content and relation with depressive, anxious and obsessional symptoms. *Behaviour Research and Therapy, 31*, 713–720.

Rachman, S. (1997). A cognitive theory of obsessions. *Behaviour Research and Therapy, 35*, 793–802.

Radmosky, A. S., & Rachman, S. (2004). Symmetry, ordering and arranging compulsive behavior. *Behaviour Research and Therapy, 42*, 893–913.

Rorschach, H. (1942). *Psychodiagnostics: A diagnostic test based on perception.* Oxford: Hans Huber.

Rossi, A., & Daneluzzo, E. (2002). Schizotypal dimensions in normals and schizophrenic patients: A comparison with other clinical samples. *Schizophrenia Research, 54*, 67–75.

Salkovskis, P. M. (1985). Obsessional–compulsive problem: A cognitive–behavioral analysis. *Behaviour Research and Therapy, 23*, 571–583.

Salkovskis, P. M., & Westbrook, D. (1989). Behaviour therapy and obsessional ruminations: Can failure be turned into success? *Behaviour Research and Therapy, 27*, 141–160.

Sanavio, E. (1988). Obsessions and compulsions: The Padua Inventory. *Behaviour Research and Therapy, 26*, 169–177.

Spielberger, C. D., Gorsuch, R. L., Luchene, R. E., Vagg, P. R., & Jacobs, G. A. (1970). *Manual for the state–trait anxiety inventory*. Palo Alto, CA: Consulting Psychologists Press.

Stanley, M. A., & Turner, S. M. (1995). Schizotypal features in obsessive–compulsive disorder. *Comprehensive Psychiatry, 31*, 511–518.

Stöber, J., & Joormann, J. (2001). A short form of the worry domain questionnaire: construction and factorial validation. *Personality and Individual Differences, 31*, 591–598.

Thordarson, D. S., Radomsky, A. S., Rachman, S., Shafran, R., Sawchuk, C. N., & Hakstian, A. R. (2004). The Vancouver Obsessional Compulsive Inventory (VOCI). *Behaviour Research and Therapy, 42*, 1289–1314.

Tolin, D. F., Abramowitz, J. S., Kozak, M. J., & Foa, E. B. (2001). Fixity of belief, perceptual aberration, and magical ideation in obsessive–compulsive disorder. *Journal of Anxiety Disorders, 15*, 501–510.

Turner, S. M., Beidel, D. C., & Stanley, M. A. (1992). Are obsessional thoughts and worry different cognitive phenomenon? *Clinical Psychology Review, 12*, 257–270.

Weiner, I. B. (1998). *Principles of Rorschach interpretation*. Mahwah, NJ: Lawrence Erlbaum Associates.

Wells, A., & Davies, M. (1994). The thought control questionnaire: a measure of individual differences in the control of unwanted thoughts. *Behaviour Research and Therapy, 32*, 871–878.

World Health Organization (1993). *The ICD-10 Classification of Mental and Behavioural Disorders: Diagnostic Criteria for Research*. Geneva: WHO.

8

DISCUSSION: CONCEPTUALIZING SUBTYPES OF OBSESSIVE–COMPULSIVE DISORDER

DEAN MCKAY[1], JONATHAN S. ABRAMOWITZ[2], AND STEVEN TAYLOR[3]

[1]*Department of Psychology, Fordham University;*
[2]*Department of Psychology, University of North Carolina at Chapel Hill;*
[3]*Department of Psychiatry, University of British Columbia*

Although the *Diagnostic and Statistical Manual of Mental Disorders* (*DSM-IV*) (American Psychiatric Association, 2000) suggests that obsessive–compulsive disorder (OCD) is a coherent syndrome, the chapters in Part I of this volume offer a compelling case that OCD is highly heterogeneous. Obsessional fears, compulsive rituals, avoidance patterns, and covert neutralizing strategies are as idiosyncratic as the personal concerns and life experiences of individuals seeking evaluation and treatment, thus making it difficult to identify a single 'textbook' profile of OCD. Yet because this wide variation in symptom presentation is generally limited to certain themes (e.g., contamination, symmetry), there are collections of typical clinical profiles or 'subtypes'.

As the table of contents for Part I illustrates, the most common OCD subtyping schemes at present are concerned with overt symptom theme (for a review see McKay et al., 2004). This approach has proven clinically fruitful because various

Correspondence to: Dean McKay, Department of Psychology, Fordham University, 441 East Fordham Road, Bronx, NY 10458.

symptoms show differential responses to particular interventions (Abramowitz, Franklin, Schwartz, & Furr, 2003). Nevertheless, reliance purely on symptoms as a basis for subtyping is not without limitations. In this discussion we integrate material from the chapters in Part I to arrive at conclusions regarding the conceptualization of OCD in terms of its heterogeneity. We begin by summarizing relevant theoretical issues and highlighting the historical context in which recent research in this area has occurred. Next, we discuss the possibilities of moving beyond overt symptom themes in conceptualizing the heterogeneity of OCD. Finally, we draw conclusions regarding the status of OCD as comprised of subtypes and offer a look to the future.

WHY SUBTYPES?

The reason researchers and clinicians are interested in identifying subtypes of OCD is similar to the reason we delineate psychiatric syndromes in the first place. Blashfield and Livesley (1999) noted that this process facilitates (a) communication among mental health professionals, (b) the development of theories to explain psychopathology, (c) the prediction of clinical course, and (d) the matching of patients to effective treatments. Numerous proposals for classifying psychiatric disorders have been studied. As it is in the *DSM-IV*, the idea that psychiatric disorders can be usefully classified into categories is implied in research on OCD subtyping: the categorical approach works best 'when all members of a diagnostic class are homogeneous, when there are clear boundaries between classes, and when the different classes are mutually exclusive' (American Psychiatric Association, 2000, p. xxxi).

As with the *DSM*'s approach to defining separate psychiatric disorders, OCD subtyping efforts have been based, to some extent, on the notion that advances in understanding and treating such disorders are most likely to occur if we study homogeneous groups (Robins & Guze, 1970). Specifically, Robins & Guze (1970) proposed:

> Homogeneous diagnostic grouping provides the soundest base for studies of etiology, pathogenesis, and treatment. The roles of heredity, family interactions, intelligence, education, and sociological factors are most simply, directly, and reliably studied when the group studied is as homogeneous as possible. (p. 984)

To identify and validate such groups, Robins & Guze outlined five phases that interact with one another so that new findings in any one of the phases may lead to modifications in one or more of the other phases. The process has as its aim ongoing self-rectification and increasing refinement, which may lead to more homogeneous diagnostic grouping. The five phases are as follows:

1. *Clinical observations.* The clinical description of a proposed diagnostic syndrome (or subtype) may be based on some striking clinical feature, or on a combination of descriptive features thought to be associated with one another (e.g., signs and symptoms and demographic features).

2. *Laboratory studies.* These include chemical, physiological, neuroimaging, and anatomical (e.g., biopsy and autopsy) findings. Psychological studies (e.g., tests of cognitive abilities or functioning) may also be included. When laboratory tests are consistent with the defined clinical picture, they permit a more refined classification.

3. *Exclusion of other disorders.* Exclusionary criteria (including criteria for discriminating subtypes) are developed on the basis of clinical descriptions and laboratory findings. The criteria should permit exclusion of borderline or doubtful cases so that the index group may be as homogeneous as possible.

4. *Follow-up studies.* These studies can be used to determine whether the diagnostic category or subtype is stable over time. Do patients with one putative OCD subtype, for example, tend to switch to another subtype over time? Follow-up studies can also investigate whether members from a putative homogeneous group differ in their course of disorder or treatment response. A putative subtype may not be homogeneous if it can be clearly divided into patients with good versus poor prognosis.

5. *Family studies.* The validity of a proposed type or subtype of psychiatric disorder would be supported by showing that it runs in families or is of increased prevalence in first-degree relatives, reflecting the effects of genetic or shared environmental factors.

As McKay and colleagues (2004) have pointed out, researchers interested in identifying subtypes of OCD have used a number of the approaches outlined above, with a focus on clinical descriptions being the most often employed method. Other investigators have focused on comorbidity or laboratory tests. As a result, proposed OCD subtype schemes have included early vs. later onset OCD, presence vs. absence of ties, presence vs. absence of childhood streptococci-related autoimmune disorders, and presence vs. absence of psychotic or neurological features (e.g. Albert, Maina, Ravizza, Bogetto, & Leonard, 2002; Allen, Leonard, & Swedo, 1995; Calamari, Wiegartz, & Janeck, 1999; Eichstedt & Arnold, 2001; Geller et al., 1998; Sobin et al., 2000). The merits of various subtyping schemes depend on a number of factors, including the methodology, empirical support for each subtype, and whether some subtypes have advantages over others.

SYMPTOMS AS SUBTYPES: CATEGORICAL OR DIMENSIONAL?

Does a system consisting of multiple syndromal categories (subtypes) have advantages over a dimensional model in which clinical features are classified in terms of a quantification of attributes? A subtyping system might be superior in cases where a critical attribute is not dimensional. For example, if some sorts of OCD arise from streptococcal infections, a categorical system would seem more appropriate (i.e., you either have the infection or you don't). We next consider methodological issues in subtyping OCD. One of the chief methods employed for determining subtypes has relied upon statistical methods designed to form broad categories from a larger number of disparate observations.

STATISTICAL ISSUES IN SUBTYPING

The empirical literature related to subtypes of OCD has relied primarily on factor analytic approaches in determining groups of symptoms that form larger, internally consistent categories. The majority of this literature has relied on the Yale–Brown Obsessive Compulsive Scale (YBOCS) symptom checklist (Goodman et al., 1989). However, factor analyses do not identify groups of individuals that are distinguishable on the basis of symptoms, but instead identifies groups of symptoms that typically occur together; individuals can, and often do, have more than one set of symptoms according to this approach. Therefore, the factor analytic models serve the purpose of identifying dimensions of symptoms, not separate groups of patients with particular symptom profiles (McKay et al., 2004).

Recent findings do suggest that some symptoms may be unique subtypes of OCD, based on either symptoms or cognitions. Using taxometric methods, Haslam et al. (2005) found that OCD may be comprised of three symptom-based subtypes (contamination, checking, and obsessions) and three subtypes based on cognitions (responsibility, perfectionism, and importance of thoughts). Taxometric analyses (Waller & Meehl, 1998) allow for the identification of distinctions between groups of respondents on the basis of profiles from indicator variables. An important limitation of taxometric analysis is the reliance on large sample sizes to establish stable estimates of taxonicity from sets of indicator variables. Since the identification of symptom subtypes in OCD is best conducted with individuals diagnosed with the disorder, this procedure typically requires coordination among several research groups. For example, in the Haslam et al. (2005) study, the data was obtained from groups contributing to the larger Obsessive Compulsive Cognitions Working Group validation study related to the Obsessive Beliefs Questionnaire (OCCWG, 2005). Even in the context of obsessive–compulsive cognitions there is the potential for subtyping, since a subgroup of individuals diagnosed with the disorder do not endorse cognitions theoretically related to the disorder (Taylor et al., 2006).

A problem with using taxometric methods to identify putative OCD subtypes is that taxometrics only tests two kinds of models; a model in which a construct is continuous (dimensional) and a model in which a construct consists of two groups (the taxon and its complement). Taxometric methods were not designed to test whether a construct consists of three or more groups. If a construct defined by, say, severity of contamination obsessions and washing compulsions was subjected to a taxometric analysis, then the results might spuriously indicate the washing/contamination construct was dimensional, when in fact it may consist of three or more categories or subtypes (e.g., mild symptoms, moderately severe symptoms, and very severe symptoms associated with overvalued ideation). Thus, researchers should not be overly reliant on taxometric methods, or any statistical method for that matter, to investigate OCD subtypes. Researchers should consider using statistical methods that enable investigators to identify three or more groups, such as latent class analysis or cluster analysis (e.g., see Hagenaars & McCutcheon, 2002).

MEASUREMENT ISSUES IN SUBTYPING

The literature examining subtypes based on symptoms has generally supported the following major dimensions: obsessions (such as sexual, aggressive, religious, or somatic) and checking; symmetry, ordering, and arranging; contamination obsessions and cleaning compulsions; and hoarding (Abramowitz, McKay, & Taylor, 2005). Of these, one stands out for its difference from the others. Hoarding has been conceptualized in a manner that is distinct from other symptoms associated with OCD (Frost & Hartl, 1996), and the treatment of hoarding is quite different from approaches for other forms of OCD (Steketee & Frost, 2006). Further, the prognosis for outcome associated with hoarding is significantly poorer than for other symptom clusters when exposure with response prevention is applied (Abramowitz et al., 2003). This suggests that hoarding is syndromally different from OCD, and possibly an entity separate from OCD itself.

The question of interest here is whether hoarding belongs in the category of OCD at all. Each study that isolates hoarding as a 'subtype,' in relying on the Y–BOCS symptom checklist, has applied either factor analysis or cluster analysis. These statistical procedures rely on covariance matrices of items to determine broader groupings (Gorsuch, 1983). The procedures, however, are at the mercy of the items and the conceptualization of the assessment tool. In this case, the inclusion of hoarding, as with all the other symptoms listed, was based on clinical observations. However, were there items on the Y–BOCS checklist for pyromania, we would be considering pyromania a subtype, because items for this problem are unlikely to load on any other symptom dimension factor. This is not enough to support its inclusion as a subtype however, since other syndromal signs are necessary for inclusion. In the case of hoarding, the evidence is increasingly pointing away from OCD, despite its inclusion on the Y–BOCS checklist and its persistent presence as a symptom subtype.

BEYOND SYMPTOM SUBTYPES

THEORETICAL MODELS

As noted above, the utility in examining symptoms of OCD in isolation from the disorder itself is for the development of interventions. The chapters in this section robustly support this assertion. However, classification of subtypes of OCD on the basis of symptoms appears to have limited utility. An examination of the literature suggests that other approaches may be viable in subtyping OCD, ones based on conceptual frameworks derived from the very nature of obsessions and compulsions rather than from their manifest symptoms.

One prominent example is the distinction between autogenous and reactive obsessions (Lee & Telch, Chapter 7). This approach has the benefit of conceptualizing core symptoms of OCD across symptom domains. This eliminates the problem of multiple 'subtypes' in a single individual with OCD, and allows for model testing associated with hypothesized presentations of the disorder. This model appears promising in light of preliminary research and the link to clinical interventions inherent in its conceptualization.

The importance of such etiology-based classification is underscored by considering classificatory systems in the biological sciences. The most widely used system for classifying organisms is based on cladistics (Kitching, Forey, Humphries, & Williams, 1998), which emphasizes the process of evolution. The merits of this approach for classifying OCD (and psychopathology in general) remain to be investigated. There are several challenges in applying cladistics to the classification of psychopathology. However, one aspect of the cladistic approach that can be used is the emphasis on theory; that is, the theory of evolution. The fact that cladistics is the dominant school of biological classification suggests that classification of psychopathology eventually must incorporate theories into a psychiatric classification system (Blashfield & Livesley, 1999).

DIAGNOSTIC COMORBIDITY MODELS

There are other potential approaches to conceptualizing subtypes without resorting to a symptom profile approach. One approach involves the examination of pathology that occurs with significantly higher frequency in conjunction with OCD when compared to other disorders. For example, tic disorders, particularly Tourette's syndrome, appear to have a higher rate of comorbid OCD compared to other diagnoses (Olatunji et al., Chapter 6). Approaches of this sort allow for the development of models, both psychological and pathophysiological, of treatment for common presentations of the disorder.

Some conceptualizations of the disorder have not been pursued extensively, despite the accumulation of evidence in their favor. Although not represented in this text, the proposed schizotype model represents one such example (Enright & Beech, 1997). Enright argued that OCD, in its entirety, was more akin to a schizotype on the basis of performance on particular cognitive processing tasks. While this may be an overstatement, there is reason to suggest that OCD may present with schizotypal features. For example, recent evidence has suggested that some individuals with OCD have high levels of magical ideation, a putative indicator for schizotypy (Einstein & Menzies, 2004). Further, a significant subgroup of individuals with OCD was determined to also have positive signs of schizotypy (Sobin et al., 2000). It has also been noted for some time in the literature that a common comorbid presentation of OCD is with schizotypal personality, which in turn presents a significant complication in the treatment of the condition (Stanley, Turner, & Borden, 1990). These findings suggest that this, and possibly other, conceptually derived subtype schemes exist that would robustly describe the various presentations of OCD.

CONCLUSIONS

Nearly 3 decades ago the prominent British psychiatrist Robert E. Kendell wrote that:

> Few psychiatric disorders have yet been adequately validated and it is still an open issue whether there are genuine boundaries between the clinical syndromes recognized in contemporary classifications, or between these syndromes and normality. In the long run validation depends on the elucidation of aetiological processes. (1989, p. 45)

His conclusions are as relevant today as they were then, and are particularly applicable to OCD. A growing body of research suggests that OCD is not a unitary syndrome; it is heterogeneous both in terms of symptoms and quite probably in terms of etiology. In the process of carving up OCD symptom subtypes the question arises as to the number and scope of each subtype. The more subtypes, the smaller the number and type of symptoms contained in each subtype. The most fine-grained 'subtyping' scheme would be to focus on the etiology and treatment of individual types of symptoms (e.g., sexual obsessions) rather than on groups of symptoms. Persons (1986) identified several advantages to focusing on symptoms and other psychological phenomena as the level of analysis (i.e., the *symptom approach* – SA) instead of focusing on psychiatric syndromes, including symptom subtypes or diagnoses (the *diagnostic category approach* – DA). The advantages of the SA for understanding psychopathology include the following: (a) the SA permits a more detailed or fine-grained analysis of phenomena that might be ignored or overlooked by the DA; (b) the SA contributes to the development of theories of psychopathology, particularly to the development of elaborate hypotheses linking specific clinical phenomena to underlying mechanisms; (c) the SA, unlike the DA, recognizes the possibility of the continuity of clinical phenomena and normal phenomena, both in terms of phenomenology and possible mechanisms; and (d) the SA contributes to the refinement of systems of diagnostic classification. Put in the context of OC symptom subtyping, this raises the question of whether a focus on symptoms, as in Person's SA, is more fruitful for understanding and treating OCD than current symptom-based subtyping schemes in which OCD is divided into groups of symptoms (i.e., a form of DA). Further research is required to address this important question.

There are no models that completely account for the diversity of symptom presentations of OCD (for discussion, see Taylor, McKay, & Abramowitz, 2005). Therefore, a potentially more fruitful approach lies in describing subsets of clinical presentations that are within the diagnostic confines of OCD. At this point, the symptom-based approach to subtyping has led to important findings to inform treatment development (Sookman, Abramowitz, Calamari, Wilhelm, & McKay, 2005). However, there are important limitations to the symptom-based approach. Future research devoted to conceptually derived models of valid groupings of patients within the larger diagnosis of OCD appears promising in this regard. This will eventually permit the development of OCD subtypes based on etiology or based on other important considerations such as treatment response. Etiological-based subtyping would be used primarily for understanding the myriad ways in which obsessions and compulsions arise, whereas treatment-based subtyping would be used for the clinical goal of selecting the intervention that is most likely to be beneficial for a given individual. Etiology-based and treatment response-based subtyping schemes may turn out to be quite similar to one another. For example, a schizotypal subtype would presumably be treated with a different therapy than a hoarding subtype. Although an etiology-based approach to subtyping may eventually prove to be more useful than a symptom-based approach, this does not mean that the content of symptoms is irrelevant for understanding OCD. A full understanding of this disorder requires, for example, an understanding of how cultural factors and other social influences interact with psychobiological mechanisms to shape the form and content of obsessions and compulsions (Sica et al., in press).

Finally, as research goes forward, it will be important to remember that OCD subtyping is not simply an academic exercise akin to classifying different kinds of butterflies or frogs. Rather, an important goal of OCD subtyping is to better understand and help people afflicted by the often severe and debilitating symptoms of the syndrome currently called OCD.

REFERENCES

Abramowitz, J. S., Franklin, M. E., Schwartz, S. A., & Furr, J. M. (2003). Symptom presentation and outcome of cognitive–behavioral therapy for obsessive–compulsive disorder. *Journal of Consulting and Clinical Psychology, 71*, 1049–1057.

Abramowitz, J. S., McKay, D., & Taylor, S. (2005). Special series: Subtypes of obsessive–compulsive disorder. Introduction. *Behavior Therapy, 36*, 367–369.

Albert, U., Maina, G., Ravizza, L., & Bogetto, F. (2002). An exploratory study on obsessive–compulsive disorder with and without a familial component: Are there any phenomenological differences? *Psychopathology, 35*, 8–16.

Allen, A. J., Leonard, H. L., & Swedo, S. E. (1995). Case study: A new infection-triggered, autoimmune subtype of pediatric OCD and Tourette's syndrome. *Journal of the American Academy of Child and Adolescent Psychiatry, 34*, 307–311.

American Psychiatric Association (2000). *Diagnostic and Statistical Manual of Mental Disorders* (4th ed., text rev.) (*DSM-IV-TR*). Washington, DC: APA.

Blashfield, R. K., & Livesley, W. J. (1999). Classification. In T. Millon, P. H. Blaney, & R. D. Davis (Eds.), *Oxford textbook of psychopathology* (pp. 3–28). New York: Oxford University Press.

Calamari, J. E., Wiegartz, P. S., & Janeck, A. S. (1999). Obsessive–compulsive disorder subgroups: A symptom-based clustering approach. *Behaviour Research and Therapy, 37*, 113–125.

Eichstedt, J. A., & Arnold, S. L. (2001). Childhood-onset obsessive–compulsive disorder: A tic-related subtype of OCD? *Clinical Psychology Review, 21*, 137–158.

Einstein, D. A., & Menzies, R. G. (2004). The presence of magical thinking in obsessive–compulsive disorder. *Behaviour Research and Therapy, 42*, 539–549.

Enright, S., & Beech, A. (1997). Schizotypy and obsessive–compulsive disorder. In G. Claridge (Ed.), *Schizotypy: Implications for illness and health* (pp. 202–223). New York: Oxford.

Frost, R. O., & Hartl, T. L. (1996). A cognitive-behavioral model of compulsive hoarding. *Behaviour Research and Therapy, 14*, 341–350.

Geller, D., Biederman, J., Jones, J., Park, K., Schwartz, S., Shapiro, S., & Coffey, B. (1998). Is juvenile obsessive–compulsive disorder a developmental subtype of the disorder? A review of the pediatric literature. *Journal of the American Academy of Child and Adolescent Psychiatry, 37*, 420–427.

Goodman, W. K., Price, L. H., Rasmussen, S. A., Mazure, C., Delgado, P., Heninger, G. R., et al. (1989). The Yale–Brown Obsessive–Compulsive Scale: Development, use, reliability, and validity. *Archives of General Psychiatry, 46*, 1006–1011.

Gorsuch, R. L. (1983). *Factor analysis* (2nd ed.). Mahwah, NJ: Erlbaum.

Hagenaars, J. A., & McCutcheon, A. L. (2002). *Applied latent class analysis.* Cambridge: Cambridge University Press.

Haslam, N., Williams, B. A., Kyrios, M., McKay, D., & Taylor, S. (2005). Subtyping obsessive–compulsive disorder: A taxometric analysis. *Behavior Therapy, 36*, 381–391.

Kendell, R. E. (1989). Clinical validity. *Psychological Medicine, 19*, 45–55.

Kitching, I. J., Forey, P. L., Humphries, C. J., & Williams, D. M. (1998). *Cladistics: The theory and practice of parsimony analysis* (2nd ed.). Oxford: Oxford University Press.

McKay, D., Abramowitz, J., Calamari, J., Kyrios, M., Radomsky, A., Sookman, D., et al. (2004). A critical evaluation of obsessive–compulsive disorder subtypes: Symptoms versus mechanisms. *Clinical Psychology Review, 24*, 283–313.

OCCWG (Obsessive Compulsive Cognitions Working Group) (2005). Psychometric validation of the obsessive belief questionnaire and interpretation of intrusions inventory – part 2: Factor analyses and testing of a brief version. *Behaviour Research and Therapy, 43*, 1527–1542.

Persons, J. B. (1986). The advantages of studying psychological phenomena rather than psychiatric diagnoses. *American Psychologist, 41*, 1252–1260.

Robins, E., & Guze, S. B. (1970). Establishment of diagnostic validity in psychiatric illness: Its application to schizophrenia. *American Journal of Psychiatry, 126*, 983–987.

Sica, C., Taylor, S., Arrindell, W. A., & Sanavio, E. (in press). A cross-cultural test of the cognitive theory of obsessions and compulsions: A comparison of Greek, Italian, and American individuals. *Cognitive Therapy and Research.*

Sobin, C., Blundell, M. L., Weiller, F., Gavigan, C., Haiman, C., & Karayiorgou, M. (2000). Evidence of a schizotypal subtype of obsessive–compulsive disorder. *Journal of Psychiatric Research, 34*, 15–24.

Sookman, D., Abramowitz, J. S., Calamari, J. E., Wilhelm, S., & McKay, D. (2005). Subtypes of obsessive–compulsive disorder: Implications for specialized cognitive behavior therapy. *Behavior Therapy, 36*, 393–400.

Stanley, M. A., Turner, S. M., & Borden, J. W. (1990). Schizotypal features in obsessive–compulsive disorder. *Comprehensive Psychiatry, 31*, 511–518.

Steketee, G. & Frost, R. O. (2006). *Compulsive hoarding and acquiring: Therapist guide.* Oxford: Oxford University Press.

Taylor, S., Abramowitz, J., McKay, D., Calamari, J., Sookman, D., Kyrios, M., et al. (2006). Do dysfunctional beliefs play a role in all types of obsessive–compulsive disorder? *Journal of Anxiety Disorders, 20*, 85–97.

Taylor, S., McKay, D., & Abramowitz, J. (2005). Is obsessive–compulsive disorder a disturbance of security motivation? Comment on Szechtman & Woody (2004). *Psychological Review, 112*, 650–656.

Waller, N. G., & Meehl, P. E. (1998). *Multivariate Taxometric Procedures: Distinguishing Types from Continua.* Thousand Oaks, CA: Sage.

PART

II

POSSIBLE OBSESSIVE– COMPULSIVE SPECTRUM DISORDERS

9

TRICHOTILLOMANIA

MARTIN E. FRANKLIN[1], DAVID F. TOLIN[2], AND GRETCHEN J. DIEFENBACH[3]

[1]University of Pennsylvania School of Medicine; [2]The Institute of Living & University of Connecticut School of Medicine; [3]The Institute of Living

Trichotillomania (TTM) is a chronic impulse control disorder characterized by repetitive pulling out of one's hair, resulting in noticeable hair loss. In this chapter we will describe the phenomenology of TTM in adults and youth, consider its similarities and differences with obsessive–compulsive disorder (OCD), and discuss how our proposed biopsychosocial theory of TTM (Franklin, Tolin, & Diefenbach, 2006) relates to treatment. Where possible, empirical evidence for these theoretical claims will be provided; unfortunately, TTM research continues to lag behind what has been done in OCD, and thus the model must still be considered quite tentative. Notably, current cognitive–behavioral treatment programs for TTM diverge from those for OCD in some important ways, primarily concerning the degree to which patients are encouraged to stay in situations that evoke urges to engage in repetitive behaviors. In TTM this is typically discouraged, whereas in OCD it is encouraged. We will discuss the theoretical rationale for this distinction, and will address differences in the theoretical models underlying both disorders that have clinical implications for managing TTM over the long run, and for the treatment of 'urge-driven' compulsive behaviors such as those elicited by 'not just right' experiences in OCD.

Correspondence to: Martin E. Franklin, Center for Treatment and Study of Anxiety, 3535 Market Street 6th Floor, Philadelphia, PA 19104.

139

PHENOMENOLOGY OF TTM

DEFINITIONS AND VARIATIONS OF TTM

The Diagnostic and Statistical Manual of Mental Disorders (4th edition, text revision) (*DSM-IV-TR*) (American Psychiatric Association, 2000) defines TTM as: (a) recurrent pulling out of one's hair resulting in noticeable hair loss; (b) an increasing sense of tension immediately before pulling or when attempting to resist the behavior; (c) pleasure, gratification or relief when pulling; (d) not better accounted for by another mental disorder and not due to a general medical condition (e.g., a dermatological condition); and (e) clinically significant distress or impairment in social, occupational, or other important areas of functioning. Criteria B and C are somewhat controversial given that a significant minority of adults who pull their hair do not meet these criteria. Christenson, Mackenzie, and Mitchell (1991) reported that in an adult sample of 60 chronic hair pullers, 5% failed to endorse a feeling of tension prior to pulling, and 12% did not report gratification or tension release subsequent to pulling. Similarly, Schlosser, Black, Blum, and Goldstein (1994) indicated that 23% of their clinical sample failed to meet the diagnostic criteria of tension and gratification. The applicability of *DSM-IV-TR* criteria B and C may be even more tenuous in youth. For example, Hanna (1997) found that only half of his small sample of 11 children and adolescents endorsed both rising tension and relief associated with hair pulling, although endorsement of these criteria is more common in older children and adolescents (King et al., 1995). On the whole, findings on the *DSM-IV-TR* criteria for TTM suggest that the current diagnostic classification scheme may be overly restrictive, particularly with respect to pediatric samples. Accordingly, many researchers who are studying TTM do not require that all participants endorse criteria B and C, defining their samples instead as individuals with any repetitive hair pulling leading to visible alopecia that is not the result of another psychiatric or medical condition.

With respect to other possible subtypes within TTM, approximately 75% of adult TTM patients report that most of their hair pulling behavior takes place 'automatically' or outside of awareness, whereas the remaining 25% describe themselves as primarily focused on hair pulling when they pull (Christenson & Mackenzie, 1994). However, the distinction between focused and unfocused pulling is complicated by the fact that most patients engage in both types of pulling behavior (Flessner et al., 2006). The subset of patients who primarily engage in focused hair pulling are more likely to pull hair from the pubic area and report more shame as a result of hair pulling than unfocused pullers (du Toit, van Kradenburg, Niehaus, & Stein, 2001). Whether these two observations are related to one another is unclear, because du Toit et al. did not report whether focused pullers who do not pull from the pubic region were more ashamed than unfocused pullers. Some researchers have postulated that TTM patients who engage primarily in focused hair pulling are more 'OCD-like' and also may be more responsive to pharmacological interventions found effective for OCD (Christenson & O'Sullivan, 1996; du Toit et al., 2001), a potential distinction that will be discussed in detail below. In general, the issue of TTM subtyping is one both of considerable importance and ongoing debate, and no formal subtyping system has been advanced as yet.

Much less information is available on how TTM presents in children and adolescents, but the little that has been published suggests similarity to adult hair pulling. As with adults, the scalp is the most common pulling site in children and adolescents, followed by eyelashes and eyebrows (Reeve, 1999). We (Tolin, Franklin, Diefenbach, Anderson, & Meunier, 2006) found that 11 of 47 (23%) children and adolescents pulled from two or more sites, 23 (49%) pulled scalp hair exclusively, and 13 (28%) pulled eyelashes exclusively. Nearly a third of children reported that the site of pulling had changed over time. The absence of body hair on younger children precludes pulling from certain sites, but clinical work with adolescents appears consistent with the adult data in that pulling from sites other than the face and scalp is also common.

EPIDEMIOLOGY AND COMORBIDITY

Once thought to be extremely rare (Mannino & Delgado, 1969), survey research with nonclinical samples has indicated that hair pulling is more common than had been originally suggested. In studies involving college samples, 10–13% of students reported hair pulling, with the prevalence of clinically significant pulling ranging between 1% and 3.5% (Christenson, Pyle, & Mitchell, 1991; Rothbaum et al., 1993). One epidemiological survey of 17-year-olds in Israel suggests a lifetime hair pulling prevalence of 1%, with fewer reporting noticeable hair loss or distress from these symptoms (King et al., 1995). A large study of TTM and skin picking using the Massachusetts General Hospital Hairpulling Scale and the Massachusetts General Hospital Skin Picking Scale, both psychometrically sound self-report instruments, in a large sample of college freshmen suggested that TTM and skin picking with associated distress and impairment were present in about 2% of the sample; notably, there was little overlap between the two groups (Hajcak, Franklin, Simons, & Keuthen, 2006). Epidemiological research on TTM is extremely limited both in terms of number of studies and in methodology. The generalization of these data to more representative epidemiological research is unclear, and there remains a need for epidemiological research on TTM.

In general, psychiatric comorbidity appears to be quite common among adults with TTM. Christenson, Mackenzie, and Mitchell (1991) found that approximately 82% of an adult clinical sample with TTM met criteria for a past or current comorbid Axis I disorder. Specifically, of these patients with comorbid disorders, there was a lifetime prevalence rate of 65% for mood disorders, 57% for anxiety disorders, 22% for substance abuse, 20% for eating disorders, and 42% for personality disorders. The most frequently cited comorbid personality disorders are histrionic, borderline, and obsessive–compulsive (Christenson, Chernoff-Clementz, & Clementz, 1992; Schlosser et al., 1994; Swedo & Leonard, 1992). In a large sample of adults seeking treatment for TTM, Christenson (1995) found comorbidity rates of 57% for major depression, 27% for generalized anxiety disorder, 20% for eating disorders, 19% for alcohol abuse, and 16% for other substance abuse. In a mixed sample of children, adolescents, and adults with TTM, Swedo and Leonard (1992) found comorbidity rates of 39% for unipolar depression, 32% for generalized anxiety disorder, 16% for OCD, and 15% for substance abuse.

In pediatric clinical samples, Reeve, Bernstein, and Christenson (1992) and King et al. (1995) found, respectively, that 7 of 10 (70%) and 9 of 15 (60%) children with TTM had at least one comorbid Axis I disorder. Conversely, Tolin et al. (2006) found that only 18 of 48 (38%) of their child and adolescent sample met criteria for a comorbid disorder. Sampling issues most likely underlie these observed differences, in that our samples were subject to a telephone screen prior to entering the study, which may have led to the exclusion of some cases with severe comorbid psychopathology.

FUNCTIONAL IMPAIRMENT AND QUALITY OF LIFE

From a clinical standpoint it is clear that TTM can significantly impact functioning, especially when onset occurs during the sensitive years of early adolescence (Christenson et al., 1991). Significant rates of avoidance and distress involving public activities, sexual intimacy, and athletic endeavors have been reported in clinical samples (e.g., Stemberger, Thomas, Mansueto, & Carter, 2000), and other studies have indicated that many TTM patients spend over one hour per day extracting hair (e.g., Mansueto, 1990). That being said, it was only recently that functional impairment has been systematically evaluated using psychometrically sound instruments. Functional limitations were examined in a cohort of adult hair pullers ($n = 58$) attending a national TTM conference using survey questions and standardized self-report scales (Keuthen et al., 2001). Seventy-one percent of the sample endorsed TTM-related distress or impairment in social functioning such as the following: Decreased contact with friends (40%), decreased dating activity (47%), loss of intimacy (40%), and negative impact on family relationships (50%). In addition, 55% of the sample endorsed TTM-related distress or impairment in occupational functioning including the following: Job avoidance (29%), lateness to work (22%), decreased coworker contact (28%), and decreased career aspirations (34%). Lastly, 69% of the sample endorsed avoidance of specific leisure activities. The Medical Outcomes Study 36-Item Short-Form Health Survey (Ware, 1993) reflected quality of life impairment on all mental health subscales. Severity of hair pulling was negatively correlated with scores on all four subscales and, importantly, depression was found to mediate the relationship between TTM and impaired quality of life. Similar results were reported in a sample of treatment-seeking adults with TTM (Diefenbach, Tolin, Hannan, Crocetto, & Worhunsky, 2005).

RELATIONSHIP WITH OCD, SKIN PICKING, AND NAIL BITING

One of the key theoretical debates within the field pertains to whether TTM should be conceptualized as an impulse control disorder or as a variant of OCD.

Many have likened TTM to OCD given the apparent behavioral similarity between the repetitive and perceived uncontrollable nature of hair pulling with that of compulsions, and because of the possible selective responsiveness of TTM to serotonin reuptake inhibitors (SRIs). The classification of TTM as an OCD spectrum disorder is also supported by evidence showing elevated rates of OCD in patients with TTM (Christenson, Mackenzie, & Mitchell, 1991). Swedo (1993; Swedo & Leonard, 1992) suggested that both OCD and TTM patients see their hair pulling/compulsive behaviors as unreasonable, and describe an irresistible urge and anxiety that cause them to perform the behaviors. The percentage of TTM patients who fail to endorse criteria in the *DSM* specifying tension and relief associated with hair pulling, though relatively low, supports some researchers' inclination to conceptualize TTM as a variant of OCD (Jenike, 1989; Swedo & Leonard, 1992), and not as an impulse-control disorder, at least in adult populations.

Other researchers, however, have argued instead that TTM and OCD are separate, distinct diagnoses (e.g., Stanley & Cohen, 1999). Unlike the repetitive and intrusive nature of obsessions in OCD, they propose that TTM is not at all characterized by persistent and intrusive thoughts regarding hair pulling, and that hair pulling often occurs outside awareness. The nature of the repetitive behavior in TTM is generally limited to the topography of hair pulling, whereas compulsions in OCD often consist of a variety of behaviors performed to alleviate anxiety. Moreover, individuals with OCD describe their compulsions as unpleasant but necessary to reduce negative affect, whereas most with TTM describe hair pulling as pleasurable or satisfying in some way. Thus, OCD is maintained by *negative reinforcement* (decrease in negative affect) and compulsions rarely elicit positive affect, whereas TTM is more likely to be maintained by *positive reinforcement* (increase in pleasurable experience).

In further support of the distinction between the two disorders, phenomenology and epidemiology also differ with respect to OCD and TTM. Age of onset is generally later for OCD than for TTM (Himle, Bordnick, & Thyer, 1995; Swedo, 1993; Tukel, Keser, Karali, Olgun, & Calikusu, 2001). Additionally, OCD patients report higher levels of overall anxiety than do TTM patients (Himle et al., 1995; Tukel et al., 2001), and TTM is associated with a broader range of affective states than is OCD (Diefenbach, Mouton-Odum, & Stanley, 2002; Stanley & Cohen, 1999). The proposed difference in conceptualizations of OCD and TTM has critical implications for treatment that lead to the use of different cognitive–behavioral therapy (CBT) strategies for each disorder. In CBT for OCD, individuals are encouraged to remain in anxiety-provoking situations to promote habituation. Theoretically, those receiving CBT for TTM might be better served by reducing urges by altering hair pulling cues (e.g., exiting high-risk situations, using competing response strategies) rather than completing focused exposures without adjunctive efforts to reduce anxiety (as in exposure and response prevention for OCD), given that positive rather than negative reinforcement is more likely to underlie TTM behaviors. In order to weaken pulling urges, TTM patients must learn not to seek positive reinforcement from pulling; out of this conceptualization comes *habit reversal*, which is essentially the substitution of an alternative behavior that is incompatible with pulling.

One dimension on which we (e.g., Franklin, Tolin, & Diefenbach, 2006; Franklin & Tolin, in press) and other researchers (e.g., Christenson & Mansueto, 1999; Stanley & Cohen, 1999) have noted important differences between TTM and OCD is in the centrality of cognition in the maintenance of the disorder. TTM is generally not characterized by intrusive thoughts, ideas, or images *per se*, and in fact many individuals with TTM report that their pulling occurs outside of conscious awareness and without any obvious preceding cognition (e.g., Flessner et al., 2006). With the notable exception of the 'not just right' experience, cognitions in the form of frequent and distressing obsessions play a pivotal role in OCD. Compulsions are characterized as behaviors or mental acts that are engaged in intentionally in order to reduce the likelihood of a feared outcome or to reduce obsessional distress. The majority of adult patients with OCD endorse the presence of a feared consequence that would occur if they did not engage in these rituals (Foa et al., 1995); this is very rarely the case in TTM and, we would argue, would warrant a possible alternative diagnosis of OCD if present. Conversely, repetitive behaviors without a clear cognitive prompt for them would be suggestive to some researchers as complex tic phenomenology rather than as OCD (e.g., Piacentini & Chang, 2005). The overlap and relationships between 'not just right' OCD, complex tics, and TTM may well be an important area for future study.

Although a detailed consideration of other body-focused impulse control disorders such as skin picking and severe nail biting is beyond the scope of this chapter, many experts (e.g., Christenson & Mansueto, 1999) have noted similarities among these conditions as well as common co-occurrence. As with TTM, it is important conceptually to determine the function of the behavior in order to decide how to define and treat it. If the skin picking and nail biting are largely negatively reinforcing – that is, reducing anxiety associated with specific obsessional thoughts and/or reducing the likelihood of feared outcomes – they may be better conceptualized as OCD and treated accordingly. In our clinical experience, however, these conditions are much more likely to functionally resemble TTM as described above and thus may very well fit the conceptual model we describe in the chapter. Nevertheless, much more research is needed to determine how these conditions differ in order to say with confidence whether they are all one entity or conceptually distinct conditions that require separate theoretical consideration and treatment approaches.

TREATMENT

PHARMACOLOGICAL APPROACHES

In general, knowledge about TTM treatments is limited by small sample sizes, lack of specificity regarding sample characteristics, non-random assignment to treatment, dearth of long-term follow-up data, exclusive reliance on patient self-report measures, and lack of information regarding rates of treatment refusal and drop-out. Pharmacotherapy trials have focused primarily on examining the efficacy of SRIs, whereas psychotherapy studies have focused on behavioral and cognitive–behavioral protocols. Other treatments are used in service settings to treat TTM (e.g., hypnosis), but have not yet been subjected to empirical study. Of the six randomized controlled trials (RCTs) evaluating the efficacy of pharmacotherapy conducted to date, five involved the evaluation of SRIs. This may reflect the previously prevailing view that TTM is a variant of OCD, and thus ought to be responsive to the same pharmacologic agents that have proven successful in ameliorating OCD symptoms. Swedo et al. (1989) conducted a double-blind crossover study with 14 women, and found clomipramine (CMI) superior to desipramine at post-treatment. However, long-term response to CMI varied widely, with an overall 40% reduction in symptoms at 4-year follow-up (Swedo, Lenane, & Leonard, 1993). At follow-up, patients were evenly divided between those without discernible long-term benefits and those with at least moderate improvements; those with a comorbid anxiety disorder or with comorbid borderline personality disorder fared more poorly with respect to long-term TTM symptom reduction. Christenson, Mackenzie, Mitchell, and Callies (1991) failed to demonstrate the superiority of fluoxetine (FLU) over placebo (PBO) in a double-blind crossover study; in that trial, neither condition reduced hair pulling significantly. Following from Christenson et al. (1991), Streichenwein and Thornby (1995) also failed to show any difference between FLU and PBO in reducing hair pulling despite having lengthened the treatment phase and increasing the maximum FLU dose to 80 mg. In the first study to examine the efficacy of pharmacotherapy and a comparison treatment, Ninan, Rothbaum, Marstellar, Knight, and Eccard (2000) compared CMI, CBT, and PBO. Compared to both CMI and PBO, CBT produced greater reductions in hair pulling severity and associated impairment, and yielded a significantly higher responder rate. Differences between CMI and PBO approached but did not achieve statistical significance. Similarly, another RCT found CBT superior to FLU and wait-list, and failed to show a significant treatment effect for FLU (van Minnen, Hoogduin, Keijsers, Hellenbrand, & Hendriks, 2003). Taken together, results from these controlled studies of SRIs are equivocal at best, although in view of the small sample sizes more controlled research should still be conducted to determine their efficacy more definitively.

Although double-blind discontinuation studies have not been conducted in TTM, accumulating evidence from open studies suggests that treatment response gained from pharmacotherapy may not be maintained in the long run. For example, an uncontrolled study by Pollard and colleagues (1991) indicated that the majority of a small sample of patients treated with CMI lost their treatment gains even while being maintained on a previously therapeutic dose of the drug. A retrospective study by Iancu, Weizman, Kindler, Sasson, and Zohar (1996) found that of patients receiving treatment with serotonergic drugs, 75% achieved a clinically significant response during the first two months, but symptoms returned to pretreatment levels during the third month with continued medication.

As is evident from the above review, the TTM pharmacotherapy literature to date is both underdeveloped and equivocal. SRIs, the class of medication found efficacious in OCD, have generally not resulted in promising outcomes for TTM. Perhaps, as we discussed above, important differences between OCD and TTM may underlie this apparent difference in treatment response. Intriguingly, naltrexone, an opioid-blocking compound thought to decrease positive reinforcement by preventing the binding of endogenous opiates to relevant receptor sites in the brain, has also been found superior to PBO in reducing TTM symptoms (Christenson, Crow, & Mackenzie, 1994). In addition, several case studies have indicated that augmentation of SRIs with atypical antipsychotics may be beneficial (Epperson, Fasula, Wasylink, Price, & McDougle, 1999; Stein & Hollander, 1992), and an open trial suggested that olanzapine may be efficacious as a monotherapy for TTM (Stewart & Nejtek, 2003). Clearly there is much more work to be done in the area of pharmacotherapy development and outcome evaluation. Of particular note, we are aware of no RCTs of pharmacotherapy for children and adolescents with TTM.

BEHAVIORAL AND COGNITIVE–BEHAVIORAL APPROACHES

With respect to behavioral approaches and CBT packages, a variety of specific techniques have been applied, including awareness training, self-monitoring, aversive conditioning, covert sensitization, negative practice, relaxation training, habit reversal, competing response training, stimulus control, and overcorrection. Although the state of the CBT literature justifies only cautious recommendations, habit reversal, awareness training, and stimulus control are generally purported as the core efficacious interventions for TTM, with other interventions such as cognitive techniques to be used on an as-needed basis.

Three randomized trials with adults have been conducted regarding the efficacy of CBT. As mentioned above, Ninan et al. (2000) found CBT superior to both CMI and PBO at post-treatment, which is the same pattern reported by van Minnen et al. (2003) in their RCT involving behavior therapy, FLU, and wait-list. Two studies have compared CBT interventions to other psychosocial interventions. Azrin, Nunn, & Frantz (1980) found that habit reversal (HR) was more effective than negative practice at post-treatment and at 2-year follow-up. Although encouraging, methodological issues limit the study's ultimate utility, including exclusive reliance upon patient self-report, substantial attrition (7 of 19) during the follow-up phase, and the absence of a formal treatment manual to allow for replication. In a study of group-based interventions for TTM, Diefenbach and colleagues (Diefenbach, Tolin, Hannan, Maltby, & Crocetto, 2006) found manualized CBT to be superior to a nondirective supportive therapy using CGI Improvement as the primary outcome measure. However, treatment response was rather modest in both conditions when examining clinically significant change as defined by a post-treatment score of 6 or below on the Massachusetts General Hospital Hairpulling Scale total score, with 22% of group CBT patients and 30% of supportive therapy patients achieving this standard, which contrasts with findings from van Minnen et al.'s (2003) study, in which 64% of BT patients met this more stringent definition for improvement.

The significant problem of relapse following CBT approaches, which is certainly a common problem reported clinically, was highlighted in an open study in which patients received nine sessions of CBT involving HR (Lerner, Franklin, Meadows, Hembree, & Foa, 1998). Twelve of 14 patients were classified as responders at post-treatment (>50% reduction on the NIMH–Trichotillomania Severity Scale total score), yet only 4 of 13 met this criterion an average of 3.9 years post-treatment. Keuthen et al.'s (2001) naturalistic follow-up of patients who received pharmacotherapy or behavior therapy further underscored concern about maintenance of gains. Similarly, Mouton and Stanley (1996) found 4 of 5 patients benefiting initially from group HR, but only 2 of 5 patients maintained clinically significant gains at 6-month follow-up.

To date, only one study has examined the efficacy of CBT for children and adolescents with TTM (Tolin et al., 2006). Twenty-two children and adolescents were enrolled in an open trial of individual CBT with particular attention toward relapse prevention. TTM severity decreased significantly, and 77% of children were classified as treatment responders at post-treatment and 64% at 6-month follow-up. The lack of a control group, however, limits the strength of conclusions that can be drawn.

Generally speaking, the limited and equivocal treatment literature strongly suggests that there is neither a universal nor complete response to any treatments for TTM. Given that monotherapy with CBT or pharmacotherapy is likely to produce only partial symptom reduction in the long run, it might be argued that these therapies yield superior improvement when combined. Controlled studies examining the efficacy of CBT treatments involving HR, pharmacotherapy, and their combination have yet to be completed, although at this point the decision as to which pharmacotherapy option to consider for such a study is not yet clear.

TOWARD AN EMPIRICAL UNDERSTANDING OF TTM

There is a clear need for improved efficacy of psychological and pharmacological treatments for TTM. To date, there has been insufficient experimental study of the psychopathology of hair pulling, which results in critical gaps in our understanding of the factors that cause and/or maintain this behavior. The corollary of this idea is that an enhanced empirical understanding of hair pulling will lead to a more comprehensive biopsychosocial model of TTM, which will in turn inform the next generation of therapeutic interventions (Foa & Kozak, 1997).

Figure 9.1 shows a schematic diagram of a preliminary biopsychosocial model of TTM. We stress that this model, which was presented in greater detail elsewhere (Franklin, Tolin, & Diefenbach, 2006) is preliminary, as the available experimental and descriptive psychopathology research in TTM is relatively sparse. Furthermore, given the emphasis in the current chapter on the similarities

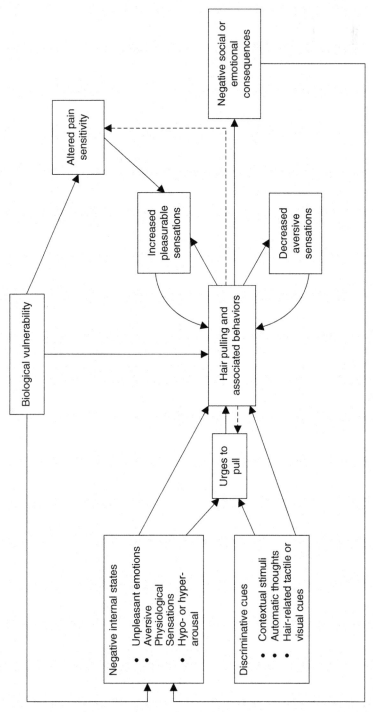

FIGURE 9.1 Schematic diagram of a preliminary biopsychosocial model of trichotillomania

and differences between TTM and OCD, we intersperse our comments about this conceptual model of TTM with data on OCD in order to highlight areas of convergence and divergence.

BIOLOGICAL VULNERABILITY

It is likely that biological vulnerabilities increase the probability that a person will develop TTM. Familial research suggests that TTM may be associated with elevated rates of OCD or other excessive habits among first-degree relatives (Bienvenu et al., 2000; King et al., 1995; Lenane et al., 1992). This finding is consistent with the notion of a genetic basis for a spectrum of excessive grooming behaviors that includes TTM, although environmental factors such as social learning cannot be ruled out as yet. The familial basis of OCD is already well established (e.g., Lipsitz et al., 2005) and a possible candidate gene has recently been identified (Arnold, Sicard, Burroughs, Richter, & Kennedy, 2006; Dickel et al., 2006); such work has yet to be conducted in TTM.

Neuroimaging research has demonstrated hyperactivity in the left cerebellum and right superior parietal lobe (Swedo et al., 1991), as well as possible structural abnormalities in the left putamen (O'Sullivan et al., 1997), left inferior frontal gyrus, and right cuneal cortex (Grachev, 1997). Furthermore, TTM patients have been shown to make errors in spatial processing (Rettew, Cheslow, Rapoport, Leonard, & Lenane, 1991), divided attention (Stanley, Hannay, & Breckenridge, 1997), and nonverbal memory and executive functioning (Keuthen et al., 1996). Studies such as these do not necessarily imply that preexisting brain abnormalities cause the symptoms of TTM; it is entirely possible that chronic TTM or its associated features lead to changes in brain structure or function, or that both TTM and the brain abnormalities are caused by a third, as yet unknown, variable. There is a more extensive neurobiological literature on OCD, and although some overlap with TTM has been found with respect to abnormalities in the basal ganglia and in the frontal lobes for both conditions, visuospatial and visuoconstructional dysfunction that are quite robust in OCD have not been identified in TTM (Stanley & Cohen, 1999).

We also suspect that a nonspecific biological vulnerability is manifested in difficulty tolerating discomfort. That is, individuals who feel a need to control or eliminate their uncomfortable emotions or sensations might be at greater risk to develop TTM and perhaps other disorders as well. This notion of 'experiential avoidance' has been forwarded as a vulnerability factor for general psychopathology by Hayes and colleagues (e.g., Hayes, Strosahl, & Wilson, 1999), and intolerance of aversive states has been noted in anxiety disorders (Ladouceur, Gosselin, & Dugas, 2000; Reiss, Peterson, Gursky, & McNally, 1986; Tolin, Abramowitz, Brigidi, & Foa, 2003). A preliminary investigation of experiential avoidance in TTM suggested that a tendency to avoid unpleasant emotions was related to severity of hair pulling urges (Begotka, Woods, & Wetterneck, 2004). However, the relationship, while statistically significant, was relatively weak. This may relate to the fact that the investigators used a questionnaire that assessed primarily anxiety- and depression-related avoidance, rather than an avoidance of physiological arousal or other sensations that may be more directly applicable to TTM. This study also did not use a nonclinical control group; thus, range restriction may have been a factor. Clearly more research is needed to investigate the relationship between experiential avoidance and hair pulling and, more broadly, to examine whether experiential avoidance is related to biological factors and whether it represents a global diathesis for the development of maladaptive behaviors.

ALTERED PAIN SENSITIVITY

Individuals with TTM often report that hair pulling is not painful (Christenson et al., 1991; Sanderson & Hall-Smith, 1970), or in many cases that it feels good or pleasurable (Stanley, Swann, Bowers, Davis, & Taylor, 1992). It is possible that alterations in pain sensitivity influence the reinforcing quality of pulling behavior. One possible mechanism for such alterations is upregulation of the endogenous opioid system; this model has not been supported by challenge tasks (Frecska & Arato, 2002), although some evidence suggests that pulling may decrease with administration of opiate receptor antagonists (Carrion, 1995; Christenson, Crow, & MacKenzie, 1994). Intriguingly, dogs with acral lick dermatitis (a potential animal model of TTM) show reductions in evoked sensory nerve action potentials (van Nes, 1986), possibly suggesting decreased pain sensitivity. However, TTM patients do not appear to show reduced pain in non-pulling areas such as the fingertips (Christenson, Raymond et al., 1994). It may be that pain sensations are not globally altered in TTM, but rather are diminished only at the sites of pulling. This may result from habituation of the pain response caused by repeated pulling over time. In a survey of children and adolescents with TTM, participants reported that their first pulling episode resulted in a mixture of pleasurable and painful sensations. However, more recent pulling episodes were reportedly associated with the same degree of pleasure, but a much lower degree of pain (Meunier, Tolin, & Franklin, 2006). For those patients who do experience pulling-related pain, the pain itself may be reinforcing by distracting the individual from negative emotional or physiological states; such a possible function of pain in TTM has been discussed by clinical experts (e.g., Christenson & Mansueto, 1999) but has yet to be evaluated empirically.

HAIR PULLING CUES

The behavioral model of hair pulling suggests that pulling begins as a normal response to stress, but eventually becomes associated with a variety of internal and external cues through conditioning mechanisms (Azrin & Nunn, 1973; Mansueto, Stemberger, Thomas, & Golomb, 1997). Descriptive research has indicated that situations associated with hyperarousal (e.g., negative affective states) or hypoarousal (e.g., boredom, fatigue, sedentary activities) are common cues for hair pulling. For example, Christenson, Ristvedt, and Mackenzie (1993) identified two factors of hair pulling cues: negative affect and sedentary/contemplative cues.

The negative affect component was composed of feeling terms (e.g., feeling angry or hurt) and situations associated with negative self-evaluation (e.g., weighing yourself, interpersonal conflicts). The sedentary/contemplative component was comprised of situations associated with fatigue (e.g., lack of sleep) and directed attention (e.g., reading, television). However, the relationship between pulling cues and TTM 'subtypes' requires further examination. Physical sensations have also been identified as arousal cues for hair pulling. For example Mansueto (1990) found that a substantial minority of patients reported skin sensitivity (25%), itching (23%), irritation (16%), pressure (14%), and burning sensations (5%) as preceding pulling episodes; however, these may well be nonspecific correlates of neuroticism or negative affectivity as suggested by Watson and Clark (1984), so the specificity of these overlapping symptoms needs therefore to be examined more closely.

Cognitive components are also involved at least to some extent in conceptualizing this disorder, in that cognitions may serve as cues and consequences to the behavioral sequence. In some cases negative cognitions about the pulling habit itself, such as fear of negative evaluation, may also play a role in the perpetuation of pulling, as these cognitions result in increased negative emotion which in turn may increase urges to pull. Additionally, patients sometimes worry that the urges to pull will either never go away or will escalate indefinitely unless pulling occurs (despite their being able to provide ample evidence to the contrary from their own experience with urges). Beliefs in the positive effects of hair pulling (e.g., 'hair pulling will make me feel better') or pulling facilitative thoughts (e.g., 'I'll just pull *one*') may also cue pulling episodes (Gluhoski, 1995).

Another category of potential pulling triggers is contextual cues, which may not have originally been associated with pulling or pulling-related feelings or sensations, but by the process of associative conditioning have become linked with these factors through repetitive pulling episodes. Common contextual cues for pulling include visual signs that hair is misshapen or unattractive (e.g., asymmetrical hair, gray hair), tactile sensations (e.g., feeling a coarse hair), places or activities where pulling has occurred in the past (e.g., bathroom, bed, watching television), being alone, or the presence of pulling implements (e.g., tweezers). Both arousal and contextual cues may be either associated with pulling directly or through the mediation of a hair pulling 'urge'. Over time, hair pulling urges that are reinforced by pulling lead to stronger urges to pull, which perpetuates the behavioral cycle.

REINFORCEMENT

As described earlier, hair pulling is often preceded by general negative internal states such as unpleasant emotions, aversive physiological sensations, or dysregulated arousal. Hair pulling, in turn, appears to result in a decrease of these states. In retrospective reports, individuals with TTM report that pulling leads to reduced feelings of tension, boredom, and anxiety (e.g., Woods et al., in press), and report experiencing larger reductions in sadness and anger (Stanley, Borden, Mouton, & Breckenridge, 1995). In these cases, hair pulling is negatively reinforced and is thus functionally similar to the compulsive behaviors seen in OCD. However, to the extent that hair pulling evokes pleasurable sensations, the pulling habit is also be strengthened via *positive* reinforcement (Azrin & Nunn, 1973; Mansueto et al., 1997). Pleasure may be obtained not only through pulling, but also through associated behaviors such as playing with or inspecting the hair, oral stimulation, or trichophagia (Christenson & Mansueto, 1999). Thus, pulling may be maintained by either negative or positive reinforcement, or both. Our clinical observations suggest that some TTM patients may experience one or the other form of reinforcement, or different kinds of reinforcement may be active for the same person at different times. We propose that careful attention to the specific hair pulling contingencies is critical in developing a functional analysis and planning therapeutic interventions for TTM.

DELAYED CONSEQUENCES OF PULLING

Although hair pulling is immediately reinforced via its consequent emotional or interoceptive changes, longer-term negative consequences of pulling also exist. The most obvious delayed consequence of hair pulling is the negative impact on physical appearance, which many hair pullers make great efforts to conceal. Concealment of hair loss can take the form of wigs or special make-up, which can be costly, time-consuming, and uncomfortable. Increases in negative emotional states including guilt, sadness, and anger also occur following pulling episodes for TTM patients. Hair pulling has also been associated with negative self-evaluation, frustrations with being out of control of pulling, and low self-esteem (Casati, Toner, & Yu, 2000; Soriano et al., 1996; Stemberger et al., 2000). Hair pulling can also lead to negative social consequences. In an experimental study, adolescents viewing videotapes of individuals pulling hair rated hair pullers lower in social acceptability than those who were not pulling hair (Boudjouk, Woods, Miltenberger, & Long, 2000). Consequently, hair pullers have reported interpersonal conflicts, social isolation, and loneliness (Casati et al., 2000; Stemberger et al., 2000). However, as with many maladaptive behaviors (e.g., smoking, overeating) the short-term reinforcement value often overpowers the delayed aversive consequences, resulting in continued pulling. In fact, the longer-term consequences may even serve to escalate the pulling cycle by providing a new stimulus cue (e.g., negative self-evaluative thoughts, negative affect) that can prompt additional pulling episodes. Given the importance of pulling resistance and tolerance of subsequent uncomfortable affect to the eventual discontinuation of pulling (through extinction of reinforcing consequences), investigations into interventions that maximize these factors (e.g., acceptance and commitment therapy, motivational interviewing) may be fruitful.

SUMMARY

At present, the experimental and descriptive psychopathology literature in TTM is quite 'young' and there is a clear need for additional research in this area. However, preliminary data are converging on a tentative biopsychosocial model in which biologically vulnerable individuals become trapped in cycles of hair pulling that are triggered by internal and contextual discriminative cues, and that are subsequently reinforced by reduction of a variety of negative internal stimuli or by eliciting positive sensations. This cycle persists despite clear negative social and emotional consequences because such consequences are delayed and thus are outweighed by more immediate and salient reinforcers. We fully expect that additional research will result in the modification of this preliminary model and we hope, in the spirit of Foa and Kozak (1997), that a more comprehensive and empirically informed model will break the apparent 'efficacy ceiling' of TTM treatment and lead to more effective interventions.

With respect to the relationship between TTM and OCD, although the two conditions may well be part of a larger group of disorders characterized by inability to resist urges to engage in repetitive behaviors, important differences between the two conditions have also emerged. In particular, the centrality of cognition in OCD but not in TTM, the affective function of the repetitive behavior, and specifically the degree to which pleasurable sensations are a primary consequence of engaging in pulling but not in compulsions, and some of the observed differences in the underlying neurobiology warrant attention as well.

FUTURE DIRECTIONS

Several steps can be taken to rectify the dearth of TTM research, and to clarify the nature of its relationship to OCD. A large-scale epidemiological study should be conducted to determine the point and lifetime prevalence rates of the disorder in pediatric and adult samples. Although some small-scale prevalence studies have hinted that TTM is a surprisingly common condition, a larger epidemiological effort would clarify the need to direct resources towards the scientific study of this problem. Inclusion of instruments that measure focused and unfocused pulling and also OCD symptom measures in such a study is imperative, since some researchers have speculated that TTM that is more focused and 'OCD-like' (e.g., done intentionally to reduce negative affect) could be more responsive to SRIs (O'Sullivan, Christenson, & Stein, 1999). Epidemiology studies that include measures of all of these symptom domains may well allow us to better estimate what percentage of the TTM population can be characterized in this way, and hence these data can be used to help inform the development of a more targeted treatment intervention approach.

Another essential issue to be addressed is the improved assessment of functional impairment measures in TTM. Those who treat TTM patients know from clinical experience that these patients are often isolated, avoidant of situations in which their alopecia and pulling behavior might be discovered (e.g., swimming, dating), and frequently feel inferior or 'weird,' but as yet there is little empirical research documenting dysfunction in these important dimensions. Use of existing psychometrically sound measures (e.g., Medical Outcomes Survey) and development of new TTM-specific interference instruments may be used to accompany symptom measures to improve understanding of TTM's impact upon hair pullers as well as the effects of treatments. A recent Internet-based survey study of individuals who self-identified as having TTM indicated moderate levels of functional impairment and an association between hair pulling severity and impairment (Woods et al., in press); moreover, participants' levels of self-reported stress, depression, and anxiety as measured by the DASS-21 were comparable to a sample of treatment-seeking OCD patients (Antony et al., 1998), suggesting further that TTM is not a trivial concern. Future studies of treatment-seeking and epidemiological samples will be needed to further clarify the relationship between TTM symptoms, functional impairment, stress, and affective disturbances.

Longitudinal research is also needed to determine the percentage of TTM sufferers whose hair pulling remits without intervention, and examination of factors associated with maintenance of pulling behavior over time may help determine which hair pullers ought to be targeted for earlier intervention. These types of studies are both contingent upon the development of psychometrically sound interviews and self-report measures, a process which has already begun in adult TTM (Keuthen et al., 1995; O'Sullivan et al., 1995) and is now under way with younger samples (Diefenbach, Tolin, Franklin, & Anderson, 2003). Once available, the measures will set the stage for the epidemiological and longitudinal studies described above. Experimental psychopathology studies linking psychological and biological methods would also go a long way towards closing the current knowledge gaps and perhaps would stimulate a more interdisciplinary approach to the treatment of this condition. The prevailing biological theory of dysfunction, namely a serotonin dysregulation, may require reconsideration given the relatively poor treatment response demonstrated thus far with medications that are selective for that neurotransmitter. It may be especially useful to examine psychological and biological measures while a patient is pulling, or resisting urges to pull. For example, psychophysiological research may explore the modulation function of hair pulling to establish a relationship between changes in subjective experiences (e.g., decreased urge, decreased tension) and physiological responding over the hair pulling cycle. Additionally, studies of pulling site-specific pain tolerance may very well shed light on an ongoing area of controversy, namely whether TTM patients experience pain at the pulling site when pulling and whether there are biological correlates to the subjective experience that may help us better understand TTM.

The meager treatment outcome literature and the equivocal findings from RCTs suggest that there is much to do with respect to TTM intervention research. Preliminary evidence suggests that CBT is effective for many TTM patients; however, additional RCTs comparing CBT with alternative psychological (e.g., supportive counseling) and pharmacological (e.g., SRI medications, opioid antagonists) treatments are needed. Given the possible role of experiential avoidance in the etiology and/or maintenance of TTM, the addition of mindfulness/acceptance strategies may also prove fruitful; recent evidence suggests that a combined treatment protocol of habit reversal plus Acceptance and Commitment Therapy was superior to a wait-list control (Woods et al., 2006), but dismantling studies will be needed to isolate which elements of the protocol were most effective. Next, dismantling research is critical for identifying the efficacious elements of CBT; additional research on which patients respond to which elements would also be helpful in the construction of treatment-planning algorithms. Additional biological research is needed to examine patterns of abnormal neurotransmitter and brain metabolic activity in TTM patients, and the effect of specific compounds on these factors; it is also important to determine whether the glutamate transporter gene recently identified as a potential candidate gene for OCD is also implicated in TTM.

Most pharmacotherapy research to date in TTM has focused on serotonergic medications; however, research into other strategies (e.g., opioid blockers, glutamatergic compounds) may also be useful. Following this, effectiveness research is needed to determine the degree to which CBT and pharmacologic algorithms can be successfully implemented in front-line mental health settings with less-rigidly selected patients. These research steps will be greatly facilitated by improved theoretical models of TTM based on additional experimental psychopathology findings, epidemiological evidence, and functional impairment data. In many ways the OCD literature serves as a model for how to programmatically move from the study of etiology and phenomenology to psychopathology, neurobiology, and treatment; much would be accomplished in TTM if this same model is followed, regardless of whether the two conditions turn out to be diagnostically, functionally, and biologically distinguishable.

ACKNOWLEDGEMENT

This article was supported in part by a grant from the National Institute of Mental Health (MH61457).

REFERENCES

American Psychiatric Association (2000). *Diagnostic and statistical manual of mental disorders* (4th ed., text revision) *(DSM-IV-TR)*. Washington, DC: APA.

Antony, M. M., Bieling, P. J., Cox, B. J., Enns, M. W., & Swinson, R. P. (1998). Psychometric properties of the 42-item and 21-item versions of the depression anxiety stress scales in clinical groups and a community sample. *Psychological Assessment, 10,* 176–181.

Arnold, P. D., Sicard, T., Burroughs, E., Richter, M. A., & Kennedy, J. L. (2006). Glutamate transporter gene *SLC1A1* associated with obsessive–compulsive disorder. *Archives of General Psychiatry, 63,* 769–776.

Azrin, N. H., & Nunn, R. G. (1973). Habit-reversal: A method of eliminating nervous habits and tics. *Behaviour Research and Therapy, 11,* 619–628.

Azrin, N. H., Nunn, R. G., & Frantz, S. E. (1980). Treatment of hairpulling (trichotillomania): A comparative study of habit reversal and negative practice training. *Journal of Behavior Therapy and Experimental Psychiatry, 11,* 13–20.

Begotka, A. M., Woods, D. W., & Wetterneck, C. T. (2004). The relationship between experiential avoidance and the severity of trichotillomania in a nonreferred sample. *Journal of Behavior Therapy and Experimental Psychiatry, 35,* 17–24.

Bienvenu, O. J., Samuels, J. F., Riddle, M. A., Hoehn-Saric, R., Liang, K. Y., Cullen, B. A., et al. (2000). The relationship of obsessive–compulsive disorder to possible spectrum disorders: Results from a family study. *Biological Psychiatry, 48*, 287–293.

Boudjouk, P. J., Woods, D. W., Miltenberger, R. G., & Long, E. S. (2000). Negative peer evaluation in adolescents: Effects of tic disorders and trichotillomania. *Child & Family Behavior Therapy, 22*, 17–28.

Carrion, V. G. (1995). Naltrexone for the treatment of trichotillomania: A case report. *Journal of Clinical Psychopharmacology, 15*, 444–445.

Casati, J., Toner, B. B., & Yu, B. (2000). Psychosocial issues for women with trichotillomania. *Comprehensive Psychiatry, 41*, 344–351.

Christenson, G. A. (1995). Trichotillomania: From prevalence to comorbidity. *Psychiatric Times, 12*, 44–48.

Christenson, G. A., Chernoff-Clementz, E., & Clementz, B. A. (1992). Personality and clinical characteristics in patients with trichotillomania. *Journal of Clinical Psychiatry, 53*, 407–413.

Christenson, G. A., Crow, S. J., & Mackenzie, T. B. (1994, May). A placebo controlled double blind study of naltrexone for trichotillomania. *New Research Program and Abstracts of the 150th Annual Meeting of the American Psychiatric Association*, Philadelphia, PA, NR597.

Christenson, G. A., & Mackenzie, T. B. (1994). Trichotillomania. In M. Hersen & R.T. Ammerman (Eds.), *Handbook of prescriptive treatments for adults* (pp. 217–235). New York: Plenum.

Christenson, G. A., Mackenzie, T. B., & Mitchell, J. E. (1991). Characteristics of 60 adult chronic hair-pullers. *American Journal of Psychiatry, 148*, 365–370.

Christenson, G. A., Mackenzie, T. B., Mitchell, J. E., & Callies, A. L. (1991). A placebo-controlled, double-blind crossover study of fluoxetine in trichotillomania. *American Journal of Psychiatry, 148*, 1566–1571.

Christenson, G. A., & Mansueto, C. S. (1999). Trichotillomania: Descriptive characteristics and phenomenology. In D. J. Stein, G. A. Christenson, & E. Hollander (Eds.), *Trichotillomania* (pp. 1–41). Washington, DC: American Psychiatric Press.

Christenson, G. A., & O'Sullivan, R. L. (1996). Trichotillomania: Rational treatment options. *CNS Drugs*, 6, 23–34.

Christenson, G. A., Pyle, R. L., & Mitchell, J. E. (1991). Estimated lifetime prevalence of trichotillomania in college students. *Journal of Clinical Psychology, 52*, 415–417.

Christenson, G. A., Raymond, N. C., Faris, P. L., McAllister, R. D., Crow, S. J., Howard, L. A., et al. (1994). Pain thresholds are not elevated in trichotillomania. *Biological Psychiatry, 36*, 347–349.

Christenson, G. A., Ristvedt, S. L., & MacKenzie, T. B. (1993). Identification of trichotillomania cue profiles. *Behaviour Research and Therapy, 31*, 315–320.

Dickel, D. E., Veenstra-VanderWeele, J., Cox, N. J., Wu, X., Fischer, D. J., Van Etten-Lee, M., et al. (2006). Association testing of the positional and functional candidate gene *SLC1A1/EAAC1* in early-onset obsessive–compulsive disorder. *Archives of General Psychiatry, 63*, 778–785.

Diefenbach, G. J., Mouton-Odum, S., & Stanley, M. A. (2002). Affective correlates of trichotillomania. *Behaviour Research and Therapy, 40*, 1305–1315.

Diefenbach, G. J., Tolin, D. F., Franklin, M. E., & Anderson, E. R. (2003, November). *The Trichotillomania Scale for Children (TSC): A new self-report measure to assess pediatric hair pulling.* Presented to the Annual Meeting of the Association for Advancement of Behavior Therapy, Boston, MA.

Diefenbach, G. J., Tolin, D. F., Hannan, S., Crocetto, J., & Worhunsky, P. (2005). Trichotillomania: Impact on psychosocial functioning and quality of life. *Behaviour Research and Therapy, 43*, 869–884.

Diefenbach, G. J., Tolin, D. F., Hannan, S., Maltby, N., & Crocetto, J. (2006) Group treatment of trichotillomania: Behavioral therapy versus supportive therapy. *Behavior Therapy, 37*, 353–363.

du Toit, P. L., van Kradenburg, J., Niehaus, D. H. J., & Stein, D. J. (2001). Characteristics and phenomenology of hair pulling: An exploration of subtypes. *Comprehensive Psychiatry, 42*, 247–256.

Epperson, N. C., Fasula, D., Wasylink, S., Price, L. H., & McDougle, C. J. (1999). Risperidone addition in serotonin reuptake inhibitor-resistant trichotillomania: Three cases. *Journal of Child and Adolescent Psychopharmacology, 37*, 353–363.

Flessner, C. A., Woods, D. W., Franklin, M. E., Cashin, S.E., Keuthen, N. J., & The Trichotillomania Learning Center Scientific Advisory Board (2006). The Milwaukee–Dimensions of Trichotillomania Survey (M–DOTS): Development, exploratory factor analysis, and psychometric properties. Manuscript submitted for publication.

Foa, E. B., & Kozak, M. J. (1997). Beyond the efficacy ceiling? Cognitive behavior therapy in search of theory. *Behavior Therapy, 28,* 601–611.

Foa, E. B., Kozak, M. J., Goodman, W. K., Hollander, E., Jenike, M. A., & Rasmussen, S. (1995). DSM-IV filed trial: Obsessive compulsive disorder. *American Journal of Psychiatry, 152,* 90–96.

Franklin, M. E., & Tolin, D. F. (in press). *Treating trichotillomania: Cognitive behavioral therapy for hair pulling and related problems.* New York, NY: Springer.

Franklin, M. E., Tolin, D. F., & Diefenbach, D. (2006). Trichotillomania. In E. Hollander & D. J. Stein (Eds.), *Handbook of impulse control disorders* (pp. 149–173). Washington, DC: American Psychiatric Publishing.

Frecska, E., & Arato, M. (2002). Opiate sensitivity test in patients with stereotypic movement disorder and trichotillomania. *Progress in Neuro-Psychopharmacology & Biological Psychiatry, 26,* 909–912.

Gluhoski, V. L. (1995). A cognitive approach for treating trichotillomania. *Journal of Psychotherapy Practice and Research, 4,* 277–285.

Grachev, I. D. (1997). MRI-based morphometric topographic parcellation of human neocortex in trichotillomania. *Psychiatry and Clinical Neuroscience, 51,* 315–321.

Hajcak, G., Franklin, M. E., Simons, R. F., & Keuthen, N. J. (2006). Hairpulling and skin picking in relation to affective distress and obsessive–compulsive symptoms. *Journal of Psychopathology and Behavioral Assessment, 28,* 179–187.

Hanna, G. L. (1997). Trichotillomania and related disorders in children and adolescents. *Child Psychiatry and Human Development, 27,* 255–268.

Hayes, S. C., Strosahl, K. D., & Wilson, K. G. (1999). *Acceptance and commitment therapy: An experiential approach to behavior change.* New York: Guilford Press.

Himle, J. A., Bordnick, P. S., & Thyer, B. A. (1995). A comparison of trichotillomania and obsessive–compulsive disorder. *Journal of Psychopathology and Behavioral Assessment, 17,* 251–260.

Iancu, I., Weizman, A., Kindler, S., Sasson, Y., & Zohar, J. (1996). Serotonergic drugs in trichotillomania: Treatment results in 12 patients. *Journal of Nervous and Mental Disease, 184,* 641–644.

Jenike, M. A. (1989). Obsessive–compulsive and related disorders: A hidden epidemic. *New England Journal of Medicine, 321,* 539–541.

Keuthen, N. J., Fraim, C., Deckersbach, T. D., Dougherty, D. D., Baer, L., & Jenike, M. A. (2001). Longitudinal follow-up of naturalistic treatment outcome in patients with trichotillomania. *Journal of Clinical Psychiatry, 62,* 101–107.

Keuthen, N. J., O'Sullivan, R. L., Ricciardi, J. N., Shera, D., Savage, C. R., Borgmann, A. S., et al. (1995). The Massachusetts General Hospital (MGH) Hairpulling Scale: 1. Development and factor analyses. *Psychotherapy and Psychosomatics, 64,* 141–145.

Keuthen, N. J., Savage, C. R., O'Sullivan, R. L., Brown, H. D., Shera, D. M., Cyr, P., et al. (1996). Neuropsychological functioning in trichotillomania. *Biological Psychiatry, 39,* 747–749.

King, R. A., Scahill, L., Vitulano, L. A., Schwab-Stone, M., Tercyak, K. P., & Riddle, M. A. (1995). Childhood trichotillomania: clinical phenomenology, comorbidity, and family genetics. *Journal of the American Academy of Child and Adolescent Psychiatry, 34,* 1451–1459.

Ladouceur, R., Gosselin, P., & Dugas, M. J. (2000). Experimental manipulation of intolerance of uncertainty: A study of a theoretical model of worry. *Behaviour Research and Therapy, 38,* 933–941.

Lenane, M. C., Swedo, S. E., Rapoport, J. L., Leonard, H., Sceery, W., & Guroff, J. J. (1992). Rates of obsessive compulsive disorder in first degree relatives of patients with trichotillomania: A research note. *Journal of Child Psychology and Psychiatry, 33,* 925–933.

Lerner, J., Franklin, M. E., Meadows, E. A., Hembree, E., & Foa, E. B. (1998). Effectiveness of a cognitive-behavioral treatment program for trichotillomania: An uncontrolled evaluation. *Behavior Therapy, 29,* 157–171.

Lipsitz, J. D., Mannuzza, S., Chapman, T., Foa, E. B., Franklin, M. E., Goodwin, R. D., et al. (2005). A direct interview family study of obsessive–compulsive disorder II: Contribution of proband informant information. *Psychological Medicine, 35,* 1–9.

Mannino, F. V., & Delgado, R. A. (1969). Trichotillomania in children: A review. *American Journal of Psychiatry, 126,* 505–511.

Mansueto, C. S. (1990, November). *Typography and phenomenology of trichotillomania.* Presented at the annual meeting of the Association for Advancement of Behavior Therapy, San Francisco, CA.

Mansueto, C. S., Stemberger, R. M. T., Thomas, A. M., & Golomb, R. G. (1997). Trichotillomania: A comprehensive behavioral model. *Clinical Psychology Review, 17,* 567–577.

Meunier, S. A., Tolin, D. F., & Franklin, M. E. (2006). Affective and sensory correlates of pediatric hair pulling. Manuscript submitted for publication.

Mouton, S. G., & Stanley, M. A. (1996). Habit reversal training for trichotillomania: A group approach. *Cognitive and Behavioral Practice, 3,* 159–182.

Ninan, P. T., Rothbaum, B. O., Marsteller, F. A., Knight, B. T., & Eccard, M. B. (2000). A placebo-controlled trial of cognitive-behavioral therapy and clomipramine in trichotillomania. *Journal of Clinical Psychiatry, 61,* 47–50.

O'Sullivan, R., Christenson, G. A., & Stein, D. J. (1999). Pharmacotherapy of trichotillomania. In D. J. Stein, G. A. Christenson, & E. Hollander (Eds.), *Trichotillomania* (pp. 134–167). Washington, DC: American Psychiatric Press.

O'Sullivan, R. L., Keuthen, N. J., Hayday, C. F., Ricciardi, J. N., Buttolph, M. L., Jenike, M. A., et al. (1995). The Massachusetts Hospital (MGH) Hairpulling Scale: 2. Reliability and validity. *Psychotherapy and Psychosomatics, 64,* 146–148.

O'Sullivan, R. L., Rauch, S. L., Breiter, H. C., Grachev, I. D., Baer, L., Kennedy, D. N., et al. (1997). Reduced basal ganglia volumes in trichotillomania measured via morphometric magnetic resonance imaging. *Biological Psychiatry, 42,* 39–45.

Piacentini, J., & Chang, S. (2005). Habit reversal training for tic disorders in children and adolescents. *Behavior Modification, 29,* 803–822.

Pollard, C. A., Ibe, I. O., Krojanker, D. N., Kitchen, A. D., Bronson, S. S., & Flynn, T. M. (1991). Clomipramine treatment of trichotillomania: A follow-up report on four cases. *Journal of Clinical Psychiatry, 52,* 128–130.

Reeve, E. (1999). Hair pulling in children and adolescents. In D. J. Stein, G.A. Christenson, & E. Hollander (Eds.), *Trichotillomania* (pp. 201–224). Washington, DC: American Psychiatric Association Press.

Reeve, E. A., Bernstein, G. A., & Christenson, G. A. (1992). Clinical characteristics and psychiatric comorbidity in children with trichotillomania. *Journal of the American Academy of Child and Adolescent Psychiatry, 31,* 132–138.

Reiss, S., Peterson, R. A., Gursky, D. M., & McNally, R. J. (1986). Anxiety sensitivity, anxiety frequency and the prediction of fearfulness. *Behaviour Research and Therapy, 24,* 1–8.

Rettew, D. C., Cheslow, D. L., Rapoport, J. L., Leonard, H. L., & Lenane, M. C. (1991). Neuropsychological test performance in trichotillomania: A further link with obsessive–compulsive disorder. *Journal of Anxiety Disorders, 5,* 225–235.

Rothbaum, B. O., Shaw, L., Morris, R., & Ninan, P. T. (1993). Prevalence of trichotillomania in a college freshman population [Letter]. *Journal of Clinical Psychiatry, 54,* 72.

Sanderson, K. V., & Hall-Smith, P. (1970). Tonsure trichotillomania. *British Journal of Dermatology, 82,* 343–350.

Schlosser, S., Black, D. W., Blum, N., & Goldstein, R. B. (1994). The demography, phenomenology, and family history of 22 persons with compulsive hair pulling. *Annals of Clinical Psychiatry, 6,* 147–152.

Soriano, J. L., O'Sullivan, R. L., Baer, L., Phillips, K. A., McNally, R. J., & Jenike, M. A. (1996). Trichotillomania and self-esteem: A survey of 62 female hair pullers. *Journal of Clinical Psychiatry, 57,* 77–82.

Stanley, M. A., Borden, J. W., Mouton, S. G., & Breckenridge, J. K. (1995). Nonclinical hair pulling: Affective correlates and comparison with clinical samples. *Behaviour Research and Therapy, 33,* 179–186.

Stanley, M. A., & Cohen, L. J. (1999). Trichotillomania and obsessive–compulsive disorder. In D. J. Stein, G. A. Christenson, & E. Hollander (Eds.), *Trichotillomania* (pp. 225–261). Washington, DC: American Psychiatric Press.

Stanley, M. A., Hannay, H. J., & Breckenridge, J. K. (1997). The neuropsychology of trichotillomania. *Journal of Anxiety Disorders, 11,* 473–488.

Stanley, M. A., Swann, A. C., Bowers, T. C., Davis, M. L., & Taylor, D. J. (1992). A comparison of clinical features in trichotillomania and obsessive–compulsive disorder. *Behaviour Research and Therapy, 30,* 39–44.

Stein, D. J., & Hollander, E. (1992). Low-dose pimozide augmentation of serotonin reuptake blockers in the treatment of trichotillomania. *Journal of Clinical Psychiatry, 53,* 123–126.

Stemberger, R. M. T., Thomas, A. M., Mansueto, C. S., & Carter, J. G. (2000). Personal toll of trichotillomania: Behavioral and interpersonal sequelae. *Journal of Anxiety Disorders, 14,* 97–104.

Stewart, R. S., & Nejtek, V. A. (2003). An open-label, flexible-dose study of olanzapine in the treatment of trichotillomania. *Journal of Clinical Psychiatry, 64,* 49–52.

Streichenwein, S. M., & Thornby, J. I. (1995). A long-term, double-blind, placebo-controlled crossover trial of the efficacy of fluoxetine for trichotillomania. *American Journal of Psychiatry, 152,* 1192–1196.

Swedo, S. E. (1993). Trichotillomania. *Psychiatric Annals, 23,* 402–407.

Swedo, S. E., & Leonard, H. L. (1992). Trichotillomania: An obsessive compulsive spectrum disorder? *Psychiatric Clinics of North America, 15,* 777–790.

Swedo, S. E., Leonard, H. L., Rapoport, J. L., Lenane, M., Goldberger, E. L., & Cheslow, D. (1989). A double-blind comparison of clomipramine and desipramine in the treatment of trichotillomania (hair pulling). *New England Journal of Medicine, 321,* 497–501.

Swedo, S. E., Lenane, M. C., & Leonard, H. L. (1993). Long-term treatment of trichotillomania (hair pulling) [Letter]. *New England Journal of Medicine, 329,* 141–142.

Swedo, S. E., Rapoport, J. L., Leonard, H. L., Schapiro, M. B., Rapoport, S. I., & Grady, C. L. (1991). Regional cerebral glucose metabolism of women in trichotillomania. *Archives of General Psychiatry, 48,* 828–833.

Tolin, D. F., Abramowitz, J. S., Brigidi, B. D., & Foa, E. B. (2003). Intolerance of uncertainty in obsessive–compulsive disorder. *Journal of Anxiety Disorders, 17,* 233–242.

Tolin, D. F., Franklin, M. E., Diefenbach, G. J., Anderson, E., & Meunier, S. A. (2006). Pediatric trichotillomania: Descriptive psychopathology and an open trial of cognitive–behavioral therapy. Manuscript submitted for publication.

Tukel, R., Keser, V., Karali, N. T., Olgun, T. O., & Calikusu, C. (2001). Comparison of clinical characteristics in trichotillomania and obsessive–compulsive disorder. *Journal of Anxiety Disorders, 15,* 433–441.

van Minnen, A., Hoogduin, K. A., Keijsers, G. P., Hellenbrand, I., & Hendriks, G. (2003). Treatment of trichotillomania with behavioral therapy or fluoxetine. *Archives of General Psychiatry, 60,* 517–522.

van Nes, J. J. (1986). Electrophysiological evidence of sensory nerve dysfunction in 10 dogs with acral lick dermatitis. *Journal of the American Animal Hospital Association, 22,* 157–160.

Ware, J. E. Jr. (1993). *SF-36 Health survey manual and interpretation guide.* Boston: The Health Institute, New England Medical Center.

Watson, D., & Clark, L. A. (1984). Negative affectivity: The disposition to experience aversive emotional states. *Psychological Bulletin, 96,* 465–490.

Woods, D. W., Flessner, C. A., Franklin, M. E., Keuthen, N. J., Goodwin, R., Stein, D. J., et al. (in press). The Trichotillomania Impact Project (TIP): Exploring phenomenology, functional impairment, and treatment utilization. *Journal of Clinical Psychiatry.*

Woods, D. W., Wetterneck, C. T., & Flessner, C. A. (2006). A controlled evaluation of acceptance and commitment therapy plus habit reversal for trichotillomania. *Behaviour Research and Therapy, 44,* 639–656.

10

SHOULD PATHOLOGICAL GAMBLING BE CONSIDERED AN OBSESSIVE–COMPULSIVE SPECTRUM CONDITION?

HEATHER DURDLE[1] AND SHERRY H. STEWART[2]

[1]*Department of Psychology, University of Windsor;* [2]*Departments of Psychiatry & Psychology, Dalhousie University*

Pathological gambling is a chronic disorder that involves the failure to resist urges or impulses to gamble. This leads to serious disruptions in personal, family, and occupational functioning. According to the *DSM-IV-TR* (American Psychiatric Association, 2000), the diagnostic criteria for pathological gambling include preoccupation with gambling; 'chasing' losses (i.e., gambling with increasing amounts of money in an attempt to break even); lying to conceal the extent of involvement in gambling-related activities; the commission of illegal acts to finance gambling; and gambling as a way to escape problems or relieve dysphoric mood (e.g., guilt, anxiety, depression).

The prevalence of pathological gambling has increased in the past 20 years, with current estimates placing the North American lifetime prevalence rate at 1.7% (Shaffer, Hall, & Vander Bilt, 1999). Pathological gambling typically begins in adolescence or early adulthood, with a later age of onset for females than for males. As the frequency of gambling increases, there are often severe implications, as these individuals struggle to cover gambling-related debts and meet their

Correspondence to: Heather Durdle, Department of Psychology, University of Windsor, 401 Sunset Ave, Windsor, ON, Canada, N9B 3P4.

other financial obligations. This in turn has an effect on society, as up to 60% of pathological gamblers commit illegal acts to support their gambling (Rosenthal & Lorenz, 1992).

Rates of comorbid psychiatric diagnoses amongst pathological gamblers are relatively high. These individuals, compared to people who do not suffer from pathological gambling, have greater rates of depression, attention-deficit hyperactivity disorder, antisocial, narcissistic, and borderline personality disorders, substance use disorders, and anxiety disorders (see Raylu & Oei, 2002 for a review). Several health problems related to stress (such as hypertension and migraines) are also found to be elevated in these individuals. These psychiatric and health problems, coupled with financial or legal difficulties, likely contribute to the elevated rates of suicidal ideation and attempts amongst pathological gamblers (Petry & Kiluk, 2002).

Pathological gambling is currently classified in the *DSM-IV-TR* as an impulse control disorder (alongside such disorders as intermittent explosive disorder, kleptomania, pyromania, and trichotillomania). However, on the basis of elevated comorbidity rates and similar clinical features, some authors have suggested that pathological gambling may best be conceptualized in psychiatric nosology as either an addictive disorder alongside substance use disorders, or an obsessive–compulsive (OC) spectrum disorder (e.g., Blanco, Moreyra, Nunes, Sáiz-Ruiz, & Ibáñez, 2001).

In this chapter, we will begin by reviewing the literature linking pathological gambling to substance use and impulsivity before expanding on the similarities and differences between pathological gambling and obsessive–compulsive disorder (OCD). Finally, we will attempt to integrate these research findings and comment on the appropriateness of including pathological gambling as an OC spectrum condition.

PATHOLOGICAL GAMBLING AND SUBSTANCE USE DISORDERS

Several criteria for pathological gambling have been directly modeled after the diagnostic criteria for substance abuse and dependence (American Psychiatric Association, 2000). These criteria include repeated unsuccessful efforts to cut back or stop gambling, as well as criteria related to tolerance and withdrawal (i.e., the need to gamble with increasing amounts of money in order to achieve desired excitement, and restlessness or irritability when attempting to cut down or stop gambling, respectively). Research supports these clinical similarities of pathological gambling to the substance use disorders. Pathological gamblers evidence tolerance by increasing the size of their bets over time (Spunt, 2002), as well as physical withdrawal symptoms such as insomnia, headaches, or loss of appetite when attempting to quit or cut back on gambling (Rosenthal & Lesieur, 1992). More recent research also indicates that pathological gamblers abstaining from gambling endorse levels of craving that are even higher than abstinent alcoholics (Tavares, Zilberman, Hodgins, & el-Guebaly, 2005).

Pathological gambling and substance use disorders are commonly comorbid with one another, which would be expected to occur if the two disorders had etiologic mechanisms in common. The findings of several studies (e.g., Lesieur, Blume, & Zoppa, 1986; Toneatto & Brennan, 2002) suggest that relative to the general population, the rates of pathological gambling are 2 to 14 times higher among various groups of treatment-seeking substance abusers. Similarly, Lesieur (1998) reports that between 47 and 52% of pathological gamblers receive a substance abuse diagnosis at some point in their lives.

PATHOLOGICAL GAMBLING AND IMPULSIVITY

Although there appear to be many similarities between pathological gambling and the substance use disorders, pathological gambling is classified in the *DSM-IV-TR* as an impulse control disorder. All of the disorders in this category share the common core features of difficulty in resisting an impulse, a desire or temptation to perform a detrimental behavior (either to self or others), an emotional discomfort or tension before performing the act, and pleasurable feelings while performing the behavior. Often the impulsive act is followed by feelings of regret or guilt.

The similarities between pathological gambling and impulsivity are supported by the clinical observations of pathological gamblers as restless and easily bored (e.g., Graham & Lowenfeld, 1986), with problems delaying gratification (Rugle & Melamed, 1993). Empirical research provides more mixed evidence, however. Some studies support a relationship between pathological gambling and higher rates of impulsivity (e.g., Steel & Blaszczynski, 1998) and impulse control disorders (Specker, Carlson, Christenson, & Marcotte, 1995), while other studies report no relationship (e.g., Allcock & Grace, 1988).

PATHOLOGICAL GAMBLING AND THE OC SPECTRUM

A third possible conceptualization of the nosological classification of pathological gambling places it on the OC spectrum of disorders (Hollander & Wong, 1995). The latter spectrum of conditions are said to share similar characteristics to OCD, such as phenomenology, presumed etiology, associated features (e.g., age of onset, comorbidity), clinical course, familial history, and response to pharmacological or behavioral treatments (Bienvenu et al., 2000; Hollander, 2005). The common core feature of all disorders in this spectrum of conditions is the presence of repetitive thoughts and behaviors. These symptoms are manifested differently across the distinct diagnostic entities, but in each case the patient typically realizes that the obsessions are irrational and inappropriate, yet they find them extremely difficult to resist (Hollander, 2005).

The theoretical placement of pathological gambling amongst this spectrum of conditions does take into account the disorder's relationship to impulsivity. For example, Hollander (2005) identifies three distinct clusters of OC spectrum conditions: Preoccupation with bodily sensations or appearance (e.g., body dysmorphic disorder, anorexia nervosa, and hypochondriasis); impulsive disorders (e.g., trichotillomania, pathological gambling, kleptomania); and neurological disorders (e.g., Tourette's syndrome, autism). This conceptualization categorizes pathological gambling with other impulse control disorders, as in the current diagnostic system (American Psychiatric Association, 2000), and recognizes the distinct features of this class of conditions.

A more dimensional conceptualization of the OC spectrum of conditions also acknowledges the link between pathological gambling and impulsivity. In this model, the various disorders are classified along a dimension that has compulsive features at one pole and impulsive features at the other. The distinction between these two extremes is that compulsivity is driven by an attempt to alleviate tension or anxiety, while impulsivity is driven by the desire to obtain pleasure, arousal, or gratification (Hollander & Rosen, 2000). Pathological gambling is conceptualized as being closer to the impulsive end of the spectrum, with only self-injurious behavior, sexual compulsions, and the impulsive–aggressive personality disorders conceptualized as having more impulsive characteristics. In contrast, OCD is conceptualized as being at the extreme of the compulsive end of the spectrum.

The inclusion of pathological gambling as an OC spectrum condition highlights the disorder's similarities to OCD, while its placement along the dimensional conceptualization acknowledges that there are many distinct features of the two disorders. Research and clinical observations support both these similarities and differences.

SIMILARITIES AND DIFFERENCES

One key similarity between pathological gambling and OCD is the apparent inability to delay or inhibit repetitive behavior (Hollander & Wong, 1995). In the case of pathological gambling, these individuals report persistent urges and impulses to gamble. These urges are such an important and recognizable feature of the disorder that pathological gambling is often referred to as 'compulsive gambling' by lay people (Blanco et al., 2001). For pathological gamblers as well as individuals with OCD, these compulsions often lead to excessive and harmful behavior that causes significant distress or disruption to everyday life (Black, Goldstein, Noyes, & Blum, 1994).

Both pathological gambling and OCD involve an excessive preoccupation with intrusive thoughts. In the case of pathological gambling, these individuals often report repetitive thoughts related to gambling that they cannot resist. In fact, these intrusive thoughts are considered to be a defining feature of this disorder in the current diagnostic system (American Psychiatric Association, 2000). There is emerging empirical support for the role of obsessive thoughts in pathological gambling. Blaszczynski (1999) showed that 40 pathological gamblers scored higher than 40 nonpathological gamblers on the two obsession factors (but not on the two compulsion factors) of the Padua Inventory (Sanavio, 1988) – a validated measure of OCD symptoms. A later study by Frost, Meagher, and Riskind (2001) also found that pathological gamblers scored higher than light gamblers on the obsessions subscale (as well as the compulsions subscale) of another validated measure of OCD symptoms, the Yale–Brown Obsessive–Compulsive Scale (Y–BOCS; Goodman et al., 1989).

One important difference between pathological gambling and OCD appears to be in the type of reinforcement involved in each disorder. OCD involves negative reinforcement. Compulsive rituals are thought to be maintained because they provide relief from the anxiety created by the obsessive thoughts. In contrast, pathological gambling is thought to involve mainly positive reinforcement such as the rewards received or anticipated from gambling (e.g., money or positive affect). However, negative reinforcement processes are also thought to be involved in maintaining problem gambling behavior, just as has been found for other impulse control disorders (McElroy, Hudson, Phillips, Keck, & Pope, 1993; Rasmussen & Eisen, 1992). The role of negative reinforcement is highlighted in the current diagnostic criteria for pathological gambling (i.e., gambling to escape problems or relieve guilt, anxiety, or depression; American Psychiatric Association, 2000). Given that pathological gambling is often associated with high levels of anxiety (e.g., Petry, Stinson, & Grant, 2005), many pathological gamblers may experience decreased negative affect as a result of their gambling. Therefore, both positive and negative reinforcement seem to be potential maintaining factors for pathological gambling behavior, while negative reinforcement is the sole reward system involved in OCD.

Because of the types of rewards they receive, pathological gamblers experience their repetitive gambling behavior as ego-syntonic. That is, they generally describe their repetitive gambling behavior as pleasurable. This is in contrast to the ego-dystonic nature of the symptoms of a person with OCD, who experiences their thoughts as alien or not within their control (McElroy et al., 1993). While pathological gamblers may also experience ego-dystonic aspects of their gambling, this tends to relate to longer-term consequences of their maladaptive behavior (e.g., inability to meet financial obligations, relationships problems due to their gambling).

DYSFUNCTIONAL COGNITIONS

Individuals with pathological gambling and OCD show some similar dysfunctional cognitions that may be important in understanding the possible link between these disorders. Several gambling-specific cognitive distortions have been identified (e.g., Toneatto, 1999; Toneatto, Blitz-Miller, Calderwood, Dragonetti, & Tsanos, 1997) that may be involved in the development and maintenance of pathological gambling (Raylu & Oei, 2002). However, one cognitive distortion that is found in both pathological gamblers and individuals with OCD involves an illusion of control over the outcome of their repetitive behavior. Although an illusion of control appears to be present in both disorders, it appears to present in somewhat different forms. Pathological gamblers believe that they can influence the outcome of their wager, either directly or indirectly (Raylu & Oei, 2002). This distorted belief amounts to an illusion of control over luck (Toneatto, 1999). A similar illusion of control also appears to be present in individuals with OCD. In this case, this cognitive distortion tends to manifest as the belief that their repetitive behaviors gain them some control over their environment.

Another important way that pathological gamblers and individuals with OCD evidence similar cognitive distortions relates to their beliefs in the possibility of improbable events. In the case of OCD, these individuals are dominated by thoughts and worries about the possibility of a one-in-a-million chance that something terrible will happen to them (Rasmussen & Eisen, 1992). In a similar way, pathological gamblers are consumed with the belief that regardless of the odds stacked against them, their gambling will have a positive monetary outcome. Toneatto et al. (1997) label this as a probability error, and it appears to be present in both disorders, although in different forms.

It has also been argued that pathological gamblers and individuals with OCD are preoccupied with worries about lost opportunity (Frost & Steketee, 1998). Frost et al. (2001) found that pathological gamblers scored higher than a light gambling comparison sample on the compulsive buying and compulsive hoarding subscales of the Y–BOCS. Compulsive hoarding occurs in 20–30% of individuals with OCD, and is characterized by the failure to discard objects that appear to be useless or of a limited value (Frost & Gross, 1993). Compulsive buying is a related disorder associated with the excessive acquisition of unnecessary possessions.

These findings have been used to suggest that pathological gambling is associated with the specific OC symptoms of compulsive buying and compulsive hoarding (Frost et al., 2001). It has been further suggested that both pathological gambling and these compulsive behaviors relate to acquisition. In the case of OCD, each possession represents an opportunity that would be lost if it were discarded (i.e., compulsive hoarding) or not acquired (i.e., compulsive buying). In the case of pathological gambling, these individuals have difficulty refraining from gambling because each unplayed game represents a similar lost opportunity for financial acquisition. Therefore, it is argued that the same underlying concern with acquisition is manifested differently in both pathological gambling and OCD (Frost et al., 2001).

Although there are many similar cognitive distortions between the disorders, another important way that they appear to differ pertains to cognitions regarding susceptibility to threat/harm. One of the core cognitive characteristics of OCD is an overestimation of threat (OCCWG, 1997) or an exaggerated sense of harm, whereas the behavior of pathological gamblers suggests just the opposite – beliefs that they are impervious to harm. It has been proposed that across the various OC spectrum conditions, there is a continuum ranging from an exaggerated sense of harm at the compulsive end of the spectrum, to an underestimated sense of harm at the impulsive end of the spectrum (Hollander & Rosen, 2000). Because the two disorders fall on different ends of this spectrum, pathological gambling is often associated with risk-taking behavior (Blanco et al., 2001), while OCD is associated with risk aversion, harm avoidance, anticipatory anxiety (Blanco et al., 2001), and excessive doubt (Rasmussen & Eisen, 1992).

COMORBIDITY

If pathological gambling is appropriately conceptualized as an OC spectrum condition, it should follow that there is a high comorbidity between pathological gambling and OCD. The evidence in the literature is mixed on this subject, with the prevalence rates varying greatly. A general population study showed that the rate of OCD was elevated among pathological gamblers (16%) (Bland, Newman, Orn, & Stebelsky, 1993). In contrast, the lifetime rate of OCD amongst the general population is estimated to be 1.5% (American Psychiatric Association, 2000). Reported rates of OCD among pathological gamblers in treatment range from a high of 20% (Linden, Pope, & Jonas, 1986) to rates as low as 0% (Black et al., 1994). More moderate rates of 10% have been reported by other authors (Black & Moyer, 1998). Conversely, the rates of pathological gambling in individuals receiving treatment for OCD have been found to be similar to the lifetime prevalence rate of 1.7% in the general population (Shaffer et al., 1999). For example, one study found that the lifetime prevalence rate of pathological gambling amongst OCD patients was 1.2% (Du Toit, van Kradenburg, Niehaus, & Stein, 2001), while another found no past or current diagnoses of pathological gambling in 80 individuals with OCD (Bienvenu et al., 2000). Therefore, although the reported rates vary across studies, there does appear to be an elevation of OCD amongst pathological gamblers in both general population studies and samples of pathological gamblers in treatment. However, the rate of pathological gambling amongst individuals receiving treatment for OCD appears to be similar to the base rate in the general population. This pattern of findings suggests that if there is an elevated comorbidity of pathological gambling and OCD, individuals with this form of dual disorder may be more likely to be referred or to seek services for their pathological gambling disorder.

Several studies have also examined the family history of individuals with either disorder in an attempt to find evidence of a familial link between the two disorders. Thus far, this approach has failed to find any such relationship. Research has found neither any past or present diagnoses of pathological gambling amongst first-degree relatives of those with OCD (Bienvenu et al., 2000; Black et al., 1994), nor elevated rates of OCD among the first-degree relatives of pathological gamblers (Black, Moyer, & Schlosser, 2003).

Some authors have also examined the possible link between pathological gambling and the OC spectrum condition of obsessive–compulsive personality disorder (OCPD). It is consistently reported that pathological gamblers have higher than average rates of personality disorders, with the percentage of pathological gamblers meeting criteria for at least one personality disorder ranging from 25% (Specker, Carlson, Edmonson, Johnson, & Marcotte, 1996) to as high as 87% and 92% (Black & Moyer, 1998; Blaszczynski & Steel, 1998, respectively). There is mixed evidence, however, whether pathological gambling is linked specifically to OCPD. The rate of diagnosis varies widely across studies. One study found that OCPD was among the least frequently diagnosed personality disorders in pathological gamblers (Blaszczynski & Steel, 1998), whereas another found that it was among the most diagnosed personality disorders (Black & Moyer, 1998). A third study found comparable rates of all personality disorders in their pathological gambling sample (Specker et al., 1996). Therefore, although rates of personality disorders are elevated overall in pathological gamblers, there does not appear to be consistent evidence suggesting a specific link to OCPD.

While the study of diagnostic criteria provides mixed evidence, the findings using dimensional assessments appear to more favourably support a link between pathological gambling and OC spectrum disorders. Using the Symptom Checklist-90-Revised (Derogatis, 1977), several studies provide evidence that, relative to normal controls, pathological gamblers have elevated scores on the OC subscale (e.g., Martinez-Pina et al., 1991; Petry, 2000).

Similarly, it has been found that pathological gamblers reported more neurotic and obsessive thoughts on the Maudsley Obsessive–Compulsive Inventory (MOCI; Hodgson & Rachman, 1977) than a matched control sample (Burton, Netemeyer, & Andrews, 2000). Furthermore, scores on the South Oaks Gambling Screen (SOGS; Lesieur & Blume, 1987) (a measure of pathological gambling symptoms) were significantly correlated with the neurotic and obsessive thoughts measured by the MOCI. On face value it does not appear that the SOGS is assessing any criteria that may be shared aspects of the two disorders. Therefore, the findings of Burton et al. (2000) appear to indicate that individuals with more dysfunctional gambling behavior evidence more OC traits. This is supported by the findings of the Frost et al. (2001) study, discussed earlier, that pathological gamblers reported more obsessions and compulsions on the Y–BOCS relative to light gamblers.

Only two studies provide evidence that pathological gambling may not be associated with OC traits. In both these instances, this lack of a relationship is only evidenced on some, but not all, of the measures employed. Anholt et al. (2004) reported that relative to pathological gamblers, individuals with OCD had higher scores on the Padua Inventory – Revised. However, no difference was found between these groups on the Obsessive–Compulsive Beliefs Questionnaire-87, a measure of maladaptive cognitions associated with OCD (OCCWG, 1997). Pathological gamblers also did not score higher on the Lynfield Scale, a measure of OCD symptoms (Allen & Tune, 1975), than normal controls, yet they had higher OC subscale scores on the Symptom Checklist-90 (Martinez-Pina et al., 1991). Therefore, whenever there is evidence to suggest that pathological gambling may not be associated with a greater prevalence of OC traits and symptoms, there is further evidence from different measures given to the same participants to suggest that there is in fact a link between pathological gambling and OCD.

A recent meta-analysis attempted, in part, to summarize these research findings linking pathological gambling and OCD (Durdle, 2005). This research examined studies that compared pathological gamblers with controls on comorbidity rates of OCD, as well as their scores on dimensional measures that assess OC traits. The weighted effect size linking pathological gambling and OC traits was found to be in the medium to large range, suggesting that there is a substantial relationship between pathological gambling and OCD. This relationship was found to not differ from the strength of the relationship between pathological gambling and impulsivity, but both were significantly stronger than the association between pathological gambling and substance use disorders (Durdle, 2005).

COMMON RISK FACTORS

The exact reasons for why one develops pathological gambling or OCD remain unknown. A recent theoretical model lends itself to the suggestion that anxiety may be a common causal link between pathological gambling and OCD. Several researchers have found high rates of obsessive thoughts amongst pathological gamblers (e.g., Frost et al., 2001). It has been proposed that the effect of these thoughts on gambling behavior is likely to be indirect via their effects on anxiety (Burton et al., 2000). That is, these neurotic or obsessive thoughts become a major source of anxiety or tension until an act relieves them. Just as individuals with OCD engage in repetitive behavior to relieve anxiety caused by obsessive thoughts, pathological gamblers may gamble as a way to relieve tension caused by similar cognitions. Therefore, for some individuals, gambling may be a behavioral outlet to reduce the anxiety resulting from obsessive thinking (Burton et al., 2000). It is hypothesized that there is likely a threshold level of anxiety that must be reached before the individual is strongly motivated to relieve the resulting tension through gambling (Burton et al., 2000).

This theorized model of psychological risk factors for pathological gambling was tested by conducting a structural equation model on the self-report scores of 44 pathological gamblers and 164 individuals from a matched consumer sample who varied naturally on their gambling behaviors (Burton et al., 2000). The pathway from neurotic/obsessive thoughts to anxiety was significant for both samples. However, the pathway from anxiety to SOGS scores was significant only for the pathological gamblers. Another significant pathway from neurotic/obsessive thoughts to impulsivity was also found for both samples. However, the pathway from impulsivity to SOGS scores was only significant for pathological gamblers. Therefore, these findings suggest that across all individuals, neurotic or obsessive thoughts may lead to anxiety or impulsivity. However, it seems that for pathological gamblers only, this anxiety or impulsivity is linked to their gambling behavior. This finding supports a common developmental or maintaining link between OC symptoms and pathological gambling that involves both anxiety and impulsivity, although longitudinal research is needed to more fully understand these relationships.

TREATMENT RESPONSE

The study of both pharmacological and psychological treatment responses indicates that pathological gambling and OCD respond to some common treatments, which is consistent with the possibility of a common underlying pathology. Both of these disorders have been linked to serotonergic dysfunction, and both disorders have been found to respond to treatment with selective serotonin reuptake inhibitors (SSRIs). Although sample sizes are generally small, studies of pathological gamblers have reported significant improvement in symptoms following treatment with such SSRIs as fluvoxamine, paroxetine, and citalopram (see Hollander, Sood, Pallanti, Baldini-Rossi, & Baker, 2005 for a review). These symptom improvements include fewer thoughts and urges to gamble, better ability to resist these urges, and often complete abstinence from gambling during the treatment period. Studies of individuals with OCD have reported similar treatment responses to SSRIs such as paroxetine, setraline, and fluvoxamine (see Stanley & Turner, 1995 for a review). Improvements for these individuals include decreased severity of their OCD symptoms and improved daily functioning.

Although SSRIs are the primary pharmacological treatment for OCD, pathological gambling has been found to also respond to a variety of other medications. This is likely because in addition to the hypothesized serotonergic dysregulation, pathological gambling has also been linked to dysfunctions in the dopaminergic (e.g., Bergh, Eklund, Södersten, & Nordin, 1997) and noradrenergic systems (Roy et al., 1988). Therefore, pathological gamblers have also been reported to evidence symptom improvements in response to the noradrenergic/serotonergic reuptake inhibitor nefazodone; the norepinephrine dopamine reuptake inhibitor bupropion; and even the opiate antagonist naltrexone, which blocks the release of dopamine in the nucleus accumbens (see Hollander et al., 2005 for a review). Research has failed to find similar results for individuals with OCD, and therefore pathological gambling appears to respond to a wider range of pharmacological treatments. This is congruent with the observation that the rewards are different between the two disorders, with pathological gamblers receiving both potentially positive and negative reinforcement, and individuals with OCD receiving only potentially negative reinforcement for their behavior.

Studies of psychological treatments show that both disorders respond to some similar approaches, as well. In fact, some treatments for pathological gambling have been explicitly modeled after those known to be effective for OCD. One highly effective psychological treatment for OCD involves cue exposure and response prevention (ERP). In this approach, individuals are exposed to cues normally associated with triggering their obsessive thoughts (or are exposed to the obsessive thoughts themselves) and are prevented from acting on their compulsions. Over time, this disconfirms mistaken associations, promotes habituation to the fearful thoughts and situations, and eventually helps extinguish the compulsive behavior amongst individuals with OCD (Hollander, 2005).

Limited research suggests that this approach is also useful in the treatment of pathological gambling. In a case series study of two pathological gamblers, ERP led to a significant reduction in gambling behavior and urges to gamble in both individuals (Symes & Nicki, 1997). In addition to ERP, research suggests that both pathological gambling (e.g., Ladouceur et al., 2001) and OCD (e.g., Salkovskis, 1999) respond well to a broader range of cognitive–behavioral interventions including cognitive restructuring techniques involving identification and challenging of some of the problematic beliefs thought to contribute to maintaining these disorders.

While cognitive–behavioral therapy appears to be a promising treatment for both disorders, other successful psychosocial approaches to treat pathological gambling such as relapse prevention (Ladouceur et al., 2001) and self-help groups such as Gamblers Anonymous (Petry, 2005a) are not used in the treatment of OCD. Therefore, while pathological gambling appears to respond well to psychological treatments modeled after those for OCD, pathological gamblers also often respond well to interventions commonly used in the treatment of substance abuse.

AREAS FOR FURTHER RESEARCH

Research evaluating the proposal that pathological gambling is best viewed as an OC spectrum condition is in its infancy. Thus, there are many exciting avenues of future research that will help clarify the validity of this proposal. We will consider a few of these potential avenues in this section.

One approach that may help clarify the degree of relationship of pathological gambling to OCD is the approach currently being taken by Robert Krueger and his colleagues in studying the structure of psychopathology. On the basis of a meta-analysis, Krueger and Markon (2006) concluded that research supports the existence of a broad 'internalizing' cluster of disorders including depression and anxiety disorders, and a broad 'externalizing' cluster including substance use and antisocial behavior disorders. Moreover, it appears that negative affectivity traits (e.g., anxiety) may be risk factors for both internalizing and externalizing disorders, but traits involving disinhibition (e.g., impulsivity) may be risk factors specifically for externalizing disorders (Krueger & Tackett, 2003). Previous research has shown that OCD belongs in the internalizing cluster (Krueger, Caspi, Moffitt, & Silva, 1998) but no research using this approach has yet attempted to model where pathological gambling lies in this conceptualization. A simplistic version of the OC spectrum perspective would predict that pathological gambling should fall in the internalizing cluster of disorders along with OCD. But pathological gambling's genetic links with alcohol dependence (Slutske et al., 2000), and its links with both anxiety and impulsivity (e.g., Burton et al., 2000), would suggest it may be more likely to cluster with the externalizing disorders.

Another area for future research is the possibility that the OC spectrum may encompass only some, but not all, forms of pathological gambling. For instance, it has been suggested by several authors (e.g., Blaszczynski, Winter, & McConaghy, 1986; Specker et al., 1996; Stewart, Zack, Klein, Loba, & Fragopoulous, 2003) that pathological gambling may have different subtypes. This means that pathological gambling may not be a homogenous disorder, and while some cases may closely resemble OCD, this is not necessarily true for all individuals. This theory could help explain some of the mixed evidence linking the two disorders and is congruent with the placement of at least some cases of pathological gambling along the spectrum continuum. Future research could examine the similarities and differences between pathological gamblers of different subtypes and patients with OCD. It could be predicted that those in Blaszczynski et al.'s (1986) 'emotionally-vulnerable' gambler subtype would hold much more in common with OCD patients than those in their 'impulsive, antisocial' gambler subtype, for example.

Another theory suggests that impulsivity may begin the gambling cycle, while compulsivity maintains the disorder (DeCaria, Begaz, & Hollander, 1998). Again, this theory could help explain some of the mixed evidence regarding the relationship of pathological gambling to OCD and is consistent with the placement and inclusion of pathological gambling as an OC spectrum condition, at least at certain stages. Future research could examine the similarities and differences between pathological gamblers at different stages of the disorder and patients with OCD. It could be predicted that gamblers at later stages of the disorder would hold much more in common with OCD patients than those at earlier stages of the disorder.

An additional area for future research is the role of depression in helping explain the observed relations between pathological gambling and OCD. Major depression is commonly comorbid with pathological gambling (Petry, 2005b) and with OCD (Abramowitz, 2004). Obsessions in particular are associated with depression (Bhar & Kyrios, 2005). There are many potential research questions within this particular area. One example is examining the degree to which depression (as opposed to anxiety and/or impulsivity) may account for the relation of obsessional thoughts and problem gambling symptoms among pathological gamblers (cf. Burton et al., 2000).

Finally, laboratory-based methodologies could be used to examine the degree to which the processes causing and maintaining compulsive behaviors in OCD are similar to or different than those causing and maintaining excessive gambling in pathological gambling. For example, pathological gamblers could have their mood, physiological arousal, thoughts, and gambling behavior monitored prior to and during gambling play. The OC spectrum perspective would suggest that prior to a gambling bout, obsessive thoughts about gambling would lead to higher self-reported anxiety and anxious arousal (e.g., skin conductance) which would in turn prompt gambling behavior. Engaging in gambling behavior should result in decreased self-reported anxiety and anxious arousal. Although no study to date has examined this full sequence of predicted events, laboratory-based studies of video lottery terminal play by our group provide more support for the role of positive reinforcement than negative reinforcement in maintaining gambling behavior (e.g., Stewart, Collins, Blackburn, Ellery, & Klein, 2005).

CONCLUSIONS

The evidence linking pathological gambling and OCD is to some degree mixed. As a result, there is debate in the literature surrounding the appropriateness of including pathological gambling as a spectrum condition. Evidence suggesting that pathological gambling should not be included as an OC spectrum condition includes findings that individuals with each disorder receive potentially different rewards for their behaviors, and the fact that the two disorders involve very different estimates of threat. Authors such as Black et al. (1994) also use the lack of evidence supporting a familial-genetic link between the two disorders to suggest that there is no relationship between pathological gambling and OCD. Other authors acknowledge that while there are some similarities, they feel that there is not yet enough evidence to suggest that the two disorders are part of a familial spectrum of disorders (e.g., Bienvenu et al., 2000).

Research that supports a link between the two disorders includes the finding that individuals with each disorder experience both obsessive thoughts and compulsive behaviors (e.g., Frost et al., 2001) as well as the observation that there are similar cognitive distortions in each disorder that involve illusions of control (e.g., Toneatto, 1999) and the possibility of improbable events (e.g., Rasmussen & Eisen, 1992). There is also mixed evidence of higher than average comorbidity rates between the disorders, at least of elevated rates of OCD among pathological gamblers (e.g., Bland et al., 1993), as well as high OC traits in pathological gamblers (e.g., Petry, 2000). Similar treatment responses to SSRIs, cognitive–behavioral therapy, and possibly ERP, in addition to evidence that the disorders may share common risk factors (Burton et al., 2000), provide further evidence that OCD and pathological gambling share several features.

Although much data still needs to be gathered, examination of the available evidence does appear to support the inclusion of pathological gambling as an OC spectrum disorder. One of the strengths of this theory is that it acknowledges that there are important differences among the various disorders comprising this spectrum of conditions. Therefore, the inclusion of pathological gambling as a spectrum condition is not compromised by the fact that the disorder of pathological gambling evidences a wider range of symptoms. For example, the findings that pathological gamblers evidence tolerance and withdrawal (e.g., Tavares et al., 2005), often suffer from a wider range of cognitive distortions (e.g., Toneatto et al., 1997), and respond to pharmacological treatments that do not target only the serotonergic system (e.g., Bergh et al., 1997), are not necessarily at odds with the proposal of pathological gambling as an OC spectrum disorder.

A second strength of the spectrum theory is that it acknowledges and incorporates pathological gambling's close association with impulsivity and substance abuse. As previously discussed, a recent meta-analysis provided evidence that pathological gambling is strongly associated with both OC traits and impulsivity (Durdle, 2005). These meta-analytic findings are in congruence with the placement of pathological gambling between the compulsive and impulsive poles of the continuum proposed by Hollander and Wong (1995). The demonstrated association between pathological gambling and substance use disorders (e.g., Lesieur et al., 1986; Toneatto & Brennan, 2002) also fits within the confines of this model, as the spectrum theory does not exclude the possibility that pathological gambling also shares similar features to substance use disorders. In fact, a model by Donovan (1988) posits a relationship between OCD and addictive disorders more generally (including substance use disorders and pathological gambling as a behavioral addiction).

Overall, the evidence appears to suggest that the inclusion of pathological gambling as an OC spectrum condition is consistent with both research findings and clinical observations. While it is evident that the two disorders share similar key features, pathological gambling evidences a wider range of symptoms and set of effective treatments. This is congruent with the theorized placement of pathological gambling along the continuum of disorders comprising the OC spectrum. This spectrum theory also appears to be in agreement with current theories and research findings regarding pathological gambling. While further investigation of the OC spectrum of disorders is required, this theory should prove to be a useful tool in the current conceptualization and treatment of both OCD and pathological gambling.

ACKNOWLEDGEMENTS

Heather Durdle is supported by a Canada Graduate Doctoral Scholarship from the Social Sciences and Humanities Research Council of Canada. Sherry H. Stewart is supported by a Canadian Institutes of Health Research Investigator Award and a Killam Professorship. Some of the work described herein was supported by the Ontario Problem Gambling Research Council and the Social Sciences and Humanities Research Council of Canada (Durdle) and the Ontario Problem Gambling Research Council and the Nova Scotia Gaming Foundation (Stewart).

REFERENCES

Abramowitz, J. S. (2004). Treatment of obsessive compulsive disorder in patients who have comorbid major depression. *Journal of Clinical Psychology, 60*, 1133–1141.

Allcock, C. C., & Grace, D. M. (1988). Pathological gamblers are neither impulsive nor sensation seekers. *Australian and New Zealand Journal of Psychiatry, 22*, 307–311.

Allen, J. J., & Tune, G. S. (1975). The Lynfield obsessional compulsive questionnaire. *Scottish Medical Journal, 20*, 21–24.

American Psychiatric Association (2000). *Diagnostic and statistical manual of mental disorders* (4th ed., text revision) *(DSM-IV-TR)*. Washington, DC: APA.

Anholt, G. E., Emmelkamp, P. M. G., Cath, D. C., van Oppen, P., Nelissen, H., & Smit, J. H. (2004). Do patients with OCD and pathological gambling have similar cognitive dysfunctions? *Behaviour Research and Therapy, 42*, 529–537.

Bergh, C., Eklund, T., Södersten, P., & Nordin, C. (1997). Altered dopamine function in pathological gambling. *Psychological Medicine, 27*, 473–475.

Bhar, S. S., & Kyrios, M. (2005). Obsessions and compulsions are associated with different cognitive and mood factors. *Behaviour Change, 22*, 81–96.

Bienvenu, O. J., Samuels, J. F., Riddle, M. A., Hoehn-Saric, R., Liang, K. Y., Cullen, B. A. M., et al. (2000). The relationship of obsessive–compulsive disorder to possible spectrum disorders: Results from a family study. *Biological Psychiatry, 48*, 287–293.

Black, D. W., Goldstein, R. B., Noyes, R., & Blum, N. (1994). Compulsive behaviors and obsessive–compulsive disorder (OCD): Lack of a relationship between OCD, eating disorders, and gambling. *Comprehensive Psychiatry, 35*, 145–148.

Black, D. W., & Moyer, T. (1998). Clinical features and psychiatric comorbidity of subjects with pathological gambling behavior. *Psychiatric Services, 49*, 1434–1439.

Black, D. W., Moyer, T., & Schlosser, S. (2003). Quality of life and family history in pathological gambling. *Journal of Nervous and Mental Disease, 191*, 124–126.

Blanco, C., Moreyra, P., Nunes, E. V., Sáiz-Ruiz, J., & Ibáñez, A. (2001). Pathological gambling: Addiction or compulsion? *Seminars in Clinical Neuropsychiatry, 6*, 167–176.

Bland, R. C., Newman, S. C., Orn, H., & Stebelsky, G. (1993). Epidemiology of pathological gambling in Edmonton. *Canadian Journal of Psychiatry, 38*, 108–112.

Blaszczynski, A. (1999). Pathological gambling and obsessive–compulsive spectrum disorders. *Psychological Reports, 84*, 107–113.

Blaszczynski, A., & Steel, Z. (1998). Personality disorders among pathological gamblers. *Journal of Gambling Studies, 14*, 51–71.

Blaszczynski, A. P., Winter, S. W., & McConaghy, N. (1986). Plasma endorphin levels in pathological gambling. *Journal of Gambling Behavior, 2*, 3–14.

Burton, S., Netemeyer, R. G., & Andrews, J. C. (2000). Modeling potential psychological risk factors of pathological gambling. *Journal of Applied Social Psychology, 30*, 2058–2078.

DeCaria, C. M., Begaz, T., & Hollander, E. (1998). Serotonergic and noradrenergic function in pathological gambling. *CNS Spectrums, 3*, 38–47.

Derogatis, L. R. (1977). *SCL-90 administration, scoring, and procedures manual, I*. Baltimore, MD: Johns Hopkins University School of Medicine.

Donovan, D. M. (1988). Assessment of addictive behaviors: Implications for an emerging biopsychosocial model. In D. M. Donovan & G. A. Marlatt (Eds.), *Assessment of Addictive Behaviors* (pp. 3–48). New York: Guilford.

Durdle, H. (2005). A meta-analysis examining the relationship of pathological gambling to impulsivity, substance use, and obsessive–compulsive traits. Unpublished Master's thesis, University of Windsor, Ontario, Canada.

Du Toit, P. L., van Kradenburg, J., Niehaus, D., & Stein, D. J. (2001). Comparison of obsessive–compulsive disorder patients with and without comorbid putative obsessive–compulsive spectrum disorders using a structured clinical interview. *Comprehensive Psychiatry, 42*, 291–300.

Frost, R. O., & Gross, R. C. (1993). The hoarding of possessions. *Behaviour Research and Therapy, 31*, 367–381.

Frost, R. O., Meagher, B. M., & Riskind, J. H. (2001). Obsessive–compulsive features in pathological lottery and scratch-ticket gamblers. *Journal of Gambling Studies, 17*, 5–19.

Frost, R. O., & Steketee, G. (1998). Hoarding: Clinical aspects and treatment strategies. In M. A. Jenike, L. Baer, & W. E. Minichiello (Eds.), *Obsessive compulsive disorder: practical management* (3rd ed.). St Louis, MO: Mosby.

Goodman, W. K., Price, L. H., Rasmussen, S. A., Mazure, C., Fleischmann, R. L., Hill, C. L., et al. (1989). The Yale–Brown Obsessive Compulsive Scale. I. Development, use, and reliability. *Archives of General Psychiatry, 46*, 1006–1011.

Graham, J. R., & Lowenfeld, B. L. (1986). Personality dimensions of the pathological gambler. *Journal of Gambling Behavior, 2*, 58–66.

Hodgson, R. J., & Rachman, S. J. (1977). Obsessional–compulsive complaints. *Behaviour Research and Therapy, 15*, 389–395.

Hollander, E. (2005). Obsessive–compulsive disorder and spectrum across the life span. *International Journal of Psychiatry in Clinical Practice, 9*, 79–86.

Hollander, E., & Rosen, J. (2000). Impulsivity. *Journal of Psychopharmacology, 14*, S39–S44.

Hollander, E., Sood, E., Pallanti, S., Baldini-Rossi, N., & Baker, B. (2005). Pharmacological treatments of pathological gambling. *Journal of Gambling Studies, 21*, 101–110.

Hollander, E., & Wong, C. M. (1995). Obsessive–compulsive spectrum disorders. *Journal of Clinical Psychiatry, 56 (Suppl 4)*, 3–6.

Krueger, R. F., Caspi, A., Moffitt, T. E., & Silva, P. A. (1998). The structure and stability of common mental disorders (DSM-III-R): A longitudinal–epidemiological study. *Journal of Abnormal Psychology, 107*, 216–227.

Krueger, R. F., & Markon, K. E. (2006). Reinterpreting comorbidity: A model-based approach to understanding and classifying psychopathology. *Annual Review of Clinical Psychology, 2*, 111–133.

Krueger, R. F., & Tackett, J. L. (2003). Personality and psychopathology: Working toward the bigger picture. *Journal of Personality Disorders, 17*, 109–128.

Ladouceur, R., Sylvain, C., Boutin, C., Lachance, S., Doucet, C., Leblond, J., et al. (2001). Cognitive treatment of pathological gambling. *Journal of Nervous and Mental Disease, 189*, 774–780.

Lesieur, H. R. (1998). Costs and treatment of pathological gambling. *Annals of the American Academy of Political and Social Science, 556*, 152–171.

Lesieur, H. R., & Blume, S. B. (1987). The South Oaks Gambling Screen (SOGS): A new instrument for the identification of pathological gamblers. *American Journal of Psychiatry, 144*, 1184–1188.

Lesieur, H. R., Blume, S. B., & Zoppa, R. M. (1986). Alcoholism, drug abuse, and gambling. *Alcoholism: Clinical and Experimental Research, 10*, 33–38.

Linden, R. D., Pope, H. G., & Jonas, J. M. (1986). Pathological gambling and major affective disorder: Preliminary findings. *Journal of Clinical Psychiatry, 47*, 201–203.

Martinez-Pina, A., Guirao de Parga, J. L., Fusté, I., Vallverdú, R., Serrat Planas, X., Martin Mateo, M., & Moreno Aguado, V. (1991). The Catalonia survey: Personality and intelligence structure in a sample of compulsive gamblers. *Journal of Gambling Studies, 7*, 275–299.

McElroy, S. L., Hudson, J. I., Phillips, K. A., Keck, P. E., & Pope, H. G. (1993). Clinical and theoretical implications of a possible link between obsessive–compulsive and impulse control disorders. *Depression, 1*, 121–132.

OCCWG (Obsessive Compulsive Cognitions Working Group) (1997). Cognitive assessment of obsessive–compulsive disorder. *Behaviour Research and Therapy, 35*, 667–681.

Petry, N. M. (2000). Psychiatric symptoms in problem gambling and non-problem gambling substance abusers. *The American Journal on Addictions, 9*, 163–171.

Petry, N. M. (2005a). Gamblers Anonymous and cognitive-behavioral therapies for pathological gamblers. *Journal of Gambling Studies, 21*, 27–33.

Petry, N. M. (2005b). *Pathological Gambling: Etiology, Comorbidity, and Treatment.* Washington, DC: American Psychological Association.

Petry, N. M., & Kiluk, B. D. (2002). Suicidal ideation and suicide attempts in treatment-seeking pathological gamblers. *Journal of Nervous and Mental Disease, 190*, 462–469.

Petry, N. M., Stinson, F. S., & Grant, B. F. (2005). Comorbidity of DSM-IV pathological gambling and other psychiatric disorders: Results from the National Epidemiological Survey on alcohol and related conditions. *Journal of Clinical Psychiatry, 66*, 564–574.

Rasmussen, S. A., & Eisen, J. L. (1992). The epidemiology and differential diagnosis of obsessive compulsive disorder. *Journal of Clinical Psychiatry, 53*, S4–S9.

Raylu, N., & Oei, T. P. S. (2002). Pathological gambling: A comprehensive review. *Clinical Psychology Review, 22*, 1009–1061.

Rosenthal, R. J., & Lesieur, H. R. (1992). Self-reported withdrawal symptoms and pathological gambling. *American Journal on Addictions, 1*, 150–154.

Rosenthal, R. J., & Lorenz, V. C. (1992). The pathological gambler as criminal offender. *Clinical Forensic Psychiatry, 15*, 647–660.

Roy, A., Adinoff, B., Roehrich, L., Lamparski, D., Custer, R., Lorenz, V., et al. (1988). Pathological gambling: A psychobiological study. *Archives of General Psychiatry, 45*, 369–373.

Rugle, L., & Melamed, L. (1993). Neuropsychological assessment of attention problems in pathological gamblers. *Journal of Mental and Nervous Disease, 181*, 107–112.

Salkovskis, P. (1999). Understanding and treating obsessive–compulsive disorder. *Behaviour Research and Therapy, 37*, S29–S52.

Sanavio, E. (1988). Obsessions and compulsions: The Padua Inventory. *Behaviour Research and Therapy, 26*, 169–177.

Shaffer, H. J., Hall, M. N., & Vander Bilt, J. (1999). Estimating the prevalence of disordered gambling behavior in the United States and Canada: A research synthesis. *American Journal of Public Health, 89*, 1369–1376.

Slutske, W. S., Eisen, S., True, W. R., Lyons, M. J., Goldberg, J., & Tsuang, M. (2000). Common genetic vulnerability for pathological gambling and alcohol dependence in men. *Archives of General Psychiatry, 57*, 666–673.

Specker, S. M., Carlson, G. A., Christenson, G. A., & Marcotte, M. (1995). Impulse control disorders and attention deficit disorder in pathological gamblers. *Annals of Clinical Psychiatry, 7*, 175–179.

Specker, S. M., Carlson, G. A., Edmonson, K. M., Johnson, P. E., & Marcotte, P. E. (1996). Psychopathology in gamblers seeking treatment. *Journal of Gambling Studies, 12*, 67–81.

Spunt, B. (2002). Pathological gambling and substance misuse. *Substance Use & Misuse, 37*, 1299–1304.

Stanley, M. A., Turner, S. M. (1995). Current status of pharmacological and behavioral treatment of obsessive–compulsive disorder. *Behavior Therapy, 26*, 163–186.

Steel, Z., & Blaszczynski, A. (1998). Impulsivity, personality disorders and pathological gambling severity. *Addiction, 93*, 895–905.

Stewart, S. H., Collins, P., Blackburn, J. R., Ellery, M., & Klein, R. M. (2005). Heart rate increase to alcohol administration and video lottery terminal (VLT) play among regular VLT players. *Psychology of Addictive Behaviors, 19*, 94–98.

Stewart, S. H., Zack, M., Klein, R., Loba, P., & Fragopoulous, F. (2003, September). *Gambling motives and drinking motives in pathological gamblers who drink when gambling.* Paper presented at the Responsible Gambling Council of Ontario Annual Conference, Toronto, Ontario, Canada.

Symes, B. A., & Nicki, R. M. (1997). A preliminary consideration of cue-exposure, response-prevention treatment for pathological gambling behaviour: Two case studies. *Journal of Gambling Studies, 13*, 145–157.

Tavares, H., Zilberman, M. L., Hodgins, D. C., & el-Guebaly, N. (2005). Comparison of craving between pathological gamblers and alcoholics. *Alcoholism: Clinical and Experimental Research, 29*, 1427–1431.

Toneatto, T. (1999). Cognitive psychopathology of problem gambling. *Substance Use and Misuse, 34*, 1593–1604.

Toneatto, T., Blitz-Miller, T., Calderwood, K., Dragonetti, R., & Tsanos, A. (1997). Cognitive distortions in heavy gambling. *Journal of Gambling Studies, 13*, 253–266.

Toneatto, T., & Brennan, J. (2002). Pathological gambling in treatment-seeking substance abusers. *Addictive Behaviors, 27*, 465–469.

11

BODY DYSMORPHIC DISORDER

DEAN MCKAY, JENNIFER T. GOSSELIN,
AND SAPNA GUPTA

Fordham University, New York

Most individuals can identify aspects of their appearance they wish were different, and may even engage in grooming strategies to enhance their appearance. For some, however, the anxiety and worry associated with negative perceptions of their physical features are extreme and interfere with everyday functioning. The measures taken to compensate for their perceived defects are time-consuming and can be expensive and even painful, from excessive hair tweezing to plastic surgery (Sarwer, Gibbons, & Crerand, 2004).

In 1891, the Italian psychiatrist Morselli coined the term 'dysmorphophobia' to describe the condition in which patients demonstrated an obsessive concern or fear about a physical flaw or deformity that is actually minor or undetectable, coupled with an irresistible impulse to self-examine (see Jerome's 2001 translation; see also Berrios & Kan, 1996). In 1980, dysmorphophobia was included in the *DSM-III* under the label 'atypical somatoform disorder'. In the *DSM-III-R* it was renamed Body Dysmorphic Disorder (BDD), which continues to be the diagnostic category used in the *DSM-IV-TR* (American Psychiatric Association, 2000).

This chapter provides an overview of BDD and its clinical features, etiology, and treatment approaches. We also examine whether BDD should be considered part of the *obsessive–compulsive spectrum* (OCS); a set of disorders that some think overlap on the basis of their obsessive–compulsive features. The OCS has

Correspondence to: Dean McKay, Department of Psychology, Fordham University, 441 East Fordham Road, Bronx, NY 10458.

been developed in an effort to describe conditions that fall along a continuum from compulsive to impulsive, with the central feature being an inability to exert regulatory control over behavior (Hollander & Rosen, 2000).

CLINICAL FEATURES OF BODY DYSMORPHIC DISORDER

In the *DSM-IV-TR*, BDD is described as a clinically distressing preoccupation with an imagined or slight defect in appearance that results in impairment in daily functioning (American Psychiatric Association, 2000). A diagnosis is not given if the individual's concern is a manifestation of an eating disorder, gender identity disorder, or another disorder that better accounts for the symptoms. BDD is categorized in the *DSM* as a somatoform disorder, along with other disorders involving bodily concerns that are believed to be psychogenic, such as somatization disorder, conversion disorder, pain disorder, and hypochondriasis. When the belief that particular aspects of the body are malformed or ugly is held with strong conviction, despite contradictory evidence, a diagnosis of delusional disorder, somatic type may be applied, although it has been suggested that this is simply a more severe or less insightful variant of BDD (DeMarco, Li, Phillips, & McElroy, 1998; Phillips, 2004a; Phillips, McElroy, Keck, Hudson, & Pope, 1994). The current edition of the *DSM* accounts for this by inclusion of the modifier 'with poor insight' for a diagnosis of BDD.

The categorization of BDD has been problematic in that it shares features of, and is often comorbid with, many other disorders. Examples include disorders that involve impulsivity and/or compulsivity – such as trichotillomania, psychogenic excoriation, tic disorders, substance abuse disorders, and obsessive–compulsive disorder (OCD) (Arnold, Auchenbach, & McElroy, 2001; Grant, Menard, Pagano, Fay, & Phillips, 2005). Within the somatoform disorders, BDD patients and patients with hypochondriasis tend to share a process of worry about their bodies, poor insight, and repetitive reassurance-seeking (Lochner et al., 2005). Despite these similarities, BDD has a low rate of comorbidity with other somatoform disorders (Hollander, Cohen, & Simeon, 1993; Phillips et al., 1994; Phillips, Nierenberg, Brendel, & Fava, 1996).

The distorted perception of one's body and extreme measures taken to change one's appearance provides a link between eating disorders and BDD. Although eating disorders are a rule-out condition for BDD, when the criteria have been adjusted to allow these conditions to co-occur, the rate of comorbidity is high (Grant, Kim, & Eckert, 2002; Gupta & Johnson, 2000; Phillips & Diaz, 1997; Rosen & Ramirez, 1998). BDD also typically includes interpersonal impairment and is commonly comorbid with social anxiety disorder and avoidant personality disorder (Nierenberg et al., 2002; Phillips et al., 1994; Phillips, McElroy, Keck, Pope, & Hudson, 1993). The near delusional quality of the beliefs in BDD has raised the issue of whether BDD falls along the spectrum of psychotic disorders, although this idea has not received much empirical support (Phillips et al., 1994; Phillips et al., 1993).

COGNITIVE, EMOTIONAL, BEHAVIORAL, AND
INTERPERSONAL FEATURES OF BDD

The cognitive and emotional features of BDD include a strongly held belief about the repugnance of the disliked physical characteristics and concomitant feelings of shame and embarrassment. The most common body areas focused upon include parts of the head, such as facial skin, hair, or nose; and other body areas such as buttocks, breasts, and sex organs (Phillips et al., 1993; Veale et al., 1996). Perseveration about the defects leads to excessive time and energy spent on checking, concealing, or camouflaging the flaws, as well as increased self-consciousness. Attempts to reduce the anxiety associated with the recurrent defect-related thoughts – such as looking in mirrors, seeking reassurance from others, and grooming behaviors – often paradoxically sustain the individual's anxiety and self-focused attention, and are experienced as difficult to control or diminish (Phillips, 2002). Even medical treatments and procedures tend to leave an individual with BDD dissatisfied. In some cases, individuals undergo repeated treatments or surgeries, but they maintain a persistent view of the outcome as unacceptable (Crerand et al., 2004; Phillips & Diaz, 1997).

The attentional and perceptual biases involved with BDD contribute to the perpetuation of the disorder. According to Veale's (2004) cognitive behavioral model of BDD, negative internal self-images are cued by external stimuli such as seeing oneself in a reflective surface. The negative affect that results leads to urges to camouflage, check one's appearance, and related behaviors, as well as increased rumination. The person's negative body image also reinforces or strengthens the tendency to focus on oneself excessively, which in turn increases the process of selective attention to the defect as the person looks in the mirror. This completes a vicious cycle of self-focus, seeing a reflection of oneself, rumination and negative affect, self-focus, and so on. The self may be perceived as an esthetic object to be scrutinized (Veale, 2004); in fact, individuals with BDD are more likely than other individuals to have an education and/or employment in art or design (Phillips & Menard, 2004; Veale, Ennis, & Lambrou, 2002).

Like individuals with social phobia, those with BDD often attribute negative social interactions or outcomes (e.g., rejection) to their perceived physical defects, and may be quick to interpret another's ambiguous behavior as a sign of rejection or negative judgment (Buhlmann, Wilhelm et al., 2002). Rather than attending to the interpersonal interaction, they may instead attend to their own appearance and become preoccupied with the concern that others are taking similar notice of their perceived defect. This self-presentational apprehension may interfere with social ease and effectiveness, leading to increased social anxiety and even limited social contact, which diminishes the opportunity for positive social experiences. Moreover, research has demonstrated that BDD sufferers are prone to misinterpret others' facial expressions (Buhlmann, McNally, Etcoff, Tuschen-Caffier, & Wilhelm, 2004). This may lead to increased suspicion that others notice their perceived defects. In some cases, BDD presents with delusions and ideas of reference – such as assuming that others are talking about them at a distance – which may further perpetuate their avoidance of others (Phillips, 1999; Phillips et al., 1993).

IMPAIRMENT

Several studies have attested to the debilitating nature of BDD. Compared to general population norms, individuals with BDD demonstrate significantly lower scores on measures of well being, adjustment, mental health, and psychosocial functioning; moreover, BDD sufferers' scores on these scales were even significantly lower than the scores for individuals with clinical depression, as well as those with debilitating medical conditions such as diabetes; or among those with recent myocardial infarction (Phillips, Menard, Fay, & Pagano, 2005). For individuals with BDD and a history of substance use disorder, a majority reported that their BDD was a contributor to the development of their substance use (Grant, Menard, Pagano, Fay, & Phillips, 2005). Demographic assessments have shown that those with BDD are more likely to be unemployed and to have achieved less academically than both healthy controls and those with OCD (Frare, Perugi, Ruffolo, & Toni, 2004).

Significant social impairment among those with BDD is supported by the findings that many such patients have been housebound for a week or more (Phillips et al., 1994), that social anxiety disorder is a common comorbid diagnosis, and that most have never married or are presently divorced (Phillips & Diaz, 1997; Phillips et al., 2005; Veale et al., 1996). BDD sufferers are also at increased risk for hospitalization and suicide attempts (Phillips et al., 1993; Veale et al., 1996). Almost one-quarter of patients had attempted suicide in one study (Veale et al., 1996), and close to half of BDD patients in another study reported lifetime suicidal ideation (Altamura, Paluello, Mundo, Medda, & Mannu, 2001). It is important to note that the rate of suicide in BDD is considerably greater than in OCD, where it has been shown to be as low as 0.08% in a meta-analysis of suicide risk among anxiety disorder patients (Khan, Leventhal, Khan, & Brown, 2002).

PREVALENCE AND CLINICAL COURSE

Prevalence estimates of BDD range from 1% to 5%. Researchers have reported a prevalence of 0.7% among adult females 36–44 years of age (Otto, Wilhelm, Cohen, & Harlow, 2001), 2.2% among an ethnically diverse group of adolescents (Mayville, Katz, Gipson, & Cabral, 1999), 4.8% among a group of Turkish female nursing program students (Cansever, Uzun, Dönmez, & Ozşahin, 2003), and 5.3% among German college students (Bohne et al., 2002). BDD is over-represented among clinical populations and among individuals seeking cosmetic surgery or dermatological treatment, as compared to the general population (Altamura et al., 2001; Crerand et al., 2004; Phillips, Dufresne, Wilkel, & Vittorio, 2000). Factors contributing to the under-recognition of BDD, however, include: (a) the presence of a separate clinical disorder that is more primary (Grant, Kim, & Crow, 2001); (b) embarrassment about and hesitancy to divulge BDD symptoms (Phillips, 1991); and (c) a tendency to minimize the associated distress and impairment, leading to underutilization of psychological and psychiatric treatment (Phillips, Nierenberg, Brendel, & Fava, 1996).

The initial onset of BDD is typically during adolescence, with a chronic course in most cases, lasting approximately 9–18 years (Perugi et al., 1997; Phillips et al., 1993, 1994, 2005; Phillips, Pagano, Menard, Fay, & Stout, 2005). The severity of symptoms may fluctuate, and symptoms may even remit over time, although partial remission is more likely than full remission (Phillips et al., 2005). The physical characteristic of concern may also change over time, either with additions of perceived defects or substitutions of defects (American Psychiatric Association, 2000; Phillips et al., 1993).

BDD seems to occur roughly equally in men and women (Phillips & Diaz, 1997; Phillips et al., 2000), although some studies have suggested gender differences. When self-referred, females tend to outnumber males (Veale et al., 1996). Another study showed that across various ethnic groups adolescent females had more symptoms of BDD than adolescent males (Mayville et al., 1999). In an Italian sample, males with BDD had more severe BDD symptoms than females, although no other gender differences were found (Altamura et al., 2001).

The particular physical complaint often differs by gender, although there tends to be an equal number of body parts of focus among the genders, typically three to four (Phillips & Diaz, 1997). For example, whereas both men and women complain about their skin, hair, and nose, women are more likely to be preoccupied with their hips, buttocks, and breasts, and men commonly report concern about their body build, genitals, and height (Mayville et al., 1999; Perugi et al., 1997; Phillips & Diaz, 1997). In fact, some researchers have proposed the separate categorization of muscle dysmorphia – the obsessive concern about not being muscular enough, primarily found in males – in a similar manner to anorexia nervosa, which is primarily found in females (Olivardia, 2001).

ETIOLOGIC AND CONCEPTUAL MODELS

PSYCHOLOGICAL AND SOCIOCULTURAL ETIOLOGY

The etiology of BDD is likely to be a complex interaction between psychological, genetic, physiological, and sociocultural forces. Childhood experiences of rejection, as well as physical, sexual, and emotional abuse have been implicated (Cororve & Gleaves, 2001; Neziroglu & Khemlani-Patel, 2003; Veale, 2004). Similar to eating disorders, BDD is likely influenced by the messages one receives from family, peers, and society about standards of attractiveness and the value of appearance (Neziroglu, Roberts, & Yaryura-Tobias, 2004; Rivera & Borda, 2001). Critical messages may be internalized and held with increasing tenacity over time. When asked to recall images associated with anxiety about their appearance, patients with BDD, relative to healthy individuals, reported images that were more negative, emotionally laden, vivid, and recurrent (Osman, Cooper, Hackmann, & Veale, 2004). The images reported by BDD patients also tended to include a somatic component and be associated with negative, appearance-related childhood or adolescent memories; whereas such image–memory association was rare among controls (Osman et al., 2004).

As noted previously, BDD typically begins in adolescence, a developmental stage that commonly involves heightened attention to one's appearance, greater insecurity, and greater attention to others' perceptions of oneself (Bell & Bromnick, 2003). Individuals at risk for psychiatric disorders may have a particularly difficult time negotiating the demands of adolescence, making them more vulnerable to developing BDD at this stage of development (Neziroglu et al., 2004; Veale et al., 1996).

From a behavioral perspective, BDD may result from a combination of classical and operant conditioning, similar to the processes by which phobias develop (Neziroglu et al., 2004). According to such a model, negative experiences, such as peers' ridicule of a body part, become associated with that body part through classical conditioning such that seeing or thinking of the body part is enough to elicit a negative emotional response. Behaviors such as camouflaging, seeking reassurance, and social avoidance serve as negative reinforcers, reducing negative affect temporarily, but preventing the natural extinction of the conditioned negative emotional response.

NEUROPSYCHOLOGICAL FACTORS AND PHYSIOPATHOLOGY

Research has begun to address the physiological components of the cognitive, emotional, and behavioral phenomena in BDD. Primary lines of research have used task performance to evaluate BDD, such as tasks involving information processing, planning, memory, and motor functioning. These measures are assumed to reflect functioning in certain brain regions. Another research approach is the use of brain imaging to identify structural or functional deviance in BDD. Although in an early stage of investigation, brain imaging results have implicated a variety of brain areas, including areas that are directly or indirectly involved with executive and perceptual abilities (Carey, Seedat, Warwick, van Heerden, & Stein, 2004; Rauch et al., 2003).

Research evaluating task performance among those with BDD has generally demonstrated impaired executive function, as well as memory deficits (Deckersbach et al., 2000; Hanes, 1998). For example, BDD patients had difficulty organizing stimuli into clusters or attending to larger features of stimuli, which may have impaired their ability to encode and then recall the stimuli (Deckersbach et al., 2000). This finding is consistent with the tendency in BDD to exclusively focus on minute details of one's appearance, while ignoring one's overall appearance. The impaired executive functioning and repetitive behaviors among patients with BDD implicate the prefrontal cortex and striatum in the pathophysiology of the disorder (Hanes, 1998; Hollander, 2005; van den Heuvel et al., 2005).

Among patients with BDD, the belief that the particular physical feature is unsightly may be due to dysfunction in the initial processing of sensory input and/or dysfunction in perception. For example, when presented with an undistorted computer image of their own face, half of the participants with BDD viewed the image as distorted and altered the image on the computer, while healthy controls made no changes to the image (Yaryura-Tobias, Neziroglu, & Torres-Gallegos, 2002).

Additional research on BDD patients' misperception of the emotions conveyed by facial expressions lends further support to the view that a major component of BDD is distortion in perception (Buhlmann et al., 2004).

Eating disorders also include perceptual disturbances, and several brain structures been tied to eating and body image disturbances including limbic system structures, the prefrontal area (Shirao, Okamoto, Mantani, Okamoto, & Yamawaki, 2005; Shirao, Okamoto, Okada, Okamoto, & Yamawaki, 2003) and parietal regions (see Kaye et al., 2005 for a review). Similar regions, such as the parietal, parietal-occipital, prefrontal, and temporal areas have been implicated in BDD, suggesting that BDD and eating disorders share a similar pathophysiology, although this research area requires much additional investigation (Carey et al., 2004; Yaryura-Tobias et al, 2002). In contrast, many of the aforementioned areas are not implicated or have a lesser role in the pathophysiology of OCD (with the exception of the prefrontal cortex; see Greisberg & McKay, 2003; Rauch, Whalen, Dougherty, & Jenike, 1998).

The neuropsychological research on BDD includes major caveats. Many of these studies – particularly brain imaging studies – are based on very small samples, often including less than 20 participants, and in some cases, only including females. Samples of BDD patients often included individuals with additional comorbid disorders, and many of the participants were taking psychotropic medications during the study, serving as a potential confound. For those studies measuring executive functioning through behavioral tasks, anxiety may have interfered with performance. Lastly, research in this area has yielded somewhat inconsistent and mixed results in terms of the particular deficits or relevant brain regions in BDD (Carey et al., 2004; Deckersbach et al., 2000; Rauch et al., 2003).

PERSONALITY FACTORS

The clinical descriptions of individuals with BDD are strikingly similar to descriptions of individuals who struggle with pathological perfectionism. Individuals with BDD spend a great deal of time inspecting their perceived defects and trying to make the area look 'perfect', only to conclude that the area remains flawed. A similar process occurs in perfectionism, such as selectively attending to a mistake and concluding that the finished product is not good enough, despite repeated and often excessive efforts (Frost et al., 1995). Perfectionism is also associated with rumination about the perceived failure to meet overly high standards, leading to excessive self-criticism (Flett, Hewitt, Blankstein, & Gray, 1998; Shafran, Cooper, & Fairburn, 2002). The domain of concern in BDD is, of course, body features. Individuals with BDD not only wish their bodies could be flawless, but they also place a great deal of importance on attractiveness as a personal quality, perhaps overestimating its value and influence (Neziroglu, Roberts, & Yaryura-Tobias, 2004).

Self-discrepancy theory has been used to describe the cognitive processes involved in BDD (Veale, 2004). This theory describes three personal constructs individuals use to make judgments about themselves: the 'actual self', 'ideal self', and 'ought self' (Higgins, 1987). Respectively, these domains of self-beliefs are defined as one's 'true' or actual qualities, qualities one would ideally like to have, and qualities one is obligated to have or should have. When a discrepancy exists between one's perception of how one *is* and how one *would like to be* or *ought to be*, one may be susceptible to negative emotions, such as dejection, and may attempt to reduce this discrepancy, although true flawlessness is never achieved (Higgins, 1987). Research using self-discrepancy theory revealed significant discrepancies between the actual versus ideal selves and actual versus ought/should selves among those with BDD (Veale, Kinderman, Riley, & Lambrou, 2003). Similarly, maladaptive perfectionism has been described and measured as the discrepancy between perceptions of one's actual performance and one's idealistic goal of a perfect performance (Slaney, Rice, & Ashby, 2002).

BDD AND THE OBSESSIVE–COMPULSIVE SPECTRUM

SUPPORT FOR INCLUSION IN THE OC SPECTRUM

The concept of the obsessive–compulsive spectrum (OCS) asserts that several disorders that have been variously categorized in the DSM share important features of OCD and are therefore related (Hollander, 2005). Hollander and Rosen (2000) suggest that the unifying feature of the OCS is an inability to regulate behavior, and that many otherwise disparate disorders from the DSM fall along a continuum from compulsive to impulsive. The disorders along this continuum constitute the OCS. By extension, an implication of the spectrum conceptualization is that the classification system of disorders might be reorganized according to putative etiological similarities (Phillips, 2002). Disorders often included in the OCS are hypochondriasis, Tourette's disorder, BDD, and trichotillomania. Other impulse control disorders, eating disorders, borderline personality disorder, and neurological disorders, such as autism, have also been proposed (Hollander, 2005; Phillips, 2002). Criteria for inclusion in the spectrum are shared overt symptoms, clinical course, gender ratio, familial patterns of disorders, treatment response, and indicators of pathogenic similarities (Hollander, 2005; Phillips, McElroy et al., 1995; but also see McKay & Neziroglu, in press for recommendations for methodological improvements).

Does BDD share characteristics with OCD? The anxiety/distress evoking nature of the recurrent, distressing thoughts involved in BDD bear similarities to clinical obsessions, and the irresistible urges to repetitively engage in examining or hiding the defect in order to reduce distress are similar to compulsions in OCD. This supports the view that BDD is related to OCD. Moreover, there is frequent comorbidity between BDD and OCD (particularly among samples of patients with BDD), and a relatively high rate of family history of OCD among BDD probands (Altamura et al., 2001). Among samples of patients with BDD, 37–39% had OCD previously or concurrently (Hollander et al., 1993; Phillips et al., 1993) and among samples of patients with OCD, 12–19% had comorbid BDD or a history of BDD (Bienvenu et al., 2000; Diniz et al., 2004; Simeon, Hollander, Stein, Cohen, & Aronowitz, 1995), and 4% of OCD patients' relatives had BDD at some point in their lives (Bienvenu et al., 2000). The similarities between OCD and BDD patients in terms of demographic and phenomenological characteristics, such as gender, age of onset, course, treatment response, and severity of their disorders also support a possible association between BDD and OCD (Saxena et al., 2001; Simeon et al., 1995).

Researchers have also argued that since patients with OCD and those with BDD respond to similar specific treatment techniques, such as exposure and response prevention (McKay et al., 1997), as well as similar psychotropic medications, BDD belongs in the OCS. Serotonin reuptake inhibitors (SRIs) have been effective for the treatment of BDD and OCD (Fallon, 2004; Hollander et al., 1999; Phillips, Grant et al., 2005; Phillips & Najjar, 2003). The similarity between OCD and BDD in response to medication has been used to support the concept that these disorders share similar dysfunction in the transmission of particular neurotransmitters, such as serotonin and dopamine. Nevertheless, this is a tenuous argument since etiologic factors cannot necessarily be deduced simply from knowledge of a treatment's effectiveness. Moreover, OCD and BDD patients are likely to respond to higher doses of SRIs compared to other disorders (Dougherty, Rauch, & Jenike, 2004; Phillips, 2004b).

The cognitive impairments characteristic of OCD and BDD patients also support the inclusion of BDD in the OCS. For example, both groups of patients have shown difficulty organizing stimuli into a meaningful pattern that can later be recalled (Deckersbach et al., 2000; Kuelz, Hohagen, & Voderholzer, 2004). These results also dovetail with the hypothesis that OCD and BDD share a similar dysfunction in the frontostriatal system, which is involved in executive functioning, learning, and memory (Deckersbach et al., 2000).

SUPPORT FOR EXCLUSION FROM THE OC SPECTRUM

Despite the similarities between OCD and BDD, a clear difference between the two disorders is that the themes of obsessions for individuals with OCD tend to focus on responsibility for harm (or its prevention) rather than self-presentational and appearance concerns of those with BDD (Phillips, McElroy et al., 1995). Researchers have also differentiated between OCD and BDD on the basis of insight into the senselessness of symptoms; BDD patients demonstrating significantly less insight than OCD patients (Eisen, Phillips, Coles, & Rasmussen, 2004; Hollander, 2005; Mackley, 2005; McKay, Neziroglu, & Yaryura-Tobias, 1997). Moreover, patients with comorbid BDD and OCD demonstrate less insight with respect to their BDD symptoms compared to their OCD symptoms (Simeon et al., 1995). The recurrent thoughts in BDD are often less similar to the unwanted obsessions commonly seen in OCD and more similar to overvalued ideas and even delusional thinking, which are held with greater conviction (Frare et al., 2004;

Phillips, McElroy et al., 1995). Moreover, the delusional thought processes in some individuals with BDD may include ideas of reference (for example, feeling that strangers notice, and object to, the perceived bodily defect), which is a symptom not typically seen in OCD (Phillips et al., 1993). Research supports greater degrees of obsessions and compulsions among those with OCD compared to those with BDD and, conversely, greater degrees of overvalued ideation among those with BDD compared to OCD (McKay et al., 1997).

Although both OCD and BDD may be quite distressing, the cognitions and behaviors involved in OCD may be considered to be more ego-dystonic than those in BDD. For example, on the one hand, individuals with BDD may believe their obsessive thoughts to be true and may view their camouflaging and checking behaviors as necessary and as a way to improve one's appearance. On the other hand, individuals with OCD may question the validity of their obsessive thoughts or view these thoughts as appalling and may resent the need to perform admittedly unnecessary or impractical behaviors. In OCD, tension and anxiety tend to precede compulsions, which often then reduce anxiety. In BDD, however, tension and anxiety prior to checking in the mirror can be exacerbated by their behaviors, particularly by lengthy sessions of gazing in the mirror, as the belief that the defect is hideous and obvious may be confirmed by the image they perceive (Phillips, McElroy et al., 1995; Veale & Riley, 2001). The behaviors in BDD therefore are not completely analogous to compulsions in OCD. Furthermore, individuals who engage in repetitive forms of grooming, such as skin picking, may actually alter their appearance for the worse, potentially creating a cyclical process (Arnold, Auchenbach, & McElroy, 2001).

Although BDD and OCD are often comorbid, many other disorders have higher rates of comorbidity with BDD and OCD, respectively. Among OCD patients in one study, only 19% had lifetime BDD, which was much lower than a history of major depression (62%), tic disorders (39%), social phobia (39%), and simple phobia (25%; Diniz et al., 2004). BDD patients have a higher rate of comorbid depression compared to individuals with OCD (Phillips, Grant et al., 2005). One study showed that BDD was more common among individuals with Tourette's disorder than among individuals with OCD, leading the researchers to question the inclusion of BDD in the OCS (Coffey et al., 1998). Research on the similarities between BDD and eating disorders has also supported BDD as a variant of body image disturbance (Rosen & Ramirez, 1998). The comorbidity between BDD and OCD versus the comorbidity between BDD and others disorders thus does not lend clear support to the inclusion of BDD in the OCS.

In addition to the use of comorbidity and family history data to classify disorders in the OCS, researchers have also used neurological and treatment response data. The effective treatment of OCD and BDD with SRI antidepressants has been used to support the inclusion of BDD in the OCS. However, whereas both disorders respond to SRI medication, the degree of symptom relief may not be the same and response to augmentation strategies has not been comparable. For example, adding pimozide – a neuroleptic often prescribed for tic disorders – to an existing regimen of fluoxetine was *not* an effective treatment for BDD patients (Phillips, 2005), although the addition of a neuroleptic to an SRI *was* effective for OCD patients in two studies (McDougle et al., 1990; McDougle, Epperson, Pelton, Wasylink, & Price, 2000). These comparative medication response studies do not persuasively lend support for inclusion in the OCS. As noted elsewhere, even if two disorders were to respond to the same medication, this result would not necessarily mean that the same mechanism is causing both disorders (Abramowitz & Deacon, 2006).

The pathophysiology of OCD has received far more attention than that of BDD. The primary areas of the brain emphasized in OCD research are the orbitofrontal cortex (part of the prefrontal cortex that receives sensory input), basal ganglia (especially the caudate nucleus of the striatum), and the thalamus (Pian et al., 2005; Tekin & Cummings, 2002). There is scant research comparing the brain structures implicated in OCD and BDD, and the brain imaging studies of BDD have relied on small samples and have produced mixed findings. A neuroimaging study of eight female BDD patients revealed brain abnormalities in regions that were similar to previous studies of OCD (specifically, asymmetry of the caudate nucleus and atypical white matter volume), although the particular type of abnormalities was different in the BDD group compared to that observed in the extant OCD research (Rauch et al., 2003). A second imaging study of six BDD patients demonstrated a variety of abnormalities, including occipital and parietal irregularities, although many of the findings were not consistent across participants (Carey et al., 2004). Additional brain imaging studies of BDD are needed to draw substantive conclusions, but the data thus far do not suggest that the two disorders are comparable in this sense.

Unlike OCD, BDD patients' primary symptom of distortion of body features may involve impaired parietal lobe functioning, which serves to interpret and integrate sensory information (Rivera & Borda, 2001). Body perceptual disturbances other than BDD – from the phantom limb phenomenon to anorexia nervosa – have provided additional evidence of the role of the connections between the parietal and occipital regions in their cerebral pathology, and BDD is likely to involve similar pathophysiology (Yaryura-Tobias et al., 2002). This again sets BDD apart from OCD.

TREATMENT

BDD tends to be a difficult condition to treat, in part because beliefs about one's appearance and how important appearance is to one's self-worth tend to be stable. Clinicians face the challenge of fostering investment in the therapeutic process and in the therapeutic goals, even though these goals counter many patients' perception that their defect is the true problem. Patients often do not present for psychological treatment with BDD as their primary concern. Rather, friends, family members, or physicians (dermatologists and plastic surgeons, for example) typically refer such individuals for therapy (Sarwer et al., 2004). Given the high comorbidity between BDD and other disorders, clinicians are challenged with creating treatment plans that alleviate patients' complex symptom presentations.

For example, since the majority of individuals with BDD struggle with major depression (Phillips et al., 1993), clinical conceptualizations should include attention to how these disorders interact and potentially exacerbate one another.

In predicting symptom remission, the severity of symptoms at baseline assessment tends to be a useful prognostic indicator. Other factors such as the presence and severity of delusions, demographic characteristics, duration of symptoms, and comorbid disorders may also predict clinical course (Phillips, Grant et al., 2005; Phillips, Pagano et al., 2005). Of the psychological treatment approaches, cognitive–behavior therapy (CBT) and behavior therapy (BT) have received the most research attention and have demonstrated the greatest efficacy in treating BDD (McKay et al., 1997; Neziroglu & Khemlani-Patel, 2003; Rosen, Reiter, & Orosan, 1995a). A recent meta-analysis supported the effectiveness of CBT over medication, although both CBT and BT resulted in similar levels of clinical improvement (Williams, Hadjistavropoulos, & Sharpe, 2006).

COGNITIVE–BEHAVIOR THERAPY

The cognitive–behavioral model of BDD posits that this disorder is maintained through biased information processing, which leads one to repeatedly confirm the negative, distorted beliefs about one's physical features that constitute the core of the disorder (Buhlmann & Wilhelm, 2004; Phillips, 1993; Sarwer, Gibbons, & Crerand, 2004; Veale et al., 1996). The individual attends to information that supports the belief that the body part is flawed, such as inspecting every pore on one's face or watching for someone to glance at one's nose. Information that does not support the belief about the defect is discounted, such as a comment from a friend that one's appearance is fine. Positive interpersonal experiences, such as a compliment, can be attributed to the camouflaging or hiding of the defect, again leaving the distorted belief intact and reinforcing the compensatory strategies.

Both individual and group CBT based on the model described above have been effective in treating BDD (Rosen, Reiter, & Orosan, 1995a,b; Wilhelm, Otto, Lohr, & Deckersbach, 1999; Veale et al., 1996). Treatment involves psychoeducation to help patients understand their disorder and to orient them to the CBT model; this process includes reframing symptoms in cognitive–behavioral terms. Patients may engage in self-monitoring in the form of journaling maladaptive thoughts and behaviors to provide an assessment of target symptoms. Symptoms are reduced through challenging distorted thoughts and beliefs and teaching the patient to reduce attentional focus on the perceived defect. Clinicians may explore patients' core beliefs and assumptions about the value of appearance and the meaning attached to the defect in terms of personal worth. Patients learn to stop negative thoughts as they emerge in daily life and to replace these with positive, nonjudgmental self-statements. CBT also includes behavioral techniques, such as exposure and response prevention, to reduce appearance-related rituals and to provide experiences that counter negative beliefs (Rosen, Reiter, & Orosan, 1995a,b; Sarwer et al., 2004; Veale, 2004; Veale et al., 1996). It should be noted, however, that in many ways the approach to treatment using CBT differs significantly from that for OCD. For example, recent models of cognitive therapy for OCD focus on inflated responsibility and thought action fusion (Clark, 2004), whereas cognitive therapy in BDD focuses on distorted thinking about one's physical appearance.

BEHAVIOR THERAPY

Behavior therapy of BDD emphasizes repeated exposure to feared imagery, situations, or stimuli (McKay, 1999; Neziroglu & Khemlani-Patel, 2003; Sarwer et al., 2004). As in anxiety disorders, avoidance of threatening situations – particularly situations in which one's appearance might be judged by others – deprives the individual with BDD of a potentially corrective experience. Thus, prolonged and repeated exposure helps the patient to learn that (a) such fears are excessive, and (b) anxiety naturally declines if the situation is not avoided. Behaviors such as excessive mirror-gazing or self-inspection (or mirror-avoidance in some cases), wearing hats to hide one's face or hair, or excessively eliciting reassurance from others are considered 'safety behaviors', designed to protect one from a presumed disastrous outcome (Grant & Phillips, 2005; Neziroglu, Roberts, & Yaryura-Tobias, 2004; Veale, 2004). Response prevention incorporates abstinence from such behaviors as they interfere with the correction of dysfunctional cognitions and the extinction of fear.

Examples of exposure exercises for individuals with BDD include wearing clothing that reveals or accentuates the imagined defect, wearing no makeup in public, and calling attention to the defect with makeup (Rosen, Reiter, & Orosan, 1995a,b). One technique that has shown preliminary success involves exposing patients to an image of him- or herself in a distorted (curved) mirror while preventing safety behaviors such as checking in a normal mirror (Gorbis, 2004). Similar techniques involve the use of computerized images of the person that can be manipulated (Neziroglu, Hsia, & Yaryura-Tobias, 2000). In order to sustain therapeutic progress over time, patients may need to learn to anticipate and cope with situations that could reactivate their symptoms, and occasional follow-up sessions may be helpful (McKay, 1999; Sarwer et al., 2004).

PHARMACOTHERAPY

As mentioned previously, individuals with BDD seem to respond well to antidepressants that inhibit the reuptake of the neurotransmitter serotonin, termed serotonin reuptake inhibitors (SRIs). These medications include antidepressants such as clomipramine, which affects both serotonin and norepinephrine transmission. This is true of other SRIs, such as fluoxetine, fluvoxamine, and citalopram (Hollander et al., 1993; Phillips, 2004b; Phillips, McElroy, Dwight, Eisen, & Rasmussen, 2001; Phillips & Najjar, 2003; Williams, Hadjistavropoulos, & Sharpe, 2006). Although particular individuals may respond to non-SRI antidepressants, such as bupropion (Nardi, Lopes, & Valenca, 2005), the data generally indicate that SRIs are superior to non-SRIs for the treatment of BDD (Hollander et al., 1999; Phillips, 2004b).

Moreover, SRIs have been shown to be efficacious in treating individuals with delusional levels of BDD, suggesting that SRIs – rather than antipsychotic medications – be administered as an initial treatment regimen (Phillips et al., 2002). The use of medication in combination with CBT emphasizing exposure and response prevention and psychoeducation has been shown to be effective in treating BDD in one study (Saxena et al., 2001). Other research suggests, however, that patients showed a similar treatment response to SRIs with or without combined CBT (Phillips, Albertini, Siniscalchi, Khan, & Robinson, 2001). Psychiatrists should consider a few caveats when administering medication for BDD. Individuals with BDD may require higher doses of SRIs than patients with other disorders, such as depression, and BDD patients tend to remain on SRIs for a long duration. When BDD patients decide to discontinue their medication, they have high rates of relapse of symptoms (Phillips, 2004b; Phillips, Albertini et al., 2001).

SUMMARY AND FUTURE DIRECTIONS

Although BDD has gained clinical and research attention in recent years, additional work is needed to better understand the etiology, physiopathology, and effective treatment options for this disorder. The proposed inclusion of BDD in the OCS carries important implications. Reclassification of any disorder within a new nomenclature should serve the ultimate purpose of making research, diagnosis, and treatment of the disorder more effective. As with any diagnostic classification issue, there are no definitive answers of inclusion or exclusion of a disorder apart from the opinions of the researchers who define the disorders, create the classification system, and determine the criteria for inclusion or exclusion (Maddux, Gosselin, & Winstead, 2005). The OCS concept is problematic in that it lacks a clear definition as well as agreed-upon conditions that must be met for a disorder to be included in the spectrum (Phillips, 2002). Even among researchers who agree that BDD should be considered part of the spectrum, there is some disagreement about how it is related to the spectrum or which BDD-related spectrum disorders together with BDD make up a cluster of OCS disorders (Hollander, 2005). Just as BDD has been considered part of the OCS, it has also emerged as a candidate for inclusion in the affective spectrum and the social anxiety spectrum (Schneier, Blanco, Anita, & Liebowitz, 2002). Additional epidemiological, etiological, neuropsychological, and pharmacological research is needed to better understand to what extent BDD belongs in the OCS.

REFERENCES

Abramowitz, J. S., & Deacon, B. (2006). The OC spectrum: A closer look at the arguments and the data. In J. S. Abramowitz & A. C. Houts (Eds.), *Concepts and controversies in obsessive–compulsive disorder* (pp. 141–149). New York: Springer.

Altamura, C., Paluello, M. M., Mundo, E., Medda, S., & Mannu, P. (2001). Clinical and subclinical body dysmorphic disorder. *European Archives of Psychiatry and Clinical Neuroscience, 251*(3), 105–108.

American Psychiatric Association (2000). *Diagnostic and statistical manual of mental disorders* (4th ed., text revision) *(DSM-IV-TR)*. Washington, DC: APA.

Arnold, L. M., Auchenbach, M. B., & McElroy, S. L. (2001). Psychogenic excoriation: Clinical features, proposed diagnostic criteria, epidemiology and approaches to treatment. *CNS Drugs, 15*(5), 351–359.

Bell, J. H., & Bromnick, R. D. (2003). The social reality of the imaginary audience: A grounded theory approach. *Adolescence, 38*(150), 205–219.

Berrios, G. E., & Kan, C. S. (1996). A conceptual and quantitative analysis of 178 historical cases of dysmorphophobia. *Acta Psychiatrica Scandinavica, 94*, 1–7.

Bienvenu, O. J., Samuels, J. F., Riddle, M. A., Hoehn-Saric, R., Liang, K. Y., Cullen, B. A. M., et al. (2000). The relationship of obsessive–compulsive disorder to possible spectrum disorders: Results from a family study. *Biological Psychiatry, 48*(4), 287–293.

Bohne, A., Wilhelm, S., Keuthen, N. J., Florin, I., Baer, L., & Jenike, M. A. (2002). Prevalence of body dysmorphic disorder in a German college student sample. *Psychiatry Research, 109*, 101–104.

Buhlmann, U., McNally, R. J., Etcoff, N. L., Tuschen-Caffier, B., & Wilhelm, S. (2004). Emotion recognition deficits in body dysmorphic disorder. *Journal of Psychiatric Research, 38*, 201–206.

Buhlmann, U., & Wilhelm, S. (2004). Cognitive factors in body dysmorphic disorder. *Psychiatric Annals, 34*(12), 922–926.

Buhlmann, U., Wilhelm, S., McNally, R. J., Tuschen-Caffier, B., Baer, L., & Jenike, M. A. (2002). Interpretive biases for ambiguous information in body dysmorphic disorder. *CNS Spectrums, 7*(6), 435–436.

Cansever, A., Uzun, O., Dönmez, E., & Ozşahin, A. (2003). The prevalence and clinical features of body dysmorphic disorder in college students: A study in a Turkish sample. *Comprehensive Psychiatry, 44*(1), 60–64.

Carey, P., Seedat, S., Warwick, J., van Heerden, B., & Stein, D. J. (2004). SPECT imaging of body dysmorphic disorder. *Journal of Neuropsychiatry and Clinical Neurosciences, 16*(3), 357–359.

Clark, D. A. (2004). *Cognitive–behavioral therapy for OCD*. New York: Guilford.

Coffey, B. J., Euripedes, C. M., Biederman, J., Baer, L., Rauch, S. L., O'Sullivan, R. L., et al. (1998). Tourette's disorder with and without obsessive–compulsive disorder in adults: Are they different? *The Journal of Nervous and Mental Disease, 186*(4), 201–206.

Cororve, M. B., & Gleaves, D. H. (2001). Body dysmorphic disorder: A review of conceptualizations, assessment, and treatment strategies. *Clinical Psychology Review, 21*(6), 949–970.

Crerand, C. E., Sarwer, D. B., Magee, L., Gibbons, L. M., Lowe, M. R., Bartlett, S. P., et al. (2004). Rate of body dysmorphic disorder among patients seeking facial plastic surgery. *Psychiatric Annals, 34*(12), 958–965.

Deckersbach, T., Savage, C. R., Phillips, K. A., Wilhelm, S., Buhlmann, U., Rauch, S. L., et al. (2000). Characteristics of memory dysfunction in body dysmorphic disorder. *Journal of the International Neuropsychological Society, 6*, 673–681.

DeMarco, L. M., Li, L. C., Phillips, K. A., & McElroy, S. L. (1998). Perceived stress in body dysmorphic disorder. *Journal of Nervous and Mental Disease, 186*(11), 724–726.

Diniz, J. B., Rosario-Campos, M., Shavitt, R. G., Curi, M., Hounie, A. G., Brotto, S. A., et al. (2004). Impact of age at onset and duration of illness on the expression of comorbidities in obsessive–compulsive disorder. *Journal of Clinical Psychiatry, 65*(1), 22–27.

Dougherty, D. D., Rauch, S. L., & Jenike, M. A. (2004). Pharmacotherapy for obsessive–compulsive disorder. *Journal of Clinical Psychology, 60*(11), 1195–1202.

Eisen, J. L., Phillips, K. A., Coles, M. E., & Rasmussen, S. A. (2004). Insight in obsessive compulsive disorder and body dysmorphic disorder. *Comprehensive Psychiatry, 45*(1), 10–15.

Fallon, B. A. (2004). Pharmacotherapy of somatoform disorders. *Journal of Psychosomatic Research, 56*, 455–460.

Flett, G. L., Hewitt, P. L., Blankstein, K. R., & Gray, L. (1998). Psychological distress and the frequency of perfectionistic thinking. *Journal of Personality and Social Psychology, 75*, 1363–1381.

Frare, F., Perugi, G., Ruffolo, G., & Toni, C. (2004). Obsessive–compulsive disorder and body dysmorphic disorder: a comparison of clinical features. *European Psychiatry, 19*, 292–298.

Frost, R. O., Turcotte, T. A., Heimberg, R. G., Mattia, J. I., Holt, C. S., & Hope, D. A. (1995). Reactions to mistakes among subjects high and low in perfectionistic concerns over mistakes. *Cognitive Therapy and Research, 19*, 195–205.

Gorbis, E. (2004). Crooked mirrors: The externalization of self-image in body dysmorphic disorder. *The Behavior Therapist, 27*(4), 74–76.

Grant, J. E., Kim, S. W., & Crow, S. J. (2001). Prevalence and clinical features of body dysmorphic disorder in adolescent and adult psychiatric inpatients. *Journal of Clinical Psychiatry, 62*(7), 517–522.

Grant, J. E., Kim, S. W., & Eckert, E. D. (2002). Body dysmorphic disorder in patients with anorexia nervosa: Prevalence, clinical features, and delusionality of body image. *International Journal of Eating Disorders, 32*, 291–300.

Grant, J. E., Menard, W., Pagano, M. E., Fay, C., & Phillips, K. A. (2005). Substance use disorders in individuals with body dysmorphic disorder. *Journal of Clinical Psychiatry, 66*(3), 309–316.

Grant, J. E., & Phillips, K. A. (2005). Recognizing and treating body dysmorphic disorder. *Annals of Clinical Psychiatry, 17*(4), 205–210.

Greisberg, S. & McKay, D. (2003). Neuropsychology of obsessive compulsive disorder: A review and treatment implications. *Clinical Psychology Review, 23*, 95–117.

Gupta, M. A., & Johnson, A. M. (2000). Nonweight-related body image concerns among female eating-disordered patients and nonclinical controls: Some preliminary observations. *International Journal of Eating Disorders, 27*(3), 304–309.

Hanes, K. R. (1998). Neuropsychological performance in body dysmorphic disorder. *Journal of the International Neuropsychological Society, 4*(2), 167–171.

Higgins, E. T. (1987). Self-discrepancy: A theory relating self and affect. *Psychological Review, 94*(3), 319–340.

Hollander, E. (2005). Obsessive–compulsive disorder and spectrum across the life span. *International Journal of Psychiatry in Clinical Practice, 9*(2), 79–86.

Hollander, E., Allen, A., Kwon, J., Aronowitz, B., Schmeidler, J., Wong, C., et al. (1999). Clomipramine vs. despipramine crossover trial in body dysmorphic disorder. *Archives of General Psychiatry, 56*(11), 230–233.

Hollander, E., Cohen, L. J., & Simeon, D. (1993). Body dysmorphic disorder. *Psychiatric Annals, 23*(7), 359–364.

Hollander, E., & Rosen, J. (2000). Obsessive–compulsive spectrum disorders: A review. In M. Maj, N. Sartorius, A. Okasha, & J. Zohar (Eds.), *Obsessive–compulsive disorder* (pp. 203–224). Chichester, UK: Wiley.

Kaye, W. H., Frank, G. K., Bailer, U. F., Henry, S. E., Meltzer, C. C., Price, J. C., et al. (2005). Serotonin alterations in anorexia and bulimia nervosa: New insights from imaging studies. *Physiology & Behavior, 85*, 73–81.

Khan, A., Leventhal, R. M., Khan, S., & Brown, W. A. (2002). Suicide risk in patients with anxiety disorders: A meta-analysis of the FDA database. *Journal of Affective Disorders, 68*, 183–190.

Kuelz, A. K., Hohagen, F., & Voderholzer, U. (2004). Neuropsychological performance in obsessive–compulsive disorder: A critical review. *Biological Psychology, 65*, 185–236.

Lochner, C., Hemmings, S. M. J., Kinnear, C. J., Niehaus, D. J. H., Nel, D. G., Corfield, V. A., et al. (2005). Cluster analysis of obsessive–compulsive spectrum disorders in patients with obsessive–compulsive disorder: clinical and genetic correlates. *Comprehensive Psychiatry, 46*(1), 14–19.

Mackley, C. L. (2005). Body dysmorphic disorder. *Dermatologic Surgery, 31*(5), 553–558.

Maddux, J. E., Gosselin, J. T., & Winstead, B. A. (2005). Conceptions of psychopathology: A social constructionist perspective. In J. E. Maddux & B. A. Winstead (Eds.), *Psychopathology: foundations for a contemporary understanding* (pp. 3–18). Mahwah, NJ: Lawrence Erlbaum.

Mayville, S., Katz, R. C., Gipson, M. T., & Cabral, K. (1999). Assessing the prevalence of body dysmorphic disorder in an ethnically diverse group of adolescents. *Journal of Child and Family Studies, 8*(3), 357–362.

McDougle, C. J., Epperson, C. N., Pelton, G. H., Wasylink, S., & Price, L. H. (2000). A double-blind, placebo-controlled study of risperidone addiction in serotonin reuptake inhibitor-refractory obsessive–compulsive disorder. *Archives of General Psychiatry, 57,* 794–801.

McDougle, C. J., Goodman, W. K., Price, L. H., Delgado, P. L., Krystal, J. H., Charney, D. S., et al. (1990). Neuroleptic addition in fluvoxamine-refractory obsessive–compulsive disorder. *The American Journal of Psychiatry, 147*(5), 652–654.

McKay, D. (1999). Two-year follow-up of behavioral treatment and maintenance for body dysmorphic disorder. *Behavior Modification, 23*(4), 620–629.

McKay, D. & Neziroglu, F. (in press). The spectrum of obsessive–compulsive disorders: methodological issues, with body dysmorphic disorder and hypochondriasis as examples. *Psychiatry Research.*

McKay, D., Neziroglu, F., & Yaryura-Tobias, J. A. (1997). Comparison of clinical characteristics in obsessive–compulsive disorder and body dysmorphic disorder. *Journal of Anxiety Disorders, 11*(4), 447–454.

McKay, D., Todaro, J., Neziroglu, F., Campisi, T., Moritz, E. K., & Yaryura-Tobias, J. A. (1997). Body dysmorphic disorder: A preliminary evaluation of treatment and maintenance using exposure with response prevention. *Behaviour Research and Therapy, 35*(1), 67–70.

Morselli, E. (Jerome, L., trans.). (2001). Dysmorphophobia and taphephobia: Two hitherto undescribed forms of insanity with fixed ideas. *History of Psychiatry, 12*(45), 103–114.

Nardi, A. E., Lopes, F. L., & Valenca, A. M. (2005). Body dysmorphic disorder treated with bupropion: Cases report. *Australian and New Zealand Journal of Psychiatry, 39*(1–2), 112.

Neziroglu, F., Hsia, C., & Yaryura-Tobias, J. A. (2000). Behavioral, cognitive, and family therapy for obsessive–compulsive and related disorders. *Psychiatric Clinics of North America, 23*(3), 657–670.

Neziroglu, F., & Khemlani-Patel, S. (2003). Therapeutic approaches to body dysmorphic disorder. *Brief Treatment and Crisis Intervention, 3*(3), 307–322.

Neziroglu, F., Roberts, M., & Yaryura-Tobias, J. A. (2004). A behavioral model for body dysmorphic disorder. *Psychiatric Annals, 34*(12), 915–920.

Nierenberg, A. A., Phillips, K. A., Peterson, T. J., Kelly, K. E., Alpert, J. E., Worthington, J. J., et al. (2002). Body dysmorphic disorder in outpatients with major depression. *Journal of Affective Disorders, 69,* 141–148.

Olivardia, R. (2001). Mirror, mirror on the wall, who's the largest of them all? The features and phenomenology of muscle dysmorphia. *Harvard Review of Psychiatry, 9*(5), 254–259.

Osman, S., Cooper, M., Hackmann, A., & Veale, D. (2004). Spontaneously occurring images and early memories in people with body dysmorphic disorder. *Memory, 12*(4), 428–436.

Otto, M. W., Wilhelm, S., Cohen, L. S., & Harlow, B. L. (2001). Prevalence of body dysmorphic disorder in a community sample of women. *American Journal of Psychiatry, 158*(12), 2061–2063.

Pearlstein, T. (2002). Eating disorders and comorbidity. *Archives of Women's Mental Health, 4,* 67–78.

Perugi, G., Akiskal, H. S., Giannotti, D., Frare, F., Di Vaio, S., & Cassano, G. B. (1997). Gender-related differences in body dysmorphic disorder (dysmorphophobia). *Journal of Nervous and Mental Disease, 185*(9), 578–582.

Phillips, K. A. (1991). Pimozide in clinical psychiatry. *Journal of Clinical Psychiatry, 52*(12), 514–515.

Phillips, K. A. (1999). Body dysmorphic disorder and depression: Theoretical considerations and treatment strategies. *Psychiatric Quarterly, 70*(4), 313–331.

Phillips, K. A. (2002). *Disorders of body image.* Petersfield, UK: Wrightson Biomedical Publishing.

Phillips, K.A. (2004a). Psychosis in body dysmorphic disorder. *Journal of Psychiatric Research, 38,* 63–72.

Phillips, K.A. (2004b). Treating body dysmorphic disorder using medication. *Psychiatric Annals, 34,* 945–953.

Phillips, K. A. (2005). Placebo-controlled pimozide augmentation of fluoxetine in body dysmorphic disorder. *American Journal of Psychiatry, 162,* 377–379.

Phillips, K. A., Albertini, R. S., Siniscalchi, J. M., Khan, A., & Robinson, M. (2001). Effectiveness of pharmacotherapy for body dysmorphic disorder: A chart-review study. *Journal of Clinical Psychiatry, 62*(9), 721–727.

Phillips, K. A., & Diaz, S. F. (1997). Gender differences in body dysmorphic disorder. *Journal of Nervous and Mental Disease, 185*, 570–577.

Phillips, K. A., Dufresne, R. G., Jr., Wilkel, C. S., & Vittorio, C. C. (2000). Rate of body dysmorphic disorder in dermatology patients. *Journal of the American Academy of Dermatology, 42*, 436–441.

Phillips, K. A., Grant, J. E., Siniscalchi, J. M., Stout, R., & Price, L. H. (2005). A retrospective follow-up study of body dysmorphic disorder. *Comprehensive Psychiatry, 46*, 315–321.

Phillips, K. A., McElroy, S. L., Dwight, M., Eisen, J., & Rasmussen, S. A. (2001). Delusionality and response to open-label fluvoxamine in body dysmorphic disorder. *Journal of Clinical Psychiatry, 62*(2), 87–91.

Phillips, K. A., McElroy, S. L., Hudson, J. I., & Pope, H. G., Jr. (1995). Body dysmorphic disorder: An obsessive–compulsive spectrum disorder, a form of affective spectrum disorder, or both? *Journal of Clinical Psychiatry, 56*(4), 41–51.

Phillips, K. A., McElroy, S. L., Keck, P. E., Jr., Hudson, J. I., & Pope, H. G., Jr. (1994). A comparison of delusional and nondelusional body dysmorphic disorder in 100 cases. *Psychopharmacology Bulletin, 30*(2), 179–186.

Phillips, K. A., McElroy, S. L., Keck, P. E., Jr., Pope, H. G., Jr., & Hudson, J. I. (1993). Body dysmorphic disorder: 30 cases of imagined ugliness. *American Journal of Psychiatry, 150*(2), 302–308.

Phillips, K. A., & Menard, W. (2004). Body dysmorphic disorder and art background. *American Journal of Psychiatry, 161*(5), 927–928.

Phillips, K. A., Menard, W., Fay, C., & Pagano, M. E. (2005). Psychosocial functioning and quality of life in body dysmorphic disorder. *Comprehensive Psychiatry, 46*, 254–260.

Phillips, K. A., & Najjar, F. (2003). An open-label study of citalopram in body dysmorphic disorder. *Journal of Clinical Psychiatry, 64*(6), 715–720.

Phillips, K. A., Nierenberg, A. A., Brendel, G., & Fava, M. (1996). Prevalence and clinical features of body dysmorphic disorder in atypical major depression. *Journal of Nervous and Mental Disease, 184*(2), 125–129.

Phillips, K. A., Pagano, M. E., Menard, W., Fay, C., & Stout, R. L. (2005). Predictors of remission from body dysmorphic disorder: A prospective study. *Journal of Nervous and Mental Disease, 193*(8), 564–567.

Pian, H. K. L., van Megan, H. J. G. M., Ramsey, N. F., Mandl, R., van Rijk, P. P., Wynne, H.J., et al. (2005). Decreased thalamic blood flow in obsessive-compulsive disorder patients responding to fluvoxamine. *Psychiatric Research: Neuroimaging, 138*, 89–97.

Rauch, S. L., Phillips, K. A., Segal, E., Makris, N., Shin, L. M., Whalen, P. J., et al. (2003). A preliminary morphometric magnetic resonance imaging study of regional brain volumes in body dysmorphic disorder. *Psychiatry Research: Neuroimaging, 122*, 13–19.

Rauch, S. L., Whalen, P. J., Dougherty, D., & Jenike, M. A. (1998). Neurobiologic models of obsessive–compulsive disorder. In M. A. Jenike, L. Baer, & W. E. Minichiello (Eds.), *Obsessive–compulsive disorders: Practical management* (3rd ed.) (pp. 222–253). St Louis, MO: Mosby.

Rivera, R. P., & Borda, T. (2001). The etiology of body dysmorphic disorder. *Psychiatric Annals, 31*(9), 559–563.

Rosen, J. C., & Ramirez, E. (1998). A comparison of eating disorders and body dysmorphic disorder on body image and psychological adjustment. *Journal of Psychosomatic Research, 44*(3/4), 441–449.

Rosen, J. C., Reiter, J., & Orosan, P. (1995a). Cognitive-behavioral body image therapy for body dysmorphic disorder. *Journal of Consulting and Clinical Psychology, 63*(2), 263–269.

Rosen, J. C., Reiter, J., & Orosan, P. (1995b). 'Cognitive–behavioral body image therapy for body dysmorphic disorder': Correction. *Journal of Consulting and Clinical Psychology, 63*(3), 437.

Sarwer, D. B., Gibbons, L. M., & Crerand, C. E. (2004). Treating body dysmorphic disorder with cognitive–behavior therapy. *Psychiatric Annals, 32*(12), 934–941.

Saxena, S., Winograd, A., Dunkin, J. J., Maidment, K., Rosen, R., Vapnik, T., et al. (2001). A retrospective review of clinical characteristics and treatment response in body dysmorphic disorder versus obsessive–compulsive disorder. *Journal of Clinical Psychiatry, 62*(1), 67–73.

Schneier, F. R., Blanco, C., Anita, S. X., & Liebowitz, M. R. (2002). The social anxiety spectrum. *Psychiatric Clinics of North America, 25*, 757–774.

Shafran, R., Cooper, Z., & Fairburn, C. G. (2002). Clinical perfectionism: a cognitive-behavioural analysis. *Behaviour Research and Therapy, 40*, 773–791.

Shirao, N., Okamoto, Y., Mantani, T., Okamoto, Y., & Yamawaki, S. (2005). Gender differences in brain activity generated by unpleasant word stimuli concerning body image: An fMRI study. *British Journal of Psychiatry, 186*, 48–53.

Shirao, N., Okamoto, Y., Okada, G., Okamoto, Y., & Yamawaki, S. (2003). Temporomesial activation in young females associated with unpleasant words concerning body image. *Neuropsychobiology, 48*(3), 136–142.

Simeon, D., Hollander, E., Stein, D. J., Cohen, L., & Aronowitz, B. (1995). Body dysmorphic disorder in the DSM-IV field trial for obsessive–compulsive disorder. *American Journal of Psychiatry, 152*(8), 1207–1209.

Slaney, R. B., Rice, K. G., & Ashby, J. S. (2002). A programmatic approach to measuring perfectionism: The Almost Perfect Scales. In G. L. Flett & P. L. Hewitt (Eds.), *Perfectionism: theory, research, and treatment* (pp. 63–88). Washington, DC: American Psychological Association.

Tekin, S., & Cummins, J. L. (2002). Frontal-subcortical neuronal circuits and clinical neuropsychiatry: An update. *Journal of Psychosomatic Research, 53*, 647–653.

van den Heuvel, O. A., Veltman, D. J., Groenwegen, H. J., Witter, M. P., Merckelbach, J., Cath, D. C., et al. (2005). Disorder specific neuroanatomical correlates of attentional bias in obsessive-compulsive disorder, panic disorder, and hypochondriasis. *Archives of General Psychiatry, 62*, 922–933.

Veale, D., Boocock, A., Gournay, K., Dryden, W., Shah, F., Willson, R., et al. (1996). Body dysmorphic disorder: A survey of fifty cases. *British Journal of Psychiatry, 169*, 196–201.

Veale, D., Ennis, M., & Lambrou, C. (2002). Possible association of body dysmorphic disorder with an occupation or education in art and design. *American Journal of Psychiatry, 159*, 1788–1790.

Veale, D., Gournay, K., Dryden, W., Boocock, A., Shah, F., Willson, R., et al. (1996). Body dysmorphic disorder: A cognitive behavioural model and pilot randomized controlled trial. *Behaviour Research and Therapy, 34*(9), 717–729.

Veale, D., Kinderman, P., Riley, S., & Lambrou, C. (2003). Self-discrepancy in body dysmorphic disorder. *British Journal of Clinical Psychology, 42*, 157–169.

Veale, D., & Riley, S. (2001). Mirror, mirror on the wall, who is the ugliest of them all? The psychopathology of mirror gazing in body dysmorphic disorder. *Behaviour Research and Therapy, 39*, 1381–1393.

Wilhelm, S., Otto, M. W., Lohr, B., & Deckersbach, T. (1999). Cognitive behavior group therapy for body dysmorphic disorder: A case series. *Behaviour Research and Therapy, 37*, 71–75.

Williams, J., Hadjistavropoulos, T., & Sharpe, D. (2006). A meta-analysis of psychological and pharmacological treatments for body dysmorphic disorder. *Behaviour Research and Therapy, 44*, 99–111.

Yaryura-Tobias, J. A., Neziroglu, F., & Torres-Gallegos, M. (2002). Neuroanatomical correlates and somatosensorial disturbances in body dysmorphic disorder. *CNS Spectrums, 7*(6), 432–434.

12

HYPOCHONDRIASIS

THEO K. BOUMAN

University of Groningen, The Netherlands

PHENOMENOLOGY

In his 1986 movie *Hannah and Her Sisters*, Woody Allen's character Mickey Sachs suffers from hearing loss in one ear. He attributes this to a brain tumor and so consults a number of doctors, only to find his preoccupation with the fatal disease progressively worsens. This movie provides a fine example of the thoughts and behaviors of a typical hypochondriacal patient. It shows that even when medical investigations do not reveal any serious disease, hypochondriacal patients remain convinced of its existence.

Many contemporary authors prefer the concept of 'health anxiety' to the historical term 'hypochondriasis', although most of them use these terms interchangeably. Hypochondriasis is regarded as a severe and clinically significant type of health anxiety. Although excessive health anxiety is the hallmark of hypochondriasis, it is also a common feature of other disorders, such as panic disorder, illness phobia, somatic delusions, and mood disorders.

Although the large majority of people benefit from medical care, a significant proportion show persistent manifestations of health anxiety even though they have been properly evaluated and assured that they don't have a serious medical disease. Prevalence studies have mainly been conducted in primary care settings, yielding lifetime prevalence figures of excessive health anxiety (hypochondriasis) that range from 0.8% (Gureje, Ustun, & Simon, 1997) to 4.5% (Faravelli et al., 1997).

Correspondence to: Theo K. Bouman, Department of Clinical and Developmental Psychology, University of Groningen, Grote Kruisstraat 2-1, 9712 TS Groningen, The Netherlands.

196

In many ways the cognitive and behavioral presentations of hypochondriacal patients resemble those of patients with obsessive–compulsive disorder (OCD). In this chapter we will explore the similarities and differences between these two conditions. In order to do so, first the phenomenology of hypochondriasis will be described in some detail and placed in theoretical and empirical framework.

DIAGNOSTIC CRITERIA

Contemporary diagnostic systems consider fear to be a prominent feature of hypochondriasis. The *DSM-IV-TR* (American Psychiatric Association, 2000) definition reads as follows, with A and B being the main criteria:

A. Preoccupation with fears of having, or the idea that one has, a serious disease based on the person's misinterpretation of bodily symptoms.
B. The preoccupation persists despite appropriate medical evaluation and reassurance.
C. The belief in Criterion A is not of delusional intensity (as in Delusional Disorder, Somatic Type) and is not restricted to a circumscribed concern about appearance (as in Body Dysmorphic Disorder).
D. The preoccupation causes clinically significant distress or impairment in social, occupational, or other important areas of functioning.
E. The duration of the disturbance is at least 6 months.

The *ICD-10* (World Health Organization, 1993) research diagnostic criteria define the central aspects of the 'hypochondriacal disorder' (F45.2) as:

A. A persistent belief, of at least 6 months' duration, of the presence of a maximum of two serious physical diseases (of which a least one must be specifically named by the patient).
B. Preoccupation with the belief and symptoms cause persistent distress or interference with personal functioning in daily living, and leads the patient to seek medical treatment or investigations (or equivalent help from local healers).
C. Persistent refusal to accept medical advice that there is no adequate physical cause for the symptoms or physical abnormality, except for short periods up to a few weeks at a time immediately after or during medical investigations.

Although the two sets of diagnostic criteria share a number of similarities, there are also significant differences. *ICD-10* requires a maximum of two diseases whereas *DSM-IV* places no such restriction. *ICD-10* includes circumscribed concerns about physical appearance as part of hypochondriacal disorder, whereas *DSM-IV* explicitly excludes this clinical presentation, categorizing it as a distinct clinical condition, Body Dysmorphic Disorder. Most importantly, the criteria seem to suggest that *ICD-10* focuses on disease conviction ('persistent belief of …'), whereas *DSM-IV* incorporates both disease conviction ('the idea that one has …') as well as health anxiety ('fears of having …').

As may be apparent from the above description, these criteria are too global and atheoretical to allow for a deep understanding of the nature and interpersonal dynamics of hypochondriasis. Therefore, the next sections will highlight the somatic, cognitive, and behavioral manifestations of the disorder.

BODILY SENSATIONS

Both classification systems mentioned above heavily emphasize the nature of somatic sensations or perceived changes in the dynamics of hypochondriasis in particular and somatoform in general. According to the *DSM-IV-TR* general description, somatoform disorders are characterized by somatic sensations or changes that cannot be sufficiently medically explained. In the case of hypochondriasis, however, explained as well as unexplained bodily reactions may be the focus of the patient's concern. Basically, each and every bodily sensation or change may develop into the subject of the hypochondriacal preoccupation, since the fear is associated with a *misinterpretation* of harmless bodily changes and sensations. These somatic manifestations are quite diverse and vary from person to person and may include (variations in) bodily functions (e.g., palpitations, sweating, bloating), minor physical abnormalities (e.g., blemishes, irregularities of the skin, sore throat), vague and ambiguous physical sensations (e.g., tired or heavy limbs, general feeling of malaise, fatigue). The patient's focus may be stable and pertain to only one specific body system or it may change over time, shifting from the fear of one disease to the other.

One of our patients, for example, continued to be preoccupied with heart failure, no matter what else happened. Even when she was to undergo abdominal surgery to remove a large mass, she was not a bit concerned that it might be malignant. In contrast, another patient was very worried about contracting any disease for fear of losing his dignity in the terminal phase of the illness. This led him to present with a wide variety of bodily complaints and disease convictions over a period of time.

An additional problem is the need for adequate medical evaluation in order to be able to make the diagnosis. The question is who is to determine what is considered adequate: the general practitioner, the medical specialist, the patient, or the therapist? All these parties hold different opinions on the definition of 'adequate medical evaluation'. In this respect it is quite feasible (and the rule rather than the exception) that there is a discrepancy between the patient's opinion and that of the doctor; that is, the patient is convinced of a serious medical condition whereas the doctor is not.

COGNITIVE PROCESSES

According to the *DSM-IV* and *ICD-10* diagnostic criteria as well as to contemporary theoretical models (Warwick & Salkovskis, 1990), the misinterpretation of bodily sensations, rather than the nature of the sensations themselves, is the core feature of hypochondriasis. The hypochondriacal patient typically harbors the conviction that bodily changes or sensations imply a serious (and often a potentially lethal) disease. The core of the misinterpretation of bodily sensations is a cognitive process in which attributional and attentional processes and biases play a key role.

A prominent feature of hypochondriasis is the *overestimation of dangerousness* of relatively harmless bodily changes and sensations. More specifically, hypochondriacal patients consider changes and sensations to be the precursors or signs of a known or unknown physical disaster. Therefore, the emphasis is more on the preoccupation with the belief that there is an underlying serious disease, rather than with the bodily manifestations themselves. Basically any such sensation can be conceived as meaning something fatal. In most patients the fear concentrates on cancer, heart failure or a combination of both. Fear of death in general or of less lethal diseases (e.g., sexually transmitted diseases, neurodegenerative diseases) are less common. Apart from that, danger may also be perceived in medical information, information from other people, and in private events (thoughts and images).

Confirmatory bias is considered an important maintaining factor, because patients attend to and encode information that is consistent with their private disease theory, thereby dismissing inconsistent information. If a doctor discusses the lab results and remarks that fortunately there is no trace of malignancy, the patient just remembers the latter word and starts wondering why the doctor brought this up in the first place. Was the doctor trying to suggest something, without wanting to reveal the gruesome truth?

Although many hypochondriacal patients are considerably concerned about the catastrophic nature of the bodily changes or sensations, they also experience a persistent element of doubt about this and are basically uncertain of their fate. Many of their behaviors are inspired by this *intolerance for uncertainty*. This becomes visible in their quest for the ultimate medical test, the newest diagnostic method, just another scan, etc., just about anything to transform uncertainty into certainty. Anecdotal accounts have it that some patients were quite relieved when after some years a 'real' disease was discovered, making an end to a long period of uncertainty.

Thought–action fusion may be present in the form of the conviction that when you mention the feared disease you will call it upon yourself. This notion may in turn lead to the avoidance of mentioning a certain word, such as 'cancer'. It may easily be seen that this will obscure communication between the patient and doctors or psychologists.

In some patients the thoughts are held with such great conviction and tenacity, that there are only a few moments of uncertainty. This may lead to the DSM diagnostic specifier '*with no insight*', bordering at a somatic (i.e., hypochondriacal) delusion in which patients hardly have any doubt about their feared disease.

A good example is one of our patients who was convinced he was suffering from AIDS and went as far as joining a support group, taking AIDS medication, and leading the life of a terminally ill patient. His doctor had in vain tried to reassure him that nothing was wrong and that the many HIV-tests the patient had taken could only be interpreted in his advantage.

This case illustrates that the stronger the conviction and the greater the fear, the more the concern takes a prominent place in the person's life, dominating thinking, behaving and relating to other people, and has the quality of overvalued ideation.

Apart from the attributional factors, *attentional distortions* also play a great role in the clinical picture. This can be observed in the hypochondriacal patient's strong tendency to selectively attend to bodily changes or sensations, medical information in the media, medical topics in social encounters, as well as in attending to personally relevant (i.e., illness confirming) information in medical consultations. The opposite can also be observed, in that many patients go to great lengths to divert their attention away from the issues mentioned above. These attentional approach and avoidance strategies are in line with and supported by the behavioral features of hypochondriasis.

BEHAVIORAL MANIFESTATIONS

Many hypochondriacal behaviors can be regarded as safety behaviors, because they are performed with the purpose of reducing anxiety, distress, or uncertainty. Patients go to great lengths to discover what is the matter with their bodies, and persistently seek reassurance from significant others (e.g., partner, children, general practitioner, nurse, specialist). These behaviors may seem exaggerated at first glance, but they can be readily understood from the patient's point of view. Specific safety behavior leads to a short-term reduction of anxiety, but also to the maintenance of hypochondriasis in the long run. In general, three types of safety behaviors are distinguished:

- *Avoidance and escape behaviors* (e.g., physical exercise, medical information, touching body parts, meeting ill people, any social interaction).
- *Checking behavior* (e.g., pulse, excrement, urine, abdominal or rectal checking).
- *Reassurance seeking* (e.g., from partner, children, general practitioner, nurse, medical specialist, psychologist). The provision of reassurance seems to be the most sensible thing a doctor could do, and is the most frequently administered psychotherapeutic intervention. Ideally, the doctor explains to the patient that nothing serious is wrong and the patient goes home completely reassured. In hypochondriacal patients this reassurance is short-lived and the need for reassurance will only increase, thus leading to the maintenance of the condition, because of the inability to reassure themselves. Many researchers and clinicians agree that the provision of adequate information is a preferred line of action (Warwick & Salkovskis, 1985).

Many safety behaviors reflect the themes of *responsibility* and *control* that patients experience in relation to their health. They try to check every potential risk factor (in the specific domain they are preoccupied with). 'If I haven't done everything to check if I have throat cancer, I wouldn't forgive myself,' one woman remarked. Responsibility is in some patients directed towards their own health behavior, but in others toward significant others, in particular their children. 'If I die, my children will end up in the gutter, since nobody will really care about them,' a 33-year-old divorced mother feared.

Control is manifested in many ways, such as trying to persuade the doctor to organize a specific referral, forcing the partner to provide reassurance, avoiding illness-related topics in a conversation. On the other hand, it is quite possible that for many people health anxiety is associated with excessive avoidance, including avoidance of medical consultations. They hardly ever go to see a doctor for fear of discovery of a fatal disease. By definition these people cannot be given the *DSM-IV* diagnosis of hypochondriasis, because criterion B has not been fulfilled.

In sum, the somatic, attributional, attentional, and behavioral features of hypochondriasis and health anxiety are functionally and meaningfully related and focus on the theme of self-assessed ill health.

ETIOLOGICAL AND CONCEPTUAL MODELS AND ISSUES

ETIOLOGY

To date a comprehensive and empirically tested model of the onset and course of hypochondriasis is lacking. Many studies that have been reported thus far focus upon one or more combinations of putative etiological factors versus hypochondriasis.

It is generally believed that the age of onset for hypochondriasis lies in early childhood, although in individual patients any age may be the start of the disorder. A few studies have concentrated on a genetic and familial component in hypochon-driasis (e.g., Noyes et al., 1997; Taylor et al., 2006; Torgerson, 1986), suggesting that there is, at best, only a moderate genetic contribution. However, in a family study Bienvenue et al. (2000) found hypochondriacal patients to have a relatively high prevalence in case probands.

In the current cognitive behavioral conceptualization of hypochondriasis, the dis-order is assumed to originate from threatening situations that form maladaptive health-related assumptions (Salkovskis & Warwick, 2001; Warwick & Salkovskis, 1990). These assumptions are triggered under circumstances in which ambiguous bodily sensations are experienced, or in the event of critical incidents (such as being confronted with somebody else's symptoms or even death). Next, the assumptions may be consolidated by further health-related experiences, by selective attention to illness-related information, and by confirmatory reasoning bias.

The course is often chronic, but remission (also known as transient hypochon-driasis) also occurs. Barsky et al. (1993), for example, found that 36.5% of patients no longer met criteria for hypochondriasis in a 5-year prospective study. The reasons for this transient state are not well understood (Williams, 2004).

Recently it has been hypothesized that attachment style may be associated to the disorder. Noyes and colleagues (2003) tested this hypothesis in a large sample of hypochondriacal patients and found insecure (fearful) attachment to be positively correlated with hypochondriasis and somatic complaints and negatively related to satisfaction with medical care. The authors interpret their findings as support for an interpersonal model of hypochondriasis.

MAINTENANCE

The central part of the cognitive behavioral model is the misinterpretation of innocuous bodily changes and sensations (Salkovskis & Warwick, 2001). The model states that innocuous bodily sensations (but also external stimuli or events) are catastrophically misinterpreted, leading to anxiety and other negative affective states such as depression and distress. This in turn provokes physical reactions and safety-seeking behaviors that maintain the original misinterpretations. To date only components of the model have undergone empirical testing. In general the results are in line with a cognitive formulation of the disorder.

MISINTERPRETATION OF INNOCUOUS SENSATIONS

In several self-report and experimental studies the general tendency to misinterpret ambiguous bodily sensations has been investigated. The overall conclusion is that hypochondriacal patients have specific and unique dysfunctional beliefs about illness (see for an overview Williams, 2004). The hypochondriacal patients in the study by MacLeod, Haynes, & Sensky (1998) gave more somatic attributions to common physical sensations than anxious and non-anxious controls. Barsky et al. (1993) found hypochondriacal patients were more likely to consider bodily sensations indicative of a disease than non-hypochondriacal patients. In an analogue study using students, Marcus and Church (2003) found hypochondriasis to be the only variable to predict participant's estimates of their likelihood of developing serious illness, even after controlling for other variables. Similar findings were reported by Haenen, de Jong, Schmidt, Stevens, & Visser (2000). Furthermore, hypochondriacal patients tend to worry more and have less control about hypochondriacal themes than about other topics (Bouman & Meijer, 1999). Not all studies have replicated these findings. De Jong, Haenen, Schmidt, & Mayer (1998) did not find a specific danger confirming reasoning pattern in hypochondriacal patients compared to healthy controls.

ATTENTIONAL BIAS

Hypochondriasis is related to a preferential attention allocation to health-relevant information (Williams, 2004). This has been found in experimental studies using, for example, the modified Stroop task and word recognition tasks (Haenen, Schmidt, Kroeze, & van den Hout, 1996; Hitchcock & Mattews, 1992; Owens,

Asmundson, Hadjistravropoulos, & Owens, 2004), as well as self-report question-naires (Vervaeke, Bouman, & Valmaggia, 1999).

In a study by Brown and colleagues (1999) no support of an attentional bias was found because hypochondriacal patients did not perceive more health-related words than words unrelated to health. In contrast, they found a bias against report-ing health-related items, interpreting this as a manifestation of perceptual defense.

RELATIONSHIP TO OBSESSIVE–COMPULSIVE DISORDER

PARALLELS BETWEEN OCD AND HYPOCHONDRIASIS

At first glance, hypochondriasis and OCD share many similarities. In both condi-tions obsessions, intrusions, preoccupied thinking, rumination and attentional biases characterize the patients' cognitive processes. Functionally, these processes lead to high levels of anxiety and distress, in turn prompting for purposeful anxiety-reducing behavior and/or rituals. These behaviors have a ritualistic and compulsive character.

In many patients both disorders do not manifest themselves via anxious mood *per se*, but via persistent behavioral patterns (checking in OCD and reassurance seeking in hypochondriasis). Only when the patient is prevented from carrying out these rituals do they become anxious.

Despite its defining nature, concern about health is not solely restricted to hypochondriasis. Savron et al. (1996) reported the presence of mild abnormal illness behavior in OCD, because all scales on Kellner's Illness Attitude Scales (Kellner, 1986) were clinically elevated in OCD patients compared to healthy controls. An Indian study by Jaisoorya, Janardhan Reddy, & Srinath (2003) also showed the prevalence of hypochondriasis (and a number of other disorders) to be higher in OCD patients than in healthy controls. In a more specific study, Abramowitz and colleagues (1999) compared OCD patients with and without health concerns. The results showed that the OCD plus health concern patients scored higher on contam-ination obsessions and washing compulsions, whereas the 'pure' OCD patients were more engaged in harming obsessions and checking compulsions.

DIFFERENCES BETWEEN OCD AND HYPOCHONDRIASIS

Hypochondriacal cognitions and behaviors

Hypochondriasis is thematically organized around one theme: the feared dis-ease. Most conspicuous is the role of bodily changes and sensations as input in hypochondriasis. The assumed hypersensitivity to interoceptive cues (bodily sen-sations) in hypochondriasis results in a vicious circle of more anxiety, which increases arousal, thus producing more bodily sensations, similar to the processes in panic disorder (cf. Salkovskis & Clark, 1993).

The thoughts and behaviors are often considered more ego-syntonic for the hypochondriacal patient. They suffer from a disease conviction that they consider completely justified. For them, the ensuing behaviors are quite understandable and a logical corollary of the feared disease. For that reason hypochondriacal patients typically do not resist these compulsive behaviors, as is the case in OCD.

> A male patient had the strong conviction he was (or could be) suffering from prostate cancer. He was very much upset by this prospect and engaged in checking behavior in the form of daily self-performed rectal examinations. Despite the secrecy and stigma attached to his checking behavior, he kept performing it in order to monitor any changes in the pelvic area in general and his prostate in particular.

This patient exemplifies the motto for most hypochondriacal patients: their behaviors are of life-saving value. It is the purpose that counts and to a lesser extent the precise way in which the behaviors are carried out.

As a further example, one patient engaged in her reassurance rituals at bedtime. The husband had to check his wife's back for irregularities of the skin and then he had to say the 'magic word': 'It's OK, nothing is wrong with your skin.' Both knew that the ritual made sense in the wife's hypochondriacal belief system, and both knew that the husband had to perform his ritual in order to make her reassured enough to go to sleep.

OCD cognitions

Intrusive thoughts in OCD relate to many topics, mostly harm, responsibility, violating moral or social norms, etc. According to current cognitive behavioral conceptualizations, these intrusions are evaluated (i.e. misinterpreted), leading to emotional and behavioral responses. The evaluation often takes place against a moral or probabilistic standard; that is, something dreadful that might happen is either morally despicable, or highly probable. In OCD patients the content of the obsessions has become a cognitive ritual in which the same verbal or pictorial content is repeated time and again.

> This was seen, for example, in the case of a woman who struggled with unwanted sexually oriented thoughts in which she wondered whether she had slept with her male colleagues. The thoughts kept entering her mind on a daily basis and grew in intensity upon confrontation with her colleagues and her husband. To get rid of the associated distress she had picked up an elaborate ritual in which she checked most things she had laid her hands on, such as keys, doors, microwave, bills, or paper work. She became very upset and tired about her rituals, which she considered to be bizarre and a real burden. Not being able to perform her rituals would lead to an increased level of distress, and an even stronger urge to perform the checking rituals.

It seems that OCD is more ego-dystonic in nature, compared to the more ego-syntonic features of hypochondriasis. According to Barsky (1992), OCD patients hold a more disconnected set of ideas, experience these as abnormal mental events, and hence tend to keep these ideas (intrusions) to themselves. Hypochondriacal patients, on the other hand, view their thoughts as more realistic and hold them in an internally consistent cognitive network. Because of this they are less inclined to be secretive about these thoughts.

OCD behaviors

Typically behavioral rituals or compulsions in OCD have to be performed in a very precise ('just right') and stereotyped way because of their symbolic value with the aim of preventing some dreaded consequences (such as the death of a loved one). Unlike hypochondriasis, the rituals in OCD have become a purpose in their own right, and not being able to perform them properly induces a high level of distress in patients.

Differences in insight

Neziroglu, McKay, & Yaryura-Tobias (2000) compared hypochondriacal patients, OCD patients, and those with both diagnoses. They found 'pure' hypochondriacal patients to score highest on overvalued ideation and (together with the mixed diagnosis group) higher on panic and agoraphobic symptoms. Furthermore, the OCD group scored highest on obsessions. Hypochondriacal patients display less insight in their condition than OCD patients (Abramowitz et al., 1999). In a cluster analytic study on obsessive–compulsive spectrum disorders, Lochner et al. (2005) found three clusters, one of which being the 'somatic' cluster (including body dysmorphic disorder and hypochondriasis). Patients in this cluster exhibited less insight and more somatic obsessions and compulsions than those in the other two clusters called 'reward deficiency' and 'impulsivity'. The reported lack of insight and the ego-syntonic nature of hypochondriasis may well be related. The hypochondriacal patient finds their interpretations and reasoning to make sense, and therefore consider their thoughts and actions to be quite reasonable. It is possible that the patients' core beliefs differ between these disorders, hypochondriasis being primarily associated with 'bodily vulnerability and mortality' and OCD with 'responsibility and control'.

From the above it can be concluded that hypochondriasis and OCD share many similarities on a phenomenological as well as functional level. Phenomenologically speaking, both conditions overlap in their content in the sense that some OCD patients are engaged in health-related themes, and some hypochondriacal patients display general harm avoidance themes. Functionally speaking, the similarities are also manifold. The initial triggers (either internal or external) give rise to misinterpretations that promote negative emotions (mostly anxiety and distress, but also depression and anger). Specific safety behaviors are used to reduce these unwanted emotions in the short term, but ironically in the long run contribute to their maintenance.

FUTURE DIRECTIONS

A modest number of studies have been carried out into the relations between hypochondriasis and OCD. Most of them involve relatively small groups that have been defined using diagnostic interviews or cut-off scores on questionnaire. For that reason the reliability of the diagnostic groups is questionable. Future research would probably benefit more from a dimensional and transdiagnostic approach (Harvey et al., 2004). This seems to be more fruitful than a categorical perspective. The latter too much emphasizes the assumption of nosological entities and their interrelations, for example by comparing groups of patients with different diagnoses. As patients possess a wide variety of features, this type of research is not the prime candidate for studying the functional and etiological mechanisms underlying specific disorders. The dimensional approach on the other hand allows more insight into the mechanisms and components of, in this case, OCD and hypochondriasis. Such an approach would also pave the way for a more integrated cognitive behavioral model of disorders in which preoccupation and rumination prevails. For one, a model in which the many aspects of hypochondriasis are accounted for needs yet to be formulated (Williams, 2004). The same holds for a model in which the general vulnerability for OCD-spectrum disorders is encompassed.

Additional recommendations pertain to the idiosyncratic nature of hypochondriasis. From experimental studies it has become apparent that not all health-related stimuli (e.g., threat words in modified Stroop task) have the same meaning (and therefore effect) for all hypochondriacal participants. Averaging out the experimental effects can be counteracted by using idiosyncratic measures. Research would also profit from the application of experimental paradigms (rather than self-report questionnaires) to get more insight in nonconscious automatic features of information processing (e.g., Williams, 2004).

The present interest in subtyping in the field of OCD should also be transferred to the domain of hypochondriasis and health anxiety. Splitting rather than lumping may help to find more precise mechanisms in the latter disorders and in their relation with other disorders such as OCD, generalized anxiety disorder, and somatization. These mechanisms may, for example, be non-specific (e.g., the strong belief in dangerousness, responsibility, thought–action fusion) or specific (e.g., certain bodily sensations, or mental events). Most studies hardly take into account the discrimination between disease fear and disease conviction (Barsky, 1992), or disease phobia, thanatophobia, and health anxiety (Fava & Magnelli, 2001), as well as various other phenomenological of etiological subtypes (Fallon, Quereshis, Laje, & Klein, 2000).

TREATMENT

Until the late 1980s psychological treatments for hypochondriasis were generally considered a waste of time. Some authors went as far as stating that there was no specific treatment and patients would not profit from any treatment whatsoever. In the 1990s research into the nature and treatment of hypochondriasis has increased. In particular the cognitive behavioral conceptualization of the disorder (Warwick & Salkovskis, 1990) has been stimulating to both researchers and clinicians. For the latter the clinical picture became more understandable because the model allowed for hypotheses as starting points for treatment. In particular cognitions and behaviors are therapeutic targets, and even attentional processes seem promising candidates in this respect. Here we will briefly summarize results from outcome studies. Further details, including the results of a meta-analysis, can be found in Taylor and Asmundson (2004).

In the 1960s to 1980s a number of case studies were published in which various interventions from the emerging behavioral and (later) cognitive therapies were demonstrated, such as systematic desensitization, exposure in vivo, hypnotherapy, relaxation, thought-stopping, and response prevention. Lacking a specific model for hypochondriasis, the philosophy behind these treatments was based upon that from analogue problem areas, in particular anxiety disorders.

The first study of cognitive–behavior therapy (CBT) consisted of a case series using cross-over design with six patients. Visser and Bouman (1992) compared six sessions of cognitive therapy with six sessions of behavior therapy (exposure and response prevention; ERP), and found both treatments to have beneficial effects.

Warwick, Clark, Cobb, & Salkovskis (1996) published the first wait-list controlled trial, in which 32 patients with *DSM-III-R* hypochondriasis were randomly assigned to either CBT or wait-list. CBT consisted of 16 one-hour sessions in which the hypochondriacal misinterpretations were challenged. Patients in the active treatment condition improved on all hypochondriacal measures, and improvement was maintained at 3 months follow-up. According to a blind assessor, 76% of the patients in the treatment condition improved, against 5% in the wait-list condition. Despite a number of methodological limitations, this study suggested the therapeutic potential of CBT for hypochondriasis.

In a subsequent study, Clark et al. (1998) compared the effects of CBT with those of behavioral stress management (BSM), and wait-list. Forty-eight patients were randomly assigned to each of these three conditions, and received 16 individual one-hour sessions. BSM consisted of relaxation exercises, psychoeducation about stress and the acquisition of problem-solving skills. Although CBT led to a quicker treatment response, both active treatment conditions performed equally well at 1-year follow-up on nearly all measures.

Bouman and Visser (1998) compared the efficacy of 'pure' cognitive therapy with that of 'pure' behavior therapy (i.e., ERP) by randomly assigning 17 patients to either of these treatment conditions. Cognitive therapy encompassed 12 one-hour sessions and consisted of detecting dysfunctional thoughts, by means of Socratic questioning and thought records. The thoughts were challenged and the patients were assisted in formulating more functional thoughts. No behavioral interventions were carried out in the cognitive condition. ERP consisted of the formulation of a hierarchy of hypochondriacal themes, such as repeated checking, asking for reassurance, avoiding of exercise and medical information. Gradual exposure and refraining from anxiety-reducing behaviors resulted in a decrease of fear for the situations. It was concluded that both treatments were equally effective.

Following this, Visser and Bouman (2001) conducted a study comparing CBT, ERP, and wait-list. In this multi-center study in regular outpatient health care institutions 78 patients participated, 20% of whom eventually dropped out. In the CBT condition hypochondriacal thoughts were challenged both verbally and using behavioral experiments. The ERP condition was the same as that used the 1998 study. Results showed patients in the active treatment condition to improve at 1 and 6 month follow-up, against no such gain in the wait-list condition.

To date, the largest randomized, control trial has been carried out by Barsky and Ahern (2004), who included 102 patients in a CBT-condition compared to 85 patients in a condition consisting of standard medical care. Participants were selected from a sample of 6307 general hospital patients who were screened for hypochondriasis and of whom 8% satisfied research criteria. Active treatment consisted of six manualized sessions and a consultation letter to each patient's general practitioner. At the end of treatment and at 6 and 12 month follow-up patients exhibited a significant decrease in hypochondriacal fears, convictions, and behaviors, whereas their social functioning and general daily activities showed improvement.

Greeven et al. (in press) were the first to carry out a randomized controlled trial in which CBT was compared to paroxetine and placebo. Initially 112 hypochondriacal patients were randomly assigned to three conditions, and 30 (27%) eventually dropped out of the treatment. On average CBT and paroxetine led to more improvement than placebo. The number of therapy sessions was individually determined, ranging from 6 to 16 sessions with an average number of 7.3 sessions.

EFFECTIVE INTERVENTIONS

From these controlled studies at independent research centers it can be concluded that various CBT interventions have proven to be effective for hypochondriasis. However, the studies differ considerably in a number of methodological and clinical aspects, such as patient recruitment, therapist selection, setting, and outcome measures. Leaving this aside, *behavioral interventions*, and in particular the combination of exposure and response prevention, are effective in reducing safety behaviors and hypochondriacal anxiety. Most studies on the treatment of hypochondriasis emphasize cognitive change; that is, the modification of maladaptive assumptions about the patient's personal health and bodily functions. The procedure consists of challenging the dysfunctional beliefs by checking them against objective evidence. This can be done verbally, by, for example, examining and balancing the arguments in favor and against the patient's disease theory.

Overall, great similarity can be observed between the general treatment approaches for both OCD and hypochondriasis. ERP and cognitive interventions have proven to be effective in both disorders. Treatment studies of OCD support the efficacy of ERP. The relative paucity of cognitive therapy studies in OCD may be attributable to the fact that the conceptualization and treatment development of OCD started earlier than that of hypochondriasis. The latter later gained attention with the rise of cognitive models of psychopathology, along with an absence of a broadly supported behavioral model for hypochondriasis. A difference between the treatment of both disorders relates to the setting in which many patients are seen. Especially the medical context, in which hypochondriacal patients are often treated, makes a proper introduction and referral to a psychological treatment a very important and crucial first step.

An important theme for a future research agenda is the isolation of active ingredients of psychological treatments. This type of study helps to elucidate the maintaining factors of both hypochondriasis and OCD and subsequently throws light on their similarities and differences. Clinically speaking, correcting misinterpretation of innocuous bodily changes and sensations may seem a compelling candidate. However, other factors are equally plausible; for example, promoting changes on a process level rather than a content level, such as by reducing cognitive elaboration (e.g., stopping worrying; Brown et al., 1999) and integration (i.e., the automatic processes that strengthen adaptive cognitive schemata).

CONCLUSIONS

Hypochondriasis and OCD share many similarities on a phenomenological (notably cognitive and behavioral) and functional level. Most differences seem to pertain to the specific nature of the preoccupation. This may be the reason that an increasing number of authors consider hypochondriasis a good example of an OCD spectrum disorder (e.g., Abramowitz, Schwartz, & Whiteside, 2002; Castle & Phillips, 2006).

Despite this impression we need more research into the precise mechanisms that play a role in the origin and maintenance of these disorders. To date, the number of studies addressing this area is only limited and may profit from methodological improvements. The increasing emphasis on studying psychological processes across disorders rather than comparing diagnostic groups is very promising and will no doubt further our knowledge on the ties between OCD and hypochondriasis. This will contribute to the formulation of a comprehensive model of hypochondriasis, including both individual as well as interpersonal aspects.

REFERENCES

Abramowitz, J. S., Brigidi, B. D., & Foa, E. B. (1999). Health concerns in patients with obsessive–compulsive disorder. *Journal of Anxiety Disorders, 13*, 529–539.

Abramowitz, J. S., Schwartz, S. A., & Whiteside, S. P. (2002). A contemporary conceptual model of hypochondriasis. *Mayo Clinic Proceedings, 77*, 1323–1330.

American Psychiatric Association (2000). *Diagnostic and statistical manual of mental disorders* (4th ed., text revision) (*DSM-IV-TR*). Washington, DC: Author.

Barsky, A. J. (1992). Hypochondriasis and obsessive–compulsive disorder. *Psychiatric Clinics of North America, 15*, 791–801.

Barsky, A. J., & Ahern, D. K. (2004). Cognitive behavior therapy for hypochondriasis. *JAMA, 291*, 1464–1470.

Barsky, A. J., Cleary, P. D., Sarnie, M. K., & Klerman, G. L. (1993). The course of transient hypochondriasis. *American Journal of Psychiatry, 150*, 484–488.

Bienvenue, O. J., Samuels, J. F., Riddle, M. A., Hoehn-Saric, R., Liang, K-Y, Cullen, B. A. M., et al. (2000). The relationship of obsessive–compulsive disorder to possible spectrum disorders: Results from a family study. *Biological Psychiatry, 48*, 287–293.

Bouman, T. K., & Meijer, K. J. (1999). A preliminary study of worry and metacognitions in hypochondriasis. *Clinical Psychology and Psychotherapy, 6*, 96–101.

Bouman, T. K., & Visser, S. (1998). Cognitive and behavioural treatments of hypochondriasis. *Psychotherapy and Psychosomatics, 67*, 214–221.

Brown, H. D., Kosslyn, S. M., Delamater, B., Fama, J., & Barsky, A. J. (1999). Perceptual and memory biases for health-related information in hypochondriacal individuals. *Journal of Psychosomatic Research, 47*, 67–78.

Castle, D. J., & Phillips, K. A. (2006). Obsessive–compulsive spectrum of disorders: A defensible construct? *Australian and New Zealand Journal of Psychiatry, 40*, 114–120.

Clark, D. M., Salkovskis, P. M., Hackman, A., Wells, A., Fennell, M., Ludgate, J., et al. (1998). Two psychological treatments for hypochondriasis: A randomized controlled trial. *British Journal of Psychiatry, 173*, 218–225.

De Jong, P. J., Haenen, M-A., Schmidt, A., & Mayer, B. (1998). Hypochondriasis: the role of fear-confirming reasoning. *Behaviour Research and Therapy, 36*, 65–74.

Fallon, B. A., Qureshi, A. I., Laje, G., & Klein, B. (2000). Hypochondriasis and its relationship to obsessive–compulsive disorder. *Psychiatric Clinics of North America, 23*, 605–616.

Faravelli, C., Salvatori, S., Galassi, F., Aiazzi, L., Drei, C., & Cabras, P. (1997). Epidemiology of somatoform disorders: A community survey in Florence. *Social Psychiatry and Psychiatric Epidemiology, 32*, 24–29.

Fava, G. A., & Magnelli, L. (2001). Hypochondriasis and anxiety disorders. In V. Starcevic & D. R. Lipsitt (Eds.), *Hypochondria: Modern perspectives on an ancient malady* (pp. 89–102). Oxford: Oxford University Press.

Greeven, A., van Balkom, A. J. L. M., Visser, S., Merkelbach, J.W., van Rood, Y.R., van Dyck, R., et al. (in press). Cognitive behavior therapy and paroxetine in the treatment of hypochondriasis: A randomized controlled trial. *American Journal of Psychiatry.*

Gureje, O., Ustun, T. B., & Simon, G. E. (1997). The syndrome of hypochondriasis: A cross-national study in primary care. *Psychological Medicine, 27*, 1001–1010.

Haenen, M. A., de Jong, P. J., Schmidt, A. J. M., Stevens, S., & Visser, L. (2000). Hypochondriacs' estimation of negative outcomes: Domain-specificity and responsiveness to reassuring and alarming information. *Behaviour Research and Therapy, 38*, 819–833.

Haenen, M. A., Schmidt, A. J. M., Kroeze, S., & van den Hout, M. A. (1996). Hypochondriasis and symptom reporting: The effect of attention versus distraction. *Psychotherapy and Psychosomatics, 65*, 43–48.

Harvey, A., Watkins, E., Mansell, W., & Shafran, R. (2004). *Cognitive behavioral processes across psychological disorders: A transdiagnostic approach to research and treatment.* Oxford: Oxford University Press.

Hitchcock, P. B., & Mattews, A. (1992). Interpretation of bodily symptoms in hypochondriasis. *Behaviour Research and Therapy, 20*, 223–234.

Jaisoorya, T. S., Janardhan Reddy, Y. C., & Srinath, S. (2003). The relationship of obsessive–compulsive disorder to putative spectrum disorders: Results from an Indian study. *Comprehensive Psychiatry, 44*, 317–323.

Kellner, R. (1986). *Somatization and hypochondriasis.* New York: Praeger.

Lochner, C., Hemmings, S. M. J., Kinnear, C. J., Niehaus, D. J. H., Nel, D. G., Corfield, V. A., et al. (2005). Cluster analysis of obsessive–compulsive spectrum disorders in patients with obsessive–compulsive disorder: Clinical and genetic correlates. *Comprehensive Psychiatry, 46*, 14–19.

MacLeod, A. K., Haynes, C., & Sensky, T. (1998). Attributions about common bodily sensations: Their associations with hypochondriasis and anxiety. *Psychological Medicine, 28*, 225–228.

Marcus, D. K., & Church, S. E. (2003). Are dysfunctional beliefs about illness unique to hypochondriasis? *Journal of Psychosomatic Research, 54*, 543–547.

Neziroglu, F., McKay, D., & Yaryura-Tobias, J. A. (2000). Overlapping and distinctive features of hypochondriasis and obsessive–compulsive disorder. *Journal of Anxiety Disorders, 6*, 603–614.

Noyes, R., Holt, C. S., Happel, R. L., Kathol, R. G., & Yagla, S. J. (1997). A family study of hypochondriasis. *Journal of Nervous and Mental Disease, 185*, 223–232.

Noyes, R., Kathol, R. G., Fisher, M. M., Phillips, B. M., Suelzer, M. T., & Woodman, C. L. (1994). Psychiatric comorbidity among patients with hypochondriasis. *General Hospital Psychiatry, 16*, 78–87.

Noyes, R., Stuart, S. P., Langbehn, D. R., Happel, R. L., Longley, S. L., Muller, B. A., et al. (2003). Test of an interpersonal model of hypochondriasis. *Psychosomatic Medicine, 65*, 292–300.

Owens, K. M. B., Asmundson, G. J. G., Hadjistavropoulos, T., & Owens, T.J. (2004). Attentional bias toward illness threat in individuals with elevated health anxiety. *Cognitive Therapy and Research, 28*, 57–66.

Salkovskis, P. M., & Clark, D. M. (1993). Panic disorder and hypochondriasis. *Advances in Behaviour Research and Therapy, 15*, 23–48.

Salkovskis, P. M., & Warwick, H. M. C. (2001). Making sense of hypochondriasis: A cognitive model of health anxiety. In G. J. G. Asmundson, S. Taylor, & B. Cox (Eds.), *Health anxiety: Clinical and research perspectives on hypochondriasis and related conditions* (pp. 46–64). Chichester: Wiley.

Savron, G., Fava, G. A., Grandi, S., Rafanelli, C., Raffi, A. R., & Belluardo, P. (1996). Hypochondriacal fears and beliefs in obsessive–compulsive disorder. *Acta Psychiatrica Scandinavica, 93*, 345–348.

Taylor, S., & Asmundson, G. J. G. (2004). *Treating health anxiety: A cognitive behavioral approach.* New York: Guilford.

Taylor, S., Thordarson, D. S., Jang, K. L., & Asmundson, G. J. G. (2006). Genetic and environmental origins of health anxiety: A twin study. *World Psychiatry, 5*, 47–50.

Torgerson, S. (1986). Genetics of somatoform disorders. *Archives of General Psychiatry, 43*, 502–505.

Vervaeke, G. A. C., Bouman, T. K., & Valmaggia, L. R. (1999). Attentional correlates of health anxiety in a non-clinical sample. *Psychotherapy and Psychosomatics, 68*, 22–25.

Visser, S., & Bouman, T. K. (1992). Cognitive behavioural approaches in the treatment of hypochondriasis: Six single case cross-over studies. *Behaviour Research and Therapy, 24*, 597–602.

Visser, S., & Bouman, T. K. (2001). The treatment of hypochondriasis: Exposure and response prevention vs. cognitive therapy. *Behaviour Research and Therapy, 39*, 423–442.

Warwick, H. M. C., Clark, D. M., Cobb, A., & Salkovskis, P. M. (1996). A controlled trial of cognitive-behavioural treatment of hypochondriasis. *British Journal of Psychiatry, 169*, 189–195.

Warwick, H. M. C., & Salkovskis, P. M. (1985). Reassurance. *British Medical Journal, 290*, 1028.

Warwick, H. M. C., & Salkovskis, P. M. (1990). Hypochondriasis. *Behaviour Research and Therapy, 24*, 597–602.

Williams, P. G. (2004). The psychopathology of self-assessed health: A cognitive approach to health anxiety and hypochondriasis. *Cognitive Therapy and Research, 28*, 629–644.

World Health Organization (1993). *The ICD-10 classification of mental and behavioural disorders: Research diagnostic criteria.* Geneva: WHO.

13

Tic Disorders and Tourette Syndrome

Kieron O'Connor and Julie Leclerc

Fernand–Seguin Research Centre

CLINICAL FEATURES

Tics are not precisely defined, however, diagnostic nosology considers them as sudden, repetitive, recurrent, and non-rythmic unintentional motor movements or phonic productions that involve one or more muscle groups (American Psychiatric Association, 2000). They have been described along two dimensions. One dimension pertains to the nature of activity reflected in the tic: motor, phonic, sensory, or cognitive. The other pertains to the degree of muscle involvement: 'simple' tics involve only one muscle group whereas 'complex' tics involve more than one muscle group. Tics are distinguished from routine habits such as playing with a paper clip or a piece of paper, and from the behaviors associated with clinical habit disorders such as compulsive hair pulling (trichotillomania), scratching, and teeth grinding. In contrast to tics, routine habits are voluntary, even if automated, and can easily be brought under control through awareness. Finally, tics can also cause marked distress and significant impairment in social and occupational life because of their frequency and intensity. One particular source of psychological distress is the social embarrassment that arises from difficulty controlling tic behavior in public. For this reason, secondary social anxiety, depression, and low self-esteem are commonly observed in sufferers.

Correspondence to: Kieron O'Connor, Fernand–Seguin Research Centre, Louis-H. Lafontaine Hospital, 7331 Hochelaga St, Montreal QC H1N 3V2, Canada.

TYPES OF TICS

Not surprisingly, definitions of different types of tics are not always clear and fixed, and criteria can be open to interpretation by clinicians. As an example, Jankovic (1997) proposed that the diagnostic distinction between motor and phonic tics may be artificial because phonic tics are, in fact, muscle contractions that lead to sounds and noises (larynx spasms or nasal breathing). Sensory tics are controversial because of ambiguity about their function. Some authors view these phenomena as precursors to motor tics, while others perceive such sensations as tics in their own right. In the first case, the somatic sensation (e.g., pressure, itching) might produce an impulse (i.e., *premonitory urge*) which results in a tic-like response (Banaschewski, Woerner, & Rothenberger, 2003; Cohen & Leckman, 1992; Leckman, Walker, Goodman, Paulo, & Cohen, 1994; Miguel et al., 2000). However, not all motor tics are preceded by premonitory urges and people sometimes independently report sensations such as tingling, warming, or localized irritations which could be classified as sensory tics. This fact fits with the sensory-motor regulation model of tics which emphasizes tension and heightened activation that is thought to occur immediately prior to the tic (Evers & van de Wetering, 1994). It remains unclear whether such sensations constitute a 'warning sign' or antecedent, or if they form part of the tic itself (Banaschewski et al., 2003; O'Connor, 2002). Miguel and colleagues (2000) proposed a neurological explanation wherein the physiological sensations form part of the corticostriatal dysfunctions which characterize Tourette syndrome (TS).

Cognitive or 'mental' tics, first described by Cath, Roos and van de Watering (1992) and subsequently elaborated on by O'Connor (2005a), are perhaps the least known tics. Such phenomena take the form of repeated phrases, tunes, or scenes of an almost playful nature and can be confused with obsessions or mental neutralizations as observed in obsessive–compulsive disorder (OCD). This differential diagnosis is essential because the treatment for mental tics and obsessions is quite different. Mental tics do not, for example, respond to imaginal (e.g., loop tape) exposure and response prevention, which is often effective in treating obsessions.

CATEGORICAL VERSUS CONTINUOUS CLASSIFICATION

As is shown in Table 13.1, the *Diagnostic and Statistical Manual of Mental Disorders* (*DSM-IV-TR*; American Psychiatric Association, 2000) and the International Classification Disease (*ICD-10*; World Health Organization, 1992), distinguish transitory tics from chronic tic disorders and TS. There is controversy, however, regarding the categorical nature of this diagnostic scheme. Some clinicians, for example, hold that tic disorders exist on a continuum from mild occasional tics to full-blown TS, which involves chronic motor and phonic tics. The most notorious vocal tic is coprolalia, which occurs in only about 8% of TS cases (Kurlan, 1992). There is no indication that milder tic disorders respond differently than clinical TS in behavioral treatment (O'Connor et al., 2001).

TABLE 13.1   Tic classification by *ICD-10* and *DSM-IV-TR*

	ICD-10	*DSM-IV-TR*
Transient tic disorder	Single or multiple motor or vocal tic(s) or both, that occur over a period of at least 4 weeks to 12 months or less	Presence of single or multiple motor tics and/or vocal tics for at least 4 weeks, but for no longer than 12 consecutive months
Chronic motor or vocal tic disorder	Motor or vocal tics, but not both, that occur over a period of at least 12 months with no period of remission more than 2 months	Presence of either motor tics or vocal tics, but not both, for more than 1 year
Tourette's syndrome	Combined multiple motor tics and one or more vocal and tics disorder	Presence of multiple motor tics and 1 or more vocal tics, for more than 1 year, and onset before age 18 years
Other tic disorders	Spasmodic syndrome	
Tic disorder unspecified	A residual category for a disorder that fulfils the general criteria for a tic disorder but in which the specific subcategory is not specified	Characterized by tics that do not meet criteria for a specific tic disorder or with an onset after age 18 years

The presence of tics is the sole criterion for diagnosing tic disorders. TS and chronic tic disorder are therefore differentially diagnosed solely according to frequency and type and severity of tics. TS involves multiple tics of either a vocal or motor nature, with at least one vocal tic having been present prior to age 18 years. TS is often accompanied by comorbid conditions and other behavioral problems, whereas someone with chronic tic disorder could experience a single mild tic without other comorbidity or behavioral difficulties. There is no evidence that TS and chronic tic disorder differ consistently on any performance, neuropsychological, psychophysiological or clinical variable, once tic severity is controlled. Moreover, the two conditions seem to respond equally well to the same form of psychological (behavioral) treatment. The majority of studies have included exclusively TS populations, although sometimes the inclusion criteria are unstated and degree of comorbidity, unspecified. In this chapter, when we refer to tic disorders we include both TS and chronic tic disorder.

ASSESSMENT AND DIAGNOSIS

There is no specific biological or psychological test to detect tic disorders. The diagnosis is therefore made on the basis of the individual's history and on behavioral observations. Significant others (e.g., parents, siblings) are often called on to clarify the history, severity, and nature of tics. The standard measures for effective clinical assessment of TS are semi-structured interviews that incorporate clinician-rated scales. The two most commonly used instruments are (a) the TS Global Scale, which scores the degree of tic severity and assesses disruption due to the tic multidimensionality (Harcherik, Leckman, Detlor, & Cohen, 1984), and (b) the Yale Global Tic Severity Scale (Leckman et al., 1989), which measures the frequency, intensity, complexity, and anatomical site of motor, sensory, phonic tics, and also interference in other areas of life.

Regarding differential diagnosis, tics should be distinguished from behaviors such as manual routines (e.g., playing with paper clips), stereotypies that are often present in autism (e.g., rocking movements), habit disorders such as trichotillomania and excessive nail biting, and from compulsions (as in OCD) that are performed in response to distress evoked by obsessional stimuli. Table 13.2 shows various parameters that serve to differentiate tics from these other behavioral phenomena. There is a good deal of overlap among tic disorders and habit disorders (Knell & Comings, 1993; Woods, Koch, Miltenberger, & Lumley, 1996) such that individuals with TS frequently evidence behaviors commonly observed in habit disorders (e.g., nail biting, hair pulling, skin picking; Knell & Comings, 1993). In a recent study of consecutively referred cases diagnosed with TS (n = 25) in our research clinic, 28% had a comorbid habit disorder, and 20% of those diagnosed principally with habit disorder (n = 15) had suffered from tics at some point.

COMORBIDITY

Table 13.3 shows the most common comorbid diagnoses found among individuals with tic disorders. In studies of adults, the comorbidity with OCD varies from 25% to 63% (O'Connor, 2005a). Some have observed that TS can be comorbid with bipolar disorder and schizophrenia (Berthier, Kulisevsky, & Campos, 1998; Müller, Riedel, Zawta, Günther, & Straube, 2002). Other associated symptoms include sleep disorders (e.g., insomnia) and self-injurious behaviors (Hickey & Wilson, 2000). Children and adolescents with TS often present with comorbid externalizing disorders (e.g., attention deficit–hyperactivity disorder [ADHD]) that worsen the prognosis. It is often these comorbid conditions that lead parents of affected children to seek evaluation and treatment.

When tic disorders are comorbid with OCD, OCD-related compulsions are often sensory-based and involve repetitive touching and ordering. Checking and cleaning rituals are underrepresented in such samples (Cath, Spinhoven, van Woerkom et al., 2001; George et al., 1993; O'Connor, 2005a). It has also been suggested that TS is part of a spectrum of disorders including OCD, ADHD, and habit disorders (e.g., Hollander, 1993; Shapiro & Shapiro, 1986). There is, however, no firm evidence that the behaviors involved in these conditions are related to one another, or that these conditions share any specific etiological factors, as we will discuss next.

TABLE 13.2 Characteristics to consider in differential diagnosis

	Tics	Stereotypies	Habit disorders	Compulsions
Examples	Simple: head movement Complex: shoulders shrug up and down or forward and backward	Rocking back and forward	Hairpulling Nail biting	Checking door repeatedly in case not locked Handwashing
Form	Selected muscle group Saccadic Location can change	Whole trunk or body Rythmic Fixed form and location	Involve auto-mutilation Chained flow of actions Stable sequence	Complex behaviors Follow premeditated action plan Form may vary
Degree of awareness when performing the behavior	Minimal or none at all	Slight	Medium	Full
Associated emotion	Frustration, impatience, boredom	Self-stimulation, self-focus	Complex moods (e.g., guilt, depression)	Anxiety or disgust
Triggers	Situations or activities (e.g., social) Tension/sensory activation	Internal state Movement feedback Need for stimulation	Mood and situation Need for stimulation	Obsessional fear Sense of danger if not performed

TABLE 13.3 Principal psychiatric comorbidities of Tourette's syndrome

Comorbidity	% prevalence rate	Symptoms	Comments
Attention deficit–hyperactivity disorder (ADHD)	21–90%	Impulsivity, problem behavior and tics are all exacerbated. Inattention and hyperactivity mostly appear developmentally before tics	Misdiagnosis of ADHD may occur because of the intense disruption of behavior and lack of visible evidence of tics
OCD	50–60%	Obsessions and compulsions usually begin during adolescence. The occurrence of OCD is less common in children than adults with TS	The compulsion, thought, or intrusive and recurring mental images related to anxiety can be difficult to distinguish from certain behavioral and mental tics
Anxiety disorders (other than OCD)	20–46%	Other anxiety disorders are significantly overrepresented among youth with severe tic disorder, including panic disorder (23%), schoolphobia/agoraphobia (39%), separation anxiety disorder (51%), and overanxious disorder (46%)	Tics may be exacerbated by a factor of 3.5 in anxious situations that increase stress reactivity, embarrassment and disruption in daylife activities
Mood disorders	30–60%	Major depression and bipolar disorder are the best predictors of psychiatric hospitalization for children and adolescents with TS	Depressive symptoms can partly be explained by lack of self-esteem. Patients with tics might be stigmatized or ridiculed
Learning disorders	30–60%	Impairment in language production and comprehension, disability in memorizing, visuospatial perception, and attention deficit	Rejection by peers may lead to reduction in social adaptation
Explosive (rage) outbursts	25–70% child: 35–70% adult: 8%	Episodes of sudden and recurring explosive outbursts of rage. The child can strike or break the surrounding objects, but also attack others or self. Intensity of behaviors and lack of intent distinguish rage from regular fits of anger or an emotional disorder	General aggressive behaviors have been reported in approximately 42% to 66% of children with TS. Rage attacks are the most disruptive symptoms to affect familial, educational and social aspects of the child

ETIOLOGY OF TIC DISORDERS

NEUROPSYCHOLOGICAL MODELS

There is consensus among clinicians that tic disorders are essentially neuro-biological problems (American Psychiatric Association, 2000; Leckman & Cohen, 1999). A principal hypothesis is derived from studies of basal ganglia dys-function and differences in basal ganglia volume, but there is no firm evidence of common structural deficit (Peterson et al., 1999; Rappoport, 1990). There is spec-ulation about involvement of the orbitofrontal lobes in TS, but EEG and other brain-mapping procedures do not yield consistent evidence, and most studies have not found deficits in executive function (O'Connor et al., 2005). There are, how-ever, signs of impaired visuomotor performance, especially in children with TS (Schultz et al., 1999), but the populations tested frequently have comorbid ADHD, which confounds study findings (Channon, Flynn, & Robertson, 1992; Channon, Pratt, & Robertson, 2003; Silverstein, Como, Palumbo, West, & Osborn, 1995).

In adults with TS, visuomotor processing has been assessed by tasks such as the Purdue pegboard, grooved task, and electro-physiological measurement. There is evidence of impaired performance in affected individuals relative to con-trols; and such deficits have been found to sometimes improve after successful behavioral treatment (O'Connor et al., 2006). Individuals with tic disorders also seem to adopt a particular style of action characterized by over-preparation and over-activity (described in detail below, but also see O'Connor et al., 2005). Change in style of planning has been linked both to improved motor performance and control over tics (O'Connor et al., 2006).

An initial study measuring the way people with tics plan their actions via the Style of Planning (STOP) Questionnaire revealed two major factors: over-prepa-ration and over-activity. Over-preparation involves investing too much effort physically, emotionally and cognitively. People with tics activate more muscle mass than is required for a task; and frequently activate irrelevant muscle groups (O'Connor et al., 2006). Consequently, they are less able to inhibit actions and are often less selective in controlling motor, sensory and emotional responses (Schultz et al., 1999). For example TS show little difference in both cortical and motor preparing between a simple and a complex performance (O'Connor et al., 2005). Over-activity is best represented as a tendency to always be active at the expense of relaxing and pacing tasks appropriately. Clinically, this is reflected in motor restlessness. There is also evidence that both over-preparation and over-activity are premeditated styles of planning action in adults, since they may relate to perfectionist subscales of personal organization (O'Connor, 2005). In other words, the excessive activity and preparation may be driven by perfectionistic beliefs. Hence this style of planning may produce chronic motor activation and difficulties regulating muscle contractions and tension levels, which can play a role in triggering the onset of a tic (O'Connor, 2002).

PSYCHOSOCIAL MODELS

An early learning model suggested that tics are adaptive startle reflexes initiated by an aversive event (e.g., environmental factors such as trauma), and subsequently maintained by negative reinforcement via the short-lived relief they engender (Clarke, Bray, Kehle, & Truscott, 2001; Peterson & Cohen, 1998; Roane, Piazza, Cercone, & Grados, 2002; Verdellen, Keijsers, Cath, & Hoogduin, 2004). Additional contingencies further encourage the maintenance and propagation of tics (Azrin & Nunn, 1977; Evers & van de Wetering, 1994; O'Connor, 2002). According to this model, clinically severe tic disorders arise when the tics become overlearned habits that are resistant to extinction.

Leckman and colleagues (1986) suggested a diatheses-stress hypothesis for the pathogenesis of tic disorders and TS. According to this model, tic onset is a product of the interaction of an inherited vulnerability and environmental factors. Environmental factors might include central nervous system stimulants or intermittent, uncontrollable stress during a critical period of brain development. It has been proposed that prenatal events such as the mother's level of stress during pregnancy, severe nausea and vomiting during pregnancy, and antiemetic medication, lead to changes in the sensitivity of fetal dopaminergic receptors which could partially determine the eventual severity of expression of the diathesis (Leckman et al., 1990). Evidence supporting the hypothesis that such variables precipitate the onset of tic disorders, however, is inconsistent (e.g., Leckman & Cohen, 1999; O'Connor, 2002).

Clinical observations indicate that tic frequency and intensity waxes and wanes depending on the situation or context, and that tics can occasionally be suppressed, at least temporarily (Jankovic, 1997). This variation in clinical presentation begs a behavioral explanation; for example that tics are responsive to attention and other socially relevant contingencies (Miltenberger, Fugua, & Woods, 1998). Some authors report differential social reinforcement as a key maintaining factor and, in one reported case, only four days of intervention (withdrawing attention) was effective in extinguishing the tic behavior (Watson & Sterling, 1998). On the other hand, Roane and colleagues (2002) reported that a lack of attention was a precursor to tics. So, applying time-out within a social reinforcement model could conflict with lending additional attention to positively reinforcing task engagement as a means of reducing tic frequency.

Functional analyses of tic behavior have identified social and environmental contingencies (e.g., Leckman & Cohen, 1999). That is, tic frequency can be related to engaging in certain activities and being in certain situations. A series of studies demonstrated that circumstances associated with negative emotions (e.g., anger, anxiety, depression) were most likely to elicit tics (Christensen, Ristvedt, & McKenzie, 1993; Dean, Nelson, & Moss, 1992). O'Connor and colleagues (1993a,b) found that situations could be categorized as high, medium, or low risk to the degree that they triggered tic onset, although these situations were highly idiosyncratic and unique to each person. That is, a given situation might represent high risk for one individual with a tic disorder, but low risk for another. This finding is in accord with cognitive models of emotion that posit that it is one's thoughts and beliefs *about situations* that contribute to his or her emotion (e.g., Beck, 1976). For example, the same two people could be reading a newspaper, one thinking of all the work still to be done, the other concentrating on the information in the news article. Thus, assessing cognition (i.e., automatic thoughts and interpretations) provides more information than simply making behavioral observations regarding how strongly a given situation will serve as a cue for tics (O'Connor, 2005b).

TREATMENT

BIOLOGICAL INTERVENTIONS

Psychopharmacological treatment regimes produce variable response and tics themselves are rarely eliminated by neuroleptics or other types of medication (Regeur, Pakkenberg, Fog, & Pakkenberg, 1986). The most successful agents are typical neuroleptics, such as haloperidol and pimozide, or atypical neuroleptics such as risperidone, clozapine, and olanzapine (Carter et al., 1998; Onofrj, Paci, Andreamatto, & Toma, 2000). The initial drug of choice, a low dosage of haloperidol, has the potential for unwanted extrapyramidal effects and noradrenergic side-effects. Consequently, pimozide is now preferred for its clinical efficacy and, apart from increase weight gain and a risk for depression, shows a more acceptable side-effect profile and good clinical response in some studies, but is contested in others (Sallee, Nesbitt, Jackson, Sine, & Sethuraman, 1997).

There is reason to believe, however, that the results of individual case studies inflate the effectiveness of pharmacological management of tics since more modest effects have been observed in controlled trials. Double-blind placebo-controlled studies have found tic frequency reduced by about 50% using haloperidol or pimozide (Shapiro et al., 1989) and unwanted side-effects occur in about 80% of individuals. More recent double-blind controlled trials with risperidone report decreases in symptoms of 35% (Dion, Annable, Sandor, & Chouinard, 2002), 42% (Gilbert, Batterson, Sethuraman, & Sallee, 2004) and 56% (Bruggeman et al., 2001), but with significant dropout and side-effects. According to Peterson and Azrin (1992), only about 20–30% of patients continue their medication for an extended period of time.

Single case studies on the effects of a range of stereotaxic surgical procedures have been reported. Psychosurgical techniques used to treat tic disorders have included limbic and frontal leucotomies, bilateral cerebellar dentatomy, ventrolateral thalamotomy, and gamma capsulotomy. Unfortunately, the long-term effects of these surgeries have not been documented at present (Rauch, Baer, Cosgrove, & Jenike, 1995).

BEHAVIORAL TREATMENTS

Recent studies have shown that behavior therapy can be successfully applied to the management of tic disorders (O'Connor, 2005a; Peterson & Azrin, 1992). The specific behavioral intervention depends on whether the tic is conceptualized as a classically conditioned reflex, or as part of an operantly conditionned response.

Early approaches

Initial behavioral therapy approaches for tics included the technique of extensive negative practice (Feldman & Werry, 1966), which involves voluntarily repeating the tic as quickly, and with as much effort, as possible over a fixed period of between 5 and 30 minutes with several brief rest periods (Peterson & Azrin, 1992, 1993). This approach, which is akin to a satiation paradigm, was shown to reduce tic frequency by about 58% immediately following treatment (e.g., Feldman & Werry, 1966). Unfortunately, these treatment gains were not maintained for more than a few days.

Techniques based on positive reinforcement are typically more effective in reducing undesirable behavior than are techniques based on punishment or satiation, such as aversive conditioning or negative practice. It is therefore recommended that patients with TS receive praise and encouragement (i.e., positive reinforcement) for engaging in routine activities, especially those behaviors that would commonly trigger tics, without engaging in tic behavior. This approach reduces pressure on the patient because it can alleviate the feeling of being judged.

Relaxation techniques (e.g., progressive muscle relaxation; Jacobson, 1938) also emphasize lowering tension, and can reduce tics for short periods of time. The basic idea of relaxation is to systematically train the individual to tense and relax each group of muscles (e.g., forearm, upper arm, face, etc). These exercises can be combined with calming visual images and music, and can be especially adapted for children who tend to have a smaller attention span. Bergin, Waranch, Brown, Carson, & Singer (1998) conducted a controlled trial randomly allocating 23 TS patients (mean age 11.8 years) to either a relaxation condition or a minimal therapy condition, both including awareness training. Results showed a greater improvement in the relaxation group than in the minimal group, but this advantage disappeared at three-month follow-up. Although relaxation by itself may not be an optional treatment for tics, it can be combined with other cognitive–behavioral approaches (O'Connor, 2005a).

Tension management

Evers and van de Wetering (1994) hypothesized that tics function to reduce physical tension, which is itself a reaction to aversive sensory stimulation. They suggested treatment by restructuring the stimulus or environment, and teaching the patient more appropriate and socially acceptable responses for reducing tension, thereby decreasing tic frequency. These authors reported two cases where implementation of alternative methods of tension reduction produced a significant decrease or elimination of the tic. These beneficial results were also maintained at 3-month follow-up.

Exposure-based therapy

An alternative treatment approach is exposure to the premonitory urge (i.e., to situations and stimuli known to elicit tics) while practicing resisting the tic response.

Tics, here, are viewed as voluntary responses aimed at neutralizing unpleasant sensations. Instead of trying to control the tic, this approach would encourage tolerating the urge to tic without either tensing or relaxing the muscle groups implicated in the tic. A significant decrease in tic frequency (68–75%) was reported in four cases of severe TS after 10 2-hour exposure sessions (Hoogduin, Verdellen, & Cath, 1997). Verdellen et al. (2004) reported that this exposure-based technique was comparable to habit reversal (described below) in the treatment of 43 patients with TS.

Habit reversal

The most efficient behavioral therapy for tics and TS to date is habit reversal training (HRT; Azrin & Nunn, 1973). The underlying principle of HRT is to weaken the *response chains* that play a key role in the persistence of tics. From this perspective, tics are viewed as behavioral habits that are initiated by a startle reaction and integrated into a learned response that is subsequently maintained by operant conditioning. The behavior can therefore be reversed by learning and practicing an alternative appropriately reinforced response (Azrin & Nunn, 1973; Azrin & Peterson, 1988). Contemporary HRT programs involve multiple components such as awareness training, stress management, learning to use a response that is incompatible with performing tics (considered the key element in treatment), contingency management, motivational training, and social support. The mechanism by which an incompatible response works to reduce tic frequency remains somewhat unclear. Perhaps this new learned response strengthens antagonistic muscles, distracting the person and creating a novel tic or acting as punishment. Clinical case studies involving tic disorders have reported a reduction in tic frequency of between 75% to 100% with HRT (Azrin & Peterson, 1988, 1989; Clarke et al., 2001; Miltenberger et al., 1998; Peterson, Campise, & Azrin, 1994; Woods, Twohig, Flessner, & Roloff, 2003).

Brief versions of the HRT protocol have been examined with the aim of elucidating which specific component(s) of HRT are most effective, and how they function. Results of studies on this topic indicate that awareness training, practicing a competing response, and social support are the most effective components for decreasing tic frequency and intensity (Jones, Swearer, & Friman, 1997; Miltenberger, Fugua, & McKinley, 1985; Miltenberger et al., 1998; Peterson & Azrin, 1992; Woods et al., 1996, 2003).

COGNITIVE–PSYCHOPHYSIOLOGICAL MODEL

The cognitive–psychophysiological (CP) model of understanding and treating tic disorders integrates a motor–psychophysiology approach with a cognitive–behavioral approach. It proposes that cognitive factors play an important role in both the development and maintenance of tics. This approach also builds on previous behavioral research into the development, maintenance, and modification of learned habits (O'Connor, 2005a). From this perspective, tics are best understood as a synergistic interaction between the psychological and physiological factors controlling motor action. The growth of inappropriate tension in muscle groups during specific activities is linked to a learned behavioral strategy involving a maladaptive style of preparing for action (over-activity and over-preparation) (O'Connor, 2005b).

Treatment based on the CP model follows a ten-stage program over 14 weeks, with one additional month of home practice. The program begins with awareness training that involves self-monitoring using a daily tic diary. Psychophysiological training includes education in muscle training, muscle discrimination, muscle isolation, and progressive relaxation. The next stages address hypervigilance to sensations, reattribution of interpretations of sensations, plus exposure to aid habituation to any premonitory urges. At the same time, behavioral inputs to the tension-producing style of action typical in TS and tics are addressed by reducing over-activity and over-preparation in everyday styles of planning. Cognitive restructuring addresses perfectionist beliefs and other core beliefs and appraisals that may be driving frustration, impatience, and hyperactivation associated with high-risk tic situations. Finally, alternative tension-reducing strategies are employed to restructure behavior and thinking in high-risk tic situations. These cognitive–behavioral strategies are then generalized to other tics during home practice.

The cognitive and behavioral reorganization described above addresses preparation, planning, and coping in high-risk situations (O'Connor, 2005b). Focused HRT is sometimes incorporated if an analysis of overall behavioral activity, tension, and tic function indicates that this technique would be effective for managing urges. However, we feel that a more general modification of one's *overall* behavioral repertoire provides a more comprehensive, socially acceptable, and meaningful way to diminish tics frequency as compared to HRT. Thus, for example, modifying a person's thinking and behavioral approach to a frustrating situation might automatically reduce or change their muscle tension pattern in a more naturalistic way than implementing isolated competing responses as in HRT. Competing responses do not always need to be anatomically antagonistic to the tic muscle (Verdellen et al., 2004), and changing overall behavioral activity has the advantage of modifying tic onset rather than resisting the tic after the onset. Previous work supports the claim that targeting overall behavior can affect tic onset. Clarke and colleagues (2001) reinforced adoption of competing responses with HR combined with self-modeling and feedback of self-behavior. Lamontagne (1978) reported the treatment of a vocal tic by prolonged social exposure. Paquin (1977) decreased tics by utilizing imagined mastery of tic-related situations.

A limitation of the CP approach is that sensorimotor dysregulation, as a causal agency in tic onset, has not yet been established. Psychophysiological evaluations longitudinally monitoring electroencephalogram, electromyogram, and cardiac activity would be useful measures by which to objectively evaluate the level of central motor action and peripheral tension during tic behavior. Such research would provide a clearer understanding than we currently have of the relationship between tics, motor activity, psychophysiological activation, and cognitive and behavioral stages of planning and executing action.

Another question for future research concerns the applicability of CP-based treatment programs for children. It might be more difficult to discuss abstract cognitive constructs with children than with adults; althought the constructs involved in the CP model can conceiveably be operationalized in terms of more concrete behaviors and attitudes. There have already been several reports adapting elements of HRT to children (e.g., Azrin & Peterson, 1988). Behavioral restructuring can be achieved through role-play and games; and development of a children's version of CP-based treatment program is currently under way (Leclerc, 2004).

TIC DISORDERS AND THE OBSESSIVE–COMPULSIVE SPECTRUM

Hollander (1993) proposed that a unifying factor for several impulsive and compulsive disorders was a difficulty to inhibit or delay involuntary repetitive movement. According to this point of view, obsessive compulsive disorder, chronic tic disorder, and habit disorders (i.e., impulse control disorders) were conceptualized as part of a putative spectrum of obsessive–compulsive disorders. However, the majority of research findings have thus far indicated no neurobiological evidence of similarity between OCD and tic disorders regarding deficits in the basal ganglia and frontal cortex (Busatto et al., 2000; Peterson et al., 1999). Similarly, the notion that tic disorders and OCD show similar abnormalities in serotonergic sensivity has not been supported (e.g., Cath, Spinhoven, Landman & van Kempen, 2001; Khanna, John, & Lakshmi, 2001). Electrocortical characteristics, neuropsychological findings, symptom phenomenology (i.e., behavioral analysis), and pharmacological interventions also differ between OCD and tic disorders (Johannes et al., 2002; Schultz, Carter, Seahill, & Leckman, 1999; Summerfeldt, Hood, Antony, Richter, & Swinson, 2004; Cath, Spinhoven, Landman et al., 2001). All of these findings stand in contrast to the notion that TS and tic disorders share a relationship with OCD.

Are tics similar to compulsive rituals in meaningful ways? Indeed, both are repetitive behaviors. The occurrence of a tic, however, is triggered by an increase in physical tension rather than by an obsessional thought, as is observed with compulsive rituals (Rachman & Hodgson, 1980). People are often unaware of their tics; they are simply *movements*, and there is minimal premeditation or cognitive processing involved. By contrast, OCD involves an empirically demonstrated and easily observable link between obsessional thought and compulsive behavior (e.g., Rachman & Hodgson, 1980). The compulsive action is not simply a *movement* by itself; it is a deliberate response to obsessional distress. Thus, a principal distinction between tics and OCD-related compulsions relates to the cognitive–emotional experience at the time of performing the behavior; OCD rituals reduce anxiety, tics reduce physical tension.

Further qualitative differences between TS and OCD are associated with treatment response. There are no reported studies of the use of competing response training or HRT in OCD (O'Connor et al., 2005). Such techniques would not be derived from a behavioral analysis of OCD since individuals with this condition are mostly aware of their behaviors, and such actions have a purpose as explained above (and in the chapters in the first part of this volume). Exposure and response prevention, which are the appropriate behavioral techniques in the treatment of OCD, also can be helpful for TS; although, the cognitive mechanism that mediates treatment response is different. In the treatment of TS, response prevention aims to teach the patient how to resist the urge to perform a tic when such an urge is triggered (Hoogduin et al., 1997). In OCD, response prevention facilitates the extinction of compulsive urges and the modification of dysfunctional beliefs about the need to perform compulsive rituals to prevent obsessively feared consequences (e.g., Rachman & Hodgson, 1980). Taken together, the current theoretical and research literature suggests that it is inappropriate to consider TS and OCD as part of the same spectrum of disorders.

CONCLUSIONS

A number of areas within the field of TS and tic disorders emerge as requiring future research. First, further work needs to be done to clarify differences between impulsive and compulsive phenomena (thoughts and behaviors) and to distinguish mental tics from voluntary thoughts, worries, and obsessional intrusions. Systematic application of functional analysis in tics and TS would also generate data on environmental, behavioral, cognitive, and affective associations and contingencies that maintain these problems. If an activity profile is characteristic of tics, such a profile could help to differentiate not only between tics and OCD-related phenomena, but between tics and neurological spasms. Also, a profile of activities specifically linked to tic onset or intensity might provide insights into the role of learning in the acquisition of tic disorders. A further model would integrate tension reduction and sensorimotor regulation with learning accounts of tic etiology, as well as integrating neuropsychological findings of apparent visuomotor impairment in TS (O'Connor, 2005b).

REFERENCES

American Psychiatric Association (2000). *Diagnostic and statistical manual of mental disorders* (4th ed., text rev.) *(DSM-IV-TR)*. Washington, DC: APA.

Azrin, N. H., & Nunn, R. G. (1973). Habit-reversal: A method of eliminating nervous habits and tics. *Behaviour Research and Therapy, 11*, 619–628.

Azrin, N. H., & Nunn, R. G. (1977). *Habit control in a day*. New York: Simon & Schuster.

Azrin, N. H., & Peterson, A. L. (1988). Habit reversal for the treatment of Tourette syndrome. *Behaviour Research and Therapy, 26*, 347–351.

Azrin, N. H., & Peterson, A. L. (1989). Reduction of an eye tic by controlled blinking. *Behaviour Research and Therapy, 20*, 467–473.

Banaschewski, T., Woerner, W., & Rothenberger, A. (2003). Premonitory sensory phenomena and suppressibility of tics in Tourette syndrome: Developmental aspects in children and adolescents. *Developmental Medicine and Child Neurology, 45*, 700–703.

Beck, A. T. (1976). *Cognitive therapy of the emotional disorders*. New York: International Universities Press.

Bergin, A., Waranch, H. R., Brown, J., Carson, K., & Singer, H. S. (1998). Relaxation therapy in Tourette syndrome: A pilot study. *Pediatric Neurology, 18*, 136–142.

Berthier, M. L., Kulisevsky, J., & Campos, V. M. (1998). Bipolar disorder in adult patients with Tourette's syndrome: a clinical study. *Biological Psychiatry, 43*, 364–370.

Bruggeman, R., Buitelaar, J. K., Gericke, G. S., Hawkridges, S. M., & Temlett, J. A. (2001). Risperidone versus pimozide in Tourette's disorder: A comparative double-blind parallel-group study. *Journal of Clinical Psychiatry, 62*, 50–56.

Busatto, G. F., Zamignani, D. R., Buchpiguel, C. A., Garrido, G. E., Glabus, M. F., Rocha, E. T., et al. (2000). A voxel-based investigation of regional cerebral blood flow abnormalities in obsessive-compulsive disorder using single photon emission computed tomography (SPECT). *Psychiatry Research, 99*, 15–27.

Carter, A. S., Fredine, N. J., Findley, D., Scahill, L., Zimmerman, L., & Sparrow, S. S. (1998). Pharmacological and other somatic approaches to treatment. In J. F. Leckman & D. J. Cohen (Eds.), *Tourette's syndrome, tics, obsessions, compulsions: Developmental psychopathology and clinical care* (pp. 370–398). New York: Wiley.

Cath, D., Roos, R., & van de Wetering, B. (1992). Mental play in Gilles de la Tourette's syndrome and obsessive–compulsive disorder. *British Journal of Psychiatry, 161*, 542–545.

Cath, D. C., Spinhoven, P., Landman, A. D., & van Kempen, G. M. J. (2001). Psychopathology and personality characteristics in relation to blood serotonin in Tourette's syndrome and obsessive–compulsive disorder. *Journal of Psychopharmacology, 15*, 111–119.

Cath, D. C., Spinhoven, P., van Woerkom, T. C. A. M., van de Wetering, B. J. M., Hoogduin, C. A. L., Landman, A. D., et al. (2001). Gilles de la Tourette's syndrome with and without obsessive–compulsive disorder compared with obsessive–compulsive disorder without tics: Which symptoms discriminate? *Journal of Nervous and Mental Disease, 189*, 219–228.

Channon, S., Flynn, D., & Robertson, M.M. (1992). Attentional deficits in Gilles de la Tourette syndrome. *Neuropsychiatry, Neuropsychology and Behavioral Neurology, 5*, 170–177.

Channon, S., Pratt, P., & Robertson, M. M. (2003). Executive function, memory, and learning in Tourette's syndrome. *Neuropsychology, 17*, 247–254.

Christensen, G. A., Ristvedt, S. L., & Mackenzie, T. B. (1993). Identification of trichotillomania cue profiles. *Behaviour Research and Therapy, 31*, 315–320.

Clarke, M. A., Bray, M. A., Kehle, T. J., & Truscott, S. D. (2001). A school-based intervention designed to reduce the frequency of tics in children with Tourette's syndrome. *School Psychology Review, 30*, 11–22.

Cohen, A. J., & Leckman, J. F. (1992). Sensory phenomena associated with Gilles de la Tourette's syndrome. *Journal of Clinical Psychiatry, 53*, 319–323.

Dean, J. T., Nelson, E., & Moss, L. (1992). Pathological hair pulling: A review of the literature and case reports. *Comprehensive Psychiatry, 33*, 84–91.

Dion, Y., Annable, L., Sandor, P., & Chouinard, G. (2002). Risperidone in the treatment of Tourette's syndrome: A double-blind placebo-controlled trial. *Journal of Clinical Psychopharmacology, 22*, 31–39.

Evers, R. A. F., & van de Wetering, B. J. M. (1994). A treatment model for motor tics based on a specific tension-reduction technique. *Journal of Behavior Therapy and Experimental Psychiatry, 25*, 255–260.

Feldman, R. B., & Werry, J. S. (1996). An unsuccessful attempt to treat tics by massed practice. *Behaviour Research and Therapy, 4*, 111–117.

George, M. S., Trimble, M. R., Ring, H. A., Sallee, F. R., & Robertson, M. M. (1993). Obsessions in obsessive–compulsive disorder with and without Gilles de la Tourette's syndrome. *American Journal of Psychiatry, 150*, 93–97.

Gilbert, D. L., Batterson, R., Sethuraman, G., & Sallee, F. R. (2004). Tic reduction with risperidone versus pimozide in a randomized, double-blind, crossover trial. *Journal of the American Academy of Child and Adolescent Psychiatry, 43*, 206–214.

Harcherik, D., Leckman, J., Detlor, J., & Cohen, D. (1984). A new instrument for clinical studies of Tourette's syndrome. *Journal of the American Academy of Child and Adolescent Psychiatry, 23*, 153–160.

Hickey, T., & Wilson, L. (2000). Tourette syndrome: Symptom severity, anxiety, depression, stress, social support and ways of coping. *Irish Journal of Psychology, 21*, 78–87.

Hollander, E. (1993). Obsessive–compulsive spectrum disorders: An overview. *Psychiatric Annals, 23*, 355–358.

Hoogduin, K., Verdellen, C., & Cath, D. (1997). Exposure and response prevention in the treatment of Gilles de la Tourette's syndrome: Four case studies. *Clinical Psychology and Psychotherapy, 4*, 125–135.

Jacobson, E. (1938). *Progressive relaxation*. Chicago: University of Chicago Press.

Jankovic, J. (1997). Phenomenology and classification of tics. *Neurologic Clinics of North America, 15*, 267–275.

Johannes, S., Wieringa, B. M., Nager, W., Muller-Vahl, K. R., Dengler, R., & Munte, T. F. (2002). Excessive action monitoring treatment of Tourette syndrome. *Journal of Neurology, 249*, 961–966.

Jones, K. M., Swearer, S. M., & Friman, P. C. (1997). Relax and try this instead: Abbreviated habit reversal for maladaptive self-biting. *Journal of Applied Behavior Analysis, 30*, 697–699.

Khanna, S., John, J. P., & Lakshmi Reddy, P. (2001). Neuroendocrine and behavioral responses to mCPP in obsessive–compulsive disorder. *Psychoneuroendocrinology, 26*, 209–223.

Knell, E. R., & Comings, D. E. (1993). Tourette's syndrome and attention-deficit hyperactivity disorder: Evidence for a genetic relationship. *Journal of Clinical Psychiatry, 54*, 331–337.

Kurlan, R. (1992). Tourette syndrome in a special education population: Hypotheses. *Advances in Neurology, 58*, 75–81.

Lamberg, L. (2003). ADHD often undiagnosed in adults: Appropriate treatment may benefit work, family, social life. *Journal of the American Medical Association, 290*, 1565–1567.

Lamontagne, Y. (1978). Treatment of a tic by prolonged exposure. *Behavior Therapy, 9*, 647–651.

Leckman, J. F., & Cohen, D. J. (1999). *Tourette's syndrome: Developmental psychopathology and clinical care*. New York: Wiley.

Leckman, J. F., Cohen, D. J., Price, R. A., Riddle, M. A., Minderaa, R. B., Anderson, G. M., et al. (1986). The pathogenesis of Gilles de la Tourette's syndrome: A review of data and hypotheses. In N. S. Shah & N. B. Shah (Eds.), *Movement disorders* (pp. 257–272). New York: Plenum Press.

Leckman, J. F., Dolnansky, E. S., Hardin, M. T., Clubb, M., Walkup, J. T., Stevenson, J., & Pauls, D. L. (1990). Perinatal factors in the expression of Tourette's syndrome: An exploratory study. *Journal of the American Academy of Child & Adolescent Psychiatry, 29*, 220–226.

Leckman, J. F., Riddle, M. A., Hardin, M. T., Ort, S. I., Swartz, K. L., Stevenson, J., et al. (1989). The Yale Global Tic Severity Scale: Initial testing of a clinician-rated scale of tic severity. *Journal of American Academy of Child and Adolescent Psychiatry, 28*, 566–573.

Leckman, J. K., Walker, D. E., Goodman, W. K., Pauls, D. L., & Cohen, D. J. (1994). 'Just right' perceptions associated with compulsive behavior in Tourette's syndrome. *American Journal of Psychiatry, 151*, 675–680.

Leclerc, J. (2004). *Les crises de rage*. Paper presented at the meeting of the Association Québécoise du Syndrome de la Tourette, Montreal, PQ.

Miguel, E. C., do Rosario-Campos, M. C., da Silva Prado, H., do Valle, R., Rauch, S. L., Coffey, B. J., Baer, L., et al. (2000). Sensory phenomena in obsessive–compulsive disorder and Tourette's disorder. *Journal of Clinical Psychiatry, 61*, 150–156.

Miltenberger, R. G., Fuqua, R. W., & McKinley, T. (1985). Habit reversal with muscle tics: Replication and component analysis. *Behavior Therapy, 16*, 39–50.

Miltenberger, R. G., Fuqua, R. W., & Woods, D. W. (1998). Applying behavior analysis to clinical problems: Review and analysis of habit reversal. *Journal of Applied Behavior Analysis, 31*, 447–469.

Müller, N., Riedel, M., Zawta, P., Günther, W., & Straube, A. (2002). Comorbidity of Tourette's syndrome and schizophrenia – biological and physiological parallels. *Progress in Neuro-psychopharmacology and Biological Psychiatry, 26,* 1245–1258.

O'Connor, K. P. (2002). A cognitive–behavioral/psychological model of tic disorders. *Behaviour Research and Therapy, 40,* 1113–1142.

O'Connor, K. P. (2005a). *Cognitive–behavioral management of tic disorders.* New York: Wiley.

O'Connor, K.P. (2005b). Behavioral activity and tic disorder. Submitted for publication.

O'Connor, K. P., Brault, M., Loiselle, J., Robillard, S., Borgeat, F., & Stip, E. (2001). Evaluation of a cognitive–behavioral program for the management of chronic tic and habit disorders. *Behaviour Research and Therapy, 39,* 667–681.

O'Connor, K. P., Brisebois, H., Brault, M., Robillard, S., & Loiselle, J. (2003). Behavioral activity associated with onset in chronic tic and habit disorder. *Behavior Research & Therapy, 41*(2), 241–249.

O'Connor, K. P., Gareau, D., & Blowers, G. (1993a). Change in construals of tic producing situations following cognitive and behavioral therapy. *Perceptual Motor Skills, 77,* 776–778.

O'Connor, K. P., Gareau, D., & Blowers, G. (1993b). Personal constructs amongst chronic tic sufferers. *British Journal of Clinical Psychology, 13*(2), 151–158.

O'Connor, K. P., Lavoie, M., Robert, M., Dubord, J., Stip, E., & Borgeat, F. (2005). Brain–behavior relations during motor processing in chronic tic and habit disorder. *Cognitive and Behavioral Neurology, 18,* 79–88.

O'Connor, K., Lavoie, M. E., Stip, E., Borgeat, F., & Laverdure, A. (2006). Cognitive–behaviour therapy and skilled motor performance in adults with chronic tic disorder. *Neuropsychological Rehabilitation* (in press).

Onofrj, M., Paci, C., D'Andreamatteo, G., & Toma, L. (2000). Olanzapine in severe Gilles de la Tourette syndrome: A 52-week double-blind cross-over study vs. low-dose pimozide. *Journal of Neurology, 247,* 443–446.

Paquin, M. J. (1977). The treatment of a nailbiting compulsion by covert sensitization in a poorly motivated client. *Journal of Behavior Therapy and Experimental Psychiatry, 8,* 181–183.

Peterson, A. L., & Azrin, N. H. (1992). An evaluation of behavioural treatments for Tourette syndrome. *Behaviour Research and Therapy, 30,* 167–174.

Peterson, A. L., & Azrin, N. H. (1993). Behavioral and pharmacological treatments for Tourette syndrome. *Applied and Preventive Psychology, 2,* 231–242.

Peterson, A. L., Campise, R. L., & Azrin, N. H. (1994). Behavioral and pharmacological treatments for tic and habit disorders: A review. *Developmental and Behavioural Pediatrics, 15,* 430–441.

Peterson, B. S., & Cohen, D. J. (1998). The treatment of Tourette's syndrome: Multimodal, developmental intervention. *Journal of Clinical Psychiatry, 59,* 62–72.

Peterson, B. S., Leckman, J. F., Arnsten, A., Anderson, G. M., Staib, L. H., Gore, J. C., et al. (1999). Neuroanatomical circuitry. In J. F. Leckman & D. J. Cohen (Eds.), *Tourette's syndrome – tics, obsessions, compulsions. Developmental psychopathology and clinical care* (pp. 230–260). New York: Wiley.

Rachman, S., & Hodgson, R. (1980). *Obsessions and compulsions.* New York: Prentice Hall.

Rappoport, J. L. (1990). Obsessive compulsive disorder and basal ganglia dysfunction. *Psychological Medicine, 20,* 465–469.

Rauch, S., Baer, L., Cosgrove, G. R., & Jenike, M. A. (1995). Neurosurgical treatment of Tourette's syndrome: A critical review. *Comprehesive Psychiatry, 36,* 141–156.

Regeur, L., Pakkenberg, B., Fog, R., & Pakkenberg, H. (1986). Clinical features and long-term treatment with pimozide in 65 patients with Gilles de la Tourette's syndrome. *Journal of Neurology, Neurosurgery and Psychiatry, 49,* 791–795.

Roane, H. S., Piazza, C. C., Cercone, J. J., & Grados, M. (2002). Assessment and treatment of vocal tics associated with Tourette's syndrome. *Behavior Modification, 26,* 482–498.

Salle, F. R., Nesbitt, L., Jackson, C., Sine, L., & Sethuraman, G. (1997). Relative efficacy of haloperidol and pimozide in children and adolescents with Tourette's disorder. *American Journal of Psychiatry, 154,* 1057–1062.

Schultz, R. T., Carter, A. S., Scahill, L., & Leckman, J. F. (1999). Neuropsychological findings. In J. F. Leckman & D. J. Cohen (Eds.), *Tourette's syndrome – tics, obsessions, compulsions. Developmental psychopathology and clinical care* (pp. 80–103). New York: Wiley.

Shapiro, E. S., & Shapiro, A. K. (1986). Semiology, nosology and criteria for tic disorders. *Revue Neurologique (Paris), 142,* 824–832.

Shapiro, E. S., Shapiro, A. K., Fulop, G., Hubbard, M., Mandeli, J., Nordlie, J., et al. (1989). Controlled study of haloperidol, pimozide, and placebo for the treatment of Gilles de la Tourette's syndrome. *Archives of General Psychiatry, 46,* 722–730.

Shapiro, A. K., Shapiro, E. S., Young, J. G., & Feinberg, T. E. (1988). *Gilles de la Tourette syndrome.* New York: Raven Press.

Silverstein, S. M., Como, P. G., Palumbo, D. R., West, L. L., & Osborn, L. M. (1995). Multiple sources of attentional dysfunction in adults with Tourette's syndrome: Comparison with attention deficit–hyperactivity disorder. *Neuropsychology, 9,* 157–164.

Spencer, T., Biederman, J., Harding, M., O'Donnell, D., Wilens, T., Faraone, S., et al. (1998). Disentangling the overlap between Tourette's disorder and ADHD. *Journal of Child Psychology and Psychiatry, 39,* 1037–1044.

Sukhodolsky, D. G., Scahill, L., Zhang, H., Peterson, B. S., King, R. A., Lombroso, P. J., et al. (2003). Disruptive behavior in children with Tourette syndrome: Association with ADHD comorbidity, tic severity, and functional impairment. *Journal of the American Academy of Child and Adolescent Psychiatry, 42,* 98–105.

Summerfeldt, L. J., Hood, K., Antony, M. M., Richter, M. A., & Swinson, R. P. (2004). Impulsivity in obsessive–compulsive disorder: Comparisons with other anxiety disorders and within tic-related subgroups. *Personality and Individual Differences, 36,* 539–553.

Verdellen, C. W. J., Keijsers, G. P. J., Cath, D. C., & Hoogduin, C. A. L. (2004). Exposure with response prevention versus habit reversal in Tourette's syndrome: A controlled study. *Behaviour Research and Therapy, 42,* 501–511.

Watson, T. S., & Sterling, H. E. (1998). Brief functional analysis and treatment of a vocal tic. *Journal of Applied Behavior Analysis, 31,* 471–474.

Wodrich, D. L., Benjamin, E., & Lachar, D. (1997). Tourette's syndrome and psychopathology in a child psychiatric setting. *Journal of the American Academy of Child and Adolescent Psychiatry, 36,* 1618–1624.

Woods, D. W., Koch, M., Miltenberger, R. G., & Lumley, V. A. (1996). Sequential application of major habit reversal components to treat motor tics in children. *Journal of Applied Behavior Analysis, 29,* 483–493.

Woods, D. W., Twohig, M. P., Flessner, C. A., & Roloff, T. J. (2003). Treatment of vocal tics in children with Tourette syndrome: Investigating the efficacy of habit reversal. *Journal of Applied Behavior Analysis, 36,* 109–112.

World Health Organization. (1992). *International classification of diseases* (10th ed.). Geneva: WHO.

14

SHOULD EATING DISORDERS BE INCLUDED IN THE OBSESSIVE–COMPULSIVE SPECTRUM?

KRISTEN M. CULBERT AND KELLY L. KLUMP

Department of Psychology, Michigan State University, East Lansing

It has long been recognized that eating disorders (EDs) often co-occur with other psychiatric conditions, particularly mood and anxiety disorders. In recent years, increasing attention has been placed on the specific relationship between ED and obsessive–compulsive disorder (OCD), given similarities in phenomenology, associated features, and – debatably – familial transmission. As a result of such commonalities, some have suggested that EDs are part of the 'obsessive–compulsive spectrum' (Goldsmith, Shapira, Phillips, & McElroy, 1998; Hollander, 1993; Hollander & Benzaquen, 1997). By contrast, others have argued that EDs merely co-occur with OCD but are separate disorders (Lilenfeld et al., 1998). The purpose of this chapter is to explore this controversy by examining the etiology of EDs and the mechanisms contributing to the comorbidity between EDs and OCD.

PHENOMENOLOGY OF EATING DISORDERS

ED CRITERIA

Anorexia nervosa (AN) and bulimia nervosa (BN) are the primary eating disorders that have been linked to OCD. AN is characterized by refusal to maintain body

Correspondence to: Kelly L. Klump, Michigan State University, 107B Psychology Building, East Lansing, MI 48824-1116.

weight at or above a minimally normal weight for age and height (i.e., <85% of ideal weight), and an intense fear of gaining weight or becoming fat even when one is underweight (American Psychiatric Association, 2000). Individuals with AN also have disturbances in the way in which their body weight or shape is experienced (e.g., thinking they are fat when they are emaciated), undue influence of their body weight or shape on self-esteem, and/or denial of the seriousness of the current low body weight (American Psychiatric Association, 2000). Finally, for postmenarcheal females, amenorrhea for at least three consecutive months is required (American Psychiatric Association, 2000).

Two diagnostic subtypes of AN exist. The restricting type (AN-R) is characterized by incessant avoidance of food in the absence of binge eating and/or purging (American Psychiatric Association, 2000). By contrast, the binge eating/purging type (AN-BP) includes binge eating and/or the use of compensatory behaviors (e.g., self-induced vomiting, laxative abuse), in addition to extreme food restriction. Despite shared diagnostic criteria between these subtypes, consistent differences between women with AN-R and AN-BP have been reported. Women with AN-BP have shown greater levels of impulsivity (Claes, Vandereycken, & Vertommen, 2005; Klump, Bulik et al., 2000), substance use disorders (Holderness, Brooks-Gunn, & Warren, 1994; Strober, Freeman, Bower, & Rigali, 1996), and suicidal behaviors (Favaro & Santonastaso, 1997), whereas women with AN-R tend to be more inhibited in their behaviors (Keel, 2005; Klump, Bulik et al., 2000).

BN is characterized by recurrent episodes of binge eating with loss of control over food intake during the binge (American Psychiatric Association, 2000). Bulimic individuals also engage in the use of inappropriate compensatory behaviors (e.g., self-induced vomiting, abuse of laxatives and/or diuretics, enemas, fasting, excessive exercise) in order to rid themselves of food ingested during a binge. Similar to individuals with AN, individuals with BN have a self-evaluation that is unduly influenced by body shape and weight (American Psychiatric Association, 2000).

Two subtypes of BN exist; a purging (BN-P) and nonpurging (BN-NP) subtype (American Psychiatric Association, 2000). Women with BN-P regularly engage in purging methods (i.e., self-induced vomiting, abuse of laxatives and/or diuretics, enemas) whereas women with BN-NP do not purge but instead regularly use nonpurging compensatory methods (i.e., excessive exercise or fasting) (American Psychiatric Association, 2000).

EPIDEMIOLOGY

Both AN and BN are relatively rare, occurring in approximately 0.5% and 1–3% of the population, respectively (American Psychiatric Association, 2000). Clear sex differences exist, with females outnumbering males by about 10:1 (American Psychiatric Association, 2000). Both disorders tend to develop during adolescence and young adulthood, with AN typically beginning earlier (between ages 14 and 18) then BN (during late adolescence and early adulthood) (American Psychiatric Association, 2000).

COMORBIDITY

In addition to OCD, EDs are associated with elevated rates of several psychiatric conditions. Both AN and BN are highly comorbid with major depression (e.g., Lilenfeld et al., 1998), which has led some to speculate that ED might be part of an affective spectrum (Hudson & Pope, 1990; Hudson, Pope, Jonas, & Yurgelun-Todd, 1983; Mangweth et al., 2003). In addition, EDs show high rates of lifetime comorbidity with anxiety disorders (e.g., Kaye et al., 2004; Keel, Klump, Miller, McGue, & Iacono, 2005), including separation anxiety disorder, overanxious disorder, generalized anxiety disorder, social phobia, post-traumatic stress disorder, and of course, OCD. Unlike AN, BN shows increased comorbidity with substance use disorders (e.g., Bulik et al., 2004), which likely reflects higher levels of impulsivity in these individuals (Klump et al., 2004).

ETIOLOGICAL MODELS OF EATING DISORDERS

Traditionally, researchers focused primarily on the influence of psychosocial factors on the development of EDs. However, within the past decade, there has been a major shift toward the recognition of biological and genetic factors as well. Predominating etiological models now emphasize the role of both biological and psychosocial factors in the development of EDs. These models are akin to the 'diathesis stress model' currently popular in the conceptualization of most psychiatric disorders. Interestingly, the field of EDs suffers from a lack of published theories that propose an integrative model of the factors contributing to the diathesis *and* the stress. However, a general model can be gleaned from research of each component separately.

There is growing consensus that the diathesis for EDs is a genetic vulnerability. Family studies provided initial evidence for genetic effects by showing that relatives of individuals with EDs were 7–12 times more likely to develop EDs than relatives of controls (Hudson, Pope, Jonas, Yurgelun-Todd, & Frankenburg, 1987; Kassett et al., 1989; Lilenfeld et al., 1998; Strober, Freeman, Lampert, Diamond, & Kaye, 2000; Strober, Lampert, Morrell, Burroughs, & Jacobs, 1990). Twin studies have confirmed that familial aggregation is largely due to genetic factors. Heritability estimates for both AN and BN have been found to be well over 50% (Bulik, Sullivan, & Kendler, 1998; Kendler et al., 1991; Klump, Miller, Keel, McGue, & Iacono, 2001; Wade, Bulik, Neale, & Kendler, 2000). These estimates are on a par with those for other psychiatric conditions considered to have significant biological and genetic bases (e.g., schizophrenia).

The nature of the genetic vulnerability remains unknown. Several neurobiological systems have been proposed as candidates for harboring the susceptibility, such as dopaminergic systems (Brambilla, Bellodi, Arancio, Ronchi, & Limonta, 2001; Jimerson, Lesem, Kaye, & Brewerton, 1992; Kaye, Frank, & McConaha,

1999) and gonadal hormones (Klump et al., in press). However, the serotonin (5-HT) system has received the most attention. Research suggests that women with AN and BN have dysregulated 5-HT systems that are vulnerable to dietary manipulations, yet still exhibit ED trait-like qualities (Kaye, Frank, Bailer, & Henry, 2005; Kaye, Gendall, & Strober, 1998). Candidate gene studies have provided preliminary support for a link between serotonin and EDs, as the 5-HT$_{2a}$ receptor gene has been associated with AN in a meta-analysis (Gorwood, Kipman, & Foulon, 2003). However, more recent studies have reported mixed results (Klump & Gobrogge, 2005), and other serotonin receptor genes have either not been associated with EDs or previous associations have not been replicated (Klump & Gobrogge, 2005). Thus, although the serotonin system is likely involved in the diathesis for EDs, additional work examining this and other neurobiological systems is needed.

The stressors that likely trigger the diatheses for eating disorders appear to be rather varied. Two recent meta-analyses examined psychosocial risk factors for EDs and concluded that thin-ideal internalization, negative affect, and excessive levels of drive for thinness are significant risk factors for eating pathology (Jacobi, Hayward, de Zwaan, Kraemer, & Agras, 2004; Stice, 2002). These risk factors were more significant predictors of the development of eating pathology than factors traditionally viewed as important, including family factors and dieting. However, the extent to which these risk factors can be viewed as 'stressors' as opposed to markers of the diathesis remains to be determined. For example, data suggest that drive for thinness is significantly heritable (Klump, McGue, & Iacono, 2000b; Wade, Martin, & Tiggerman, 1998) and that a common set of genetic factors may underlie associations between eating pathology and negative affect (Klump, McGue, & Iacono, 2002). Additional work is needed to clarify relationships between diatheses and stressors and, more importantly, examine their interactive influence on the development of EDs.

EDS AS OCD SPECTRUM DISORDERS

In recent years, increasing attention has been given to the theory that several nosologically distinct disorders are related to OCD, and thus these disorders comprise the 'obsessive compulsive spectrum' (Goldsmith et al., 1998; Hollander, 1993; Hollander & Benzaquen, 1997; Rasmussen, 1994). Inclusion in the spectrum is largely based on overlap with OCD in terms of clinical symptoms, etiology, treatment response, familial transmission, and associated features (e.g., age of onset, clinical course, and comorbidity). Although there is some disagreement about the inclusion criteria for the spectrum (Rasmussen, 1994), it has been suggested that both AN and BN should be included (Goldsmith et al., 1998; Hollander, 1993; Hollander & Benzaquen, 1997). As a result, investigators have aimed to further examine associations between these disorders and increase understanding of possible underlying factors influencing their co-occurrence.

COMORBIDITY AND SYMPTOM PROFILES

Comorbidity

Relationships between EDs and obsessive–compulsive symptoms have long been recognized. Palmer & Jones (1939) were the first to describe AN as a manifestation of obsessive–compulsive disorder (OCD). Likewise, DuBois (1949) suggested renaming AN as 'compulsion neurosis with cachexia' and Rothenberg (1986) called EDs a 'modern obsessive–compulsive syndrome'.

Contemporary studies of both nonclinical (Rogers & Petrie, 1996, 2001) and clinical (Anderluh, Tchanturia, Rabe-Hesketh, & Treasure, 2003; Kaye et al., 1992) populations have confirmed the presence of significant comorbidity between EDs and OCD. In a recent review, Godart et al. (2002) reported that 10–60% of individuals with AN and up to 40% of individuals with BN have a coexisting OCD diagnosis. Importantly, studies have also found elevated lifetime rates of EDs (8.3–12%) in OCD populations (Bellodi et al., 2001; Halmi et al., 1991; Hsu, Weltzin, & Kaye, 1993; Kasvikis, Tsakiris, Marks, Basoglu, & Noshirvani, 1986; Rubenstein, Pigott, L'Heureux, Hill, & Murphy, 1992), although comorbidity is not nearly as high as that observed in patients with EDs.

Some research has suggested that OCD is differentially related to AN and BN. However, results are conflicting, with some studies showing higher rates of OCD in AN than BN individuals (Lilenfeld et al., 1998; Speranza et al., 2001; Thorton & Russell, 1997), and others showing no significant differences (Fornari et al., 1992; Laessle, Wittchen, Fichter, & Pirke, 1989; Milos, Spindler, Ruggiero, Klaghofer, & Schnyder, 2002). Differential relationships across AN and BN subtypes have also been observed. Individuals with the AN-BP subtype have been found to have the highest rates of OCD (Fornari et al., 1992; Garner, Garner, & Rosen, 1993; Speranza et al., 2001), whereas individuals with AN-R have been found to have the lowest (Fornari et al., 1992; Garner et al., 1993; Speranza et al., 2001).

Taken together, findings suggest that rates of OCD are significantly elevated in all individuals with EDs, but that they may be particularly high in individuals with binge eating and purging forms of AN. Importantly, rates of EDs are also elevated in individuals with OCD, suggesting that increased OCD comorbidity in individuals with EDs is not simply a consequence of the ED or its physical manifestations.

Symptom profiles

A core issue in the debate about EDs/OCD relationships concerns the types of symptoms that qualify for OCD diagnoses in individuals with EDs. Undoubtedly, obsessive–compulsive features that are related to food and body weight are prominent in all EDs. These include relentless thoughts about thinness, body shape preoccupations, and incessant ruminations about food. Repetitive behaviors resembling compulsions are also common, including excessive exercise, methodical calorie counting, ritualistic food cutting, and repetitive weighing.

Despite the resemblance of these ED features to OCD obsessions and compulsions, clear distinctions exist. The obsessions and compulsions of OCD tend to be ego-dystonic, whereas those specific to ED tend to be ego-syntonic (Bastiani et al., 1996; Holden, 1990). Further, unlike obsessions and compulsions in OCD, repeated thoughts and behaviors about food and weight in ED patients are not necessarily viewed as intrusive (Mazure, Halmi, Sunday, Romano, & Einhorn, 1994) or senseless (Halmi et al., 2002). Reflecting these differences, food related obsessions and compulsions do not qualify as *DSM-IV-TR* symptoms of OCD in individuals with EDs (American Psychiatric Association, 2004). An additional diagnosis of OCD in ED patients is only given if the obsessions and compulsions are unrelated to food, body shape, or weight.

However, obsessions and compulsions unrelated to eating commonly occur in patients with EDs. Kaye et al. (1992) examined the presence of OCD symptoms in patients with AN, excluding core ED symptoms (i.e., body-image distortion, pathological feeding behaviors and exercise). Findings indicated that patients with AN had increased rates of the types of obsessive–compulsive symptoms (Kaye et al., 1992) that are common in patients with OCD (Goodman et al., 1989; Jenike, Buttolph, Baer, Ricciardi, & Holland, 1989). Similar results have been obtained for patients with BN (Albert, Venturello, Maina, Ravissa, & Bogetto, 2001; Rubenstein et al., 1993).

The types of OCD symptoms that are most prevalent in patients with EDs and OCD may differ. Several investigators have found symmetry and exactness obsessions to be particularly common in patients with EDs, whereas rates of other obsessions (e.g., contamination fears) and compulsions (e.g., checking, hoarding, etc.) are generally higher in patients with OCD without EDs (Bastiani et al., 1996; Halmi et al., 2002; Matsunaga et al., 1999; Srinivasagam et al., 1995; von Ranson, Kaye, Weltzin, Rao, & Matsunaga, 1999).

Elevated rates of OCD symptoms in EDs do not appear to be mere consequences of the ED pathology. The malnutrition and aberrant eating patterns that characterize EDs have been shown to increase rates of depression and food-related obsessions (Keys, Brozek, Henschel, Mickelsen, & Taylor, 1950). However, studies have found that OCD symptoms often predate the development of an ED and persist after recovery. For example, obsessive–compulsive traits in childhood have been found to precede and predict the later development of EDs in several studies (Anderluh et al., 2003; Kaye et al., 2004; Thornton & Russell, 1997). Likewise, 'recovery' designs indicate that although rates of OCD symptoms are highest in women who are ill with EDs, rates remain elevated after recovery from an ED as well (Pollice, Kaye, Greeno, & Weltzin, 1997; Srinivasagam et al., 1995; Strober, 1980; von Ranson et al., 1999).

In summary, evidence clearly supports the presence of OCD symptoms in individuals with EDs that are unrelated to food, body weight, or the status of illness. These findings suggest that general obsessive traits are not merely byproducts of the core eating pathology. However, the type of OCD symptoms that are common in ED patients (e.g., symmetry and exactness concerns) tend to be quite different from those that are common in OCD (e.g., contamination fears and checking behaviors). These differences in symptom expression might reflect important differences in etiological mechanisms that are pertinent to issues of ED/OCD spectrum definitions.

ETIOLOGY

EDs and OCD clearly meet the first 'criterion' for a common relationship by showing increased comorbidity. However, a critical consideration is whether they share etiologies. Two primary types of studies have examined this issue: family studies and studies of neurobiological mechanisms.

Family studies

Family studies provide important information about relationships amongst disorders by showing whether they aggregate in families. Disorders thought to be part of a common spectrum should, theoretically, cluster together within families. Family studies have consistently indicated that OCD aggregates in families of AN and BN probands (Halmi et al., 1991; Lilenfeld et al., 1998; Pasquale, Sciuto, Cocchi, Ronchi, & Bellodi, 1994). Studies have found morbid risks of 3.0–4.1 for OCD in first-degree relatives of both AN and BN individuals (Halmi et al., 1991; Lilenfeld et al., 1998; Pasquale et al., 1994). A family study of OCD probands also found increased rates of AN and BN in family members (Bienvenu et al., 2000), suggesting that familial aggregation is present in families of both ED and OCD patients.

An important consideration for family studies is whether proband comorbidity for an ED and OCD accounts for familial aggregation (Lilenfeld et al., 1998). A common etiology is present only if OCD aggregates within families regardless of whether the ED proband has OCD. If OCD only aggregates within families of probands with ED and OCD, then the disorders are likely transmitted independently within families and do not share a common etiology. Several studies have examined this issue for EDs and OCD, with decidedly mixed results. Lilenfeld et al. (1998) failed to find elevated rates of OCD in families of probands who had EDs only (i.e., no comorbid OCD diagnosis), whereas Cavallini et al. (2000) and Bellodi et al. (2001) observed increased rates of OCD spectrum conditions in families of ED probands, regardless of whether the ED proband had comorbid OCD.

Inconsistent findings regarding proband comorbidity make it difficult to draw conclusions about common familial relationships, although recent genetic studies provide some insight into the nature of familial and genetic effects. Devlin et al. (2002) found that subtyping ED individuals into those with high versus low levels of OCD symptoms increased evidence for linkage to several chromosomal regions. Specifically, individuals with high levels of OCD symptoms showed more significant linkage results that were different from those who did not exhibit OCD symptoms. These findings strongly suggest the presence of significant heterogeneity in ED phenotypes and that some types of EDs share genetic etiology with obsessive spectrums more than others. Diverse family study results may therefore reflect this heterogeneity and the inclusion of individuals with EDs who have differential associations with OCD.

Neurobiological mechanisms

Several investigators have postulated that ED and OCD are linked through neurobiological mechanisms (Barbarich, 2002; Yaryura-Tobias, Pinto, & Neziroglu, 2001). As described previously, the serotonin system has been found to be significantly dysregulated in patients with EDs, where low cerebrospinal fluid (CSF) levels of the serotonin metabolite 5-hydroxyindoleacetic acid (5-HIAA) have been observed during the acute phase of illness, whereas elevated CSF 5-HIAA concentrations are observed during long-term recovery (Kaye et al., 1998; Kaye, Gwirtsman, George, & Ebert, 1991). Similarly, some evidence suggests that patients with OCD have higher levels of 5-HIAA than controls (Insel, Mueller, Alterman, Linnoila, & Murphy, 1985; Thoren, Asberg, Cronholm, Jornestedt, & Traskman, 1980), although other studies have failed to find these differences (Leckman et al., 1995). Inconsistent results may be due to heterogeneity in the OCD phenotypes. Recent findings indicate that there may be several subtypes of OCD: (1) an aggressive, sexual, somatic, religious subtype; (2) symmetry, ordering, counting, arranging subtype; (3) contamination and cleaning subtype; and (4) hoarding subtype (Leckman et al., 1997). These subtypes may differ in etiological factors (Miguel et al., 2005). It is possible that only individuals with certain subtypes of OCD have elevated levels of CSF 5-HIAA, and these subtypes may be particularly related to EDs (Barbarich, 2002).

Candidate gene studies are beginning to confirm a serotonin link to both sets of disorders. Both AN and OCD have been consistently associated with the 5-HT_{2a} promoter polymorphism 1438G/A described above (Enoch et al., 1998; Enoch, Greenberg, Murphy, & Goldman, 2001; Klump & Gobrogge, 2005), although BN has been less consistently linked to this gene (Enoch et al., 1998; Ziegler et al., 1999). Notably, the 5-HT_{2a} receptor is involved in the regulation of anxiety and feeding and the action of antidepressant medications (Barnes & Sharp, 1999). Therefore, variations of the 5-HT_{2a} receptor gene may be involved in both AN and OCD, perhaps through its regulation of common behavioral and psychological characteristics. Nonetheless, it is clear that variations in this gene only influence a small proportion of cases of EDs, as the gene has not been consistently associated with BN and non-replications across all disorders are common.

In summary, studies of etiological relationships between EDs and OCD suggest that certain subtypes of EDs may be linked more strongly to OCD than others. At least part of this link is likely due to genetic factors that may influence the functioning of the serotonin system and the development of EDs, OCD, or both conditions. Additional research is needed to clarify which subtypes of EDs and OCD show etiologic relationships and identify the types of genetic and neurobiological mechanisms underlying the associations.

TREATMENT

A final consideration for examining EDs/OCD relationships is treatment response. If the disorders are part of the same spectrum, similar treatments should be effective across disorders. Evidence suggests that this is the case for BN and OCD. Selective serotonin reuptake inhibitors (SSRIs) produce recovery in a significant number of BN and OCD patients (Bellini & Merli, 2004; Greist & Jefferson, 1998; Vaswani, Ramesh, & Sagar, 2005), although cognitive–behavioral therapy (CBT) is considered the treatment of choice for both conditions. Notably, CBT results in greater than 50% symptom improvement in BN and OCD (Barlow, 2001). The focus of the CBT treatments tend to differ across disorders; in BN, the focus is on establishing control over eating using both cognitive and behavioral techniques (Fairburn, Jones, Peveler, Hope, & O'Connor, 1993), whereas exposure and response prevention (ERP) is the predominant treatment technique for OCD (Barlow, 2001). Interestingly, recent attempts to incorporate ERP for body weight and shape concerns (e.g., having patients try on swim suits) in CBT treatments for BN have shown initial promise (Bulik, Sullivan, Carter, McIntosh, & Joyce, 1998).

There is currently no treatment of choice for AN. Treatment trials examining CBT for AN have been largely disappointing (e.g., Wilson, 1999), although recent research examining family-based approaches for younger AN patients show promise (Le Grange, 1999). Medications have also been inconsistently linked with recovery in AN (Attia & Schroeder, 2005). There is some indication that SSRIs are effective for preventing relapse once weight is restored (Kaye et al., 2001), but these medications appear to have little effect when patients are low weight (Ferguson, La Via, Crossan, & Kaye, 1999; Mitchell, de Zwaan, & Roerig, 2003).

In aggregate, findings indicate similarities between BN and OCD in terms of effective treatment modalities and treatment response. CBT and SSRIs are effective for both conditions, and ERP may prove to be an important additional treatment component in BN. The striking differences in treatment response for AN are notable. The lack of effective treatment for this disorder has led some to suggest that AN shows less pathoplasticity in etiology and 'breeds true' across time more than BN (Keel & Klump, 2003). Indeed, it has been suggested that BN may be part of a broader spectrum of neurotic disorders with common etiologies, whereas AN is a categorically distinct disorder with more specific etiology and treatment response.

CONCLUSIONS

The purpose of this chapter was to examine evidence regarding whether EDs should be conceptualized as OCD spectrum conditions. Data relevant to comorbidity, symptom profiles, etiology, and treatment were reviewed. It is clear that OCD symptoms are common among individuals with EDs, and that ED symptoms occur in individuals with OCD. However, beyond these similarities, a consistent picture has yet to emerge, although data are sufficient for suggesting several possibilities regarding the link between EDs and OCD:

1. *EDs are OCD spectrum conditions*: The nature of ED pathology is very obsessive in nature, and non-food-related obsessions and compulsions are present in

EDs. Further, some studies suggest that EDs and OCD aggregate in families (regardless of proband comorbidity), and serotonin dysfunction is linked to both sets of conditions. All of these findings suggest that EDs may represent OCD spectrum conditions rather than separate disorders. However, family study data have not always confirmed shared transmission and neurobiological data have been inconsistent. Further, although treatment response is similar between BN and OCD, AN shows a very different treatment response from both conditions.

2. *Subtypes of EDs and OCD are spectrum conditions*: Genetic, neurobiological, and treatment data suggest that there is significant heterogeneity within ED and OCD syndromes. This heterogeneity was observed most consistently in genetic and treatment studies where some ED diagnoses and subtypes were linked to OCD while others were not. There is growing consensus within the ED field that AN and BN diagnoses contain heterogeneous symptom and personality profiles (Lilenfeld et al., 2000; Westen & Harnden-Fischer, 2001) that differentially relate to etiology (Devlin et al., 2002; Keel & Klump, 2003) and clinical outcomes (Westen & Harnden-Fischer, 2001). It is therefore likely that some ED subtypes are more closely related to OCD than others. Initial data in this regard would suggest that perhaps binge/purge subtypes would show stronger relationships with OCD, given the symptom and treatment outcome data described above. In addition, an OCD subtype dominated by symmetry and exactness may show stronger underlying relationships with EDs. Much more research is needed to confirm these very preliminary impressions and clarify the nature of relationships between ED and OCD subtypes.

3. *EDs are spectrum conditions with other internalizing disorders*: EDs are a common target for inclusion in 'spectrum conditions'. Currently, they are hypothesized to be part of OCD spectrum conditions, affective spectrum conditions (Hudson & Pope, 1990; Hudson et al., 1983; Mangweth et al., 2003), and to a lesser extent, obsessive–compulsive personality disorder (Lilenfeld et al., 1998). These theories are somewhat driven by a bias within the psychiatric literature to consider these disorders as symptoms of other conditions (rather than disorders in their own right), but the theories are also driven by data. Hudson and colleagues (1987) have shown that EDs do aggregate with affective disorders within families, and Lilenfeld et al. (1998) showed common familial transmission between EDs and obsessive–compulsive personality disorder (OCPD). Interestingly, extant data indicate that all forms of psychopathology can be distilled down to two empirically supported factors: an internalizing factor and an externalizing factor (e.g., Krueger, Caspi, Moffitt, & Silva, 1998). In these studies, EDs are conceptualized as internalizing disorders along with mood and anxiety disorders. Thus, one possibility is that affective disorders, anxiety disorders, and EDs can be broadly conceived as falling within the same 'spectrum' or factor. This would explain data showing that EDs fit within several spectrum conditions. Within the internalizing factor, there would likely be differential symptom, etiological, and treatment relationships both between and within disorders, but at the meta-level, the disorders are part of the same underlying internalizing dimension.

Clearly, data are insufficient for differentiating between these theories. However, they highlight several avenues for future research and the importance of thinking broadly about EDs as spectrum conditions. Specifically, future studies should examine: (1) symptom profiles, etiological factors, *and* treatment response in order to provide a comprehensive picture of shared and distinct features of the disorders; (2) subtypes of EDs and OCD and their differential associations with each other; and (3) other disorders (e.g., mood disorders) to determine whether a specific ED/OCD spectrum is present or whether findings support a meta-factor that encompasses a range of internalizing disorders. Multi-method approaches that address the above are likely to provide the strongest data for informing conceptualizations of EDs and OCD and increasing understanding of their development and treatment.

REFERENCES

Albert, U., Venturello, S., Maina, G., Ravissa, L., & Bogetto, F. (2001). Bulimia nervosa with and without obsessive–compulsive syndromes. *Comprehensive Psychiatry, 42*, 456–460.

American Psychiatric Association (2000). *Diagnostic and statistical manual of mental disorders* (4th ed., text revision) *(DSM-IV-TR)*. Washington, DC: APA.

Anderluh, M., Tchanturia, K., Rabe-Hesketh, S., & Treasure, J. (2003). Childhood obsessive–compulsive personality traits in adult women with eating disorders: Defining a broader eating disorder phenotype. *American Journal of Psychiatry, 160*, 242–247.

Attia, E., & Schroeder, L. (2005). Pharmacologic treatment of anorexia nervosa: Where do we go from here? *International Journal of Eating Disorders, 37*(Suppl.), S60–S63.

Barbarich, N. (2002). Is there a common mechanism of serotonin dysregulation in anorexia nervosa and obsessive compulsive disorder? *Eating and Weight Disorders, 7*, 221–231.

Barlow, D. H. (2001). *Clinical handbook of psychological disorders* (3rd ed). New York: Guilford Press.

Barnes, N., & Sharp, T. (1999). A review of central 5-HT receptors and their function. *Neuropharmacology, 38*, 1083–1152.

Bastiani, A., Altemus, M., Pigott, T., Rubenstein, C., Weltzin, T., & Kaye, W. (1996). Comparison of obsessions and compulsions in patients with anorexia nervosa and obsessive compulsive disorder. *Biological Psychiatry, 39*, 966–969.

Bellini, M., & Merli, M. (2004). Current drug treatment of patients with bulimia nervosa and binge-eating disorder: Selective serotonin reuptake inhibitors versus mood stabilizers. *International Journal of Psychiatry in Clinical Practice, 8*, 235–243.

Bellodi, L., Cavallini, M., Bertelli, S., Chiapparino, D., Riboldi, C., & Smeraldi, E. (2001). Morbidity risk for obsessive–compulsive spectrum disorders in first-degree relatives of patients with eating disorders. *American Journal of Psychiatry, 158*, 563–569.

Bienvenu, O., Samuels, J., Riddle, M., Hoehn-Saric, R., Liang, K., Cullen, B., et al. (2000). The relationship of obsessive-compulsive disorder to possible spectrum disorders: Results from a family study. *Biological Psychiatry, 48*, 287–293.

Brambilla, F., Bellodi, L., Arancio, C., Ronchi, P., & Limonta, D. (2001). Central dopaminergic function in anorexia and bulimia nervosa: A psychoneuroendocrine approach. *Psychoneuroendocrinology, 26*, 393–409.

Bulik, C., Klump, K., Thornton, L., Kaplan, A., Devlin, B., Fichter, et al. (2004). Comorbidity of eating disorders and alcohol use disorders. *Journal of Clinical Psychiatry, 65*, 1000–1006.

Bulik, C., Sullivan, P., Carter, F., McIntosh, W., & Joyce, P. (1998). The role of exposure with response prevention in the cognitive-behavioral therapy for bulimia nervosa. *Psychological Medicine, 28*, 611–623.

Bulik, C., Sullivan, P., & Kendler, K. (1998). Heritability of binge-eating and broadly defined bulimia nervosa. *Biological Psychiatry, 44*, 1210–1218.

Cavallini, M., Bertelli, S., Chiapparino, D., Riboldi, S., & Bellodi, L. (2000). Complex segregation analysis of obsessive–compulsive disorder in 141 families of eating disorder probands, with and without obsessive-compulsive disorder. *American Journal of Medical Genetics, 96*, 384–391.

Claes, L., Vandereycken, W., & Vertommen, H. (2005). Impulsivity-related traits in eating disorder patients. *Personality and Individual Differences, 39*, 739–749.

Devlin, B., Bacanu, S., Klump, K., Bulik, C., Fichter, M., Halmi, K., et al. (2002). Linkage analysis of anorexia nervosa incorporating behavioral covariates. *Human Molecular Genetics, 11*, 689–696.

DuBois, F. (1949). Compulsion neurosis with cachexia. *American Journal of Psychiatry, 106*, 107–115.

Enoch, M., Greenberg, B., Murphy, D., & Goldman, D. (2001). Sexually dimorphic relationship of a 5-HT$_{2a}$ promoter polymorphism with obsessive-compulsive disorder. *Biological Psychiatry, 49*, 385–388.

Enoch, M., Kaye, W., Rotondo, A., Murphy, D., & Goldman, D. (1998). 5-HT$_{2a}$ promoter polymorphism: 1438G/A, anorexia nervosa, and obsessive-compulsive disorder. *Lancet, 351*, 1785–1786.

Fairburn, C., Jones, R., Peveler, R., Hope, R., & O'Connor, M. (1993). Psychotherapy and bulimia nervosa: Longer-term effects of interpersonal psychotherapy, behavior therapy, and cognitive behavior therapy. *Archives of General Psychiatry, 50*, 419–428.

Favaro, A., & Santonastaso, P. (1997). Suicidality in eating disorders: Clinical and psychological correlates. *Acta Psychiatrica Scandinavica, 95*, 508–514.

Ferguson, C., La Via, M., Crossan, P., & Kaye, W. (1999). Are serotonin selective reuptake inhibitors effective in underweight anorexia nervosa? *International Journal of Eating Disorders, 25*, 11–17.

Fornari, V., Kaplan, M., Sandberg, D., Matthews, M., Skolnick, N., & Katz, J. (1992). Depressive and anxiety disorders in anorexia nervosa and bulimia nervosa. *International Journal of Eating Disorders, 12*, 21–29.

Garner, D., Garner, M., & Rosen, L. (1993). Anorexia nervosa 'restricters' who purge: Implications for subtyping anorexia nervosa. *International Journal of Eating Disorders, 13*, 171–185.

Godart, N., Flament, M., Perdereau, F., & Jeammet, P. (2002). Comorbidity between eating disorders and anxiety disorders: A review. *International Journal of Eating Disorders, 32*, 253–270.

Goldsmith, T., Shapira, N., Phillips, K., & McElroy, S. (1998). Conceptual foundations of obsessive–compulsive spectrum disorders. In R. Swinson, M. Antony, S. Rachman, & M. Richter (Eds.), *Obsessive-compulsive disorder: Theory, research, and treatment* (pp. 397–425). New York: Guilford Press.

Goodman, W., Price, L., Rasmussen, S., Delgado, P., Heninger, G., & Charney, D. (1989). Efficacy of fluvoxamine in obsessive–compulsive disorders. *Archives of General Psychiatry, 6*, 36–44.

Gorwood, P., Kipman, A., & Foulon, C. (2003). The human genetics of anorexia nervosa. *European Journal of Pharmacology, 480*, 163.

Greist, J., & Jefferson, J. (1998). Pharmacotherapy for obsessive–compulsive disorder. *British Journal of Psychiatry, 173*, 64–70.

Halmi, K., Eckert, E., Marchi, P., Sampugnaro, V., Apple, R., & Chen, J. (1991). Comorbidity of psychiatric diagnoses in anorexia nervosa. *Archives of General Psychiatry, 48*, 712–718.

Halmi, K., Sunday, S., Klump, K., Strober, M., Leckman, J., Fichter, M., et al. (2002). Obsessions and compulsions in anorexia nervosa subtypes. *International Journal of Eating Disorders, 33*, 308–319.

Holden, M. (1990). Is anorexia nervosa an obsessive–compulsive disorder? *British Journal of Psychiatry, 157*, 1–5.

Holderness, C., Brooks-Gunn, J., & Warren, M. (1994). Co-morbidity of eating disorders and substance abuse review of the literature. *International Journal of Eating Disorders, 16*, 1–34.

Hollander, E. (1993). Obsessive–compulsive spectrum disorders: An overview. *Psychiatric Annals, 23*, 355–358.

Hollander, E., & Benzaquen, S. (1997). The obsessive–compulsive spectrum disorders. *International Review of Psychiatry, 9*, 99–109.

Hsu, L., Weltzin, T., & Kaye, W. (1993). Are the eating disorders related to obsessive compulsive disorder? *International Journal of Eating Disorders, 14*, 305–318.

Hudson, J., & Pope, H. (1990). Affective spectrum disorder: Does antidepressant response identify a family of disorders with a common pathophysiology? *American Journal of Psychiatry, 147*, 552–564.

Hudson, J., Pope, H., Jonas, J., & Yurgelun-Todd, D. (1983). Phenomenologic relationship of eating disorders to major affective disorder. *Psychiatry Research, 9*, 345–354.

Hudson, J., Pope, H., Jonas, J., Yungelun-Todd, D., & Frankenburg, F. (1987). A controlled family history study of bulimia. *Psychological Medicine, 17*, 883–890.

Insel, T., Mueller, E., Alterman, I., Linnoila, M., & Murphy, D. (1985). Obsessive-compulsive disorder and serotonin: Is there a connection? *Biological Psychiatry, 20*, 1174–1188.

Jacobi, C., Hayward, C., de Zwaan, M., Kraemer, H., & Agras, W. (2004). Coming to terms with risk factors for eating disorders: Application of risk terminology and suggestions for a general taxonomy. *Psychological Bulletin, 130*, 19–65.

Jenike, M., Buttolph, L., Baer, L., Ricciardi, J., & Holland, A. (1989). Open trial of fluoxetine in obsessive–compulsive disorder. *American Journal of Psychiatry, 146*, 909–911.

Jimerson, D., Lesem, M., Kaye, W., & Brewerton, T. (1992). Low serotonin and dopamine metabolite concentrations in cerebrospinal fluid from bulimic patients with frequent binge episodes. *Archives of General Psychiatry, 49*, 132–138.

Kassett, J., Gerson, E., Maxwell, E., Guroff, J., Kazuba, D., Smith, A., et al. (1989). Psychiatric disorders in the first-degree relatives of probands with bulimia nervosa. *American Journal of Psychiatry, 146*, 1328–1330.

Kasvikis, Y., Tsakiris, F., Marks, I., Basoglu, M., & Noshirvani, H. (1986). Past history of anorexia nervosa in women with obsessive–compulsive disorder. *International Journal of Eating Disorders, 5*, 1069–1075.

Kaye, W., Bulik, C., Thornton, L., Barbarich, N., Masters, K., & the Price Foundation Collaborative Group (2004). Comorbidity of anxiety disorders with anorexia and bulimia nervosa. *American Journal of Psychiatry, 161*, 2215–2221.

Kaye, W., Frank, G., Bailer, U., & Henry, S. (2005). Neurobiology of anorexia nervosa: Clinical implications of alterations of function of the serotonin and other neuronal systems. *International Journal of Eating Disorders, 37*(Suppl.), S15–S19.

Kaye, W., Frank, G., & McConaha, C. (1999). Altered dopamine activity after recovery from restricting-type anorexia nervosa. *Neuropsychopharmacology, 21*, 503–506.

Kaye, W., Gendall, K., & Strober, M. (1998). Serotonin neuronal function and selective serotonin reuptake inhibitor treatment in anorexia and bulimia nervosa. *Biological Psychiatry, 44*, 825–838.

Kaye, W., Gwirtsman, H., George, D., & Ebert, M. (1991). Altered serotonin activity in anorexia nervosa after long-term weight restoration. *Archives of General Psychiatry, 48*, 556–562.

Kaye, W., Nagata, T., Weltzin, T., Hsu, L., Sokol, M., McConaha, C., et al. (2001). Double-blind placebo-controlled administration of fluoxetine in restricting and restricting-purging-type anorexia nervosa. *Biological Psychiatry, 49*, 644–652.

Kaye, W., Weltzin, T., Hsu, L., Bulik, C., McConaha, C., & Sobkiewicz, T. (1992). Patients with anorexia nervosa have elevated scores on the Yale–Brown Obsessive-Compulsive Scale. *International Journal of Eating Disorders, 12*, 57–62.

Keel, P. (2005). *Eating disorders*. Upper Saddle River, NJ: Pearson Prentice Hall.

Keel, P., & Klump, K. (2003). Are eating disorders culture-bound syndromes? Implications for conceptualizing their etiology. *Psychological Bulletin, 129*, 747–769.

Keel, P., Klump, K., Miller, K., McGue, M., & Iacono, W. (2005). Shared transmission of eating disorders and anxiety disorders. *International Journal of Eating Disorders, 38*, 99–105.

Kendler, K., MacLean, C., Neale, M., Kessler, R., Heath, A., & Eaves, L. (1991). The genetic epidemiology of bulimia nervosa. *American Journal of Psychiatry, 148*, 1627–1635.

Keys, A., Brozek, J., Henschel, A., Mickelsen, O., & Taylor, H. (1950). *The biology of human starvation*. Minneapolis, MN: University of Minnesota Press.

Klump, K., Bulik, C., Pollice, C., Halmi, K., Fichter, M., Berrettini, W., et al. (2000a). Temperament and character in women with anorexia nervosa. *Journal of Nervous and Mental Disease, 188*, 559–567.

Klump, K., & Gobrogge, K. (2005). A review and primer of molecular genetic studies of anorexia nervosa. *International Journal of Eating Disorders, 37*(Suppl.), S43–S48.

Klump, K., Gobrogge, K., Perkins, P., Thorne, D., Sisk, C., & Breedlove, S. (in press). Preliminary evidence that gonadal hormones organize and activate disordered eating. *Psychological Medicine*.

Klump, K., McGue, M., & Iacono, W. (2000b). Age differences in genetic and environmental influences on eating attitudes and behaviors in preadolescent and adolescent female twins. *Journal of Abnormal Psychology, 109*(2), 239–251.

Klump, K., McGue, M., & Iacono, W. (2002). Genetic relationships between personality and eating attitudes and behaviors. *Journal of Abnormal Psychology, 111*, 380–389.

Klump, K., Miller, K., Keel, P., McGue, M., & Iacono, W. (2001). Genetic and environmental influences on anorexia nervosa syndromes in a population-based twin sample. *Psychological Medicine, 31*, 737–740.

Klump, K., Strober, M., Bulik, C., Thornton, L., Johnson, C., Devlin, B., et al. (2004). Personality characteristics of women before and after recovery from an eating disorder. *Psychological Medicine, 34*, 1407–1418.

Krueger, R., Caspi, A., Moffitt, T., & Silva, P. (1998). The structure and stability of common mental disorders (DSM-III-R): A longitudinal-epidemiological study. *Journal of Abnormal Psychology, 107*, 216–227.

Laessle, R., Wittchen, H., Fichter, M., & Pirke, K. (1989). The significance of subgroups of bulimia and anorexia nervosa: Lifetime frequency of psychiatric disorders. *International Journal of Eating Disorders, 8*, 569–574.

Leckman, J., Goodman, W., Anderson, G., Riddle, M., Chappell, P., McSwiggan-Hardin, M., et al. (1995). Cerebrospinal fluid biogenic amines in obsessive compulsive disorder, Tourette's syndrome, and healthy controls. *Neuropsychopharmacology, 12*, 73–86.

Leckman, J., Grice, D., Boardman, J., Zhang, H., Vitale, A., Bondi, C., et al. (1997). Symptoms of obsessive–compulsive disorder. *American Journal of Psychiatry, 154*, 911–917.

Le Grange, D. (1999). Family therapy for adolescent anorexia nervosa. *Journal of Clinical Psychology, 55*, 727–739.

Lilenfeld, L., Kaye, W., Greeno, C., Merikanga, K., Plotnicov, K., Pollice, C., et al. (1998). A controlled family study of anorexia nervosa and bulimia nervosa: Psychiatric disorders in first-degree relatives and effects of proband comorbidity. *Archives of General Psychiatry, 55*, 603–610.

Lilenfeld, L., Stein, D., Bulik, C., Strober, C. M., Plotnicov, K., Pollice, C., et al. (2000). Personality traits among current eating disordered, recovered and never ill first degree female relatives of bulimic and control women. *Psychological Medicine, 30*, 1399–1410.

Mangweth, B., Hudson, J., Pope, H., Hausmann, A., De Col, C., Laird, N., et al. (2003). Family study of the aggregation of eating disorders and mood disorders. *Psychological Medicine, 33*, 1319–1323.

Matsunaga, H., Kiriike, N., Iwasaki, Y., Miyata, A., Yamagami, S., & Kaye, W. (1999). Clinical characteristics in patients with anorexia nervosa and obsessive-compulsive disorder. *Psychological Medicine, 29*, 407–414.

Mazure, C., Halmi, K., Sunday, S., Romano, S., & Einhorn, A. (1994). The Yale–Brown–Cornell eating disorder scale: Development, use, reliability and validity. *Journal of Psychiatric Research, 28*, 425–445.

Miguel, E., Leckman, J., Rauch, S., do Rosario-Campos, M., Hounie, A., Mercadante, M., et al. (2005). Obsessive–compulsive disorder phenotypes: Implications for genetic studies. *Molecular Psychiatry, 10*, 258–275.

Milos, G., Spindler, A., Ruggiero, G., Klaghofer, R., & Schnyder, U. (2002). Comorbidity of obsessive–compulsive disorders and duration of eating disorders. *International Journal of Eating Disorders, 31*, 284–289.

Mitchell, J., de Zwaan, M., & Roerig, J. (2003). Drug therapy for patients with eating disorders. *Current Drug Targets: CNS Neurological Disorders, 2*, 17–29.

Palmer, H., & Jones, M. (1939). Anorexia nervosa as a manifestation of compulsive neurosis. *Archives of Neurological Psychiatry, 41*, 856–860.

Pasquale, L., Sciuto, G., Cocchi, S., Ronchi, P., & Bellodi, L. (1994). A family study of obsessive compulsive, eating and mood disorders. *European Psychiatry, 9*, 33–38.

Pollice, C., Kaye, W. H., Greeno, C. G., & Weltzin, T. E. (1997). Relationship of depression, anxiety, and obsessionality to state of illness in anorexia nervosa. *International Journal of Eating Disorders, 21*, 67–376.

Rasmussen, S. (1994). Obsessive–compulsive spectrum disorders. *Journal of Clinical Psychiatry, 55*, 89–91.

Rogers, R., & Petrie, T. (1996). Personality correlates of anorexic and bulimic symptomatology. *Journal of Counseling and Development, 75*, 138–144.

Rogers, R., & Petrie, T. (2001). Psychological correlates of anorexic and bulimic symptomatology. *Journal of Counseling and Development, 79*, 178–187.

Rothenberg, A. (1986). Eating disorder as a modern obsessive-compulsive syndrome. *Psychiatry, 49*, 45–53.

Rubenstein, C., Pigott, T., Altemus, M., L'Heureux, F., Gray, J., & Murphy, D. (1993). High rates of comorbid OCD in patients with bulimia nervosa. *Eating Disorders: The Journal of Treatment & Prevention, 1*, 147–155.

Rubenstein, C., Pigott, T., L'Heureux, F., Hill, J., & Murphy, D. (1992). A preliminary investigation of the lifetime prevalence of anorexia and bulimia nervosa in patients with obsessive compulsive disorder. *Journal of Clinical Psychiatry, 53*, 309–314.

Speranza, M., Corcos, M., Godart, N., Loas, G., Guilbaud, O., Jeammet, P., et al. (2001). Obsessive compulsive disorders in eating disorders. *Eating Behaviors, 2*, 193–207.

Srinivasagam, N., Kaye, W., Plotnicov, K., Greeno, C., Weltzin, T., & Rao, R. (1995). Persistent perfectionism, symmetry, and exactness in anorexia nervosa after long-term recovery. *American Journal of Psychiatry, 152*, 1630–1634.

Stice, E. (2002). Risk and maintenance factors for eating pathology: A meta-analytic review. *Psychological Bulletin, 128*, 825–848.

Strober, M. (1980). Personality and symptomatological features in young, non-chronic anorexia nervosa patients. *Journal of Psychosomatic Research, 24*, 353–359.

Strober, M., Freeman, R., Bower, S., & Rigali, J. (1996). Binge eating in anorexia nervosa predicts later onset of substance use disorder: A ten-year prospective, longitudinal follow-up of 95 adolescents. *Journal of Youth and Adolescence, 25*, 519–532.

Strober, M., Freeman, R., Lampert, C., Diamond, J., & Kaye, W. (2000). Controlled family study of anorexia nervosa and bulimia nervosa: Evidence of shared liability and transmission of partial syndromes. *American Journal of Psychiatry, 157*, 393–401.

Strober, M., Lampert, C., Morrell, W., Burroughs, J., & Jacobs, C. (1990). A controlled family study of anorexia nervosa: Evidence of familial aggregation and lack of shared transmission with affective disorders. *International Journal of Eating Disorders, 9*, 239–253.

Thoren, P., Asberg, M., Cronholm, B., Jornestedt, L., & Traskman, L. (1980). Clomipramine treatment of obsessive–compulsive disorder. *Archives of General Psychiatry, 37*, 1281–1285.

Thornton, C., & Russell, J. (1997). Obsessive compulsive comorbidity in the dieting disorders. *International Journal of Eating Disorders, 21*, 83–87.

Vaswani, M., Ramesh, K., & Sagar, R. (2005). Use of selective serotonin reuptake inhibitors in neuropsychiatric disorders. In S. Shohov (Ed.), *Advances in psychology research* (Vol. 33, pp. 161–200). Hauppauge, NY: Nova Science.

von Ranson, K., Kaye, W., Weltzin, T., Rao, R., & Matsunaga, H. (1999). Obsessive–compulsive disorder symptoms before and after recovery from bulimia nervosa. *American Journal of Psychiatry, 156*, 1703–1708.

Wade, T., Bulik, C., Neale, M., & Kendler, K. (2000). Anorexia nervosa and major depression: An examination of shared genetic and environmental risk factors. *American Journal of Psychiatry, 157*, 469–471.

Wade, T., Martin, N., & Tiggerman, M. (1998). Genetic and environmental risk factors for the weight and shape concerns characteristic of bulimia nervosa. *Psychological Medicine, 28*, 761–771.

Westen, D., & Harnden-Fischer, J. (2001). Personality profiles in eating disorders: Rethinking the distinction between Axis I and Axis II. *American Journal of Psychiatry, 158*, 547–562.

Wilson, G. (1999). Cognitive behavior therapy for eating disorders: Progress and problems. *Behaviour Research and Therapy, 37*(Suppl.), S79–S95.

Yaryura-Tobias, J., Pinto, A., & Neziroglu, F. (2001). The integration of primary anorexia nervosa and obsessive–compulsive disorder. *Eating and Weight Disorders, 6*, 174–180.

Ziegler, A., Hebebrand, J., Gorg, T., Rosekranz, K., Fichter, M., Herpetz-Dahlmann, B., et al. (1999). Further lack of association between the $5\text{-}HT_{2a}$ gene promoter polymorphism and susceptibility to eating disorders and a meta-analysis pertaining to anorexia nervosa. *Molecular Psychiatry, 4*, 410–412.

15

OBSESSIVE–COMPULSIVE PERSONALITY DISORDER

ANTHONY PINTO, JANE L. EISEN, MARIA C. MANCEBO, AND STEVEN A. RASMUSSEN

Brown Medical School

Obsessive–compulsive personality traits are commonly found in the general population (Nestadt et al., 1991) and, in moderation, can be advantageous (Kline, 1967), especially in situations that reward high performance. However, the clinical diagnosis of obsessive–compulsive personality disorder (OCPD) is a chronic maladaptive pattern of excessive perfectionism, preoccupation with orderliness and detail, and need for control over one's environment that leads to significant distress or impairment, particularly in areas of interpersonal functioning. Individuals with this disorder are often characterized as rigid and overly controlling. They may find it difficult to relax, feel obligated to plan out their activities to the minute, and find unstructured time intolerable. Even though it is one of the most frequently diagnosed personality disorders across community (Ekselius, Tillfors, Furmark, & Fredrikson, 2001) and clinical (Stuart et al., 1998) samples, OCPD has received little empirical attention in the past two decades (Grilo & McGlashan, 1999; Pfohl & Blum, 1995). In fact, the OCPD research literature has been characterized as 'dying' in recent years, with fewer than 10 articles published per year (Blashfield & Intoccia, 2000; Villemarette-Pittman, Stanford, Greve, Houston, & Mathias, 2004). Recent data have shown high levels of treatment utilization by individuals with OCPD, controlling for lifetime Axis I disorders. They are three times as likely to receive individual psychotherapy as patients with major depressive disorder

Correspondence to: Anthony Pinto, Brown Medical School, Department of Psychiatry and Human Behavior, Butler Hospital, 345 Blackstone Blvd, Providence, Rhode Island 02906.

(Bender et al., 2001; Bender et al., 2006) and also report high rates of primary care utilization (Sansone, Hendricks, Gaither, & Reddington, 2004; Sansone et al., 2003). Despite this increased use of the healthcare system, to date, there is still no definitive empirically validated treatment for the disorder nor have there been any controlled treatment trials for uncomplicated OCPD. This chapter reviews the phenomenology of OCPD, the disorder's controversial relationship with OCD, and the appropriateness of its inclusion in the OCD spectrum.

PHENOMENOLOGY

DIAGNOSTIC CRITERIA

OCPD was first included in *DSM-II* (American Psychiatric Association, 1968), largely based on Freud's concept of the obsessive personality or anal-erotic character style characterized by orderliness, parsimony, and obstinacy (Freud, 1908/1963). As it is currently conceptualized in the *DSM-IV* (American Psychiatric Association, 1994), OCPD is defined by the presence of at least four of the following eight criteria: preoccupation with details, perfectionism, excessive devotion to work, hypermorality, inability to discard worn or useless items, inability to delegate tasks, miserliness, and rigidity. The *DSM-IV* categorizes OCPD on Axis II within Cluster C, along with avoidant personality disorder and dependent personality disorder, based on the overarching view that these diagnoses represent enduring and pervasive patterns of behavior characterized by excessive anxiety and fear. The diagnostic criteria for OCPD have undergone substantial changes with each *DSM* revision (see Table 15.1), which have posed obstacles to studying the disorder (Baer & Jenike, 1998). For example, the *DSM-IV* dropped two criteria present in the *DSM-III-R* (American Psychiatric Association, 1987), restricted expression of affection and indecisiveness, largely based on reviews of the empirical literature that found these traits lacked internal consistency (Pfohl, 1996).

CORE FEATURES

There have been several attempts to identify core features or dimensions of OCPD based on clinical observations, theory, and statistical approaches. A commonality among these various models is an emphasis on rigidity and perfectionism as central diagnostic features. The rigidity and perfectionism dimensions are consistent with clinical descriptions of OCPD (Pollak, 1987) that note exaggerated attempts at control. The rigidity dimension reflects the central *interpersonal* control and resistance to change aspects of OCPD, while the perfectionism dimension reflects the key cognitive or *intrapersonal* control aspect of the disorder (Grilo, 2004b). Similarly, in clinical descriptions, Shapiro (1965) noted 'cognitive rigidity' (i.e., an intense, narrow focus on details) and 'tense deliberateness' and effortfulness as important aspects of an obsessive–compulsive style. Millon (1981) identified

TABLE 15.1　Changes over time in DSM criteria for obsessive–compulsive personality disorder

Criteria	DSM-III	DSM-III-R	DSM-IV
Preoccupation with details		+	+
Perfectionism	+	+	+
Excessive devotion to work	+	+	+
Overconscientiousness regarding ethics (hypermorality)		+	+
Inability to discard worthless objects		+	+
Inability to delegate tasks*			+
Lack of generosity (miserliness)		+	+
Rigidity	+	+	+
Indecisiveness	+	+	
Restricted expression of affection	+	+	
Number of criteria for diagnosis	4 of 5 (80%)	5 of 9 (56%)	4 of 8 (50%)

*New criterion added in the *DSM-IV*.
Source: From Baer & Jenike (1998), with permission

three self-perpetuating processes, including pervasive rigidity, adherence to rules and regulations, and guilt and self-criticism, that serve to maintain and reinforce obsessive–compulsive patterns by limiting the acquisition of new perceptions of the world and the learning of more flexible strategies for living. Baer (1994) reported a two-factor solution based on the nine *DSM-III* OCPD criteria. His first factor included perfectionism, preoccupation with details, indecision, restricted affection, and inability to discard, while his second factor included rigidity, hypermorality, work devotion, and miserliness. In the Collaborative Longitudinal Study of Personality Disorders (CLPS) (Gunderson et al., 2000), a multisite study of the course and stability of *DSM-IV* personality disorders, rigidity, reluctance to delegate, and perfectionism were the most prevalent and stable OCPD criteria over a two-year follow-up period (McGlashan et al., 2005). Using *DSM-IV* criteria, Grilo, Sanislow et al. (2004) identified a three-factor solution of OCPD in a clinical sample of binge eating disorder. The three factors are 'rigidity' (rigidity, reluctance to delegate, hypermorality), 'perfectionism' (preoccupation with details, perfectionism, work devotion), and 'miserliness' (miserliness, inability to discard). Results of a confirmatory factor analysis indicate that this three-factor model also applies to a personality disorders sample (CLPS) (Pinto et al., 2007).

PREVALENCE

The *DSM-IV* estimates OCPD prevalence rates to be about 1% in community samples and 3–10% in clinical settings (American Psychiatric Association, 1994). Community-based studies reported rates of 2.0% using *DSM-III-R* criteria (Torgersen et al., 2001) and 0.9% using *DSM-IV* criteria (Samuels et al., 2002). More recently, two studies (Ekselius et al., 2001; Grant et al., 2004) using *DSM-IV* criteria, via a self-report questionnaire and lay interviewers, respectively, reported much higher rates of OCPD (7.7–7.8%), making it by far the most prevalent personality disorder in the general population. However, these unusually high rates may be an artifact of the particular assessment methods used. OCPD is one of the most frequently diagnosed in clinical samples (Sanderson, Wetzler, Beck, & Betz, 1994; Stuart et al., 1998; Wilfley et al., 2000).

Despite similar prevalence rates of OCPD cross-culturally in one epidemiological study (Karno, Golding, Sorenson, & Burnam, 1988), a recent study found that OCPD was significantly less common in Asians and Hispanics relative to Caucasians and African-Americans (Grant et al., 2004). In a clinical sample (CLPS), Chavira et al. (2003) reported equal representation of ethnic minorities across the four personality disorders studied, including OCPD.

Studies of OCPD have reported mixed results regarding gender distribution. While one community study found OCPD to be twice as common in men than women based on *DSM-III-R* criteria (Torgersen et al., 2001), another community study found no gender differences using the *DSM-IV* (Grant et al., 2004). No gender difference was reported in recent studies using clinical samples (Albert, Maina, Forner, & Bogetto, 2004; Chavira et al., 2003).

Although there is controversy as to whether personality disorders should be diagnosed in childhood, several researchers have examined the prevalence of OCPD traits in children. One study using a structured interview found that 13.5% of children aged 9–19 met criteria for OCPD, making it the most frequent disorder in this large community sample of children (Bernstein et al., 1993). This study found that OCPD, like the other personality disorders studied, was associated with a greater risk of Axis I psychopathology, depressive symptoms, and social impairment. However, unlike other personality disorders, children with OCPD were not at risk for academic impairment. In contrast, another study, using the Personality Disorder Examination (PDE) to assess personality disorders in an adolescent community sample, did not find any adolescents who met full *DSM-III-R* criteria for OCPD. Of note, this study found very low rates of the other personality disorders as well (Lewinsohn, Rohde, Sealey, & Klein, 1997).

COURSE

OCPD generally onsets in early adulthood, but patients describe having at least some of these characteristics since childhood. While there has been little systematic study to date regarding the course of this disorder, a few studies have assessed the stability of the OCPD diagnosis and each criterion over time. The available data appears to contradict clinical wisdom that persons with OCPD have a chronic and stable pattern of rigidity and perfectionism that persists throughout adulthood. In one follow-up study of adolescents with personality disorders, 32% of those initially diagnosed with OCPD met criteria two years later (Bernstein et al., 1993). Odds ratios indicated that children were four times as likely to retain the OCPD diagnosis at the 2-year follow-up if they had been initially diagnosed with moderate levels of

OCPD and 15 times more likely to continue to have the diagnosis if they initially had severe symptoms. In the CLPS, half of the participants with OCPD at baseline continued to have the diagnosis after 2 years (Grilo, Skodol et al., 2004). The presence of three of the *DSM-IV* OCPD criteria, preoccupation with details, rigidity, and reluctance to delegate, were the strongest predictors of a continued OCPD diagnosis after two years (Grilo, Skodol et al., 2004).

COMORBIDITY

There is little data on the co-occurrence of Axis I and II disorders in individuals with OCPD. In the CLPS intake sample, the most common lifetime comorbid Axis I conditions for individuals with OCPD were major depression (75.8%), generalized anxiety disorder (29.4%), alcohol abuse/dependence (29.4%), substance abuse/dependence, and OCD (20.9%) (McGlashan et al., 2000). With regard to Axis II, the most common comorbid personality disorder by far for the OCPD sample was avoidant (27.5%), followed by borderline (9.2%) and narcissistic (7.2%) (McGlashan et al., 2000).

FUNCTIONAL IMPAIRMENT

Impaired interpersonal functioning is a 'defining feature' of all personality disorders (Pincus and Wiggins, 1990), even after Axis I disorders are accounted for (Johnson, Rabkin, Williams, Remien, & Gorman, 2000), and this is especially true in OCPD. Clinical descriptions (e.g., Pollak, 1987) note that the features of OCPD, particularly the impossibly high standards, rigidity, literal compliance to authority, inflexibility in morality/ethics, and difficulty acknowledging the viewpoints of others and expressing emotion, can spark interpersonal conflicts. While ingratiating to superiors, individuals with OCPD tend to be uncompromising, demanding, and punitive with subordinates (Millon, 1981). Their need for interpersonal control can lead to hostility and occasional explosive outbursts of anger at home and work (Villemarette-Pittman et al., 2004). In fact, Stein et al. (1996) reported a greater incidence of impulsive aggression in a small sample of *DSM-III* OCPD patients compared with normal controls and noncompulsive personality disorders.

According to Skodol et al. (2002), although OCPD was associated with less overall functional impairment than the other targeted personality disorders (borderline, schizotypal, avoidant) in the CLPS, 90% of OCPD subjects in the CLPS at intake had moderate or worse impairment or poor or worse functioning in at least one life domain (occupational, family, friends, recreation, etc.) or received a global assessment of functioning rating of 60 or less. Interestingly, in a two-year follow-up study, Skodol et al. (2005) found that improvement in OCPD pathology, defined as the proportion decrease in the number of criteria met from baseline to follow-up, had little impact on functional impairment, indicating that there may be problematic personality characteristics that are not adequately captured by the current OCPD diagnostic criteria.

With regard to functional impairment, perfectionism is the feature of OCPD that has most often been examined. Recent studies suggest that maladaptive perfectionism, the tendency to feel that any less than perfect performance is unacceptable, is quite stable and a significant vulnerability factor for later depression (Rice & Aldea, 2006). One study indicates that the presence of perfectionism impedes the treatment of depression, possibly due to its relationship with rigidity (Blatt, Zuroff, Bondi, Sanislow, & Pilkonis, 1998). Socially prescribed perfectionism, the belief that others hold unrealistic expectations for one's own behaviors, has been uniquely associated with greater likelihood of suicidal ideation (Hewitt, Flett, & Weber, 1994; Hewitt, Newton, Flett, & Callander, 1997) and poorer marital adjustment (for both the individual and the partner) (Haring, Hewitt, & Flett, 2003). Further research is needed to explore the potential maladaptive effects of perfectionism, rigidity, and their interaction on both psychosocial functioning and course of OCPD.

LIMITATIONS OF THE CURRENT OCPD CONSTRUCT

Farmer and Chapman (2002) noted weaknesses in the conceptualization and assessment of the OCPD construct, including poor psychometric strength and diagnostic efficiency (sensitivity, specificity, predictive power). They contend that OCPD 'as a personality disorder concept may well benefit from additional conceptual, theoretical, and empirical development' (p. 297). In addition, Grilo (2004a; Grilo et al., 2001) found the diagnostic efficiencies of the OCPD criteria to be variable and called into question the utility of some criteria. Psychometric work on the structure and validity of the current construct of OCPD represents a pressing need (Pfohl & Blum, 1995). Such work is especially important now, considering the substantial revisions to the OCPD construct in the *DSM-IV* from earlier editions and the fact that we are just a few years away from a new edition of the *DSM*. Beyond refining the diagnostic criteria, there is also a need to develop OCPD-specific instruments. There is currently no established rater-administered measure of OCPD severity. Such a rating scale, if valid and sensitive to change, would facilitate studies of treatment and course by providing a continuous outcome score.

The arbitrary diagnostic threshold for OCPD (e.g., four of eight criteria in the *DSM-IV*), which has varied across each *DSM* edition, is another limitation of the current construct. A clinical threshold backed by compelling empirical rationale is needed to differentiate the disorder from normal personality.

The polythetic nature of the *DSM-IV* criteria for OCPD has led to substantial phenotypic heterogeneity within this diagnostic group, to the extent that two people with the diagnosis may present with very different symptom patterns. While the *DSM-IV* regards OCPD as a unitary nosological entity, the criteria reflect behavioral, cognitive, and interpersonal domains. The identification and validation of OCPD dimensions in future research will likely have important implications both for classification and treatment.

ETIOLOGICAL AND CONCEPTUAL MODELS

Researchers have developed a variety of biological and psychological models to explain the etiology of OCPD but empirical data is limited.

BIOLOGICAL MODELS

Family history

In a twin study using the *DSM-III-R*, Torgersen et al. (2000) found a heritability of 0.8 for OCPD (and 0.6 for personality disorders in general), which is higher than for most Axis I disorders, yet similar to that of OCD. Data on the familial relationship between OCPD and OCD will be reviewed in the next section of the chapter.

Genetics

In the only study to investigate the role of the serotonin transporter gene in OCPD, no differences in allelic frequencies on the serotonin transporter gene were found between OCPD individuals and controls (Perez, Brown, Vrshek-Schallorn, Johnson, & Joiner, 2006). Meanwhile, this same study reported higher frequencies of the s/s genotype in the OCD subjects versus controls, suggesting that the s/s genotype might serve as a contributory risk factor for OCD.

Brain circuitry

There have been no studies investigating imaging abnormalities in uncomplicated OCPD. In a long-term follow-up study of 16 severe and refractory OCD cases who had undergone ventromedial frontal leucotomy in the 1970s, it was noted that 3 patients with comorbid OCPD improved significantly less than the rest, implying that OCPD is associated with a more refractory form of OCD that might involve different neural pathways (Irle, Exner, Thielen, Weniger, & Ruther, 1998).

Neurochemistry

One study of serotenergic function in males with *DSM-III* OCPD found that OCPD criteria were negatively correlated with prolactin response to fenfluramine, a marker of serotonergic dysfunction (Stein et al., 1996). Those with OCPD showed significantly blunted prolactin responses to fenfluramine compared with other personality disorder patients and normal controls. Prolactin blunting after fenfluramine has been reported in several studies of OCD (Hewlett, Vinogradov, Martin, Berman, & Csernansky, 1992; Lucey, O'Keane, Butcher, Clare, & Dinan, 1992).

Neuropsychology

No study has specifically examined neurocognitive function in OCPD. However, Dinn, Harris, Aycicegi, Greene, & Andover (2002) identified associations between performance deficits on measures of frontal executive function and obsessive–compulsive traits. Prominent executive dysfunction has also been noted in OCD, both in terms of impaired inhibition of motor responses (impulsivity) and cognitive inflexibility (thought to contribute to compulsivity) (Chamberlain, Fineberg, Blackwell, Robbins, & Sahakian, 2006).

PSYCHOLOGICAL MODELS

Psychodynamic

Early psychoanalysts were the first to give significant attention to factors that contribute to the development of OCPD (Abraham, 1921/1953; Freud, 1908/1963). Conflicts stemming from issues of control at the anal stage due to inappropriate toilet training were considered to be developmentally related to the onset of OCPD (Kline, 1968). Later, family environments characterized by anger and hostility as well as inconsistent parenting were linked to the disorder (Angyal, 1965; Sullivan, 1956). In one early study, obsessional children's parents were noted to be overly controlling and conforming, with low empathy and negative responses to spontaneous affect (Adams, 1973). Salzman (1973) thought that individuals with this personality disorder were preoccupied with control over themselves and their environment as a reaction to an inner sense of helplessness. While these models remain intriguing, they lack empirical support.

Dimensional

An alternative to the categorical classification of personality disorders is a dimensional view of normal personality traits. According to this model, individuals with personality disorders represent extremes on a personality continuum. The five-factor model (Costa & McCrae, 1992a) is one of the most widely used dimensional classification systems and encompasses five basic personality traits: neuroticism, extraversion, openness to experience, agreeableness, and conscientiousness. In this model, people who carry the diagnosis of OCPD would likely be classified as having excessive conscientiousness, characterized by dutifulness, order, competence, self-discipline and deliberation (Costa & McCrae, 1992b; Widiger, 2005). One study, which supports this conceptual view of OCPD, demonstrated that OCPD was associated with high scores on all domains or facets of conscientiousness (Lynam & Widiger, 2001).

Data from the CLPS suggest a 'hybrid' model of personality disorders, consisting of more stable personality traits linked to less stable, or intermittently expressed, symptomatic behaviors or manifestations (McGlashan et al., 2005). Traits are thought to be dimensional in nature and expression, ranging from adaptive variants to pathological exaggerations in personality disorders. Meanwhile, symptomatic behaviors, conceptualized as dysfunctional adaptations used to compensate for the pathologic traits, are considered discrete (either people do them or they do not) and more likely to be intensified by life events and stress. Data from the CLPS on the prevalence and stability of *DSM-IV* personality disorder criteria sets, including OCPD, indicate that the most stable criteria (e.g., rigidity, perfectionism, and reluctance to delegate) are trait-like or attitudinal in nature, whereas the most unstable (e.g., miserliness) can be described as symptomatic behaviors. The developers of the *DSM-V* will need to address the ongoing debate as to whether personality disorders should continue to be regarded as discrete entities and to what degree dimensions should be integrated into the classification system.

Cognitive

A number of cognitive theorists have written about OCPD. Shapiro (1981) described people with OCPD as being overly focused, rigid in their thinking (considering what they *should* do as opposed to what they *would like* to do), and lacking certainty about their preferences and decisions. Guidano and Liotti (1983) hypothesized that both OCD and OCPD are fueled by beliefs about perfectionism, and the notion that there is one correct response to any given situation. These beliefs, in turn, fuel symptoms/traits of indecisiveness, procrastination and excessive doubt. Beck and Freeman (1990) described underlying assumptions, or schemas, for individuals with OCPD, such as a narrow range of acceptable feelings and actions and the critical importance of both not making a mistake and completely controlling one's environment. They postulated additional cognitive distortions with a predominant pattern of seeing things in strictly 'black-and-white terms'. Such dichotomous thinking maintains rigidity, procrastination, and perfectionism.

Behavioral

Little has been written on OCPD from a behavioral perspective. Millon (1981; Millon & Everly, 1985) postulated that OCPD is socially learned and results from the imitation and modeling of significant others, particularly overly controlling parents, during childhood, with negative consequences to the child who asserts any degree of independence. That is, the environment may reward and provide models for obsessive–compulsive patterns, leading to the development of the need to conform to strict standards, while discouraging or not reinforcing any fundamental changes in adjustment.

IS OCPD AN OCD SPECTRUM DISORDER?

Renewed interest in OCD in recent years has led researchers to attempt to define its subtypes and explore other psychiatric disorders that might have clinical and/or etiopathological links with OCD. Disorders that are posited to be linked to OCD, based on similarities in a number of domains, are referred to as 'OCD spectrum disorders'. OCPD is one of the disorders under consideration for membership in this spectrum. Despite long-standing interest in the psychiatric community, the controversial relationship between OCD and OCPD remains unclear. There has been debate as to whether these phenomena should be considered similar, overlapping entities, or whether they are better characterized as distinct. Domains of inquiry relevant to this question include the degree to which OCD and OCPD overlap both in terms of clinical characteristics and comorbidity, and whether there is a relationship between the two disorders in terms of family history, longitudinal course, and treatment response. To date, there has been both descriptive and systematic research exploring the differences and similarities between OCD and OCPD in these areas. Other important domains such as under-lying etiological similarities have not been adequately addressed to date. There is also a striking paucity of data on OCPD treatment, making it premature to com-ment on similarities in treatment response between the two disorders.

Interest in the relationship between OCD and OCPD dates back over 100 years. Janet (1904) described the development of frank obsessions and compul-sions as being preceded by a period he termed 'psychasthenic state', which was characterized by a sense that actions are performed incompletely (and the associ-ated need to do them perfectly), a strong focus on order and uniformity, indeci-siveness, and restricted emotional expression (Pitman, 1987). Following Janet's observations, Freud (1908/1963) proposed the construct of the anal character, typ-ified by obstinacy, orderliness, and parsimony. Aspects of Janet's description of the psychasthenic state and Freud's description of the anal character were later integrated into definitions of OCPD (Mancebo et al., 2005). For many years, ana-lysts used the term obsessive–compulsive neurosis to describe features of both OCD and OCPD (Angyal, 1965). While more recent psychodynamic theorists have distinguished between these disorders (Gabbard, 2005), the overlap between OCD and OCPD remains controversial.

OVERLAP BETWEEN CLINICAL PRESENTATION OF OCD AND OCPD

There is considerable overlap in the symptom presentations of OCD and OCPD, which can lead to difficulty differentiating them in clinical practice. For example, excessive list-making can be viewed as a compulsion if it is repetitive, time-consuming, and distressing; it is included in the Yale–Brown Obsessive Compulsive Scale – Symptom Checklist (Goodman et al., 1989). Excessive list-making can also be viewed as a preoccupation with details and is included in the *DSM-IV* as an exam-ple of this OCPD criterion. Similarly, perfectionism is an OCPD criterion and a symptom of OCD if it involves the need for order, symmetry, and arranging. Hoarding is also considered both a compulsion (found in OCD) and a criterion for OCPD in the *DSM-IV*. In fact, the *DSM-IV* states that if hoarding is extreme in a patient with OCPD, an additional diagnosis of OCD should be given. Although OCPD and OCD are conceptualized as separate disorders, there is clear redundancy between the two disorders regarding several symptoms. Cross-sectional and prospec-tive studies that assess specific OCPD criteria and specific OCD symptoms are needed to address this issue of overlap between definitions of the two disorders.

FUNCTIONAL CHARACTERISTICS OF SYMPTOMS

Despite the similarities between some of OCPD criteria and the obsessions and compulsions found in OCD, there are distinct qualitative differences between these disorders, particularly in the functional aspects of symptoms (i.e., what drives/motivates the individual to do them). Unlike OCPD, OCD is characterized by intrusive, distressing, time-consuming obsessions and rituals aimed at lowering the obsession-related distress. OCD symptoms are sometimes referred to as *ego-dystonic* because they are experienced as foreign and abhorrent to the affected individual. As a result, there is greater mental discomfort associated with OCD. In contrast, the symptomatic behaviors in OCPD, though they may be repetitive, are not associated with repugnant thoughts, images, or urges. OCPD traits and behaviors are considered *ego-syntonic* as individuals with the disorder view them as appropriate and correct. However, the core features of perfectionism and rigidity can each lead to significant distress in an individual with OCPD due to the associated need for control in each case (the need to control one's actions so that they are performed exactly or perfectly in perfectionism versus the need for interpersonal control in rigidity). While useful, this distinction between the disorders based on ego syntonicity is not absolute, and sometimes, as in the case of OCD hoarding, clinical presentations defy simple categorization.

A more thorough examination of the functional aspects of OCD and OCPD symptoms requires moving beyond OCD's heterogeneous phenotype to more homogeneous dimensions. Building off the model of Rasmussen and Eisen (1992), Summerfeldt et al. (2000, 2001) proposed two core dimensions of OCD, 'incompleteness' and 'harm avoidance', with unique affective, cognitive, and motivational characteristics. Based on Janet's (1904) clinical description, incompleteness refers to an inner sense of imperfection or the uncomfortable subjective state that one's actions or experiences are 'just not right'. Best regarded as a temperament-like motivational variable, incompleteness often exists in the context of OCD (typically with symmetry, counting, repeating, slowness) and has been associated with spectrum conditions such as tics and skin picking (Summerfeldt, 2004). Believed to underly obsessional personality traits, particularly pathological perfectionism and indecision (no longer a criterion for OCPD), high incompleteness scores in OCD have been shown to be predictive of meeting criteria for OCPD (Summerfeldt et al., 2000). These researchers propose that OCD symptoms motivated by feelings of incompleteness are more strongly related to OCPD than OCD symptoms motivated by harm avoidance. More research is needed to better understand the role of incompleteness in OCD and OCPD, as well as the specific relationship between incompleteness in OCD and perfectionism in OCPD.

COMORBIDITY WITH OCD

Comorbidity between OCPD and OCD has been reported in numerous studies, most of which have assessed the frequency of OCPD in clinical samples of OCD (see Table 15.2). Studies using *DSM-III* and *DSM-III-R* criteria for OCPD have shown marked variability in prevalence rates of the disorder in subjects with OCD. These earlier studies found OCPD comorbidity rates of 6–31%, with

TABLE 15.2   Co-occurrence of OCPD in OCD clinical samples

Criteria	Measure	OCD Sample size (N)	OCPD (%)
DSM-III (Baer et al., 1990)	SIDP	96	6
DSM-III (Black et al., 1993)	SIDP	32	28
DSM-III (Eisen & Rasmussen, 1991)	SIDP	114	19
DSM-III-R (Baer & Jenike, 1992)	SIDP-R	55	16
DSM-III-R (Cavedini et al., 1997)	SIDP-R	29	31
DSM-III-R (Crino & Andrews, 1996)	PDE	80	8
DSM-III-R (Diaferia et al., 1997)	SIDP-R	88	31
DSM-III-R (Horesh et al., 1997)	SCID-II	51	18
DSM-III-R (Mataix-Cols et al., 2000)	SCID-II	75	12
DSM-III-R (Matsunaga et al., 1999)	SCID-II	16	11
DSM-III-R (Matsunaga et al., 2000)	SCID-II	94	16
DSM-III-R (Sanderson et al., 1994)	SCID-II	21	5
DSM-III-R (Sciuto et al., 1991)	SIDP-R	30	3
DSM-III-R (Stanley et al., 1990)	SCID-II	25	28
DSM-III-R (Torres and Del Porto, 1995)	SIDP-R	40	18
DSM-IV (Albert et al., 2004)	SCID-II	109	23
DSM-IV (Samuels et al., 2000)	SIDP-R	72	32
DSM-IV (Pinto et al., 2006)	SCID-II	293	25

Only studies using standardized, semi-structured diagnostic interviews are listed. Abbreviations: SIDP = Structured Interview for DSM Personality Disorders, PDE = Personality Disorder Examination, SCID-II = Structured Clinical Interview for *DSM-IV* Axis II Personality Disorders.
Source: From Mancebo et al. (2005), with permission

slightly higher rates found using the more lenient *DSM-III-R* definition of OCPD. Recent studies using current *DSM-IV* criteria have consistently found elevated rates of OCPD in subjects with OCD, with estimates ranging from 23% to 32% in individuals with OCD (Albert et al., 2004; Pinto et al., 2006; Samuels et al., 2000). In studies of OCD using structured interviews of *DSM-IV* personality disorders (Pinto et al., 2006; Samuels et al., 2000), OCPD was the most frequently diagnosed personality disorder, but this was not the case in studies based on earlier editions of the *DSM* (e.g., Black et al., 1993). Some data suggest that there may be specificity in the link between OCD and OCPD. OCPD rates are consistently higher in individuals with OCD than in healthy community controls using *DSM-IV* criteria (Albert et al., 2004; Samuels et al., 2000). In addition, OCPD has been shown to occur more frequently in individuals with OCD than in individuals with other anxiety disorders (panic disorder, social phobia) (Crino & Andrews, 1996; Diaferia et al., 1997; Skodol et al., 1995) or major depressive disorder (Diaferia et al., 1997). However, one study found similar rates of OCPD in OCD and panic disorder (Albert et al., 2004). The specificity of the OCD–OCPD relationship was also not supported in the CLPS where the rate of OCD in patients with *DSM-IV* OCPD (20.9%) was similar to the rate of OCD in schizotypal personality disorder (23.3%) (McGlashan et al., 2000).

COMORBIDITY WITH OTHER PUTATIVE OCD SPECTRUM DISORDERS

Among the disorders hypothesized to be spectrum members are body dysmorphic disorder, hypochondriasis, Tourette syndrome, impulse control disorders, and eating disorders. Besides eating disorders, there is limited data on the rates of OCPD in the other putative spectrum disorders. Perfectionism is a central feature and risk factor for developing an eating disorder (Shafran & Mansell, 2001). The comorbidity of OCPD and eating disorders has been established in various eating disorder samples, including 15–26% for binge eating disorder (Grilo, 2004b; Karwautz, Troop, Rabe-Hesketh, Collier, & Treasure, 2003), and 20–61% for anorexia nervosa (Anderluh, Tchanturia, Rabe-Hesketh, & Treasure, 2003; Nilsson, Gillberg, Gillberg, & Rastam, 1999). In addition, Anderluh et al. (2003) noted that OCPD predated the onset of anorexia nervosa, and Lilenfeld et al. (1998) reported increased prevalence of OCPD in relatives of individuals with anorexia nervosa.

OCPD is the second most common comorbid personality disorder in body dysmorphic disorder, after avoidant (Phillips, Menard, Fay, & Weisberg, 2005). Despite a lack of empirical data on the comorbidity of OCPD and hypochondriasis, the disorders have been theoretically linked due to phenomenological similarities of an excessive need for control, displayed in a repetitive manner (Starcevic, 1990). OCD patients with OCPD did not differ from those without OCPD on family history for tic disorders/Tourette syndrome (Diaferia et al., 1997). Although data is not available on the prevalence of OCPD in impulse control disorders specifically, among patients seeking treatment for impulsive aggression, OCPD was the second most common Axis II diagnosis in a clinic-referred sample and the most common Axis II diagnosis in a self-referred sample (Villemarette-Pittman et al., 2004).

RELATIONSHIP OF OCPD CRITERIA TO OCD

There has been interest in examining whether specific OCPD criteria are particularly associated with OCD. Using *DSM-III-R*, Eisen and Rasmussen (1991) found that the majority of OCD patients reported perfectionism and indecisiveness (82% and 70%, respectively), suggesting the possibility that these symptoms may be developmental markers for OCD or characteristics that are part of the syndrome of OCD. In contrast, other OCPD traits such as restricted affection, excessive devotion to work, and rigidity were seen infrequently. More recently, data from the CLPS (based on *DSM-IV*) indicated that three of the eight OCPD criteria (hoarding, perfectionism, and preoccupation with details) were significantly more frequent in patients with comorbid OCD than in those without OCD (Eisen et al., 2006). The relationship between OCD and these three criteria remained significant after controlling for the presence of other anxiety disorders and major depressive disorder, showing unique associations with odds ratios ranging from 2.71 to 2.99. This finding suggests that patients with comorbid OCD and OCPD tend to have specific OCPD criteria in common.

RELATIONSHIP OF OCD CLINICAL FEATURES AND SYMPTOMS TO OCPD

Coles et al. (in press) were the first to systematically examine a range of clinical characteristics of individuals with and without comorbid OCPD in a primary OCD sample, as part of the Brown Longitudinal Obsessive Compulsive Study (BLOCS). As compared to subjects without OCPD, the OCD+OCPD subjects had a significantly younger age at onset of first OC symptoms, as well as significantly lower ratings of global functioning and more impaired social functioning, despite a lack of significant differences on overall severity of OCD symptoms. Individuals with OCD+OCPD also had higher rates of comorbid anxiety disorders and avoidant personality disorder. There was no difference in gender distribution between the OCD subjects with and without OCPD. While Diaferia et al. (1997) also reported no differences in gender or symptom severity when comparing OCD patients with and without OCPD, they did not find any differences in age of onset. In Coles et al. (in press), the OCD+OCPD subjects reported higher rate of symmetry and hoarding obsessions, and cleaning, ordering, repeating, and hoarding compulsions, as compared to OCD subjects without OCPD.

Another approach to studying the relationship between OCPD and OCD is to examine whether OCPD has a unique relationship with any of the symptom factors of OCD. Baer (1994) derived a grouping of OCPD symptoms that accounted for the majority of variance in OCPD symptoms. This primary OCPD factor was composed of preoccupation with details, perfectionism, and hoarding, the same three criteria found to be associated with OCD in Eisen (2006). Consistent with findings from Coles et al. (in press), Baer's primary OCPD symptom factor was most strongly correlated with an OCD symptom factor characterized by symmetry, ordering, repeating, counting, and hoarding. In addition, Mataix-Cols, Baer, Rauch, & Jenike (2000) reported that, independent of OCD symptom severity, hoarding symptoms predict a higher probability of having a personality disorder diagnosis, especially OCPD and avoidant.

FAMILY HISTORY

The question of a genetic link between OCD and OCPD has yet to be answered conclusively although there are indications of a familial relationship between them. Several earlier studies reported increased frequencies of OCPD traits in the parents of children with OCD (Lenane et al., 1990; Swedo et al., 1989). However, determination of the presence of these traits was made by the investigators without the use of a structured instrument. Using the Structured Interview for DSM-IIIR Personality (SIDP-R) (Pfohl, Blum, Zimmerman, & Stangl, 1989), Samuels et al. (2000) found a significantly greater frequency of OCPD in first degree relatives of OCD probands compared to relatives of control probands (11.5% vs. 5.8%, respectively). In fact, OCPD was the only *DSM-IV* personality disorder to occur more often in the relatives of OCD probands versus the relatives of control probands. Based on their data, the authors argued that OCPD and neuroticism may share a common familial etiology with OCD, and that the relationship between OCD and OCPD may be particularly strong for a subgroup of individuals with OCD. Additional research is needed to more clearly address the genetic/familial link between these disorders.

COURSE OF OCD VERSUS OCPD

Two studies evaluated individuals treated for OCD in childhood to assess the presence of OCPD in adulthood. The first study (Thomsen & Mikkelsen, 1993) assessed children who had been hospitalized for OCD and those who had been hospitalized for other psychiatric problems. Both groups had similar rates of personality disorders in general as well as OCPD in particular. OCPD was more common in those subjects whose OCD persisted into adulthood compared to the patients who no longer had OCD at follow-up. In the second study (Swedo et al., 1989), those whose OCD symptoms had remitted were just as likely to have OCPD as those with persistent OCD.

More recently, two studies have examined longitudinal associations between the disorders, with conflicting results. Using CLPS data, Shea et al. (2004) found that improvement in OCPD generally did not significantly predict remission from OCD. However, in the BLOCS clinical sample of OCD, the presence of OCPD was associated with a poorer course of OCD; those with comorbid OCPD at intake were half as likely to partially remit from OCD after two years, as compared to those without comorbid OCPD at intake (Eisen, 2006). Clearly, the longitudinal association between OCD and OCPD is an understudied area, which would shed light on the relationship between these two disorders.

TREATMENT RESPONSE

There is a striking paucity of data on the efficacy of psychological and pharmacological treatments for OCPD. Despite high levels of treatment utilization by individuals with OCPD – both in individual psychotherapy (Bender et al., 2001; Bender et al., 2006) and primary care (Sansone et al., 2003, 2004) settings – there is still no definitive empirically validated treatment for the disorder nor have there been any randomized controlled treatment trials for uncomplicated OCPD.

Various forms of psychotherapy have been described for OCPD, with very little empirical research to support them. Cognitive therapy (Bailey, 1998; Beck & Freeman, 1990; Beck, 1997) for OCPD involves challenging cognitive distortions such as 'all-or-nothing' thinking and overestimating the importance of making mistakes (catastrophizing). Because individuals with OCPD tend to show rigid thinking patterns and downplay the importance of emotional connections, establishing rapport can be difficult. In Young's schema-focused therapy (Young, 1999), the emphasis is on identifying, assessing, and challenging the patient's early maladaptive schemas as they erupt during the therapy process. Psychodynamic treatment has also been described as useful for OCPD (Gabbard, 2005; Gabbard & Newman, 2005). In one of the few psychotherapy outcome studies of OCPD, 14 *DSM-III-R* OCPD patients showed significant improvement on measures of personality disorders, depression, anxiety, general functioning, and interpersonal problems after one year of supportive-expressive psychodynamic therapy (Barber, Morse, Krakauer, Chittams, Crits-Christoph, 1997).

There have not been any direct studies of the pharmacological treatment of OCPD. The available evidence hints that OCP traits may selectively respond to serotonin reuptake inhibitors (SRIs). For example, Ekselius and von Knorring (1999) studied the effects of 24 weeks of sertraline and citalopram on 308 depressed patients with comorbid *DSM-III-R* personality disorders. Significant reductions in dysfunctional personality traits were observed in most personality disorder categories, including OCPD. In a 12-week study of clomipramine and imipramine in OCD, subjects in the clomipramine group showed a greater decrease in scores on the Self-Rating Obsessive–Compulsive Personality Inventory (SROCPI), as well as on measures of OCD and depression (Volavka, Neziroglu, & Yaryura-Tobias, 1985).

Does comorbid OCPD interfere in the clinical efficacy of gold standard OCD treatments, cognitive–behavioral therapy (CBT) and SRIs? While there are no data to answer this question with respect to CBT, the impact of comorbid OCPD on SRI treatment has been examined in three studies and results are equivocal. First, the presence of *DSM-III* OCPD was a predictor of better antidepressant response to 8 weeks of fluvoxamine in a sample of 46 outpatients seeking treatment for a major depressive episode, suggesting an enhancing therapeutic effect for OCPD comorbidity (Ansseau, Troisfontaines, Papart & von Freckell, 1991). Second, in a 12-week study of clomipramine in OCD, only the presence of schizotypal, borderline, and avoidant personality disorders predicted poorer treatment outcome; there was no effect for *DSM-III* OCPD (Baer et al., 1992). Finally, Cavedini, Erzegovesi, Ronchi, & Bellodi (1997) reported a worse outcome for patients with comorbid *DSM-III-R* OCPD (n = 9), as compared to those with uncomplicated OCD (n = 20), after 10 weeks of SRI treatment (either clomipramine or fluvoxamine). The authors concluded that comorbid OCPD may identify a subtype of OCD with a different pattern of SRI response. Future research is needed to systematically evaluate the possible influence of OCPD (and its core dimensions) on different therapeutic approaches for OCD (pharmacological, behavioral, or a combination) in larger samples.

SUMMARY OF EVIDENCE FOR AND AGAINST
OCD SPECTRUM MEMBERSHIP

Let us review the evidence for and against OCPD's membership in the OCD spectrum:

1. *Comorbidity:* While results have been varied, particularly with earlier versions of DSM, studies using *DSM-IV* criteria have found that about a fourth (to at most a third) of patients with OCD also meet criteria for OCPD. That being said, the majority of individuals with OCD (say 75%) do *not* have OCPD, which does not support theories of OCPD as a developmental precondition or prerequisite for OCD. Similarly, results from a personality disorder sample indicate that the majority of individuals with OCPD (80%) do not have OCD and are not more likely to develop OCD than other Axis I disorders, such as major depression or generalized anxiety disorder. However, the relationship between the disorders appears to have some specificity in that individuals with OCD are much more likely to have OCPD than individuals who do not have psychiatric disorders. The comorbidity of OCPD with other putative OCD spectrum disorders remains an open question because of limited data on all disorders except eating disorders. OCPD is strongly related to anorexia nervosa due to the important role of perfectionism in both disorders. The fact that OCPD shares major comorbidity with certain Axis I disorders (mood, anxiety, and eating disorders) with which OCD also has significant comorbidity is of note.

2. *Symptomatology:* While OCD symptoms are associated with greater distress and functional impairment, the symptomatic behaviors in both disorders tend to be repetitive, rule-bound or rigid, and aimed at reducing distress. The disorders also differ in terms of ego syntonicity, though this distinction is less clear when it comes to OCD hoarding. A recent study demonstrated a unique association between OCPD symptoms (hoarding, perfectionism, and preoccupation with details) and OCD. Conversely, particular OCD symptoms (symmetry, ordering, repeating, and hoarding) have shown strong associations to OCPD. Therefore, since both OCD and OCPD are heterogeneous disorders, one must look beyond the category level to understand their relationship. Specifically, the incompleteness dimension of OCD appears to be much more strongly related to the perfectionism traits and OCD-like behaviors of OCPD, rather than the rigidity/interpersonal traits of the personality disorder. Likewise, the perfectionism dimension of OCPD appears to be much more strongly related to incompleteness, rather than harm avoidance, in OCD.

3. *Course:* Both disorders have similar ages of onset and are regarded as chronic, though the diagnosis of OCPD may not be as stable as once thought. More research on the longitudinal association of the disorders would help clarify their relationship. Available data suggest that the presence of OCPD leads to poorer overall functioning and course of OCD.

4. *Family history:* There is initial evidence of a specific familial relationship between the disorders, with the rate of OCPD being twice as high in relatives of OCD probands as compared to the relatives of control probands.

5. *Genetics/neurobiology:* With only a handful of studies, research on the biological mechanisms of OCPD is severely underdeveloped. Studies of OCPD genetics, neuroimaging abnormalities, serotonergic function, and neurocognitive function are needed before any parallels can be drawn to OCD.

6. *Treatment response:* OCPD is also sorely lagging behind OCD in the area of treatment outcome research. Unlike OCD, OCPD lacks empirically validated treatments. Though there is a suggestion in the literature of a preferential response to SRIs in OCPD, this requires further investigation. In addition, there have been no attempts to study CBT response in OCPD. Further light on this question will be shed by systematic investigation of treatment response using much needed rater-administered measures of OCPD severity.

Future research is needed in several of the above domains before a more definitive conclusion can be reached regarding OCPD's membership in the OCD spectrum. For now, since categorical classifications of OCD and OCPD encompass heterogeneous groups of individuals, we propose that a subphenotype of OCPD – perfectionism – be considered as part of the OCD spectrum because of its similarities to OCD, particularly the incompleteness dimension of OCD, and anorexia nervosa, a putative spectrum member. Consistent with the hybrid model, perfectionism is thought to comprise stable personality traits and less stable symptomatic behaviors, such as list-making, ordering, repeating, all of which overlap with compulsions in OCD. The other core dimension of OCPD, rigidity, is interpersonal in nature and more likely to be related to constructs outside the OCD spectrum, such as problems related to aggression. Studying more homogeneous components, such as incompleteness in OCD and perfectionism in OCPD, may be a more fruitful way to explore the relationship between these disorders, in terms of family history, course, and treatment response. For instance, would rates of OCPD be even higher in relatives of OCD probands with primary incompleteness? Preliminary evidence suggests that ongoing OCD genetic research may be enhanced by using OCPD perfectionism as a potential marker of a specific OCD phenotype that may have a strong familial component.

CONCLUSIONS

OCPD is characterized by profound perfectionism and rigidity that leads to significant distress or impairment, particularly in areas of interpersonal functioning. There have been many theories regarding the etiology of OCPD, including biological and psychological models, but limited empirical data to support them. There are no empirically based treatments for OCPD, although there is literature describing both cognitive and psychoanalytically based approaches, as well as the possibility of a selective response to SRIs. Clearly more systematic research is needed to further investigate the treatment options for OCPD.

Despite long-standing interest in the psychiatric community, the relationship between OCD and OCPD currently remains unclear since more research is needed to compare the disorders on course, family history, neurobiology, and treatment response. Investigators have postulated that the disorders may share a common familial etiology. Patients with OCD have higher rates of OCPD than the general population. In terms of symptomatology, specific OCPD criteria (hoarding, perfectionism, and preoccupation with details) are more common in patients with OCD. In addition, particular OCD symptoms (symmetry, ordering, repeating, and hoarding) have shown strong associations to OCPD. As a result, we propose that a subphenotype of OCPD, perfectionism, be considered for inclusion in the OCD spectrum based on its similarities to OCD and OCD incompleteness.

REFERENCES

Abraham, K. (1921/1953). Contributions to the theory of the anal character. In D. Bryan & A. T. Strachey (Eds.), *Selected papers of Karl Abraham*. London: Hogarth Press.

Adams, P. (1973). *Obsessive children: A sociopsychiatric study*. New York: Brunner/Mazel.

Albert, U., Maina, G., Forner, F., Bogetto, F. (2004). DSM-IV obsessive–compulsive personality disorder: Prevalence in patients with anxiety disorders and in healthy comparison subjects. *Comprehensive Psychiatry, 45*(5), 325–332.

American Psychiatric Association (1968). *Diagnostic and statistical manual of mental disorders* (2nd ed.) *(DSM-II)*. Washington, DC: American Psychiatric Association.

American Psychiatric Association (1987). *Diagnostic and statistical manual of mental disorders* (3rd revised ed.) *(DSM-IIIR)*. Washington, DC: American Psychiatric Association.

American Psychiatric Association (1994). *Diagnostic and statistical manual of mental disorders* (4th ed.) *(DSM-IV)*. Washington, DC: American Psychiatric Association.

Anderluh, M. B., Tchanturia, K., Rabe-Hesketh, S., & Treasure, J. (2003). Childhood obsessive–compulsive personality traits in adult women with eating disorders: defining a broader eating disorder phenotype. *Am. J. Psychiatry, 160*(2), 242–247.

Angyal, A. (1965). *Neurosis and treatment: A holistic theory*. New York: John Wiley and Sons.

Ansseau, M., Troisfontaines, B., Papart, P., & von Frenckell, R. (1991). Compulsive personality as predictor of response to serotoninergic antidepressants. *BMJ, 303*(6805), 760–761.

Baer, L. (1994). Factor analysis of symptom subtypes of obsessive compulsive disorder and their relation to personality and tic disorders. *Journal of Clinical Psychiatry, 55*(Suppl.), 18–23.

Baer, L., & Jenike, M. A. (1992). Personality disorders in obsessive compulsive disorder. *Psychiatric Clinics of North America, 15*(4), 803–812.

Baer, L., & Jenike, M. A. (1998). Personality disorders in obsessive–compulsive disorder. In M. A. Jenike, L. Baer, & W. E. Minichiello (Eds.), *Obsessive Compulsive Disorders: Pratical Management* (3rd ed.). St Louis, MO: Mosby.

Baer, L., Jenike, M. A., Black, D. W., Treece, C., Rosenfeld, R., & Greist, J. (1992). Effect of axis II diagnoses on treatment outcome with clomipramine in 55 patients with obsessive–compulsive disorder. *Archives of General Psychiatry, 49*(11), 862–866.

Baer, L., Jenike, M. A., Ricciardi, J. N., 2nd, Holland, A. D., Seymour, R. J., Minichiello, W. E., & Buttolph, M. L. (1990). Standardized assessment of personality disorders in obsessive–compulsive disorder. *Archives of General Psychiatry, 47*(9), 826–830.

Bailey, G. R., Jr. (1998). Cognitive–behavioral treatment of obsessive–compulsive personality disorder. *Journal of Psychological Practice, 4*(1), 51–59.

Barber, J. P., Morse, J. Q., Krakauer, I., Chittams, J., & Crits-Christoph, K. (1997). Change in obsessive–compulsive and avoidant personality disorders following time-limited supportive-expressive therapy. *Psychotherapy, 34*, 133–143.

Beck, A. T., & Freeman, A. (1990). *Cognitive therapy of personality disorders*. New York: Guilford Press.

Beck, J. S. (1997). Cognitive approaches to personality disorders. In J. H. Wright & M. E. Thase (Eds.), *Cognitive therapy review of psychotherapy.* Washington, DC: American Psychiatric Press.

Bender, D. S., Dolan, R. T., Skodol, A. E., Sanislow, C. A., Dyck, I. R., McGlashan, T. H., et al. (2001). Treatment utilization by patients with personality disorders. *American Journal of Psychiatry, 158*(2), 295–302.

Bender, D. S., Skodol, A. E., Pagano, M. E., Dyck, I. R., Grilo, C. M., Shea, M. T., et al. (2006) Prospective assessment of treatment use by patients with personality disorders. *Psychiatric Services, 57*(2), 254–257.

Bernstein, D. P., Cohen, P., Velez, C. N., Schwab-Stone, M., Siever, L. J., & Shinsato, L. (1993). Prevalence and stability of the DSM-III-R personality disorders in a community-based survey of adolescents. *American Journal of Psychiatry, 150*(8), 1237–1243.

Black, D. W., Noyes, R., Jr., Pfohl, B., Goldstein, R. B., & Blum, N. (1993). Personality disorder in obsessive-compulsive volunteers, well comparison subjects, and their first-degree relatives. *American Journal of Psychiatry, 150*(8), 1226–1232.

Blashfield, R. K., & Intoccia, V. (2000). Growth of the literature on the topic of personality disorders. *American Journal of Psychiatry, 157*(3), 472–473.

Blatt, S. J., Zuroff, D. C., Bondi, C. M., Sanislow, C. A., 3rd, & Pilkonis, P. A. (1998). When and how perfectionism impedes the brief treatment of depression: further analyses of the National Institute of Mental Health Treatment of Depression Collaborative Research Program. *Journal of Consulting and Clinical Psychology, 66*(2), 423–428.

Cavedini, P., Erzegovesi, S., Ronchi, P., & Bellodi, L. (1997). Predictive value of obsessive–compulsive personality disorder in antiobsessional pharmacological treatment. *European Neuropsychopharmacology, 7*(1), 45–49.

Chamberlain, S. R., Fineberg, N. A., Blackwell, A. D., Robbins, T. W., Sahakian, B. J. (2006). Motor inhibition and cognitive flexibility in obsessive–compulsive disorder and trichotillomania. *American Journal of Psychiatry, 163*(7), 1282–1284.

Chavira, D. A., Grilo, C. M., Shea, M. T., Yen, S., Gunderson, J. G., Morey, L. C., et al. (2003). Ethnicity and four personality disorders. *Comprehensive Psychiatry, 44*(6), 483–491.

Coles, M. E., Pinto, A., Mancebo, M. C., Rasmussen, S. A., Eisen, J. L. (in press). OCD with comorbid OCPD: A subtype of OCD? *Journal of Psychiatric Research.*

Costa, P. T., Jr., & McCrae, R. R. (1992a). The five-factor model of personality and its relevance to personality disorders. *Journal of Personality Disorders, 6,* 343–359.

Costa, P. T., Jr., & McCrae, R. R. (1992b). *Revised NEO Personality Inventory (NEO-PI-R) and NEO Five-Factor Inventory (NEO-FFI) professional manual.* Odessa, FL: Psychological Assessment Resources.

Crino, R. D., & Andrews, G. (1996). Personality disorder in obsessive compulsive disorder: a controlled study. *Journal of Psychiatric Research, 30*(1), 29–38.

Diaferia, G., Bianchi, I., Bianchi, M. L., Cavedini, P., Erzegovesi, S., & Bellodi, L. (1997). Relationship between obsessive–compulsive personality disorder and obsessive–compulsive disorder. *Comprehensive Psychiatry, 38*(1), 38–42.

Dinn, W. M., Harris, C. L., Aycicegi, A., Greene, P., & Andover, M. S. (2002). Positive and negative schizotypy in a student sample: neurocognitive and clinical correlates. *Schizophrenia Research, 56*(1–2), 171–185.

Eisen, J. L. (2006). *OCD Subtypes based on course and clinical features.* Paper presented at the American Psychiatric Association Annual Meeting, Toronto, Canada.

Eisen, J. L., Coles, M. E., Shea, M. T., Pagano, M. E., Stout, R. L., Yen, S., et al. (2006). Clarifying the convergence between obsessive compulsive personality disorder criteria and obsessive compulsive disorder. *Journal of Personality Disorders, 20*(3), 294–305.

Eisen, J. L., & Rasmussen, S. A. (1991). *OCD and compulsive traits: phenomenology and outcome.* Paper presented at the American Psychiatric Association 144th Annual Meeting, New Orleans, LA.

Ekselius, L., Tillfors, M., Furmark, T., & Fredrikson, M. (2001). Personality disorders in the general population: DSM-IV and ICD-10 defined prevalence as related to sociodemographic profile. *Personality and Individual Differences, 30,* 311–320.

Ekselius, L., & Von Knorring, L. (1999). Changes in personality traits during treatment with sertraline or citalopram. *British Journal of Psychiatry, 174,* 444–448.

Farmer, R. F., & Chapman, A. L. (2002). Evaluation of DSM-IV personality disorder criteria as assessed by the structured clinical interview for DSM-IV personality disorders. *Comprehensive Psychiatry, 43*(4), 285–300.

Freud, S. (1908/1963). Character and anal eroticism. In P. Reiff (Ed.), *Collected papers of Sigmund Freud* (Vol. 10). New York: Collier.

Gabbard, G. O. (2005). *Psychodynamic psychiatry in clinical practice* (4th ed.). Washington, DC: American Psychiatric Publishing.

Gabbard, G. O., & Newman, C. F. (2005). Psychotherapy of obsessive compulsive personality disorder. In G. O. Gabbard, J. Beck, & J. A. Holmes (Eds.), *Oxford textbook of psychotherapy*. Oxford: Oxford University Press.

Goodman, W. K., Price, L. H., Rasmussen, S. A., Mazure, C., Fleischmann, R. L., Hill, C. L., et al. (1989). The Yale–Brown Obsessive Compulsive Scale. I. Development, use, and reliability. *Archives of General Psychiatry, 46*(11), 1006–1011.

Grant, B. F., Hasin, D. S., Stinson, F. S., Dawson, D. A., Chou, S. P., Ruan, W. J., Pickering, R. P. (2004). Prevalence, correlates, and disability of personality disorders in the United States: results from the national epidemiologic survey on alcohol and related conditions. *Journal of Clinical Psychiatry, 65*(7), 948–958.

Grilo, C. M. (2004). Diagnostic efficiency of DSM-IV criteria for obsessive compulsive personality disorder in patients with binge eating disorder. *Behavior Research and Therapy, 42*(1), 57–65.

Grilo, C. M. (2004). Factor structure of DSM-IV criteria for obsessive compulsive personality disorder in patients with binge eating disorder. *Acta Psychiatrica Scandinavica, 109*(1), 64–69.

Grilo, C. M., & McGlashan, T. H. (1999). Stability and course of personality disorders. *Current Opinion in Psychiatry, 12,* 157–162.

Grilo, C. M., McGlashan, T. H., Morey, L. C., Gunderson, J. G., Skodol, A. E., Shea, M. T., et al. (2001). Internal consistency, intercriterion overlap and diagnostic efficiency of criteria sets for DSM-IV schizotypal, borderline, avoidant and obsessive-compulsive personality disorders. *Acta Psychiatrica Scandinavica, 104*(4), 264–272.

Grilo, C. M., Sanislow, C. A., Gunderson, J. G., Pagano, M. E., Yen, S., Zanarini, M. C., et al. (2004). Two-year stability and change of schizotypal, borderline, avoidant, and obsessive–compulsive personality disorders. *Journal of Consulting and Clinical Psychology, 72*(5), 767–775.

Grilo, C. M., Skodol, A. E., Gunderson, J. G., Sanislow, C. A., Stout, R. L., Shea, M. T., et al. (2004). Longitudinal diagnostic efficiency of DSM-IV criteria for obsessive–compulsive personality disorder: a 2-year prospective study. *Acta Psychiatrica Scandinavica, 110,* 64–68.

Guidano, V. F., & Liotti, G. (1983). *Cognitive processes and emotional disorders.* New York: Guilford Press.

Gunderson, J. G., Shea, M. T., Skodol, A. E., McGlashan, T. H., Morey, L. C., Stout, R. L., et al. (2000). The Collaborative Longitudinal Personality Disorders Study: development, aims, design, and sample characteristics. *Journal of Personality Disorders, 14*(4), 300–315.

Haring, M., Hewitt, P. L., & Flett, G. L. (2003). Perfectionism, coping, and quality of intimate relationships. *Journal of Marriage and Family, 65,* 143–158.

Hewitt, P. L., Flett, G. L., & Weber, C. (1994). Dimensions of perfectionism and suicide ideation. *Cognitive Therapy and Research, 18,* 439–460.

Hewitt, P. L., Newton, J., Flett, G. L., & Callander, L. (1997). Perfectionism and suicide ideation in adolescent psychiatric patients. *Journal of Abnormal Child Psychology, 25*(2), 95–101.

Hewlett, W. A., Vinogradov, S., Martin, K., Berman, S., & Csernansky, J. G. (1992). Fenfluramine stimulation of prolactin in obsessive–compulsive disorder. *Psychiatry Research, 42*(1), 81–92.

Horesh, N., Dolberg, O. T., Kirschenbaum-Aviner, N., & Kotler, M. (1997). Personality differences between obsessive–compulsive disorder subtypes: washers versus checkers. *Psychiatry Research, 71*(3), 197–200.

Irle, E., Exner, C., Thielen, K., Weniger, G., & Ruther, E. (1998). Obsessive–compulsive disorder and ventromedial frontal lesions: clinical and neuropsychological findings. *American Journal of Psychiatry, 155*(2), 255–263.

Janet, P. (1904). *Les obsessions et al psychasthenie* (2nd ed.). Paris: Bailliere.

Johnson, J. G., Rabkin, J. G., Williams, J. B., Remien, R. H., & Gorman, J. M. (2000). Difficulties in interpersonal relationships associated with personality disorders and axis I disorders: a community-based longitudinal investigation. *Journal of Personality Disorders, 14*(1), 42–56.

Karno, M., Golding, I., Sorenson, S., & Burnam, M. (1988). The epidemiology of obsessive–compulsive disorder in five US communities. *Archives of General Psychiatry, 45*, 1094–1099.

Karwautz, A., Troop, N. A., Rabe-Hesketh, S., Collier, D. A., & Treasure, J. L. (2003). Personality disorders and personality dimensions in anorexia nervosa. *Journal of Personality Disorders, 17*(1), 73–85.

Kline, P. (1967). Obsessional traits and emotional instability in a normal population. *British Journal of Medical Psychology, 40*, 153–157.

Kline, P. (1968). Obsessional traits, obsessional symptoms and anal eroticism. *British Journal of Medical Psychology, 41*, 299–305.

Lenane, M., Swedo, S. E., Leonard, H. L., Pauls, D. L., Sceery, W., & Rapoport, J. L. (1990). Psychiatric disorders in first degree relatives of children and adolescents with obsessive-compulsive disorder. *Journal of the American Academy of Child and Adolescent Psychiatry, 29*, 407–412.

Lewinsohn, P. M., Rohde, P., Seeley, J. R., & Klein, D. N. (1997). Axis II psychopathology as a function of Axis I disorders in childhood and adolescence. *Journal of the American Academy of Child and Adolescent Psychiatry, 36*(12), 1752–1759.

Lilenfeld, L. R., Kaye, W. H., Greeno, C. G., Merikangas, K. R., Plotnicov, K., Pollice, C., et al. (1998). A controlled family study of anorexia nervosa and bulimia nervosa: psychiatric disorders in first-degree relatives and effects of proband comorbidity. *Archives of General Psychiatry, 55*(7), 603–610.

Lucey, J. V., O'Keane, V., Butcher, G., Clare, A. W., & Dinan, T. G. (1992). Cortisol and prolactin responses to d-fenfluramine in non-depressed patients with obsessive–compulsive disorder: a comparison with depressed and healthy controls. *British Journal of Psychiatry, 161*, 517–521.

Lynam, D. R., & Widiger, T. A. (2001). Using the five-factor model to represent the DSM-IV personality disorders: an expert consensus approach. *Journal of Abnormal Psychology, 110*(3), 401–412.

Mancebo, M. C., Eisen, J. L., Grant, J. E., & Rasmussen, S. A. (2005). Obessive compulsive personality disorder and obsessive compulsive disorder: clinical characteristics, diagnostic difficulties, and treatment. *Annals of Clinical Psychiatry, 17*(4), 197–204.

Mataix-Cols, D., Baer, L., Rauch, S. L., & Jenike, M. A. (2000). Relation of factor-analyzed symptom dimensions of obsessive-compulsive disorder to personality disorders. *Acta Psychiatry Scandinavica, 102*(3), 199–202.

Matsunaga, H., Kiriike, N., Matsui, T., Miyata, A., Iwasaki, Y., Fujimoto, K., et al. (2000). Gender differences in social and interpersonal features and personality disorders among Japanese patients with obsessive–compulsive disorder. *Comprehensive Psychiatry, 41*(4), 266–272.

Matsunaga, H., Miyata, A., Iwasaki, Y., Matsui, T., Fujimoto, K., & Kiriike, N. (1999). A comparison of clinical features among Japanese eating-disordered women with obsessive–compulsive disorder. *Comprehensive Psychiatry, 40*(5), 337–342.

McGlashan, T. H., Grilo, C. M., Sanislow, C. A., Ralevski, E., Morey, L. C., Gunderson, J. G., et al. (2005). Two-year prevalence and stability of individual DSM-IV criteria for schizotypal, borderline, avoidant, and obsessive–compulsive personality disorders: toward a hybrid model of axis II disorders. *American Journal of Psychiatry, 162*(5), 883–889.

McGlashan, T. H., Grilo, C. M., Skodol, A. E., Gunderson, J. G., Shea, M. T., Morey, L. C., et al. (2000). The Collaborative Longitudinal Personality Disorders Study: baseline Axis I/II and II/II diagnostic co-occurrence. *Acta Psychiatrica Scandinavica, 102*(4), 256–264.

Millon, T. (1981). *Disorders of personality: DSM-III, Axis II.* New York: Wiley.

Millon, T., & Everly, G. (1985). *Personality and its disorders.* New York: Wiley.

Nestadt, G., Romanoski, A. J., Brown, C. H., Chahal, R., Merchant, A., Folstein, M. F., et al. (1991). DSM-III compulsive personality disorder: an epidemiological survey. *Psychological Medicine, 21*(2), 461–471.

Nilsson, E. W., Gillberg, C., Gillberg, I. C., & Rastam, M. (1999). Ten-year follow-up of adolescent-onset anorexia nervosa: personality disorders. *Journal of the American Academy of Child and Adolescent Psychiatry, 38*(11), 1389–1395.

Perez, M., Brown, J. S., Vrshek-Schallhorn, S., Johnson, F., & Joiner, T. E., Jr. (2006). Differentiation of obsessive–compulsive-, panic-, obsessive–compulsive personality-, and non-disordered individuals by variation in the promoter region of the serotonin transporter gene. *Journal of Anxiety Disorders, 20*(6), 794–806.

Pfohl, B. (1996). Obsessive–compulsive personality disorder. In T. A. Widiger, H. A. Pincus, R. Ross, M. First, & W. Wakefield (Eds.), *DSM-IV Sourcebook* (Vol. 2, pp. 777–789). Washington, DC: American Psychiatric Association.

Pfohl, B., & Blum, N. (1995). Obsessive–compulsive personality disorder. In W. J. Livesley (Ed.), *The DSM-IV personality disorders*. New York: Guilford Press.

Pfohl, B., Blum, N., Zimmerman, M., & Stangl, D. (1989). *Structured interview for DSM-IIIR personality SIDP-R*. Iowa City: University of Iowa College of Medicine.

Phillips, K. A., Menard, W., Fay, C., & Weisberg, R. (2005). Demographic characteristics, phenomenology, comorbidity, and family history in 200 individuals with body dysmorphic disorder. *Psychosomatics, 46*(4), 317–325.

Pincus, A. L., & Wiggins, J. S. (1990). Interpersonal problems and conceptions of personality disorders. *Journal of Personality Disorders, 4*(342–352).

Pinto, A., Ansell, E. B., Grilo, C. M., & Shea, M. T. (2007). *A multidimensional model of obsessive–compulsive personality disorder*. Paper presented at the Annual meeting of the American Psychiatric Association, San Diego, California.

Pinto, A., Mancebo, M. C., Eisen, J. L., Pagano, M. E., & Rasmussen, S. A. (2006). The Brown Longitudinal Obsessive Compulsive Study: Clinical features and symptoms of the sample at intake. *Journal of Clinical Psychiatry, 67*, 703–711.

Pitman, R. K. (1987). Pierre Janet on obsessive–compulsive disorder (1903). *Archive of General Psychiatry, 44*, 226–232.

Pollak, J. (1987). Obsessive–compulsive personality: Theoretical and clinical perspectives and recent research findings. *Journal of Personality Disorders, 1*(3), 248–262.

Pollak, J. M. (1987). Relationship of obsessive–compulsive personality to obsessive-compulsive disorder: a review of the literature. *Journal of Psychology: Interdisciplinary and Applied, 121*(2), 137–148.

Rasmussen, S. A., & Eisen, J. (1992). The epidemiology and clinical features of OCD. In M. A. Jenike (Ed.), *Psychiatric Clinics of North America* (Vol. 15, pp. 743–758). Philadelphia, PA: W.B. Saunders Co.

Rice, K. G., & Aldea, M. A. (2006). State dependence and trait stability of perfectionism: A short-term longitudinal study. *Journal of Counseling Psychology, 53*, 205–212.

Salzman, L. (1973). *The obsessive personality*. New York: Jason Aronson.

Samuels, J., Eaton, W. W., Bienvenu, O. J., 3rd, Brown, C. H., Costa, P. T., Jr., & Nestadt, G. (2002). Prevalence and correlates of personality disorders in a community sample. *British Journal of Psychiatry, 180*, 536–542.

Samuels, J., Nestadt, G., Bienvenu, O. J., Costa, P. T., Jr., Riddle, M. A., Liang, K. Y., et al. (2000). Personality disorders and normal personality dimensions in obsessive–compulsive disorder. *British Journal of Psychiatry, 177*, 457–462.

Sanderson, W. C., Wetzler, S., Beck, A. T., & Betz, F. (1994). Prevalence of personality disorders among patients with anxiety disorders. *Psychiatry Research, 51*(2), 167–174.

Sansone, R. A., Hendricks, C. M., Gaither, G. A., & Reddington, A. (2004). Prevalence of anxiety symptoms among a sample of outpatients in an internal medicine clinic: a pilot study. *Depression and Anxiety, 19*(2), 133–136.

Sansone, R. A., Hendricks, C. M., Sellbom, M., & Reddington, A. (2003). Anxiety symptoms and healthcare utilization among a sample of outpatients in an internal medicine clinic. *International Journal of Psychiatry in Medicine, 33*(2), 133–139.

Sciuto, G., Diaferia, G., Battaglia, M., Perna, G., Gabriele, A., & Bellodi, L. (1991). DSM-III-R personality disorders in panic and obsessive-compulsive disorder: a comparison study. *Comprehensive Psychiatry, 32*(5), 450–457.

Shafran, R., & Mansell, W. (2001). Perfectionism and psychopathology: a review of research and treatment. *Clinical Psychology Review, 21*(6), 879–906.

Shapiro, D. (1965). *Neurotic styles*. New York: Basic Books.

Shapiro, D. (1981). *Autonomy and rigid character*. New York: Basic Books.

Shea, M. T., Stout, R. L., Yen, S., Pagano, M. E., Skodol, A. E., Morey, L. C., et al. (2004). Associations in the course of personality disorders and Axis I disorders over time. *Journal of Abnormal Psychology, 113*(4), 499–508.

Skodol, A. E., Gunderson, J. G., McGlashan, T. H., Dyck, I. R., Stout, R. L., Bender, D. S., et al. (2002). Functional impairment in patients with schizotypal, borderline, avoidant, or obsessive–compulsive personality disorder. *American Journal of Psychiatry, 159*(2), 276–283.

Skodol, A. E., Oldham, J. M., Hyler, S. E., Stein, D. J., Hollander, E., Gallaher, P. E., et al. (1995). Patterns of anxiety and personality disorder comorbidity. *Journal of Psychiatric Research, 5*, 361–374.

Skodol, A. E., Pagano, M. E., Bender, D. S., Shea, M. T., Gunderson, J. G., Yen, S., et al. (2005). Stability of functional impairment in patients with schizotypal, borderline, avoidant, or obsessive–compulsive personality disorder over two years. *Psychological Medicine, 35*(3), 443–451.

Stanley, M. A., Turner, S. M., & Borden, J. W. (1990). Schizotypal features in obsessive–compulsive disorder. *Comprehensive Psychiatry, 31*(6), 511–518.

Starcevic, V. (1990). Relationship between hypochondriasis and obsessive–compulsive personality disorder: close relatives separated by nosological schemes? *American Journal of Psychotherapy, 44*(3), 340–347.

Stein, D. J., Trestman, R. L., Mitropoulou, V., Coccaro, E. F., Hollander, E., & Siever, L. J. (1996). Impulsivity and serotonergic function in compulsive personality disorder. *Journal of Neuropsychiatry and Clinical Neuroscience, 8*(4), 393–398.

Stuart, S., Pfohl, B., Battaglia, M., Bellodi, L., Grove, W., & Cadoret, R. (1998). The cooccurrence of DSM-III-R personality disorders. *Journal of Personality Disorders, 12*(4), 302–315.

Sullivan, H. S. (1956). *Clinical studies in psychiatry*. New York: Norton.

Summerfeldt, L. J. (2004). Understanding and treating incompleteness in obsessive–compulsive disorder. *Journal of Clinical Psychology, 60*(11), 1155–1168.

Summerfeldt, L. J., Antony, M. M., & Swinson, R. P. (2000). *Incompleteness: a link between perfectionistic traits and OCD*. Paper presented at the Association for the Advancement of Behavior Therapy meeting, New Orleans, LA.

Summerfeldt, L. J., Kloosterman, P., Parker, J. D. A., Antony, M. M., & Swinson, R. P. (2001). *Assessing and validating the obsessive–compulsive-related construct of incompleteness*. Paper presented at the Canadian Psychological Association, Stey-foy, Quebec.

Swedo, S. E., Rapoport, J. L., Leonard, H. L., Lenane, M. C., and Cheslow, D. (1989). Obsessive–compulsive disorder in children and adolescents: clinical and phenomenology of 70 consecutive cases. *Archives of General Psychiatry, 46*, 335–341.

Thomsen, P. H., & Mikkelsen, H. U. (1993). Development of personality disorders in children and adolescents with obsessive–compulsive disorder. A 6- to 22-year follow-up study. *Acta Psychiatrica Scandinavica, 87*(6), 456–462.

Torgersen, S., Kringlen, E., & Cramer, V. (2001). The prevalence of personality disorders in a community sample. *Archives of General Psychiatry, 58*, 590–596.

Torgersen, S., Lygren, S., Oien, P. A., Skre, I., Onstad, S., Edvardsen, J., et al. (2000). A twin study of personality disorders. *Comprehensive Psychiatry, 41*(6), 416–425.

Torres, A. R., & Del Porto, J. A. (1995). Comorbidity of obsessive–compulsive disorder and personality disorders. *Psychopathology, 28*, 322–329.

Villemarette-Pittman, N. R., Stanford, M. S., Greve, K. W., Houston, R. J., & Mathias, C. W. (2004). Obsessive–compulsive personality disorder and behavioral disinhibition. *Journal of Psychology, 138*(1), 5–22.

Volavka, J., Neziroglu, F., & Yaryura-Tobias, J. A. (1985). Clomipramine and imipramine in obsessive–compulsive disorder. *Psychiatry Research, 14*(1), 85–93.

Widiger, T. A. (2005). A dimensional model of personality disorder. *Current Opinion in Psychiatry, 18*(1), 41–43.

Wilfley, D. E., Friedman, M. A., Dounchis, J. Z., Stein, R. I., Welch, R. R., & Ball, S. A. (2000) Comorbid psychopathology in binge eating disorder: relation to eating disorder severity at baseline and following treatment. *Journal of Consulting and Clinical Psychology, 68*(4), 641–649.

Young, J. E. (1999). *Cognitive therapy for personality disorders: a schema-focused approach* (3rd ed.). Sarasota, FL: Professional Resource Press.

16

IS NONPARAPHILIC COMPULSIVE SEXUAL BEHAVIOR A VARIANT OF OCD?

JONATHAN S. ABRAMOWITZ

The University of North Carolina at Chapel Hill

Variously referred to as sexual 'addictions', 'compulsions', or 'hypersexuality', nonparaphilic compulsive sexual behaviors (NCSBs) include repetitive sexual acts comprised of conventional, normative, or nondeviant sexual thoughts or behaviors that the person feels compelled or driven to perform, often in an exploitative way, which may or may not cause distress (Goldsmith, Shapira, Phillips, & McElroy, 1998). Well-known examples include the incessant use of Internet pornography, frequent masturbation (often with the aid of conventional stimuli), and continuous sexual encounters with prostitutes to the detriment of one's marital relationship. Although NCSBs are not described *per se* in the *Diagnostic and Statistical Manual of Mental Disorders* (e.g., *DSM-IV-TR*; American Psychiatric Association, 2000), people for whom this pattern of behavior persists for at least six months and interferes with their functioning are considered to meet criteria for impulse-control disorder not otherwise specified (NOS). Due in large part to the repetitive, perseverative nature of the sexual thoughts, urges, and behaviors in this condition, proponents of an obsessive–compulsive spectrum (OCS) proposal (e.g., Hollander, Friedberg, Wasserman, Yeh, & Iyengar, 2005) have drawn parallels between NCSBs and obsessive–compulsive disorder (OCD) and suggested that NCSBs are a variant of OCD. This chapter begins with a description of the essential clinical features of NCSBs.

Correspondence to: Jonathan S. Abramowitz, Department of Psychology, Campus Box 3270 (Davie Hall), University of North Carolina at Chapel Hill, Chapel Hill, NC 27514.

Next, the scant research on etiological and conceptual models of these difficulties is reviewed. The possible relationship between NCSBs and OCD is then examined in detail, before turning to a discussion of issues related to the treatment of NCSBs.

CLINICAL FEATURES

PARAPHILIC VERSUS NONPARAPHILIC SEXUAL BEHAVIOR

Table 16.1 lists paraphilic sexual disorders defined in *DSM-IV-TR*. The essential features of paraphilias are recurrent, intense, sexually arousing fantasies, urges, or behaviors that fall outside the culturally accepted realm of sexual activity. Individuals with such problems often use one or more of the following as a source of sexual gratification: Nonhuman objects; the suffering or humiliation of oneself or one's partner; and children and other nonconsenting persons. This behavior pattern persists over a period of at least six months, and in most instances it creates personal distress (although some paraphilias such as sexual sadism do not require the presence of distress for a clinical diagnosis). Individuals with paraphilias often report that these behaviors have become their primary sexual activity. When such behavior is unlawful (e.g., exhibitionism), the irresistible urges associated with it often lead to arrest and incarceration.

In contrast, nonparaphilic compulsive sexual behavior involves unrestrained practice of normative, culturally sanctioned, heterosexual or homosexual activity. It is neither culturally deviant nor illegal. Commonly identified NCSBs are listed in Table 16.2 (Coleman, 1992; Cooper & Scherer, 1999; Kafka & Prentky, 1997). The clinical vignette below further illustrates the cardinal features of NCSBs.

TABLE 16.1   Paraphilias defined in *DSM-IV-TR*

Exhibitionism: Exposure of genitals

Fetishism: Use of nonliving objects

Frotteurism: Touching or rubbing against a nonconsenting person

Sexual masochism: Receiving suffering or humiliation

Sexual sadism: Inflicting suffering or humiliation

Transvestic fetishism: Cross-dressing

Voyeurism: Observing sexual behavior

Paraphilia not otherwise specified: Includes, but is not limited to:

Necrophilia: Sexual gratification involving corpses

Zoophilia: Sexual gratification involving animals

Coprophilia: Sexual gratification involving fecal matter

Klismaphilia: Sexual gratification involving enemas

Urophilia: Sexual gratification involving urine

Matt was a 48-year-old pastor at a small suburban church. As such, he was under no authority other than that of an all male 'Board of Elders' which he had personally selected to govern the church. Matt's childhood was relatively uneventful, except that when Matt was an adolescent, his father was often ill. Because he lived in a rural area, both of his parents often traveled (sometimes for days at a time) to see doctors in far-away metropolitan areas. It was during one of these times when Matt was alone that he discovered his father's large collection of pornography in his closet. Matt regularly visited this collection and discovered masturbation. This habit continued through high school and college as Matt was not particularly sociable. At the age of 24, he met and married his wife, Karen. For the first three years of marriage, his pattern of pornography use and masturbation subsided as he and his wife engaged in regular sexual activity. Following the birth of their first (and only) child, the frequency of intercourse decreased and Matt resumed his use of pornography.

Matt's behavior had few negative consequences until the family obtained a personal computer with on-line access. Gradually, and in increasing amounts of time, Matt found himself leaving his office at the church and coming back home in the middle of the day to access pornography on the Internet and masturbate. Time alone for this behavior was readily available since the demands of his church left Matt with plenty of unscheduled and unstructured time. Moreover, his daughter was in school and Karen worked outside the home.

As time went on, Matt found himself spending more and more time thinking about and planning his autoerotic behaviors, and fantasizing about the women he had met and chatted with on-line about sex (although he never actually met them or engaged in any extramarital sexual activity). Problems began to arise, however, when several church members discovered that Matt was spending very little time at the church, and even missing Board meetings. He was also spending a great deal of money to purchase access to pornographic websites. Although Matt generally oversaw the family's accounting, his wife occasionally noticed mysterious charges on credit card statements. Matt's frequency of masturbation continued at a pace of one to three times per day; and he often accessed the Internet late at night after Karen had gone to sleep. Matt decided to seek help the very next day after Karen had walked in on him masturbating in his study late one night.

TABLE 16.2 Common forms of nonparaphilic compulsive sexual behavior

Frequent masturbation that interferes with time spent engaged in more productive activities

Persistent promiscuity that results in relationship distress or health issues

Compulsive 'cruising' for sex, including in public bathrooms, parks, bookstores

Repeated fantasies and fixation on an unobtainable partner

Dependence for sexual arousal on:
- pornography, including Internet websites, movies, videos, and telephone sex
- drugs (e.g., alcohol, stimulants such as methamphetamines, amyl nitrate or 'poppers')

PREVALENCE, COMORBIDITY, AND DEMOGRAPHIC CHARACTERISTICS

There is very little research on the epidemiology of NCSBs, and the few existing studies are limited by the lack of a consistent and validated set of diagnostic criteria, sample size, and the frequent grouping together of paraphilic and nonparaphilic conditions. Published prevalence estimates range from 3% to 5% (Coleman, 1992; Goodman, 1993; Quadland, 1985). More men than women present for treatment, and more men appear to be affected, although this may result from bias towards a male-based definition of sexuality (Coleman, 1992), and more societal tolerance of sexual nonconformity by men, which may make it easier for them to admit to these behaviors and to seek help.

With respect to patterns of comorbidity, a study of 32 men with NCSBs by Kafka and Hennen (2002) found lifetime prevalence rates of 72% and 38% for mood and anxiety disorders, respectively. The most common mood disorder was dysthymia and the most common anxiety disorder was social phobia. Comorbidity for substance abuse and impulse control disorders were 25% and 16%, respectively. Raymond, Coleman, & Miner (2003) found that among 25 adults (23 men and 2 women) with NCSBs, 96% had a lifetime diagnosis of an anxiety disorder, most commonly social phobia; and 71% had a lifetime diagnosis of a mood disorder, most commonly major depressive disorder. Comorbidity with substance abuse was 71%, and with impulse control disorders was 38%. Cluster C personality disorders, which were present in 39% of these individuals, were the most common Axis II diagnoses.

Results from two studies (Kafka & Hennen, 2002; Kafka & Prentky, 1998) suggest that relative to individuals with paraphilias, those with NCSBs report (a) fewer historical incidents of physical, nonsexual abuse; (b) higher educational achievement; less academic and occupational impairment; fewer mental health-related hospitalizations (including substance-related hospitalizations); and fewer legal difficulties. The typical person with NCSBs in these studies was a male college graduate in his middle to late 30s, employed, and earning a middle class income.

ETIOLOGIC AND CONCEPTUAL MODELS

Research on the factors that contribute to the etiology and maintenance of NCSBs is extremely sparse. Nevertheless, three conceptual models for understanding these behaviors have surfaced. These are described next.

BIOLOGICAL MODELS

A number of biological factors have been proposed as possible etiological factors in NCSBs. These include: diencephalic, frontal lobe and septal lesions (e.g., Elliott & Biever, 1996); unilateral strokes involving the temporal lobe (Monga, Monga, Raina, & Hardjasudarma, 1986); bilateral damage of the temporal lobes as seen in the Kluver–Bucy syndrome (Goscinski, Kwiatkowski, Polak, Orlowiejska, & Partyk, 1997); temporal lobe epilepsy (intraictally, postictally, or as a result of medical or surgical treatment) (e.g., Blumer & Walker, 1967); dementia, including Alzheimer's-type (Kuhn, Greiner, & Arseneau, 1998); and the use of prodopaminergic agents in the treatment of Parkinson's disease (Uitti et al., 1989). Also, substances, including alcohol, methamphetamine, cocaine, amyl nitrite ('poppers'), and gamma hydroxy-butyric acid ('date rape drug'), have all been implicated in sexual disinhibition and increased impulsivity (e.g., Colfax et al., 2005). Further, the manic phase of bipolar or schizoaffective disorder is well known to include hypersexual behavior that might be confused with a nonparaphilic sexual disorder.

It should be emphasized that very little empirical data are available to substantiate any of the above mentioned hypotheses. In addition, these biological models generally fail to explain a number of key features of NCSBs, including why these problems are more often observed in men as opposed to women, why the person develops problems with nonparaphilic behavior as opposed to paraphilias, and why these behaviors often wax and wane depending upon the availability of sexual partners (e.g., a spouse). Such models might be able to explain compulsive sexual behavior in patients with bona fide neurological disorders or those with a history of substance abuse, bipolar or psychotic disorder, but they don't seem to account for the model NCSB patient who is well-educated, gainfully employed, and physically healthy. Moreover, bipolar disorder and schizoaffective disorder are not commonly associated with NCSBs. Thus, whereas biological abnormalities might serve as general vulnerability factors, it is unlikely that they fully account for NCSBs.

ADDICTION MODELS

Some authors have considered NCSBs within an addiction model (e.g., Goodman, 1993), and as such, similar to substance abuse and dependence. The basis for similarities between NCSBs and addictive disorders is that both are by engagement in the problem behavior more frequently and for longer periods of time than intended, failure to resist or cut back, preoccupation with the behavior or with preparation for it, continuation of the behavior despite awareness of its adverse consequences, and the presence of withdrawal symptoms when the behavior is stopped. Also similar to substance dependence are the mood-enhancing properties of the behavior and the temporary escape it can provide from inner discomfort and tension.

Are NCSBs signs of 'sexual addiction'? Although NCSBs appear to share certain clinical characteristics with other behaviors considered to be addictions (e.g., alcohol dependence), empirical studies to establish the extent to which these are conceptually meaningful overlaps (as opposed to coincidental similarities) have not been conducted. In particular, it is unclear whether physiological tolerance and withdrawal, which form the cornerstone of addictive disorders, are truly present in NCSBs.

LEARNING MODELS

From a learning (conditioning) perspective NCSBs may be viewed as strongly reinforced (i.e., habitual) behavior associated with thoughts and physiologic arousal that are readily cued by external stimuli. According to this view, operant conditioning processes play a role in that sexual activity, which brings about highly pleasurable immediate emotional and physical states (e.g., orgasm), is positively reinforced by these consequences and therefore a good candidate for development into a habit. Associative learning (i.e., classical conditioning) also plays a role in that, for affected individuals, sexual thoughts (e.g., fantasies), feelings of arousal, and urges to masturbate, become strongly associated with numerous readily available trigger stimuli in the environment, including (but not limited to) certain times of day (or night), being alone, being at the computer or on the telephone, stimuli associated with sexually appetitive people, and so on. Thus, readily available external triggers cue sexual thoughts which lead to arousal and strongly reinforced urges to engage in sexual activity, which further results in pleasurable consequences that promote maintenance of the problem.

Much of the support for conditioning models of NCSBs comes from idiosyncratic clinical observations and functional analyses of behavior, rather than from empirical research. One experimental study, however, demonstrated that sexual thoughts among individuals with NCSBs were associated with sexual arousal and desire, which is consistent with the hypothesized role of positive reinforcement (Schwartz & Abramowitz, 2003). Limitations of the conditioning model include that it does not account for why NCSBs are (seemingly) more prevalent among men than women; and why, if sexual behavior is a universally reinforced behavior, the reported prevalence of NCSBs is relatively low. That is, why are some people, but not others, affected? One hypothesis that has not yet been subject to empirical study is that individual differences (possibly dictated by biological or genetic factors) regarding susceptibility to the conditioning processes described above (i.e., the propensity to associate external triggers with sexual imagery and arousal) contribute to the development of this problem.

NCSBS AND OBSESSIVE–COMPULSIVE DISORDER

OCD SYMPTOMS RELATED TO SEX

Sex has long been recognized as a content area of obsessions in OCD (Freud, 1895/1949). Data from large clinical studies (e.g., Abramowitz, 2006) indicate that as many as 20% of OCD patients experience obsessions of a sexual nature, such as impulses to perform inappropriate sexual acts, recurrent mental images of family members nude or having sex, and unrealistic doubts about one's true sexual preference. Along with such obsessions are compulsive and ritualistic efforts to reduce the discomfort or perceived risk of danger associated with such anxiety-evoking thoughts. These might take the form of overt behaviors (e.g., asking for reassurances) or mental acts (e.g., trying to replace a 'bad' thought with a 'good' one). Avoidance of stimuli that trigger sexual obsessions (e.g., pornography), and concealment of such thoughts from others (e.g., Newth & Rachman, 2001) are also commonly observed. The example below illustrates the presentation of sexual obsessions in a man with OCD.

Robert, a bank teller who had been married for 17 years, described severe sexual obsessions as his primary OCD complaint. If he saw an attractive woman at work, he experienced recurrent unwanted thoughts and images about what she might look like without her clothes on. The thoughts were utterly repugnant to Robert, who perceived them as 'highly immoral' and inconsistent with his strong love and attraction to his wife. He did not want to think about or have sex with these other women; they did not sexually arouse him; and he engaged in attempts to 'cancel out' or control these images whenever they came to mind. Among the thought control strategies Robert employed was thought suppression – attempting to stop thinking the bad thought by redirecting his attention to sexual thoughts about his wife. Robert was afraid that if he could not control his sexual thoughts it meant that he was an unfaithful husband and an adulterer. Thus, he tried to avoid places where there might be many women (e.g., shopping malls, the health club) and confessed his unwanted thoughts to his wife just to be sure she would stop him if he began to act on them.

Proponents of the hypothesis that certain impulse control, neurological, and somatoform disorders are related to OCD and comprise an OCS (e.g., Hollander et al., 2005) assert that NCSBs represent a variant of OCD. This impression is primarily derived from the observation that both NCSBs and compulsive rituals involve repetitive thoughts and behaviors. The excessive thoughts about sex in those with NCSBs are regarded as 'obsessions' and the repetitive sexual activity (e.g., masturbation), as compulsive rituals. However, the clinical examples of Robert (above) and Matt (presented at the beginning of this chapter) suggest important qualitative differences between the sexual symptoms of OCD and those of NCSBs. As Robert's case illustrates, sexual obsessions in OCD are perceived as unacceptable; they provoke anxiety, avoidance, and urges to neutralize or control the thought, or prevent feared consequences. People with OCD are exquisitely sensitive to the potential for harm and it is this that makes the occurrence of unwanted sexual thoughts especially unacceptable. In contrast, as Matt's case illustrates, people with NCSBs do not experience their sexual thoughts as distressing, and instead seem to be sexually aroused by them. In addition, such thoughts often lead to sexual behavior in people with NCSBs.

EMPIRICAL EVIDENCE

Only one study has tested the clinically derived hypotheses proposed above. In that investigation, Schwartz and Abramowitz (2003) conducted an experimental analysis of the phenomenological characteristics of sexual thoughts and behaviors in NCSBs and in patients with sexual OCD symptoms. This study focused primarily on the psychological experiences of these signs and symptoms to test whether they differ across diagnoses. If no differences in the experiences of repetitive thinking and behavior were found, it would provide evidence that NCSBs represent a variant of OCD. This study and its clinical and conceptual implications are discussed below.

Study participants were 12 adults referred to an outpatient anxiety and stress disorders clinic with the primary complaint of 'sexual obsessions'. Referral sources included physicians (including psychiatrists) and advertisements for research on OCD. Each participant was given a structured diagnostic interview as well as the Yale–Brown Obsessive Compulsive Scale (Y–BOCS; Goodman et al., 1989a, 1989b), which confirmed the presence of sexual obsessions and compulsions. Six patients (three males; three females) met *DSM-IV* criteria for OCD, whereas the other six (all males) had NCSBs and met *DSM-IV* criteria for impulse-control disorder NOS, but not OCD.

Following the diagnostic assessment the interviewer administered a semi-structured clinician-rated questionnaire designed specifically for this study. This instrument consisted of five questions addressing phenomenological aspects of sexual thoughts and related behaviors. Patients were asked (a) how much anxiety or distress their sexual thoughts caused them, (b) the extent of avoidance associated with the thoughts, (c) the strength of the urge to perform the compulsive behavior, (d) the level of sexual arousal, and (e) the amount of sexual gratification they attained from performing the compulsive behavior. Interviewers rated the participant's responses on a scale from 0 (none or never) to 8 (extremely or always). Participants were also asked to conjure up their most vivid sexual 'obsessional' thoughts and then complete the State–Trait Anxiety Inventory (STAI; Speilberger, Gorsuch, Lushene, Vagg, & Jacobs, 1983), which assesses the present ('right now') level of anxiety (state) as well as feelings of anxiety 'in general' (trait anxiety). Depression was assessed using the Beck Depression Inventory (BDI; Beck, Ward, Mendelsohn, Mock, & Erlbaugh, 1961), which measures the severity of affective, cognitive, motivational, vegetative, and psychomotor components of distress.

Figures 16.1 and 16.2 show that relative to patients with NCSBs, sexual obsessions among patients with OCD were associated with greater fear and avoidance responses. Individuals with NCSBs, in fact, evidenced very little associated fear and instead reported feeling sexually aroused. Clearly, the OCD patients reported that their sexual obsessions did not evoke sexual arousal. This suggests that whereas sexual obsessions occurring in the context of OCD are experienced as unwanted, aversive and threatening, those occurring in NPSAs are experienced as sexually arousing. These between-group differences were significant at the p < 0.01 level.

The function of repetitive behaviors also differed between groups. Although the drive to perform repetitive behaviors was not significantly different between groups, patients with NCSBs reported significantly more sexual pleasure when performing their compulsive behaviors than did OCD patients, who experienced

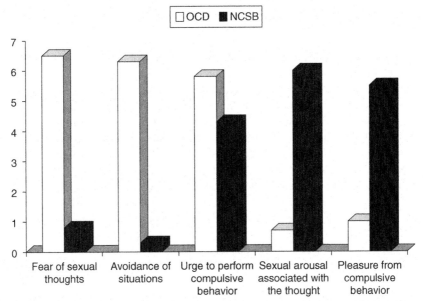

FIGURE 16.1 Mean scores for patients with OCD and NCSBs on measures of fear, avoidance, and compulsive behaviors

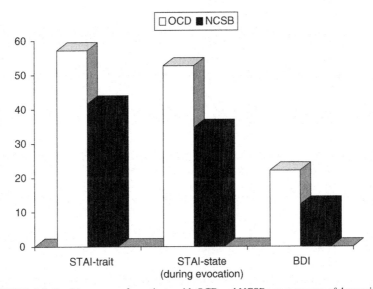

FIGURE 16.2 Mean scores for patients with OCD and NCSBs on measures of depression and anxiety

very little sexual gratification. As Figure 16.2 shows, patients with OCD also reported higher levels of trait anxiety and depression compared to those with NCSBs, who scored within the sub-clinical range of both the BDI and STAI-trait. Taken together, these findings lead to the preliminary conclusion that sexual thoughts and compulsive behaviors in NCSBs involve remarkably different psychological experiences and clinical characteristics than those observed in individuals with OCD.

Three key clinical distinctions between OCD and NCSBs that were not systematically assessed by Schwartz and Abramowitz (2003) deserve further comment. First, in NCSBs, the sexual thoughts and compulsive behaviors appear to be of greater concern to significant others (i.e., the spouse), rather than for the patient him or herself. Among OCD patients, however, the sexual thoughts and behaviors are of greatest concern to the patient him- or herself. This is supported by Schwartz and Abramowitz's (2003) finding that patients with NCSBs reported significantly less depressive and anxious symptoms than did those with OCD.

Second, whereas individuals with NCSBs do not typically report other classic types of obsessions and compulsions (e.g., contamination, aggression, checking), individuals with OCD who have sexual obsessions often report additional sorts of obsessions, such as those concerned with violence or morality (e.g., McKay et al., 2004). In the study by Schwartz and Abramowitz (2003), five of the six OCD patients reported other types of obsessions and compulsions unrelated to sex on the Y–BOCS checklist. In contrast, all six NCSB participants reported only excessive sexual thoughts or behaviors.

The third phenomenological difference between NCSBs and OCD concerns the link between repetitive thoughts and compulsive behaviors. Consistent with the diagnosis of impulse control disorder, individuals with NCSBs report deliberately planning how and where they will act on their urges to engage in the sexual activities they repetitively think about. In contrast, OCD patients with sexual obsessions commonly report beliefs such as 'thinking the sexual thoughts makes me immoral,' or 'if I think about rape it means I am a rapist'. Moreover, compulsive behaviors among OCD participants include a range of strategies (both overt and covert) aimed at resisting or neutralizing this fear by reducing the chances that the sexual obsessions will be acted upon. Thus, the phenomenological link between thought and behavior in OCD appears qualitatively distinct from that in NCSBs, further suggesting that these are unrelated conditions.

CONCLUSIONS

Overlaps between OCD and NCSBs may arise on various levels. On a superficial level, both of these conditions could be described as being typified by repetitious thinking and behavior. This is indeed the basis for including NCSBs among the OCS disorders (Hollander et al., 2005). As the empirical data and clinical observations discussed above indicate, however, the repetitive phenomena in NCSBs have qualitatively distinct phenomenological properties from those present in OCD. Therefore, incremental validity might be gained by understanding the degree of overlap at the level of psychological mechanisms underlying the repetitive behavior. In the case of sexual obsessions in OCD, the compulsive behavior is linked to threat-evoking misinterpretations of unwanted intrusive sexual thoughts as highly meaningful. The obsessive–compulsive individual worries that his or her sexual idea, image, or impulse is in some sense significant, and that action must be taken to reduce the probability of some dreaded outcome such as acting on the thought. Thus, the compulsive behavior in OCD can be conceptualized as 'neutralizing'. As is discussed above, this cognition–behavior link is not present in NCSBs. Thus, NCSBs do not appear to be related to OCD.

TREATMENT

PHARMACOLOGICAL TREATMENTS

To date, no randomized, double-blinded controlled studies of medications for NCSBs have appeared in the published literature. Two open trials, however, have examined response to selective serotonin reuptake inhibitors (SSRIs). The choice to examine SSRIs for this condition was made on the basis of seeming overlaps between NCSBs and OCD, which is known to respond to this class of medications (Kafka & Prentky, 1992).

In the first open study, Kafka and Prentky (1992) followed 10 men with NCSBs over a 12-week trial of fluoxetine. They reported statistically significant decreases in depressive and NCSB symptoms among the seven treatment completers (this was observed by week 4 of the trial). Limitations of this study included the fact that all patients had a mood disorder (major depression or dysthymia) at baseline, and that an unknown number were receiving concomitant psychotherapy. In a second trial, Kafka (1994) examined response to sertraline among 12 men with NCSBs. The mean duration of treatment was 18 weeks and 11 patients completed the study. Post-test clinician ratings on the Clinical Global Impressions Scale indicated that six patients were 'much' or 'very much' improved, although one patient experienced a worsening of symptoms. Although helpful for generating hypotheses, open trials cannot confirm that the medication caused any symptom improvement over and above nonspecific effects such as attention and expectancy (i.e., placebo effects). A second issue with the SSRIs is that reduced libido and delayed orgasm are common side-effects. Thus, it is possible that the apparent response observed in these studies is attributable to inadvertent side-effects, as opposed to the presumed mechanism of action: serotonin reuptake inhibition. Larger, controlled trials are necessary to disentangle and clarify this important issue.

Other classes of medication that do not typically produce sexual side-effects have also been examined in the treatment of NCSBs. One retrospective chart review of 14 men treated with the antidepressant nefazodone indicated that this agent was associated with long-term improvement for 6 of 11 long-term users (Coleman, Gratzer, Nesvacil, & Raymond, 2000). The opiate antagonist naltrexone, which has been shown to be effective in impulse control disorders (e.g., kleptomania) was also associated with improvement once it was added to SSRI regimens in two men with unwanted promiscuous sexual behavior (Raymond, Grant, Kim, & Coleman, 2002). Similarly, a single case history reported that topiramate, an anticonvulsant sometimes used in the treatment of impulsiveness, was helpful in treating a 32-year-old man with NCSBs (Fong, de la Garza, & Newton, 2005).

A much more controversial pharmacological approach that has been tried in sex offenders and individuals with unremitting pedophilia involves manipulation of the hypothalamic–pituitary–testicular hormonal axis to reach hypotestosteronemia, a biological state that is analogous to surgical castration (Saleh and Guidry, 2003). Such an approach lacks strong evidence for use in NCSBs, introduces ethical concerns, and can produce serious side-effects. Such an approach should be reserved for highly treatment-resistant individuals, or patients with comorbid paraphilias in which others are at risk. Moreover, this approach requires the patient's clear informed consent.

PSYCHOLOGICAL TREATMENTS

Various approaches to the psychological treatment of NCSBs have been described; although like the pharmacotherapy literature, large controlled studies that provide the most convincing evidence of treatment efficacy are lacking. The most promising psychological approaches are those derived from the behavioral model of NCSBs presented above. This form of treatment includes a collection of cognitive and behavioral procedures commonly referred to as cognitive–behavioral therapy (CBT).

In one of the only randomized controlled trials on the psychological treatment of problematic sexual behavior, McConaghy, Armstrong, & Blaszczynski (1985) compared the efficacy of two behavioral techniques: imaginal desensitization and covert desensitization. Imaginal desensitization involved a relaxation induction followed by imagining situations that lead to unwanted sexual behavior, but where this behavior is not performed. In covert desensitization, the patient imagined a scene in which an aversive event occurred which interrupted or blocked the performance of the unwanted sexual behavior (e.g., being surprised by one's roommate while masturbating). McConaghy and colleagues found that 14 treatment sessions of the former approach was more effective than the latter (89% vs. 55% reduction in unwanted sexual urges, respectively) when all treatment was delivered over the course of one week in a residential setting. Nevertheless, both of these behavioral approaches have fallen from favor in recent decades.

Contemporary CBT for NCSBs begins with a thorough behavioral assessment to determine the precise nature of the undesirable behavior (e.g., excessive masturbation), including its antecedents (e.g., using the computer) and consequences (e.g., orgasm) that might maintain the behavior. To aid in the collection of this data, the patient is often asked to self-monitor episodes of the sexual behavior between sessions. This includes recording the type of behavior, time spent performing it, and relevant environmental variables such as the situation and time of day.

A patient-specific formulation in which the assessment data is conceptualized within the framework of the behavioral model is next derived with input from the patient him- or herself. This formulation is then used in generating a treatment plan that incorporates a rationale for the various techniques to be used. Motivational interviewing strategies (e.g., Miller & Rollnick, 2002) can be used as needed to help the patient generate persuasive arguments for engaging in therapy to promote change.

The mainstay of CBT procedures for NCSBs is *habit reversal* (HR; Azrin & Nunn, 1973), which involved identifying and weakening the *behavior chains* that lead to a high risk of the undesirable and excessive sexual behavior. The patient is helped to view such behavior as a habit that is (a) cued by a series of thoughts or events (situations) and (b) maintained by positive reinforcement. The behavior can therefore be reversed by learning and practicing alternate responses at various points (in the behavior chain) leading up to the targeted behavior. The patient also learns stress management techniques, how to apply a response that is incompatible with the sexual behavior (considered the key element in treatment), contingency management, and social support. Another technique, *stimulus control*, serves to reduce exposure to triggering stimuli (e.g., making access to pornographic websites more difficult). Positive reinforcement for compliance with these strategies is also employed, and the patient is taught to understand the differences between lapses (temporary slips) and relapse (a return to baseline functioning). Lapses are reframed as opportunities to work harder on managing symptoms, rather than as occasions for self-punishment (Koran, 1999).

CONCLUSIONS

Due to the private and embarrassing nature of its associated signs and symptoms, there has been precious little research on NCSBs. Nevertheless, there is debate in the literature surrounding the appropriateness of including NCSBs as part of an OCS. The best argument for similarities between OCD and NCSBs is that both conditions involve repetitive thinking and behavior. Indeed, this is the primary reason for linking impulse control disorders with OCD (e.g., Hollander et al., 2005). Yet, upon closer inspection, the repetitive thinking and behavior in NCSBs appears to be motivated by entirely different psychological and emotional phenomena than are present in OCD. The problem of sexual obsessions in OCD is clearly identifiable: the sufferer experiences sexual thoughts that he or she finds unacceptable or repugnant, and attempts to neutralize them by engaging in some other thought or behavioral response. There is a clear phenomenological link between the occurrence of the unwanted sexual thought and the compulsive behavioral or mental ritual. This symptom picture repays careful assessment with rich and internally consistent patterns of phenomenology. We can thus regard sexual OCD symptoms as problems in which nonthreatening unwanted thoughts regarding sex have become the focus of concern; such thoughts evoke responses such as selective attention, rituals, avoidance, neutralizing, thought suppression, and other compulsive rituals, which paradoxically serve to maintain the problem (Salkovskis, 1996).

The sexual thinking and behavior in NCSBs are in sharp contrast to those observed in OCD. Individuals with NCSBs find their sexual thoughts arousing, and often deliberately conjure them up for the purposes of sexual excitement. Moreover, the repetitive behaviors represent sexual acts (which people with OCD, by contrast, are afraid to *think about*) that the individual finds highly pleasurable and thus repeats because of these consequences.

Thus, a significant problem with the existing OCS model is that it largely draws similarities between disorders such as OCD and NCSBs on the basis of superficial observations; i.e., the presence of *repetitive* symptoms. Indeed, compulsive Internet use and masturbation are repetitive behaviors in the same sense that ritualistic checking and reassurance-seeking in OCD are repetitive. But, then so is the throwing motion of a baseball pitcher and the picture-taking of a photography enthusiast. There may also be similar changes in motor areas of the brain with all of these behaviors, but few would assert that they arise from a common underlying cause or represent a common disorder. A more meaningful approach is to examine behavior more closely at the level of its antecedents and consequences (functional analysis). When this standard is used to evaluate the relationship between NCSBs and OCD, one recognizes that these two conditions bear little resemblance to one another.

Unfortunately, the insinuation that impulse control disorders such as NCSBs represent presentations of OCD is detrimental to advances in clinical treatment and experimental investigation. The OCS concept, for example, promotes the mistaken idea that NCSBs should respond to the same forms of psychological treatment that are highly successful with OCD (i.e., exposure and response prevention). As is discussed in this chapter (and in others within this section of the present volume), the treatment of NCSBs (and other impulse control disorders) is best accomplished using techniques that are not indicated for OCD (i.e., stimulus control).

Over-inclusive criteria for defining OCD also have implications for understanding this complex problem through research. As earlier chapters in this volume illustrate, OCD is a highly heterogeneous condition, and this diversity is an inherent challenge for researchers attempting to accrue patient samples. Indeed, various presentations of OCD may systematically differ from one another in one or more ways (e.g., treatment response). In efforts to maximize internal validity of both treatment and psychopathology studies, investigators sometimes deal with this heterogeneity problem by studying only a single 'type' of OCD such as 'checkers' or 'washers'. However, because of the difficulty in accumulating large samples of patients with specific OCD symptoms, most studies have necessarily included all patients meeting the criteria for OCD. If individuals with disorders such as NCSBs were to be conceptualized as having OCD, they might also be included as participants in OCD research, potentially undermining both internal and external validity. Indeed, data gathered using such contaminated samples would likely (and may already) lead to further confusion regarding the nature of OCD.

REFERENCES

Abramowitz, J. S. (2006). *Understanding and treating obsessive–compulsive disorder*. Mahwah, NJ: Lawrence Erlbaum Associates.

American Psychiatric Association (2000). *Diagnostic and statistical manual of mental disorders* (4th ed., text revision). Washington, DC.

Azrin, N. H., & Nunn, R. G. (1973). Habit-reversal: A method of eliminating nervous habits and tics. *Behaviour Research and Therapy, 11*, 619–628.

Beck, A. T., Ward, C. H., Mendelsohn, M., Mock, J., & Erlbaugh, J. (1961). An inventory for measuring depression. *Archives of General Psychiatry, 4*, 561–571.

Blumer, D., & Walker, E. (1967). Sexual behavior in temporal lobe epilepsy. *Archives of Neurology, 16*, 37–43.

Coleman, E. (1992). Is your patient suffering from compulsive sexual behavior? *Psychiatric Annals, 22*, 320–325.

Coleman, E., Gratzer, T., Nesvacil, L., & Raymond, N. C. (2000). Nefazodone and the treatment of nonparaphilic compulsive sexual behavior: A retrospective study. *Journal of Clinical Psychiatry, 61*, 282–284.

Colfax, G., Coates, T.J., Husnik, M.J., Huang, Y., Buchbinder, S., Koblin, B., et al. (2005). Longitudinal patterns of methamphetamine, popper (amyl nitrite), and cocaine use and high-risk sexual behavior among a cohort of San Francisco men who have sex with men. *Journal of Urban Health, 82*(Suppl 1), i62–i70.

Cooper, A., & Scherer, C. (1999). Overcoming methodological concerns in the investigation of online sexual activities. *Cyberpsychology and Behavior, 4*, 437–447.

Elliott, M. L., & Biever, L. S. (1996). Head injury and sexual dysfunction. *Brain Injury, 10*, 703–717.

Fong, T. W., De La Garza, R., & Newton, T. F. (2005). A case report of topiramate in the treatment of nonparaphilic sexual addiction. *Journal of Clinical Psychopharmacology, 25*, 512–514.

Freud, S. (1895/1949). Obsessions and phobias; their psychical mechanisms and aetiology. In J. Riviere (Ed. & trans.), *Collected papers of Sigmund Freud*, vol. 1 (pp. 128–137). London: Hogarth.

Goldsmith, T., Shapira, N. A., Phillips, K. A., & McElroy, S. L. (1998). Conceptual foundations of obsessive–compulsive spectrum disorders. In R. Swinson, M. Antony, S. Rachman, & M. Richter (Eds.), *Obsessive–compulsive disorder: Theory, research, and treatment* (pp. 397–425). New York: Guilford.

Goodman, A. (1993). Diagnosis and treatment of sexual addiction. *Journal of Sex and Marital Therapy, 19*, 225–251.

Goodman, W. K., Price, L. H., Rasmussen, S. A., Mazure, C., Fleischmann, R. L., Hill, C. L., et al. (1989a). The Yale–Brown Obsessive Compulsive Scale, I: Development, use, and reliability. *Archives of General Psychiatry, 46*, 1006–1011.

Goodman, W. K., Price, L. H., Rasmussen, S. A., Mazure, C., Delgado, P., Heninger, G. R., et al. (1989b). The Yale–Brown Obsessive Compulsive Scale, II: Validity. *Archives of General Psychiatry, 46*, 1012–1016.

Goscinski, I., Kwiatkowski, S., Polak, J., Orlowiejska, M.J., & Partyk, A. (1997). The Kluver Bucy syndrome. *Journal of Neurological Science, 41*, 269–272.

Hollander, E., Friedberg, J., Wasserman, S., Yeh, C., & Iyengar, R. (2005). The case for the OCD spectrum. In J. Abramowitz & A. Houts (Eds.), *Concepts and controversies in obsessive–compulsive disorder* (pp. 95–118). New York: Springer.

Kafka, M. P. (1994). Sertraline pharmacotherapy for paraphilias and paraphilia-related disorders: An open trial. *Annals of Clinical Psychiatry, 6*, 189–195.

Kafka, M. P., & Hennen, J. (2002). A DSM-IV Axis I comorbidity study of males with paraphilias and paraphilia-related disorders. *Sexual Abuse, 14*, 349–366.

Kafka, M. P., & Prentky, R. A. (1992). Fluoxetine treatment of nonparaphilic sexual addictions and paraphilias in men. *Journal of Clinical Psychiatry, 53*, 351–358.

Kafka, M. P., & Prentky, R. A. (1997). Compulsive sexual behavior characteristics. (Letter.) *American Journal of Psychiatry, 154*, 1632.

Kafka, M. P., & Prentky, R. A. (1998). Attention-deficit/hyperactivity disorder in males with paraphilias and paraphilia-related disorders: A comorbidity study. *Journal of Clinical Psychiatry, 59*, 388–396.

Koran, L. M. (1999). *Obsessive compulsive and related disorders in adults.* Cambridge: Cambridge University Press.

Kuhn, D. R., Greiner, D., & Arseneau, L. (1998). Addressing hypersexuality in Alzheimer's disease. *Journal of Gerontological Nursing, 24*, 44–50.

McConaghy, N., Armstrong, M. S., & Blaszczynski, A. (1985). Expectancy, covert sensitization and imaginal desensitization in compulsive sexuality. *Acta Psychiatrica Scandinavica, 72*, 176–187.

McKay, D., Abramowitz, J., Calamari, J., Kyrios, M., Radomsky, A., Sookman, D., et al. (2004). A critical evaluation of obsessive–compulsive disorder subtypes: Symptoms versus mechanisms. *Clinical Psychology Review, 24*, 283–313.

Miller, W. R., & Rollnick, S. (2002). *Motivational interviewing* (2nd ed.). New York: Guilford.

Monga, T. N., Monga, M., Raina, M. S., & Hardjasudarma, M. (1986). Hypersexuality in stroke. *Archives of Physical Medicine and Rehabilitation, 6*, 415–417.

Newth, S., & Rachman, S. (2001). The concealment of obsessions. *Behaviour Research and Therapy, 39*, 457–464.

Quadland, M. C. (1985). Compulsive sexual behavior: Definition of a problem and an approach to treatment. *Journal of Sex and Marital Therapy, 11*, 121–132.

Raymond, N. C., Coleman, E., & Miner, M. H. (2003). Psychiatric comorbidity and compulsive/impulsive traits in compulsive sexual behavior. *Comprehensive Psychiatry, 44*, 370–380.

Raymond, N. C., Grant, J. E., Kim, S. W., & Coleman, E. (2002). Treatment of compulsive sexual behaviour with naltrexone and serotonin reuptake inhibitors: Two case studies. *International Clinical Psychopharmacology, 17*, 201–205.

Saleh, F. M., & Guidry, L. L. (2003). Psychosocial and biological treatment considerations for the paraphilic and nonparaphilic sex offender. *Journal of the American Academy of Psychiatry and Law, 31*, 486–493.

Salkovskis, P. M. (1996). Understanding of obsessive-compulsive disorder is not improved by redefining it as something else. In R. Rapee (Ed.), *Current controversies in the anxiety disorders* (pp. 191–200). New York: Guilford.

Schwartz, S., & Abramowitz, J. (2003). Are nonparaphilic sexual addictions a variant of obsessive–compulsive disorder? A pilot study. *Cognitive and Behavioral Practice, 10*, 373–378.

Spielberger, C. D., Gorsuch, R. L., Lushene, R. E., Vagg, R. E., & Jacobs, G. A. (1983). *Manual for the State–Trait Anxiety Inventory.* Palo Alto, CA: Consulting Psychologists Press.

Uitti, R. J., Ranner, C. M., Rajput, A. H., Goetz, C. G., Klawans, H. L., & Thiessen, B. (1989). Hypersexuality with antiparkinsonian therapy. *Clinical Neuropharmacology, 12*, 275–283.

17

DISCUSSION: THE OBSESSIVE–COMPULSIVE SPECTRUM

DEAN McKAY[1], JONATHAN S. ABRAMOWITZ[2], AND STEVEN TAYLOR[3]

[1]Fordham University; [2]University of North Carolina–Chapel Hill; [3]University of British Columbia

As the chapters in Part II illustrate, there is diversity in the phenomenology, theoretical conceptualizations, and treatment approaches to the various disorders sometimes considered as part of an obsessive–compulsive spectrum (OCS). Authors of the preceding chapters have also thoroughly discussed how these putative OCS disorders overlap with, and are independent from, obsessive–compulsive disorder (OCD) itself. Which disorders should we consider as part of the OCS? Is there even enough empirical evidence that an OCS exists? We address these and related questions in the present discussion. What is interesting to note immediately is that the OCS itself has been subject to wide variation in conceptualization, with no compelling unifying themes. This is in no small way problematic for the utility of the concept of a spectrum of disorders as we endeavor to develop an empirical literature base and enumerate inclusion criteria for such a proposed clinical phenomenon.

THE OBSESSIVE–COMPULSIVE SPECTRUM

The present discussion focuses on the OCS model proposed by Hollander and colleagues (e.g., Hollander, Friedberg, Wasserman, Yeh, & Iyengar, 2005;

Correspondence: Dean McKay, Department of Psychology, Fordham University, 441 East Fordham Road, Bronx, NY 10458.

TABLE 17.1   Candidate obsessive–compulsive spectrum disorders

Impulse control disorders	Appearance/bodily sensations	Neurological disorders characterized by repetitive behaviors
Intermittent explosive disorder	Body dysmorphic disorder	Autism
Pyromania	Hypochondriasis	Asperger's syndrome
Kleptomania	Depersonalization disorder	Tourette's syndrome
Pathological gambling	Anorexia nervosa	Sydenham's chorea
Trichotillomania	Bulimia nervosa	
Paraphilias and nonparaphilic compulsive sexual behavior		
Impulsive and aggressive personality disorders such as borderline, narcissistic, and antisocial personality disorders		

Hollander & Rosen, 2000) because it is the most well articulated – if not the most vigorously promoted – example of an OCS. Hollander and colleagues describe the OCS as a set of disorders lying on a continuum from compulsive to impulsive, with the unifying feature being an inability to regulate behavior as a consequence of defects in inhibition. For example, impulsivity is said to arise from deficits in inhibition by persisting in behavior with known negative consequences. Compulsivity is said to persist as a consequence of deficits in recognizing completion of tasks.

Table 17.1 lists the disorders considered part of the OCS according to Hollander and Rosen (2000). The table shows 15 conditions proposed for inclusion, although anywhere from 9 to 21 disorders have been proposed at some time or other. Commenting on the sheer number of disorders proposed for inclusion, one author remarked, 'about a third of the DSM-IV is part of the OCS!' (Veale, 2003, p. 221). As Table 17.1 also shows, Hollander and Rosen (see also Hollander et al., 2005) also propose that the OCS disorders fall into three major clusters: impulsive disorders, disorders associated with appearance and bodily sensations, and neurological disorders characterized by repetitive behavior.

In defending their case for the existence of an OCS that includes the disorders listed in Table 17.1, Hollander et al. (2005) argue that these disorders first and foremost share overlapping signs and symptoms (e.g., obsessions and compulsions) with OCD. They also assert that although the OCS disorders fall along a continuum from compulsive (i.e., being driven by the need to attain negative reinforcement) to impulsive (i.e., driven by a need to maximize positive reinforcement), all of these conditions have in common a deficit in the ability to delay or inhibit repetitive behaviors (Hollander et al., 2005). These authors further suggest that the proposed spectrum disorders (a) are highly comorbid with OCD, (b) share common associated features (i.e., family history) with OCD, (c) have similar abnormalities in neurocircuitry and neurotransmitter functioning as OCD, and (d) respond to similar treatments as OCD (Hollander et al., 2005). Below we evaluate the case for the OCS, and which disorders should be included, by synthesizing material from the preceding chapters in this section.

EVALUATING THE CASE FOR THE OCS

SYMPTOM OVERLAP WITH OCD

Inhibitory deficits

Similarities between OCD and the OCS conditions can be viewed from different perspectives. The notion advanced by Hollander et al. (2005), that compulsive and impulsive behaviors have in common the inability to delay or inhibit repetitive behavior, implies that there is something defective with the part of the brain that controls one's ability to inhibit behavior. In seeming support of this, research shows that people with OCD, compared to healthy individuals, have an impaired ability to restrain their behavioral responses (even for affectively neutral responses; e.g., Enright, Beech, & Claridge, 1995). However, in people with OCD these impairments tend to be mild (e.g., Rosenberg, Dyck, O'Hearn, & Sweeny, 1997), and for most of the putative OCS disorders there has been no research on whether such a deficit is present. Thus, the conclusion that OCS disorders are related in this way is premature.

One problem with the assumption that general cognitive or neurological *deficits* – such as impaired inhibition – underlie OCD and the OCS is that OCD and the proposed spectrum conditions are highly heterogeneous. Along these lines, the reader will note the absence of a grand comprehensive etiologic model to adequately account for all of the symptom variations of OCD and the spectrum disorders. Instead, chapters in both sections of this volume describe highly specific 'minimodels' that can explain only specific sorts of clinical phenomena (e.g., contamination, hoarding, hair-pulling). Although there is some overlap across many of these symptom-specific models, the absence of a general model – despite decades of research on OCD – challenges the implicit assumption that a comprehensive conceptual or etiologic model for the OCS exists (Taylor, Abramowitz, & McKay, 2007; Taylor, McKay, & Abramowitz, 2005a, 2005b).

There are three additional problems with this general approach to explaining the apparent overlap in symptom presentation across the proposed OCS. First, the inhibitory deficit assumption does not account for the fact that this, and other, mild neurological deficits have been found in numerous disorders (e.g., panic, posttraumatic stress disorder; Stowe & Taylor, 2002) that are not included in the OCS. This begs the question of why such deficits give rise to OCD and the OCS disorders, as opposed to disorders not included in the spectrum. Second, the appeal to an inhibitory deficit does not elucidate the possible mechanisms by which the neurological impairment translates into the symptoms of OCD and the OCS conditions. The third problem is that the inhibitory deficit model does not predict the efficacy of treatment interventions discussed for the various OCD subtypes and spectrum conditions. Moreover, none of the contributors to this volume even describe the use of treatment procedures aimed at reversing deficits in behavioral (or cognitive) inhibition. Instead, effective treatments for the most part capitalize on (a) learning processes such as classical and operant conditioning, and (b) cognitive processes such as the effects of beliefs on emotion and behavior.

Phenomenological approaches

The chapters in this volume, which consider the specifics of each OCD subtype and putative OCS condition, present a conceptual and phenomenological picture that departs radically from the approach to understating these conditions as united on the basis of an inhibitory deficit. When this fine-grained phenomenological approach is considered, repetitive compulsive washing behavior in OCD, for example, has important characteristics that differentiate it from other repetitive behaviors sometimes colloquially labeled 'compulsive' (e.g., hair pulling in trichotillomania; TTM). Collectively, the repetitive behaviors across the OCD subtypes appear to be performed deliberately to attain reassurance and escape from obsessional fear and/or reduce the perceived probability of catastrophe. But, as the reader will note, this is not uniformly demonstrated in the OCS disorders.

Repetitive behavior in impulse-control disorders such as TTM and compulsive gambling, for example, show important distinctions from OCD: their repetitive behaviors have qualitatively different functions than do compulsive rituals in OCD. Individuals with these conditions report excitement or gratification during and after their problematic behaviors. Moreover, the antecedents of such impulsive behaviors are not anxiety-evoking obsessions. There are also clear distinctions between compulsive rituals in OCD and tics: whereas compulsive rituals are deliberate and serve as an escape from obsessional fear, tics are often spontaneous (sudden), and performed to reduce sensory discomfort or tension.

Carefully conducted phenomenological cognitive research does suggest, however, that *some* of the proposed OCS conditions share characteristics with OCD. Body dysmorphic disorder (BDD), for example, involves anxiety-evoking thoughts about physical appearance and attempts to gain reassurance (e.g., checking mirrors). Similarly, hypochondriasis (HC) involves illness-related fears and checking for reassurance of health status. However, this special relationship between anxiety-evoking thoughts and anxiety-reducing behavior appears absent from the impulse control disorders, neurological disorders, and other body-focused disorders that are included in current OCS proposals.

Some authors have noted that although OCD and many OCS behaviors involve different antecedents and consequences, anxiety and guilt are common to all of these conditions (e.g., people with compulsive gambling may feel anxious or guilty over losing money). This argument, however, ignores critical differences in the cognitive mediation underlying such anxiety in OCD and the various OCS disorders.

For example, the need to control unwanted thoughts appears to play a strong role in the maintenance of obsessional anxiety in OCD. This cognitive bias is *specific* to obsessions and is irrelevant in OCSDs such as impulse control, neurological, and body-images disorders where qualitatively different cognitive factors (or perhaps none at all) mediate any anxiety that might be present.

PATTERNS OF COMORBIDITY

The assertion that OCD and the OCS disorders are highly comorbid is not supported by existing large-scale OCD comorbidity studies. For example, in the Johns Hopkins OCD family study, Bienvenu et al. (2001) reported the following rates of OCSDs among 80 individuals with OCD: HC = 16%, BDD = 15%, anorexia nervosa = 9%, bulimia = 4%, TTM = 4%, kleptomania = 3%, pathologic gambling = 0%, and pyromania = 0%. In a larger study, Jaisoorya, Reddy, and Srinath (2003) found comorbidity rates of only 3% for Tourette's syndrome, 3% for TTM, 0.4% for sexual compulsions, compulsive buying, and anorexia, and 0% for bulimia and depersonalization among 231 OCD patients.

These findings suggest OCS disorders are quite *uncommon* among patients with OCD (HC and BDD are noteworthy exceptions, which we return to later). In fact, even if we grant that these comorbidity rates are higher than chance, a more serious problem for the OCS hypothesis is that comorbidity rates between OCD and many anxiety and mood disorders not included in the OCS are considerably higher. For example, data from the Hopkins Study indicate that 13% of OCD patients also met criteria for generalized anxiety disorder, 21% met criteria for panic disorder, 17% for agoraphobia, 36% for social phobia, 31% for specific phobias, and 54% for recurrent major depression (Nestadt et al., 2001). Thus, the comorbidity argument advanced by OCS advocates is actually supportive of the view that OCD is most closely associated with mood and anxiety disorders (on the order of 5- to 10-fold closer).

A conceptual (as opposed to empirical) problem with the appeal to comorbidity in support of an OCS is that comorbidity is common in most major mental disorders and there are numerous explanations for this phenomenon that do not require co-occurring conditions to be considered part of the same spectrum. Alcohol dependence, major depression, and posttraumatic stress disorder, for example, are all more highly comorbid than what would be expected by chance. While it is easy to recognize several potential reasons for the co-occurrence of these disorders, few would suggest alcohol dependence, depression, and posttraumatic stress disorder are etiologically related or even part of the same spectrum. To this end, Summerfeldt, Hood, Antony, Richter, and Swinson (2004) found that although OCD was associated with elevated levels of impulsivity compared to nonclinical controls, this was true across a number of anxiety disorders. In other words, elevated levels of impulsive behavior are not specific to OCD. Thus, comorbidity is of limited value in understanding the links among the proposed OCS disorders and their links to OCD itself.

COMMON ASSOCIATED FEATURES

Family histories

A comparable problem arises with the argument that OCD and the OCS conditions share associated features, such as family histories of these afflictions. Not only is this association unclear for several proposed OCSDs, but the rates of other anxiety disorders among first degree relatives of people with OCD are far higher than the rates of OCSDs among relatives of OCD sufferers (e.g., Bienvenu et al., 2000; Nestadt et al., 2001). Here again, the assertion that familial pattern is good evidence for the OCS hypothesis actually ends up supporting the notion that OCD is not as strongly related to the proposed OCS disorders as it is to other anxiety disorders.

Age of onset, course, and gender ratio

Consistent findings across numerous studies suggest that although OCD may begin at any time from childhood through old age, it has a mean age of onset in the late teenage years into the mid twenties (see Antony, Downie, & Swinson, 1998, for a review). OCD is also a chronic condition that, absent effective treatment, waxes and wanes throughout its course. Likewise, many of the disorders included in the OCS begin in late adolescence through early adulthood and follow similar courses. A noteworthy exception, however, is Tourette syndrome, which tends to begin earlier in childhood (e.g., age 6–7; Zinner, 2000). Similarity in age of onset and course is not, however, persuasive evidence that spectrum disorders are related to one another or to OCD. This is primarily because these demographic features are not in any way specific to OCD and the proposed spectrum disorders. A look through the *DSM-IV* reveals that many depressive, bipolar, anxiety, factitious, sexual, sleep, personality, psychotic, somatoform, substance abuse, and eating disorders begin during this time of life and evidence a chronic course if effective treatment is not sought. Thus, the fact that proposed spectrum disorders share these associated characteristics with OCD does not indicate anything specific about these conditions, much less that they are related to OCD.

A second problem with appeals to associated demographic features is that there are many discrepancies. For example, as mentioned above, the mean onset age in OCD and Tourette syndrome is quite different. Additionally, whereas OCD seems to affect males and females in approximately equal numbers (Karno, Golding, Sorenson, & Burnam, 1988; Kolada, Bland, & Newman, 1994), the male to female ratio in Tourette syndrome ranges from 2:1 to 4:1 (Zinner, 2000). On the other hand, kleptomania, compulsive shopping, binge eating disorder, TTM, and BDD appear to be more common in females than in males (McElroy, Keck, & Phillips, 1995; Tukel, Keser, Karali, Olgun, & Calikusu, 2001). It should be noted that only preliminary data on many spectrum disorders are available at present, and the overall reporting rates of these disorders may be underestimated due to the tendency for many individuals to hide their symptoms from others. Nevertheless, appeals to demographic characteristics such as age of onset, course, and male to female ratio do not appear to provide a cogent argument for conceptualizing the putative spectrum disorders as related to OCD.

NEUROBIOLOGY

Neurocircuitry

Although OCS advocates (e.g., Hollander et al., 2005) often contend that functional neuroimaging research has elucidated the neurocircuitry underlying OCD, few studies have addressed the neurocircuitry of OCS disorders. This precludes broad conclusions regarding similarities in neurocircuitry. Future research to examine this hypothesis should involve controlled studies that directly compare brain regions of interest in OCD and OCSDs. To date, such studies are scarce, and most of the existing research is based on very small sample sizes. Moreover, two magnetic resonance imaging (MRI) studies of TTM (O'Sullivan, Rauch, & Brieter, 1997; Stein, Coetzer, & Lee, 1997) found results that were inconsistent with MRI studies of OCD patients.

A second concern is how the available functional neuroimaging data are interpreted. Many authors imply that such data indicate the presence of 'abnormalities', 'imbalances', and 'defects' that play a role in the etiology of OCD or OCS disorders. What appears to be misunderstood is that neuroimaging studies are generally cross-sectional and therefore only describe *differences* between people with and without the disorder in question. Such study designs do not permit one to conclude that observed differences are related to etiology. In the absence of true experimental data, conclusions regarding OCD and neuroimaging findings must be restricted to those allowed by correlational data. At least three possible explanations for the current findings are that: (a) alterations in functioning in certain brain regions cause OCD; (b) OCD causes alterations in brain functioning; or (c) both phenomena are associated with a third variable. Interestingly, data from symptom provocation studies, which measure the effects of the environment on the brain in a prospective fashion, indicate that OCD patients and non-patients both evidence higher regional cerebral blood flow when exposed to anxiety-evoking, as opposed to neutral, stimuli (e.g., Cottraux et al., 1996). This leads to the conclusion that increased brain activity in OCD patients compared to controls (e.g., Rauch et al., 1994) is merely due to the differences in state and trait anxiety between individuals with and without OCD. Thus, given the inconsistent findings, paucity of comparison studies, and misinterpretation of neuropsychiatric data, the case for inclusion of OCSDs on the basis of common neurocircuitry is unconvincing.

This last point raises the issue of reductionism, which is often apparent in discussions of the OCS that contain phrases such as 'underlying brain dysfunction' and 'symptoms arising from neuroanatomical abnormalities'. These types of expressions convey that biological phenomena are somehow more fundamental than psychological phenomena. It is not a fact, however, that biological processes underlie psychological processes. Whereas neuroimaging data provide valuable information that is not obtainable through self report or behavioral means, this data is not inherently more fundamental, more accurate, or more objective than psychological data (Miller & Keller, 2000). Instead, biological and psychological approaches offer distinct types of data of potentially equal relevance for understanding OCD and potentially related phenomena. These data, however, are not simply different 'levels of analysis', except perhaps in a metaphorical (and unhelpful) sense. Neither underlies the other and neither explains away the other. They are simply two domains of information.

Neurochemistry

In large part, the problems with appeals to neurocircuitry in formulating the OCS also apply to the position that an OCS exists on the basis of overlaps in abnormal neurotransmitter function. The 'serotonin hypothesis' is often cited as the basis for neurochemical models of OCD, yet the most consistent evidence for this model comes from treatment outcome studies showing that serotonergic medication is more effective than other sorts of medications. In contrast, findings from biological marker and pharmacological challenge studies of the serotonin system in OCD have been remarkably inconsistent (Gross, Sasson, Chorpa, & Zohar, 1998). The appeal to similarly selective responses to serotonin reuptake inhibitor medication (SRIs) is only a compelling argument for the OC spectrum if this response profile is both sensitive and specific to OCD and the OCS disorders. If non-OCS disorders respond selectively to SRIs, then this appeal to neurotransmission is of little value as a means of including disorders in a spectrum. SRIs are effective for such a wide variety of disorders (including most anxiety disorders and depression) that there is little chance of meaningful pharmacological dissection of disorders with them.

A related epistemological problem with this argument is that the preferential response of a disorder to SRIs does not prove that an *abnormally* functioning serotonin system is involved in the cause of that condition. This is because specific models of etiology cannot be derived solely from knowledge of successful treatment response. Inferring such a relationship is an example of the logical error known as *ex juvantibus* reasoning, or 'reasoning backward from what helps' (a variation of the fallacy known as *post hoc ergo propter hoc*, or 'after this, therefore because of this'). Furthermore, this represents a gross oversimplification of how neurotransmitters (and SRIs) work (Leonard, 2003). The problem with such reasoning is clear in the following example: 'When I take aspirin, my headache goes away. Therefore, the reason I get headaches is that my aspirin level is too low.'

Just as there could be various mechanisms by which aspirin makes headaches go away (not the least of which is a placebo effect), there may be many possible interacting mechanisms by which SRIs decrease OCD and OCS disorder symptoms. Thus, definitive conclusions regarding causes of, and relationships between, disorders are generally not warranted on the basis of treatment response. Undoubtedly, the behavior observed in OCD and putative OCS disorders is relevant to the serotonin system (one is hard-pressed to identify many human processes that don't); yet existing evidence does not suggest that these problems are *caused* by an abnormal serotonin system (see, for examples, Inancu, Dannon, Dolberg, & Zohar, 2000,

p. 478; Leonard, 2003, p. 225), nor that an overlap in serotonin involvement justifies a spectrum. A further issue concerns whether there truly is an overlap in the response to SRIs across the proposed OCS disorders. We address this question next.

TREATMENT

Perhaps the most practical aspect of the OCS hypothesis is that a beneficial response to certain treatment approaches unites the included disorders (e.g., Hollander et al., 2005). Indeed, it would be a tremendous clinical breakthrough to identify a spectrum of disorders that could be treated with select therapies. Examination of the chapters in this volume, however, suggests that this idea has serious problems and could even result in patients being led *away from* the best treatments for their condition as we will see further below.

The appeal to a preferential response to treatments such as SRIs is only clinically useful in delineating an OCS if three conditions are satisfied: (a) preferential response to SRIs is observed uniformly across the OCS, (b) the preferential response is not observed in other disorders that are not included in the OCS, and (c) SRIs are the best treatment available for disorders of the OCS. The chapters in this volume, in concert with the existing literature base, suggest, however, that none of these parameters have empirical support.

First, whereas OCD responds preferentially to SRIs, very few controlled double-blind studies directly comparing an SRI and non-SRI have been reported for the various OCS disorders. This means that the assertion of preferential treatment response in many OCS disorders is based on open-trial study results that are not designed to answer the question of relative efficacy of medication. Moreover, non-SRIs are helpful in many of the proposed OCSDs such as kleptomania (McElroy, Keck, & Pope, 1989), compulsive shopping (McElroy, Satlin, & Pope, 1991), and pathological gambling (see Chapter 10 in this volume) to name a few. Also, antipsychotic medications (e.g., haloperidol) that are ineffective as monotherapies for OCD are often used in the treatment of Tourette's syndrome (see Chapter 13 this volume).

Second, SRIs demonstrate at least equivalent efficacy to other medications in the treatment of depressive disorders (e.g., Nemeroff & Shatzberg, 1998) and other anxiety disorders including panic disorder (e.g., Boyer, 1995) that are not included in the OCS. This illustrates the problem of lack of specificity: because SRIs help so many disorders, the observation that a group of disorders responds preferentially to these drugs cannot inform us very well about the nature of that particular disorder and whether it is related to other disorders.

Finally, research indicates that SRIs are not the most effective treatments for OCD, or for some of the proposed OCS disorders. Instead, several randomized controlled trials and meta-analyses indicate that psychological treatment involving the techniques of exposure, response prevention (ERP), and cognitive therapy is the most effective treatment approach for OCD (e.g., Foa et al., 2005), hypochondriasis (Taylor, Asmundson, & Coons, 2005), and BDD (Williams, Hadjistavropoulos, & Sharpe, 2006). Other OCS disorders respond to different sorts of cognitive–behavioral interventions, as Franklin and colleagues clearly exemplify using the case of TTM in Chapter 9 of this book.

Not only is psychological treatment often more effective than SRIs (e.g., average symptom reduction rates in OCD are 60–70% vs. 20–40% with SRIs; Jenike, 2004), it is, as many the chapters of this volume clearly illustrate, informed by specific (and empirically demonstrated) conceptual frameworks of the relevant problems. To illustrate, in the contamination subtype of OCD (see Chapter 1), compulsive washing rituals are performed to reduce inappropriate obsessional fears of germs and illnesses that might result from contact with feared contaminants. Treatment therefore requires, for example, therapeutic exposure to excessively feared contaminants and abstinence from washing rituals to demonstrate that the fear (and urge to compulsively wash) is groundless.

Because exposure and response prevention is based on the specific relationship between obsessional fear and compulsive behavior this treatment is entirely irrelevant for other proposed OCS disorders. For example, because TTM involves neither obsessional fear nor urges to perform compulsive rituals designed to escape or neutralize anxiety there would be no logic in using an exposure-based approach here: the hair pulling is cued by general tension, fatigue, or boredom; not obsessional fears as observed in OCD. Hair pulling in TTM is also not performed to reduce the probability of danger, as is observed with compulsions in OCD. Thus, the relevant therapeutic maneuvers include procedures that hinder attempts to pull (stimulus control), compete with pulling (habit reversal), and help patients avoid strong urges to pull (e.g., avoidance of cues, relaxation training). Similar procedures that aim to complicate the performance of specific undesirable behaviors are used to reduce other disorders of impulse control such as binge eating and pathological gambling.

CONCLUSIONS AND FUTURE DIRECTIONS

As this book demonstrates in Part One, OCD is a heterogeneous disorder comprised of multiple subtypes and wide diversity in presentation. Indeed, even for a single symptom subtype the functional basis can vary widely (i.e., washing rituals for germs and contaminants versus washing rituals for morality and washing away repugnant ideas). Several of the proposed OCS disorders are heterogeneous in their own right, and suggest comparison with disorders other than OCD. For example, hypochondriasis has been divided into those who primarily believe they have a nonspecific illness, and those who are fearful that they will develop an illness. These are effectively two subtypes of hypochondriasis (Noyes, Carney, & Langbehn, 2004). Further, it has been suggested that hypochondriasis is similar to panic disorder, with research attempting to distinguish the two conditions (Hiller, Leibbrand, & Fichter, 2005).

The discussion above leads to the broad conclusion that the presence of an OCS as currently conceptualized (e.g., Hollander et al., 2005) is highly tenuous. The appeal to a general inhibitory deficit to account for the presence of observed signs and symptoms, reliance on high base rates of overlapping features with poor sensitivity and specificity, misinterpretation and treatment of biological data as more fundamental than behavioral formulations, and the varied treatment response profiles largely undermine the OCS hypothesis as currently conceived. In short, each of these conceptual problems is the result of an over-inclusive and diluted spectrum proposal. On the basis of the chapters in this volume, we present some suggestions for developing a more meaningful conceptualization of an OCS. Implications of these suggestions are also discussed.

ESTABLISH A SET OF METHODOLOGICAL STANDARDS

Because of the lack of a unifying rationale for the OCS, it has been difficult to determine what exactly 'counts' as support for the spectrum. Some investigations have noted support for the inclusion of putative spectrum disorders on the basis of null findings when comparing some phenomenon between (often small) groups of patients with different disorders (which violates rule of hypothesis testing). Other investigators have claimed support for the spectrum status of a putative disorder on the basis of significant differences between the putative condition and OCD proper. Casual readers of this literature base, then, are left with no operating standards for evaluating the empirical literature on the OCS.

If the expectation were that disorders considered part of the spectrum should be non-significantly different, a more rigorous test would be determining statistical equivalence (Tryon, 2001, in press). Given that accepted methodologies exist for conducting these tests, and that the sampling required is within reach of most researchers in this area, this approach would be a desirable alternative and allow us to leave behind the unacceptable practice of attempting to 'prove the null' when researching the OCS.

RECONSIDER THE DEFINING FEATURE OF THE SPECTRUM

Following decades of research (e.g., Foa et al., 1995; Rachman & Hodgson, 1980), it has become clear that OCD involves a specific and unmistakable pattern of thinking and behavior that includes (a) intrusive senseless thoughts or ideas that evoke anxiety and distress, and (b) urges to neutralize this anxiety and distress through some purposeful action or thought (e.g., rituals, avoidance). Many sufferers engage in observable compulsive rituals (such as washing or checking), whereas others exhibit primarily mental rituals. Obsessional fear and how it is neutralized is therefore the conceptually interesting phenomenon in OCD; not the *compulsiveness* or *impulsiveness* or *repetitiveness* of this behavior. The repetitive behavior is a deliberate response to obsessions, further evidenced by the fact that some patients develop neutralizing behaviors that are brief, nonrepetitive, and entirely cognitive in nature (Ladouceur et al., 2000). Clearly such phenomena are not the main feature of many OCS disorders such as TTM, compulsive gambling, and obsessive–compulsive personality disorder.

Because the repetitive behavior observed in OCD is a response to obsessional stimuli, a valid OCS would be delineated around *obsessions*, not around compulsive or repetitive behavior. This would lead to further investigation of the psychopathology of obsessions, advancing a literature on intrusive thoughts, and potentially a meaningful subset of diagnoses that could be incrementally added to the new spectrum. In light of the fact that no model of OCD proper exists that adequately describes the heterogeneity of the disorder, a modest approach would be warranted when attempting to unify a disparate set of disorders under the heading of the OCS. In fact, perhaps not all subtypes of OCD would be included in such a spectrum. An OCS focused on obsessions would also provide treatment predictions based on specific clinical symptoms, rather than on entire diagnoses or putative biological mechanisms. There is evidence for this already, in the area of thought suppression and intrusions (Clark, 2004). This line of research has allowed for the identification of common underlying mechanisms, and has led to additional advances in the development of efficacious treatment.

FINAL CONSIDERATIONS: WHICH OCS DISORDERS ARE RELATED TO OCD?

Consistent with the current status of the research literature, the present volume has considered OCD and the OCS in the broadest sense. Whereas the notion of an OCS as put forth by its strongest advocates appears untenable, the chapters in this section of the volume do suggest that these specific disorders are more or less similar to OCD. Two conditions, BDD and hypochondriasis, appear particularly 'related to' OCD on the basis of their essential psychopathology and treatment response. In both of these conditions we find compulsive-like behavior (e.g., checking in mirrors in BDD; checking with doctors for reassurance in hypochondriasis) which is phenomenologically linked to intrusive thoughts and (obsession-like) fears (e.g., regarding appearance in BDD; regarding health in hypochondriasis). These presentations are similar to OCD; the common underlying process being the perception that some feared catastrophe will occur at some time in the future, requiring the use of avoidance or ritualistic (neutralizing) strategies to avert such negative outcomes. Finally, as the chapters in this section suggest, these conditions respond preferentially to cognitive and behavioral treatment approaches that involve exposure to fear cues and refraining from rituals. For these reasons, we suggest that of all the disorders in the proposed OCS, BDD and hypochondriasis boast the closest similarities to OCD itself.

REFERENCES

Antony, M., Downie, F., & Swinson, R. (1998). Diagnostic issues and epidemiology in obsessive–compulsive disorder. In R. Swinson, M. Antony, S. Rachman, & M. Richter (Eds.), *Obsessive–compulsive disorder: Theory, research, and treatment* (pp. 3–32). New York: Guilford.

Black, D. W. (1998). Recognition and treatment of obsessive–compulsive spectrum disorders. In R. Swinson, M. Antony, S. Rachman, & M. Richter (Eds.), *Obsessive–compulsive disorder: Theory, research, and treatment* (pp. 426–457). New York: Guilford.

Bienvenu, O., Samuels, J., Riddle, J., Hoehn-Saric, R., Liang, K., Cullen, B., et al. (2000). The relationship of obsessive–compulsive disorder to possible spectrum disorders: Results from a family study. *Biological Psychiatry, 48*, 287–293.

Boyer, W. (1995). Serotonin reuptake inhibitors are superior to imipramine and alprazolam in alleviating panic attacks. *International Clinical Psychopharmacology, 10*, 45–49.

Clark, D. A. (2004). *Intrusive thoughts in clinical disorders*. New York: Guilford.

Cottraux, J., Gerard, D., Cinotti, L., Froment, J., Deilber, M., Le Bars, D., et al. (1996). A controlled positron emission tomography study of obsessive and neutral auditory stimulation in obsessive–compulsive disorder with checking rituals. *Psychiatry Research, 60*, 101–112.

Enright, S., Beech, A., & Claridge, G. (1995). A further investigation of cognitive inhibition in obsessive–compulsive disorder. *Personality and Individual Differences, 19*, 535–542.

Foa, E. B., Kozak, M. J., Goodman, W. K., Hollander, E., Jenike, M., & Rasumssen, S. (1995). DSM-IV field trial: Obsessive–compulsive disorder. *American Journal of Psychiatry, 152*, 90–96.

Foa, E., Liebowitz, M., Kozak, M., Davies, S., Campeas, R., Franklin, M. E., et al. (2005). Treatment of obsessive–compulsive disorder by exposure and ritual prevention, clomipramine, and their combination: a randomized, placebo controlled trial. *American Journal of Psychiatry, 162*, 151–161.

Gross, R., Sasson, Y., Chorpa, M., & Zohar, J. (1998). Biological models of obsessive–compulsive disorder. In R. Swinson, M. Antony, S. Rachman, & M. Richter (Eds.), *Obsessive–compulsive disorder: Theory, research, and treatment* (pp. 141–153). New York: Guilford.

Hiller, W., Leibbrand, R., Rief, W., & Fichter, M. M. (2005). Differentiating hypochondriasis from panic disorder. *Journal of Anxiety Disorders, 19*, 29–49.

Hollander, E., Friedberg, J., Wasserman, S., Yeh, C., & Iyengar, R. (2005). The case for the OCD spectrum. In. J. S. Abramowitz & A. C. Houts (Eds.), *Concepts and controversies in obsessive–compulsive disorder* (pp. 95–118). New York: Springer.

Hollander, E., & Rosen, J. (2000). Obsessive–compulsive spectrum disorders: A review. In M. Maj, N. Sartorius, A. Okasha, & J. Zohar (Eds.), *Obsessive–compulsive disorder* (pp. 203–224). Chichester, UK: Wiley.

Hollander, E., & Wong, C. (1995). Body dysmorphic disorder, pathological gambling, and sexual compulsions. *Journal of Clinical Psychiatry, 56*(Suppl. 4), 7–12.

Inancu, I., Dannon, P. N., Dolberg, O. T., & Zohar, J. (2000). Treatment of obsessive–compulsive disorder: From theory to practice. In U. Halbreich & S. A. Montgomery (Eds.), *Pharmacotherapy for mood, anxiety, and cognitive disorders* (pp. 465–478). Washington, DC: American Psychiatric Press.

Jaisoorya, T. S., Reddy, Y. C., & Srinath, S. (2003). The relationship of obsessive–compulsive disorder to putative spectrum disorders: results from an Indian study. *Comprehensive Psychiatry, 44*, 317–323.

Jenike, M. A. (2004). Obsessive–compulsive disorder. *New England Journal of Medicine, 350*, 259–265.

Karno, M., Golding, J., Sorenson, S., & Burnam, A. (1988). The epidemiology of obsessive–compulsive disorder in five US communities. *Archives of General Psychiatry, 45*, 1094–1099.

Kolada, J., Bland, R., Newman, S. (1994). Obsessive–compulsive disorder. *Acta Psychiatric Scandinavica, 156*, 51–54.

Ladouceur, R., Freeston, M. H., Rheaume, J., Dugas, M. J., Gagnon, F., Thibodeau, N., et al. (2000). Strategies used with intrusive thoughts: A comparison of OCD patients with anxious and community controls. *Journal of Abnormal Psychology, 109*, 179–187.

Leonard, B. E. (2003). *Fundamentals of psychopharmacology* (3rd ed.). Chichester, UK: Wiley.

McElroy, S. L., Keck, P. E., & Phillips, K. A. (1995). Kleptomania, compulsive buying, and binge-eating disorder. *Journal of Clinical Psychiatry, 56*(Suppl. 4), 14–27.

McElroy, S. L., Keck, P. E., & Pope, H. G. (1989). Pharmacological treatment of kleptomania and bulimia nervosa. *Journal of Clinical Psychopharmacology, 9*, 358–360.

McElroy, S. L., Satlin, A., & Pope, H. (1991). Treatment of compulsive shopping with antidepressants: a report of three cases. *Annals of Clinical Psychiatry, 3*, 199–204.

Miller, G. A., & Keller, J. (2000). Psychology and neuroscience: making peace. *Current Directions in Psychological Science, 9*, 212–215.

Nemeroff, C., & Schatzberg, A. F. (1998). Pharmacological treatment of unipolar depression. In P. Nathan & J. Gorman (Eds.), *A guide to treatments that work* (pp. 212–225). New York: Oxford.

Nestadt, G., Samuels, J., Riddle, M., Liang, K., Bienvenu, O., Hoehn-Saric, R., Grados, M., & Cullen, B. (2001). The relationship between obsessive–compulsive disorder and anxiety and affective disorders: Results from the Johns Hopkins OCD family study. *Psychological Medicine, 31*, 481–487.

Noyes, R., Carney, C.P., & Langbehn, D.R. (2004). Specific phobia of illness: Search for a new subtype. *Journal of Anxiety Disorders, 18*, 531–545.

O'Sullivan, R. L., Rauch, S. L., Brieter, H. C. (1997). Reduced basal ganglia volumes in trichotillomania measured via morphometric MRI. *Biological Psychiatry, 42*, 39–45.

Rachman, S. J. & Hodgson, R. J. (1980). *Obsessions and compulsions.* Englewood Cliffs, NJ: Prentice-Hall.

Rauch, S., Jenike, M., Alpert, N., Baer, L., Breiter, H., Savage, C., & Fischman, A. (1994). Regional cerebral blood flow measured during symptom provocation in obsessive–compulsive disorder using oxygen-15 labeled carbon-dioxide and positron emission tomography. *Archives of General Psychiatry, 51*, 62–70.

Rosenberg, D., Dyck, E., O'Hearn, K., & Sweeney, J. (1997). Response-inhibition deficits in obsessive–compulsive disorder: an indicator of dysfunction in frontostriatal circuits. *Journal of Psychiatry and Neuroscience, 22*, 29–38.

Stein, D. J., Coetzer, R., & Lee, M. (1997). Magnetic resonance brain imaging in women with obsessive–compulsive disorder and trichotillomania. *Psychiatry Research, 74*, 177–182.

Stowe, R., & Taylor, S. (2002). Posttraumatic stress disorder. *Encyclopedia of life sciences.* London: Nature Publishing Group.

Summerfeldt, L., Hood, K., Antony, M., Richter, M., & Swinson, R. (2004). Impulsivity in obsessive–compulsive disorder: comparisons with other anxiety disorders and within tic-related subgroups. *Personality and Individual Differences, 36*, 539–553.

Taylor, S., Abramowitz, J. S., & McKay, D. (2007). Cognitive–behavioral models of OCD. In M. M. Antony, C. Purdon, & L. Summerfeldt (Eds.), *Psychological treatment of OCD: Fundamentals and beyond* (pp. 9–29). Washington, DC: American Psychological Association Press.

Taylor, S., Asmundson, G. J. G., & Coons, M. J. (2005). Current directions in the treatment of hypochondriasis. *Journal of Cognitive Psychotherapy, 19*, 291–310.

Taylor, S., McKay, D., & Abramowitz, J. (2005a). Is obsessive–compulsive disorder a disturbance of security motivation? Comment on Szechtman & Woody (2004). *Psychological Review, 112*, 650–656.

Taylor, S., McKay, D., & Abramowitz, J. (2005b). Problems with the security motivation model remain largely unresolved: Response to Woody & Szechtman (2005). *Psychological Review, 112*, 656–657.

Tryon, W. W. (2001). Evaluating statistical difference, equivalence, and indeterminacy using inferential confidence intervals: An integrated alternative method of conducting null hypothesis statistical tests. *Psychological Methods, 6*, 371–386.

Tryon, W. W. (in press). Statistical equivalence. In D. McKay (Ed.), *Handbook of research methods in abnormal and clinical psychology.* Newbury Park, CA: Sage.

Tukel, R., Keser, V., Karali, N. T., Olgun, T. O., & Calikusu, C. (2001). Comparison of clinical characteristics in trichotillomania and obsessive–compulsive disorder. *Journal of Anxiety Disorders, 15*, 433–441.

Veale, D. (2003). The obsessive–compulsive spectrum and body dysmorphic disorder. In R.G. Menzies & P.de Silva (Eds.), *Obsessive–compulsive disorder: Theory, research, and treatment* (pp. 221–236). Chichester, UK: Wiley.

Williams, J., Hadjistavropoulos, H., & Sharpe, T. (2006). A meta-analysis of psychological and pharmacological treatments for body dysmorphic disorder. *Behaviour Research and Therapy, 44*, 99–111.

Zinner, S. H. (2000). Tourette's disorder. *Pediatrics in Review, 21*, 1–22.

INDEX

CPSIA information can be obtained at www.ICGtesting.com
Printed in the USA
BVOW06*2137030916

460884BV00004B/39/P